New Zealand Wine

New Zealand Wine

The Land, the Vines, the People

Warren Moran

With cartography by Igor Drecki

hardie grant books

Contents

Guide to Maps   vii

1   The Story of New Zealand Wine   1
2   New Zealand Vines and Wines circa 1960   17
3   Regional and Varietal Revolution   31
4   Natural Environments in Human Terms   57
5   Gisborne or Poverty Bay?   83
6   Hawke's Bay   135
7   Marlborough   187
8   Central Otago   241
9   Metropolitan Vineyards and Cellars   297
10   A Natural Experiment   353

Acknowledgements   362

Sources   363

Index   371

This edition published in 2016 by Hardie Grant Books,
an imprint of Hardie Grant Publishing

Hardie Grant Books (Melbourne)
Building 1, 658 Church Street
Richmond, Victoria 3121
hardiegrantbooks.com.au

Hardie Grant Books (London)
5th & 6th Floors
52–54 Southwark Street
London SE1 1UN
hardiegrantbooks.co.uk

First published in New Zealand in 2016 by Auckland University Press

All rights reserved. No part of this publication may be reproduced, stored in a retrieval system or transmitted in any form by any means, electronic, mechanical, photocopying, recording or otherwise, without the prior written permission of the publishers and copyright holders.

The moral rights of the author have been asserted.

Copyright text © Warren Moran 2016
Copyright maps and figures © Igor Drecki and Geographx 2016

A Cataloguing-in-Publication entry is available from the catalogue
of the National Library of Australia at www.nla.gov.au

New Zealand Wine
ISBN 978 1 74379 302 2

Cover design: Carolyn Lewis
Front cover: Jim Tannock Photography
Back cover: Marti Friedlander
Page ii: Ngatarawa Wines, Hawke's Bay. *Ngatarawa Wines Collection*
Pages iv–v: Long Gully, Mt Difficulty Wines, Central Otago. *Tim Hawkins*

Printed in China by 1010 Printing International Limited

Guide to Maps

The digital oblique maps on pages 86–87, 136–7, 192–3, 212–13, 246–7, 304, 321 and 338 were drawn by Geographx. All other maps and figures are by Igor Drecki.

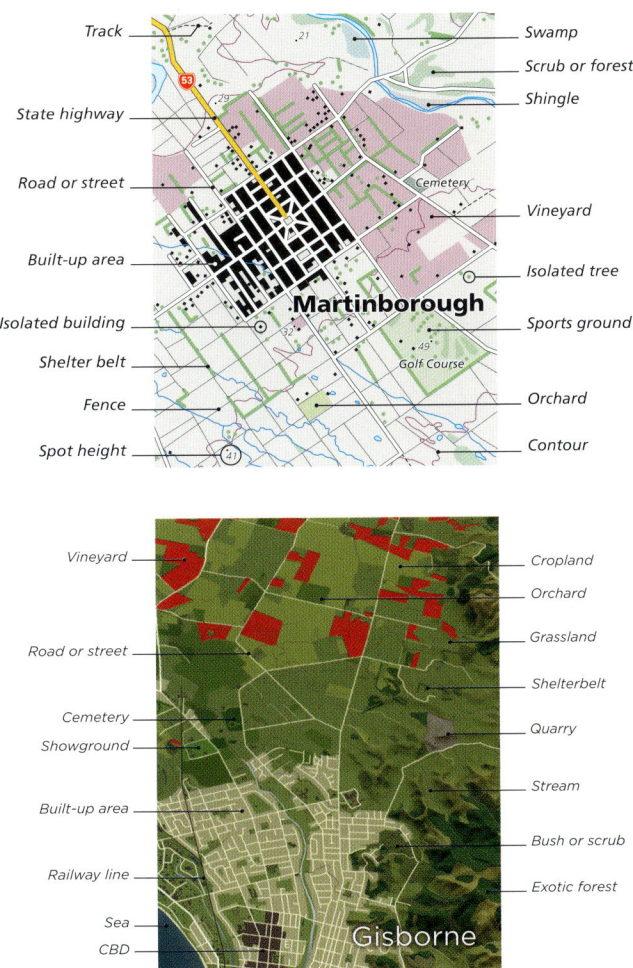

1

The Story of New Zealand Wine

I had a 'sophisticated' introduction to New Zealand wine when, in 1957, I walked into Paul Groshek's tasting room in Candia Road, West Auckland, to interview him as part of my Master's thesis on the New Zealand wine industry. Before I asked any questions, Groshek proceeded to teach me a thing or two. Grasping an open, but re-corked, bottle of Corbans Dry Red table wine resting on a noggin of his unlined tasting room, he poured a small serving into the tapered 5-ounce beer glass of the time and passed it to me to taste. I sipped and commented circumspectly. From a half-gallon jar, he then glugged a larger serving of his own red table wine, Albonez, into my glass. Again I was circumspect. Unimpressed by my commentary on the wines, he poured some of the Corbans Dry Red into his own glass, took a mouthful and promptly sprayed it all over the room, exclaiming, 'Jesus-a-Christ, boy, bloody vinegar!', and threw the rest away. He refilled his glass with Albonez, appraised its robe and bouquet, and at the first sip extolled, 'Jesus-a-Christ, boy, bloody nectar!'

Groshek was doing almost everything right. He made simple, fresh, unadulterated table wines when more than 90 per cent of New Zealand wine was fortified sherries, ports and liqueurs. His grapes came from his own, sheltered, north- and east-facing vineyard. It was organic. He fermented his reds in open vats, plunging them by hand several times each day in a form of what the French call *macération carbonique*. He added no water. His wine was stored in underground cellars dug by hand, complete

Paul Groshek sitting at his Muaga Vineyards on Candia Road in West Auckland, 1963. *Rod Harvey, Auckland War Memorial Museum – Tāmaki Paenga Hira, PH-2008-4*

with plaques for each of his dogs that had died during the excavation. Above all, he heralded – in prose and poetry – to anyone who would listen, the health qualities of unfortified table wine drunk in moderation. He even claimed to have cured the skin ailments of his dog with internal and external applications of Albonez. Groshek was much ahead of his time in all but the grape varieties he was growing. His Albonez was named after its main variety, Albany Surprise, the *labrusca* sport of the Concord grape. Albany Surprise was hardy, disease resistant and high-yielding, but it was not a grape from which you could make fine wine.

Today hardly a trace of Paul Groshek's cellar remains. He died in 1963 – the very time that New Zealanders were beginning to grasp his aspiration to make and drink table wines of quality and to plant the varieties of *Vitis vinifera* that would allow its realisation.

In the second half of the twentieth century, and into the twenty-first, the geography of international production of grapes for wine was transformed. Middle-latitude countries of the New World rapidly expanded their area in vines for the production of table wines so that many are now significant producers and exporters. This growth coincided with a decrease in the area in vines in the European Union. Persistent overproduction in Europe for much of the twentieth century was addressed under the Common Agricultural Policy by enforced reduction of the area in vines through regulation of production rights complemented by distillation of excess wine. These adjustments were sufficiently successful that, by the late 1990s, the European Union was able to consider relaxing its strict controls as it attempted to meet the competition of wine from the New World.

New Zealand is one of the New World countries to experience considerable growth in its area in vines and production of wine over the past 50 years, although with about 33,000 hectares of vines planted by 2010, it remains a small producer in global terms. New Zealand's distinctiveness lies in its successful establishment of a wine industry of quality based on its many favourable natural environments and realised by advanced viticultural and winemaking technologies. A committed group of grape growers and winemakers have shown that fine wines can be made in New Zealand from many of the *vinifera* varieties, although individual enterprises in all regions continue to seek the ideal mix of varieties for their sites. New Zealand's international status is demonstrated by its ability to sell wines of quality on some of the most competitive international markets in the world, such as Australia, the United Kingdom, the United States and Canada. The average value of New Zealand wine on the British market, for instance, has been higher than that of any other country for an extended period.

The vine has been grown in New Zealand since the early nineteenth century, but the modern commercial industry is a creation of the last four decades of the twentieth century and the first of the twenty-first. Although Paul Groshek pronounced it 'bloody nectar', his Albonez of 1957 was not fine wine. But by the end of the 1970s New Zealand winemakers Alex Corban, Denis Kasza (with Tom McDonald), Nick Nobilo, Denis Irwin, Joe and Peter Babich and others had shown that fine wines could be produced from grapes grown in three regions of New Zealand – Auckland, Gisborne and Hawke's Bay. It took about another decade – until the end of the 1980s – for the knowledge of grape growing to reach a similar level of sophistication.

Australian scientist Richard Smart, together with many receptive and innovative grape growers, had a lasting impact on viticulture by proselytising the principles of managing vine canopies in New Zealand soils and climates to ensure grapes of quality in most seasons. At the same time, the industry went through a series of regional and varietal revolutions, expanding into Marlborough, the Wairarapa, Central Otago, Nelson and Waipara, and planting a wide range of white and red varieties of *Vitis vinifera*. New Zealand now has both fine vines and fine wines that are celebrated in markets and media around the world.

Gewürztraminer vines on Seifried Estate's Redwood Valley vineyard, Nelson.

Nature versus culture?

Scholars have grappled with the question of what makes a wine great by dissecting the meanings tied up in the word *terroir*. French dictionaries always have at least two definitions of the word. The narrower, more technical, and more limited definition equates *terroir* to soil. The phrase *goût de terroir* ('taste of the soil') in relation to wine is used in the Robert dictionaries to illustrate this meaning. The second and broader meaning refers to a delimited area of land including its natural and human characteristics. This second meaning of *terroir* is linked to the word *territoire* which has a very similar meaning to the word 'territory' in English.

The advertising hype almost always adopts the narrow meaning – *terroir* as soil. In recent years we have been bombarded with so much about the soils and geology of Burgundy in particular that we are in danger of believing that the region makes great wine because the soils are ideally suited to Pinot Noir and Chardonnay. James Wilson's 1998 book *Terroir: the role of geology, climate, and culture in the making of French wines*, for instance, while an accessible description of the geology of Burgundy, is almost totally directed to this environmentally deterministic argument, despite his slipping 'culture' into the subtitle. The advertising hoardings of the Bureau Interprofessionnel des Vins de Bourgogne (BIVB) that superimpose geological cross-sections over a tasting glass perpetuate such environmental folklore. Beyond Burgundy, in recent years the publicity machine of the French industry has begun to banalise the story of wine by pumping out dubious stories about the blessings of the climates and soils of its elite appellations. Reputable English journalists and wine writers have for some time added to the myths.

Another line of thinking suggests that the advertising hype gets the causality around the wrong way. In their classic books on the French and Burgundian industries, respectively, Roger Dion and Rolande Gadille addressed the question of nature and culture. Dion opens his *Grands traits d'une géographie viticole de la France* (1943) with the bold claim that:

> *…Moeurs et croyances ont exercé, sur la distribution des vignobles à travers le monde, une influence qui a pu prévaloir sur celle du climat.*
>
> [Throughout the world, customs and beliefs have exerted an influence on the distribution of winegrowing that has prevailed over climate.]

He repeats the phrase in his *Histoire de la vigne et du vin en France des Origines au XIXème Siècle* (1959) before discussing the northern limits of the vine. By the time he published this major work, Dion's main message became even clearer. In the *avant-propos* he states:

A frosty morning's pruning at Neudorf Vineyards in Upper Moutere, Nelson.
Tim Finn

. . . il nous plairait de voir, dans les virtus de nos vignobles, l'effet d'un privilège naturel, d'une grace particulière accordée à la terre de France, comme s'il y avait eu plus d'honneur, pour notre pays, à recevoir du Ciel que de la peine des hommes cette renommée vinicole où nos ancêtres ont trouvé un sujet de fierté collective avant même que ne se fût éveillé en eux le sentiment d'une patrie française.

[It suits us to see in the qualities of our wine regions, the effect of a natural privilege, of a particular grace accorded to the land of France, as if there were greater honour for our country to receive from the heavens than from the struggles of people this renowned wine industry in which our ancestors found a collective pride even before the feeling of a French nation stirred in them.]

Gadille is more circumspect, but she establishes a similar framework as the foundation of her Burgundian study *Le vignoble de la côte bourguignonne, fondements physiques et humains d'une viticulture de haute qualité* (1967) when she states:

> *Nous touchons là aux problèmes fondamenteaux que posent la genèse individuelle des grands crus et celle des vignobles de qualité dans leur ensemble: déterminism physique originel, ou bien patiente et coûteuse création humaine, telles sont les deux explications qui peuvent être invoquées afin de justifier la localisation des vignobles prestigieux et l'aménagement interne de leurs crus.*

> [We approach here the fundamental problems posed by the distinctive origin of the grand crus and of all quality viticulture: original physical determinism or careful and costly human creation, these are the two explanations that may be invoked in order to explain the localisation of the prestigious viticultures and the internal management of their crus.]

Gadille's book remains the most comprehensive study of Burgundian winegrowing but she limits the power of her interpretation by setting the physical environment against the human, as if people are not interacting with their natural milieu. While he could never be accused of privileging the natural, Dion too, in his assertion of the greater importance of customs and beliefs over climate, establishes a dichotomy that could restrict our approaches to understanding.

Various other scholars and groups, especially from France, have probed, dissected and exposed the multiple meanings embedded in the word *terroir*. Of special importance are the investigations of the combined working group of the Institut National des Appellations d'Origine (INAO) and Institut National de la Recherche Agronomique (INRA) into the two words *terroir* and *typicité* (Vincent. 2005). Their definition of *terroir* is the most philosophically sophisticated that I know while also being eminently practical:

> *Un terroir est un espace géographique délimité où une communauté humaine a construit, au cours de l'histoire, un savoir intellectuel collectif de production, fondé sur un système d'interactions entre un milieu physique et biologique et un ensemble de facteurs humains, dans lequel les itinéraires socio-techniques mis en jeu, révèlent une originalité, confèrent une typicité et engendrent une réputation, pour un produit originaire de ce terroir.*

> [A *terroir* is a delimited geographic space where a human community has constructed, throughout the course of history, a collective intellectual knowledge of production, founded on a system of interactions among a physical and biological milieu and a set of human factors in which the socio-technical philosophies put in place establish an originality, confer a *typicité*, and engender a reputation for a product originating from this *terroir*.]

While this definition captures the essence of the term very elegantly, we also recognise that, from a wider perspective, the word *terroir* has at least six facets that interact and

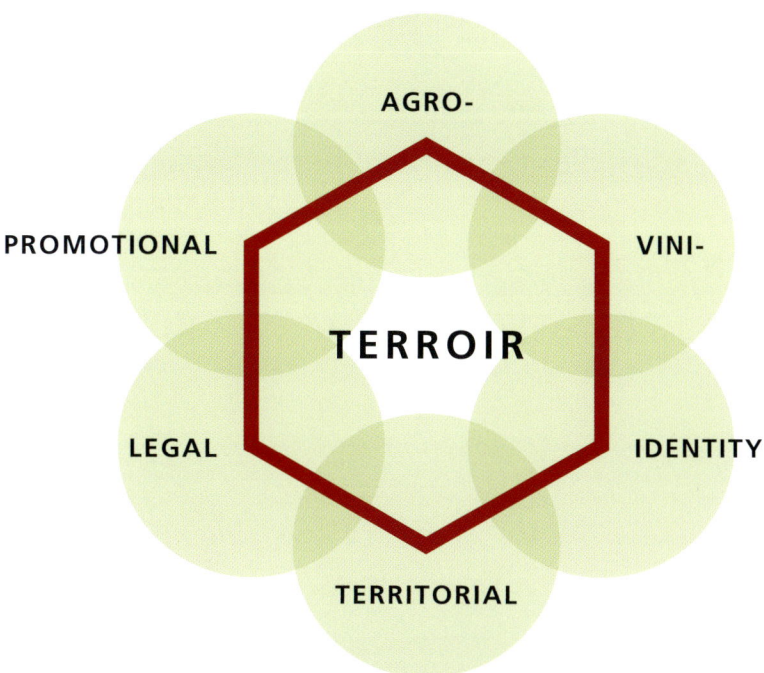

Figure 1.1 The facets of *terroir*

overlap – sometimes at the local scale, sometimes at the regional, and sometimes internationally (Figure 1.1). Each facet involves assessments and decisions by people. They are:

i   *agro-terroir* (as used by Hinnewinkel), often called ecophysiology;
ii *vini-terroir* (a term of my own coining), that captures the importance of different vinification methods in differentiating wine territories that are sometimes very important in establishing *typicité* (distinctiveness);
iii an identity *terroir* that Dion lauded;
iv a territorial *terroir* that has much wider implications than just the definition of the jurisdiction;
v   a legal *terroir* that codifies any rules associated with specific vine territories and extends as far as European Union trade agreements with other countries to protect each other's names, or even to disputes adjudicated by the World Trade Organization; and finally
vi promotional *terroir*, the facet seen by many entrepreneurs within the industry as the most important: invoking the human and natural dimensions of places sells wine.

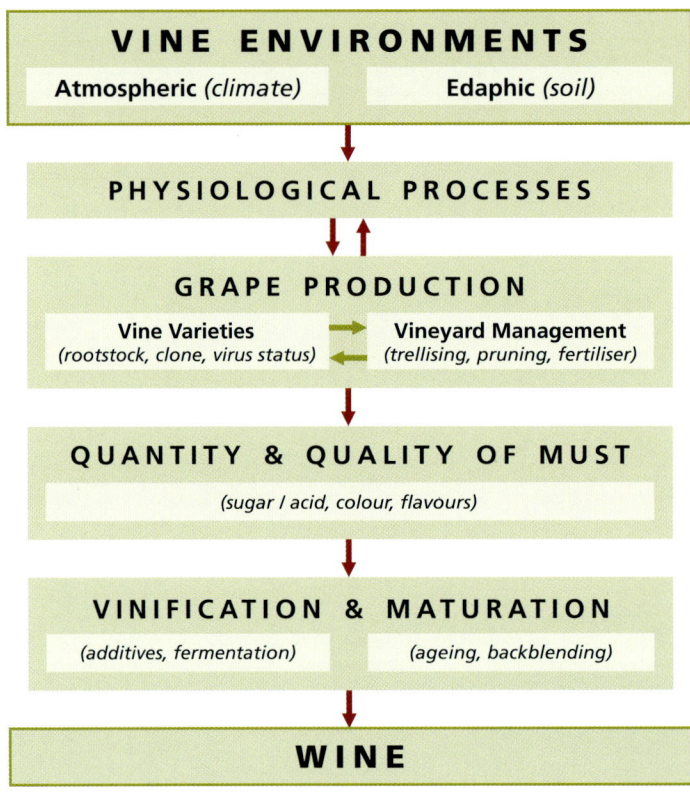

Figure 1.2 From vine to wine

The real story of wine is much more interesting than attributing success to particular soils, or to the total natural environment, or even to the competing influences of people and the natural environment (Figure 1.2). The development of great wine involves people assessing their environments, trying them out, and adapting and learning to coax the best qualities out of particular grape varieties in the vineyard and in the winery. The flavours, colours and qualities of wines are produced by interaction among components of the vine and its environments: the soil, the variety and clones of vines, their age, the atmospheric conditions of the particular season, the trellising system, the yield per vine, and the nutrients and water that are supplied to it, the balance between the photosynthetic ability of the leaves and the amount of crop on the vine, and so on (Table 1.1).

The wines of Burgundy (or rather some of them) are great wines because over centuries people learned how to select the varieties and clones, viticultural and vinification methods to express their environment in their wines. People and their effort have made Burgundy. For centuries, humans have modified the conditions in which grapes are produced. From clonal selection to plant breeding, plant spacing to canopy

Table 1.1 Terroir: approaches, sciences and explanations

Approach	Sciences/Knowledges	Type of explanation
Plant growing (*agro-terroir*)	Plant Physiology Molecular Biology Climatology / Pedology Geology	Functional (and integrative?) Functional / reductionist Varied Spatial Association Spatial Association Alchemy
Winemaking (*vini-terroir*)	Chemistry Molecular Biology	Functional / reductionist Functional / reductionist
Identity *terroir*	Geography / Humanities / Social Sciences	Cultural (*patrimoine* / *pays*)
Territorial *terroir*	Geography / Economics / Social Sciences	Functional (Economic rent / Territorial domination)
Legal *terroir*	Law / Humanities / Social Sciences	Legal argument / varied
Promotional *terroir*	Marketing	Quantitative and qualitative / Folklore

management, site selection to irrigation, copper and superphosphate to ground cows' horns, scarecrows to automated bird bangers, smudge pots to helicopters, and pruning to mechanical leaf plucking, viticulturists have modified all the physical processes influencing the vine. Irrigation, wind machines, fertilisation and soil ripping redefine *terroir* in a range of senses. The outcome of any particular visible interaction between humans and nature in viticulture carries with it a history of modification that is often buried in the empirical evidence of the here and now.

The New Zealand winegrowing revolution

The story of New Zealand wine is told in decades rather than centuries. As a result, we can observe the industry's evolution at close quarters. What does the recent experience of a New World country reveal about the role of climate and soils in association with culture and history in shaping the evolution of a wine industry? What part has empirical experience of growing vines in different environments played in the evolving nature of New Zealand winegrowing? How have enterprises and individuals influenced the rapid geographic and varietal specialisation of vines and wines in New Zealand?

Although vines were first planted in New Zealand in the early nineteenth century, the modern wine industry dates only to the late twentieth and early twenty-first centuries. In 1960, only 388 hectares were planted in grapes across New Zealand, most of that in West Auckland and Hawke's Bay. The vineyards were predominantly planted in American, disease-resistant, hybrid grape varieties and winemakers focused most of their efforts on sherry, port and liqueurs rather than table wines.

Over the last four decades of the twentieth century and the first decade of the twenty-first, the map of New Zealand viticulture and winemaking was redrawn. In 1960, two regions – West Auckland and Hawke's Bay – accounted for 85 per cent of the grapes being grown in the country. From the late 1960s, grape growers and winemakers colonised region after region and locality after locality – Gisborne, Hawke's Bay, the Wairarapa, Marlborough, Nelson, Waipara and Central Otago have seen their area in vines expand. The interaction of enterprises and cultural and ethnic groups with the natural environments of the regions and localities they have transformed is the first key theme of this book.

But the revolution after 1960 cannot be understood without confronting a second key theme: the evolution of the varietal mix. Hybrid grapes like Groshek's Albany Surprise gave way to Germanic varieties such as Müller Thurgau in the 1970s, which in turn gave way to Sauvignon Blanc and other classical varieties such as Chardonnay, Cabernet Sauvignon and Riesling in the 1980s. Pinot Noir joined the mix both as a base for sparkling wine and more recently as a still wine of quality. By the 1990s, Sauvignon Blanc, Chardonnay, Pinot Noir, Merlot, Cabernet Sauvignon and Riesling made up more than 80 per cent of all vines planted. Other *vinifera* varieties such as Gewürztraminer and Chenin Blanc rose and fell and rose again as knowledge of their vineyard management and vinification, as well as public tastes, evolved. Since 1990, more definite regional specialisation in varieties has begun to emerge in New Zealand. This is an indelible sign of the increasing knowledge accumulated by grape growers, winemakers and scientists about which varieties of grapes grow best where.

Knowledge of the natural environment and the varietal mix evolved together. In each new region, grape growers and winemakers have faced distinct natural environments. Each locality and region where vines now flourish has its own weather and climates and its own fine-grained distribution of soils. Vines have been planted progressively closer to the polar limit of their cultivation where temperatures and accumulation of energy over the growing season make it difficult to ripen some *vinifera* varieties, and early and late frosts become more of a hazard. Vines have also dispersed into regions where rainfall during the growing season is lower – an advantage in reducing the risk of fungus diseases, but a disadvantage, at least in terms of expense, in that irrigation is often necessary.

If, as many scientists suggest, some varieties produce special characteristics of flavour, texture and mouth weight closer to their environmental limit, these new localities also offer advantages. Pinot Noir is one example often cited. Such claims may need to be treated circumspectly in New Zealand, where almost the whole country may be considered as marginal for the production of some red varieties, such as Cabernet Sauvignon. Although fine Cabernet and Cabernet blends have been produced in New

Picking in Hawke's Bay.
Hawke's Bay Wine

Zealand, notably from Hawke's Bay, many growers and winemakers in Martinborough and Marlborough (and some even in parts of Auckland) have pulled out these varieties after failing to ripen them regularly.

At the very least, however, each of the new regions and localities of New Zealand is different, so that distinctive and interesting wines can be grown there. Overwhelming empirical evidence now exists, for instance, that wine made from Sauvignon Blanc grown in Marlborough achieves distinctive, zesty flavours. Its appeal on international markets saw Sauvignon Blanc provide almost half of the value of all New Zealand's export wines in 2000 and grow to three quarters by 2010. When wine writers and publicity blurbs from California, or South Africa, or even better, Australia, have begun describing their own Sauvignons as 'New Zealand' in style, a reputation has been made.

Some of the special characteristics of these and other wines derive from the soil where the grapes are grown. As with climates, the regional sequence of soils that the New Zealand vineyard has progressively occupied is revealing. But it is unwise to consider soils as if they were separate from the enveloping atmospheric environment when analysing these interactions. The vine harnesses its total environment to realise distinctive flavours and qualities in its ripe fruit.

Above all, this revolution in New Zealand winegrowing is one of people and their enterprises: the Dalmatians with their knowledge of wine but experience from a

The Story of New Zealand Wine

The harvest at Villa Maria, Hawke's Bay. *Hawke's Bay Wine*

quite different natural environment; the Anglo-Celts and their beer; the Scottish Presbyterians and their fear of the grape; the young New Zealand winemakers with their overseas experience and advanced technical knowledge and education. A nascent family tradition of winemaking and viticulture has been established as the second and third generation of Croatian, Lebanese and other New Zealand families remain in the industry alongside new investors and entrepreneurs who bring their own capital and experience from other places.

The story of New Zealand wine cannot be understood without tracing the evolution of representative enterprises in each region and their relationships with the places where they operate. Each of the enterprises has its own geography because the growing of grapes, their transformation into wine, and its bottling, packaging and distribution are often dispersed. This is most obviously the case for the large corporate firms such as Pernod Ricard (the former Montana and Corbans), Nobilo (now owned by Constellation Brands) and Villa Maria that are multi-regional in all of their operations. But it also applies to many of the smallest family firms, often located in one region, many of whom distribute to national and international markets for their survival and prosperity.

From the beginning, two main forms of enterprise – family operations and larger, often corporate, firms – have existed side by side in New Zealand's winegrowing.

Draining Pinot at the Neudorf winery in Nelson.
Tim Finn

The presence of these two has always been a source of potential tension in the industry and has influenced many aspects of its organisation including the way that the industry governs itself, initially through the Wine Institute of New Zealand, now New Zealand Winegrowers. Today, as in its growth phase, many of the larger firms rely on specialist grape growers to provide some proportion of their crop. Many of these, like a number of the smaller winemaking firms, are family-based producers.

Growing grapes, making wine and selling it is bound to result in disappointments. Frost threatens, mildews invade aggressively, birds eat the fruit, the ferments get stuck, consumers are lukewarm about the product, and show-pony wines do not win a medal. Such uncertainty might provoke some to gloom, but among the New Zealand grape growers and winegrowers I have known, it has been met instead by a tough good humour, a willingness to learn from experience, and a remarkable resilience – attributes which shine forth in their contribution to the story of New Zealand wine as it is traced throughout the course of this book.

Western Vineyards, Henderson Valley, Auckland. *Dick Scott Collection, Auckland War Memorial Museum – Tāmaki Paenga Hira, PH-2008-4*

2

New Zealand Vines and Wines circa 1960

At the 1958 New Zealand Easter Show, Class 6 of the Wine Section was for an 'Unfortified White, Hock type, not over 26 per cent proof spirit'. Four medals were awarded from fourteen entrants: McWilliam's Wines Ltd of Hawke's Bay won first prize; Josip Babich won second; Western Vineyards won third; and A. A. Corban and Sons won fourth prize.

Of these four firms, only one name persists as a commercial entity today. David, the grandson of Josip, is general manager of Babich Wines and works alongside his father Peter and his uncle Joe at their Henderson Valley winery. McWilliam's Wines is today represented on the New Zealand landscape only remotely, by the Church Road, Hawke's Bay winery of the former Montana, now owned by the French company Pernod Ricard New Zealand Ltd. A. A. Corban and Sons (by then trading as Corbans Wines Ltd) was bought by Montana in 2000. Pernod Ricard retains 'Corbans' as a brand, and the name also continues to be associated with the wine industry through Alwyn Corban of Ngatarawa Wines and his late uncle Joe who started Corbans Viticulture Ltd in 1979. The vines of Western Vineyards (third prize) are still visible on the landscape of Waitakere but only as a series of swirls on Candia Road about 2 kilometres from the Babich winery. These are the terraces of one of the most elegant vineyards of its time, still sculpted in the yellow Waitemata clays of West Auckland. Its winery is now used for yoga classes.

At nineteen, Dudley Russell began terracing land and planting grapes in the Henderson Valley. By 1960, his Western Vineyards was focusing on unfortified wines and *vinifera* grapes – the industry's future.
Dick Scott Collection, Auckland War Memorial Museum – Tāmaki Paenga Hira, PH-2008-4

If the people and firms of 1958 are now a faint memory, so too are the dominant wines. Of the 22 classes of wine judged at the 1958 Easter Show, twelve were for fortified wines and ten for unfortified or table wines such as the hock type won by McWilliam's. Considering the consumption habits of the time, the number of classes for table wine is astounding. In the late 1950s, only 13 per cent of West Auckland winery production was table wine, and among Hawke's Bay wineries the proportion was just 5 per cent. The remaining 77 per cent of wine produced in West Auckland and the remaining 95 per cent in Hawke's Bay comprised sherry, port and liqueurs.

Nevertheless, the beginnings of the modern New Zealand wine industry could be seen in faint glimmers at the 1958 show. Dudley Russell of Western Vineyards was one of the people setting the wine trends in the late 1950s and into the 1960s. Table wines ('unfortified wines' in the language of the time) made up almost a third of Western Vineyard's production in 1958 – the only large winery in New Zealand to approach this proportion. Some firms made no table wine. Two neighbours of Western Vineyards also figured in the table wine market. Sixty per cent of Paul Groshek's production at Muaga wines across Candia Road was unfortified wine and almost 20 per cent at the Josip Babich winery.

In the 'Commercial Classes' of table wines, the larger companies were also emerging to establish a preliminary pecking order. For dry table wines, sixteen prizes were available in the four classes: Corbans won eight, McWilliam's won six, and Babich and Vidal managed one each. In the 'Hock' type, Corbans won three of the four prizes – a portent of Alex Corban's Riverlea Riesling of the next decade. McWilliam's won 'Best Wine in Show' for one of their wines entered in the 'Claret' type. Their innovative Bakano and legendary 1965 Cabernet Sauvignon orchestrated by Denis Kasza for Tom McDonald were on the near horizon. Neither Villa Maria nor Montana entered wines in 1958. But in 1961 George Fistonich gave up carpentry to get involved full-time in his father's wine business at Villa Maria. In the same year, Frank and Mate Yukich contributed $250 each to float Montana Wines and develop their father's business. The transformation of the New Zealand wine industry loomed.

Geography of vines and wines from mid-century

The results of the Easter Show reveal much of the international and internal geography of the vine and wine around 1960 as well as clues to their future. Wines were named after those of other countries – Hock, Chablis, Claret, Burgundy, Sherry, Port, Vermouth, Sauterne. At least in the case of the 'Sherry' type, and especially dry sherry, the grapes were sometimes Palomino, the variety from which the genuine sherry from Jerez de la Frontera is made. By contrast, the 'Hock' type did not see many kilograms of

New Zealand wines circa 1960: 38% proof Blackberry Nip from Glenvale Wines in Bayview, Hawke's Bay; Sweet Sherry from Ballins Industries; and Spence's Sparkleburg. *Dick Scott Collection, Auckland War Memorial Museum – Tāmaki Paenga Hira, PH-2008-4*

Riesling nor the 'Chablis' type many pounds of Chardonnay. Riesling was not listed in the official data of the time, although Riesling-Sylvaner (Müller Thurgau) was. Ministry of Agriculture data for 1960 listed 6.5 acres of Pinot Chardonnay (as it was then called in New Zealand) compared with 107 acres of the hybrid Baco 22A.

A similar pattern was revealed in the reds. The dominance of Anglo settlers and thinking is evident in naming the two red wine classes 'Claret' type and 'Burgundy'. But just 16 acres of Cabernet Sauvignon, 14 of Malbec and 6.5 of Merlot – the Claret or Bordeaux varieties – are recorded in 1960, predominantly in Hawke's Bay. At the time, Albany Surprise (the New Zealand variant of the American table grape Concord) was the most common red variety with 98 acres being used for wine. Paul Groshek named his popular, dry red table wine – Albonez – after it. The hybrid Seibel 5455 is second among the reds with 68 acres. Both of these varieties were undoubtedly present in some of the wines of the red wine classes named 'Claret' type and 'Burgundy'. In fact, many red table wines were made entirely from these hybrid varieties.

While the New Zealand table wines judged at the 1958 Easter Show drew on European precedents for the names, the grapes grown had drifted far from the classical varieties that produced the major wines of France, Spain, or Italy. A few examples of classical varieties continued to be cultivated, such as the Spanish grape Palomino, but these also found their way into the popular sweet and fortified sherries and ports of the day. This pattern in New Zealand's grape production was shaped by the two major wine regions of the time – West Auckland and Hawke's Bay. Contrasts between these two winegrowing regions are not so obvious from the results of the awards, but they were considerable.

New Zealand Vines and Wines circa 1960

Auckland

West Auckland vineyards and wineries in 1960 were small, mixed holdings (Figure 2.1). All but a few of them combined growing grapes with orcharding, and most ran some livestock on the rest of their property. A few still practised market gardening. Over 90 per cent were owned by people who at the time were called Yugoslavs, after their country of origin, but colloquially known as 'Dallies' because many came from the Dalmatian coast of Croatia. They were family enterprises sometimes involving two families and more than one generation. The average size of vineyards in Henderson-Oratia was 5 acres (about 2 hectares) but much smaller if the three largest vineyards and wineries – Corbans (130 acres), Averill's (35 acres, later Penfolds) and Western Vineyards (34 acres) – all owned by non-Croats – were omitted.

On average, 70 per cent of the wine made on these Croatian holdings was sold directly to the public, mainly from the cellar but sometimes by door-to-door hawking in Auckland and other regions. Cellars were small, unpretentious buildings adjoining the family home. Brick and concrete blocks were favoured building materials. Most had a small, adjoining distillery for turning grape residues into alcohol for fortifying their ports, sherries and liqueurs. Co-operative 'stills' were illegal. The spectre of prohibition still hovered, although weakened by the experiences of the Second World War. A visit to one of these wineries – say that of Mate and Melba Brajkovich in Kumeu, or George Mazuran or Peter Fredatovich in Lincoln Road, was as friendly and welcoming as at

In Auckland, properties were small, wineries were modest, and the proprietors were often grape growers, orchardists, winemakers and shopkeepers on the same day. Yozin's building still stands on Swanson Road, no longer used and surrounded by suburban homes.
Dick Scott Collection, Auckland War Memorial Museum – Tāmaki Paenga Hira, PH-2008-4

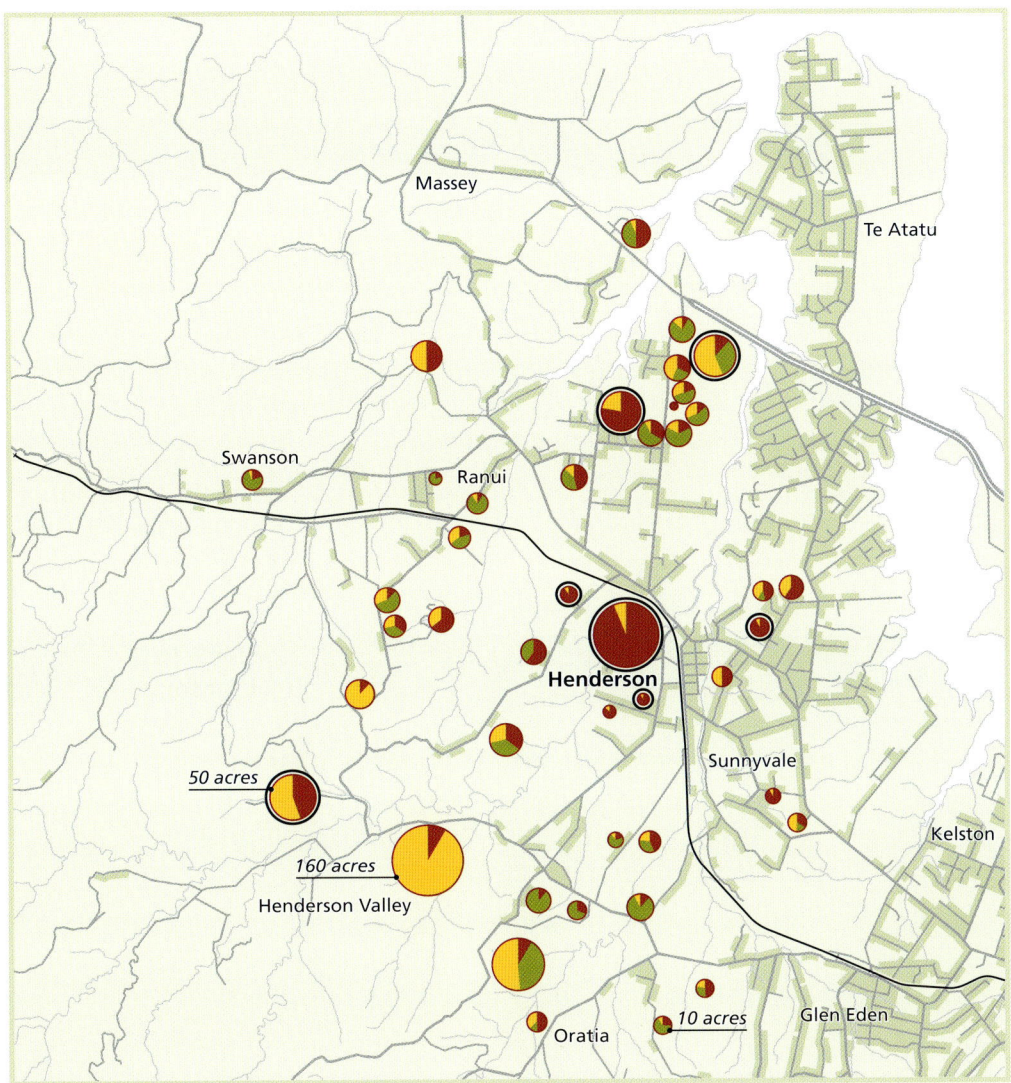

Figure 2.1 Vineyards (red), orchards (green), and other land (yellow) on mixed horticultural holdings in Henderson-Oratia, West Auckland, 1960, where circle size corresponds to the size of a holding. The seven properties with a second circle were owned by families of non-Croatian descent.

any family holding in France or Italy. At this stage of their evolution, only the wine was different. From about 1960, the second, New Zealand-born generation of Dallies were beginning to work on the family holdings. They brought change.

These West Auckland enterprises were on the doorstep of a city that was beginning to expand rapidly. The northwestern motorway opened in 1958. Roadworks to double its capacity and to widen its bridges began immediately. Although it was not obvious at the time, those Dalmatian families who owned larger parcels of land, or continued to acquire land, would become rich in assets as the land was zoned residential, industrial, or commercial. For a long period they were sufficiently politically active and valued by the community that their property taxes were calculated as if they were in a rural area. That wealth helped drive the growth of the New Zealand wine industry.

Hawke's Bay

The Hawke's Bay wine industry was so different it could have been in another country, perhaps Australia. Four enterprises – McWilliam's Wines Ltd, McDonald's Wines, Glenvale Wines and Vidal – dominated winegrowing in Hawke's Bay. Each made over 50,000 gallons (227,500 litres) of wine annually. In Henderson, Corbans (85,000 gallons) was the only winery with a similar level of production. In 1960 the four Hawke's Bay wineries were responsible for 86 per cent of the region's production. Using the categories of New Zealand Winegrowers in the twenty-first century, all of these wineries would be in Category 2 – over 200,000 litres. Only two other wineries in Hawke's Bay – Mission Vineyards and Te Mata Vineyards Ltd – produced over 5000 gallons of wine annually in 1960.

The marketing of Hawke's Bay wine was quite different from that of the West Auckland family businesses. The region's large enterprises sold almost all of their wine through wholesale liquor outlets, hotels, or wine shops. McWilliam's Wines, when merged with McDonald's in 1962 and managed by Tom McDonald, was producing over half of the Hawke's Bay wine. The two main New Zealand breweries and wholesalers of wines and spirits, New Zealand Breweries and Dominion Breweries, were substantial shareholders in McWilliam's. The sales by region of McDonald's Wines just before merger shows clearly the close relationships it had with the established retail outlets of the South Island, where some of the powerful importers and wholesalers of wine and liquor were dominant. Only 11 per cent of its wine was sold in Auckland and 14 per cent in Wellington compared with almost 50 per cent in the South Island and almost 18 per cent locally in Hawke's Bay.

None of the Hawke's Bay vineyards in 1960 were far from the coast. They formed a discontinuous belt from Bay View and the Esk Valley in the north, where Glenvale Wines of the Bird family was located, to Havelock North in the south. In between, one of Vidal's substantial vineyards was right on the coast at Te Awanga, and Mission Vineyards and the McDonald winery at Greenmeadows west of Napier formed another node. The headquarters and winery of Vidal was in Hastings and McWilliam's winery was in Napier, but both firms had vineyards in several localities.

Grapes of European origin (*Vitis vinifera*) were much more important in Hawke's Bay where they represented 64 per cent of the total area in vines. In the Auckland

'He rules by force of personality,' noted *Cooks Wine Bulletin* in April 1971. At McWilliam's Wines, Tom McDonald led a team that included Denis Kasza and Peter Hubscher to make some excellent Cabernet Sauvignons. But by the 1970s, Hubscher came to view McWilliam's as 'a sherry factory . . . based on water and sugar'. *Marti Friedlander, Auckland War Memorial Museum – Tāmaki Paenga Hira, PH-2008-4*

Table 2.1 Vineyards and wineries in Auckland and Hawke's Bay, 1960

	Auckland	Hawke's Bay
Area in vines (acres)	425	387
Winemaking licences (number)	128	16
Vines per holding (acres)	5	26
Regional wine production (%)		
Sherry	52	67
Port	35	28
Table wine	13	5
Wine production (million litres)	1.8	2.0
Vinifera varieties (% of total)	24	64

region they represented only 24 per cent. This dominance of *vinifera* varieties is partly explained by Hawke's Bay being free of the pest *Phylloxera vastatrix* at the time. Vines in North America, including *Vitis labrusca*, are resistant to this disease and hybrids of American vines and *vinifera* vines are also resistant to varying degrees. Indeed, the American vines were originally imported into France for breeding as French scientists experimented by crossing them with *vinifera* varieties. The resistance to disease of these crosses partly explains their importance in Auckland where over 75 per cent of the vines were hybrids. The hybrids and *labrusca* varieties are more robust in heavier soils and able to resist various fungus diseases in regions where rainfall and humidity are higher. Heavy soils and high humidity dominated those parts of Auckland where vines were grown at the time.

    Dalmatians who settled in West Auckland in the late nineteenth and early twentieth centuries did not choose it for the suitability of its natural environment for vines, orchards and market gardens, but rather for the opportunities that the nearby urban area offered as a market and for employment. Moreover, its heavy, largely clay soils made the land cheap. These Dalmatians had plenty of experience with clay and other difficult soils from their gumdigging in Northland and other parts of the country. Persistent hard work in clearing the land and working the soils of Henderson-Oratia made it possible to grow grapes and fruit trees (especially apples) and vegetables for the Auckland market. Chain migration to the same locality from within New Zealand and internationally brought increasing numbers of Dalmatian settlers to Henderson-Oratia and later to Kumeu-Huapai.

    Hawke's Bay, with its much lower precipitation (under 800 mm compared with over 1400 mm in West Auckland), lower humidity and higher sunshine hours, is a more suitable natural environment for growing grapes to make table wine. In addition, its soils are more varied and versatile. They include loams, clays and river-deposited gravels. These natural advantages of Hawke's Bay became clear from the 1960s when table wines became more important. But the heavier soils and higher precipitation in West Auckland have not precluded excellent wines being produced there, provided the standard of vineyard management and vinification is high. Enterprises such as Kumeu River Wines have persistently demonstrated these capacities. Moreover, West Auckland Dallies were to continue to have a major role to play in the evolution and resilience of the New Zealand wine industry.

In addition to the concentrations of viticulture in West Auckland and Hawke's Bay, two other smaller nodes are worth noting – Te Kauwhata and Gisborne. They had different origins and different local economies in the 1950s. The establishment of New Zealand's Viticultural Research Station at Te Kauwhata in 1902, with Italian-educated viticulturist Romeo Bragato heading it, had stimulated the area's viticulture and winemaking, but also orcharding and other smallholdings. By 1960, Te Kauwhata was growing primarily table grapes (Albany Surprise) and apples, although some wine

In the early days of the New Zealand industry, bushy vines produced grapes in great quantity. *Dick Scott Collection, Auckland War Memorial Museum – Tāmaki Paenga Hira, PH-2008-4*

New Zealand Vines and Wines circa 1960

was being made in the locality. This research station remained active until the middle decades of the twentieth century and Te Kauwhata later received a temporary stimulus when Cooks Wines, founded by the Auckland entrepreneur David Lucas, planted vines there in 1969 before establishing a modern winery in the 1970s.

Gisborne had a much smaller area in vines in 1960, with the Wohnsiedlers of German origin growing 20 hectares of grapes and making wine there. Wattie's established a vegetable processing plant on the Poverty Bay flats in the 1950s which stimulated horticulture more generally, and many smallholders on the Gisborne Plain became skilled in growing fruit, vegetables and other crops. Gisborne was to play a key role in the initial establishment of modern New Zealand winegrowing in the 1960s, 1970s and into the 1980s.

A transforming moment

The modern New Zealand wine industry developed out of the assortment of wines and vines established in a few regions by about 1960. In Auckland, it was also driven by a group of enthusiasts who saw the development of wine in New Zealand as one part of changing the wider culture. Its spiritual home was Paul Groshek's Muaga Vineyards in Candia Road, Henderson, where conversation flowed freely, stimulated by Groshek's wide interests and lubricated by his simple, unadulterated table wine – even on Sundays. The writer Rex Fairburn's polemical broadsheet *Crisis in the Wine Industry*, published by Pelorus Press in 1948 and reprinted in 1949, systematised some of the conversations from these symposia at Groshek's winery.

> New Zealand is probably the only country in the world with a wine-growing climate that has failed to give strong and consistent support to its wine industry. This has been due partly to the restrictive effect of the activities of certain vested interests (some of them belonging to 'the trade' and some opposed to it), and partly to lack of public knowledge and appreciation of the value of wine as a staple article of diet.
>
> Is there in New Zealand politics a man with sufficient vision to see the possibilities – economic, social and cultural – that are latent in the wine industry of this country and in the unused acres of second-class land that could be adding greatly to the wealth of the Dominion?

In the late 1950s, government action followed. From 1938 under Import Control Regulations the imports of wine and spirits were halved for several years. This reduction in supply of spirits and wine (coming mainly from Australia) coincided with increased demand for alcohol during the Second World War, partly because of the large number of American troops stationed in New Zealand. Local winegrowers responded by increasing production. But their favourable trading conditions were short-lived. Imports increased; and by 1948, overproduction in New Zealand wine was assumed to have arrived. A Royal Commission on Licensing in 1946 considered all alcohols and made recommendations on the marketing channels for wine but few were acted upon. Given the Commission's broad mandate, the power of the breweries and wine and liquor importers and merchants, this was not surprising. But the difficulties being experienced by the wine industry in both West Auckland and Hawke's Bay in the late 1940s and into the 1950s began to attract public and political attention and support.

On 26 October 1956, the New Zealand House of Representatives ordered

> that a Select Committee be appointed, consisting of ten members to enquire into and report upon the state and prospects of the wine-making industry of New Zealand, the effect of the present law upon the manufacture, distribution, sale, and consumption of New Zealand wine and all other aspects of the industry as the Committee sees fit.

Few select committees have had terms of reference so broad or made recommendations so bold. Paul Groshek gave written evidence to the Committee. His submission was by far the most colourful, visionary and unequivocal, in ideas as well as language.

> It must be understood by any practical wine-maker and wine connoisseur that most beneficial wines are natural dry table wines.
>
> ... there is no reason why these people should not be allowed to obtain table wines in grocery shops and in restaurants with meals. This would be example of how the wine should be drunk and would lead to sober drinking, as no connoisseur is a drunkard or alcoholic!
>
> It is important that any restaurant wishing to supply wine with meals should be allowed. If the place is good enough to have a meal it is good enough to have a drink.
>
> No tied house should be allowed to have a monopoly to supply prize wine with full-page advertisement in papers to a public that does not know what table wine is. The wines should strictly comply as pure grape wines and let the public find out for themselves, what is good about wine.
>
> The wine would be bottled by the wine-maker and reach the consumer direct. It would be preferable in half-size bottles.
>
> The handling and distribution laws of wine are such where wine is regarded as more dangerous than explosives and breeds lawbreakers. This is irrational.
>
> New Zealand wants more grapes to produce wine. It is of no use complaining of importing wine from cheap labour producing countries and we exploiting labour of cheap sugar producing countries. To produce more grapes we need more wine growers.
>
> This is not politics or a matter for referendum, when one half people say to other half when to drink or eat, and make liberty a mockery.

Nick Delegat and Mate Selak, under the watchful eye of customs officer Warren Leonard, draw off alcohol to fortify their ports and sherries. *Marti Friedlander, Auckland War Memorial Museum – Tāmaki Paenga Hira, PH-2008-4*

By the late 1950s, social and political attitudes – modified by more distance from the grey days of World War Two – had changed. The Select Committee that reported to the House of Representatives on 14 September 1957 recognised this shift in opinion and acted. Recommendation 27 reads 'that approved restaurants be licensed to supply New Zealand light table wine with substantial meals'. No booze was to be served with a mere snack. By 1960, legislation was in place. The nights of patrons smuggling bottles into venues under dresses or in deep pockets, and restaurants risking prosecution for serving wine, were over. That the West Auckland member H. G. R. Mason (Labour, Waitakere) moved the resolution was no coincidence.

Other recommendations took longer to realise. The cautious wording of Recommendation 15 – 'that wine-sellers' licences be more freely granted and that an application for such a licence should not be refused because of the existence, or probable existence, of other forms of licence' – looked forward to the battles to be heard before the Licensing Commission in the coming decades as the breweries and large wholesale liquor outlets protected sales of beer and imported wines and spirits for their hotels and 'off-licence' premises. Nevertheless, more wine-sellers' licences were issued, mainly to the medium-sized firms from West Auckland. Some family wineries even established small stables of wine shops across selected provincial towns, mainly in the North Island. These proved valuable marketing channels until the popularity of table wine soared in the 1970s and most outlets licensed to sell alcohol had no option but to sell New Zealand wine. Frank Yukich of Montana was at the forefront of these battles, always jousting with the breweries. They contested every one of his applications. Through Yukich's persistence, by the late 1970s Montana had accumulated 30 wine shops throughout the country.

The most far-reaching recommendation of the Select Committee – 'that wine-sellers' licences be granted to any grocer of good character who has suitable premises, and who does not sell food or drink for consumption on the premises, unless there is reasonable fear of undesirable social consequences' – sounds decidedly quaint in the freewheeling early twenty-first century. It took until 1990 before supermarkets were licensed to sell wine. Within a decade of receiving their licences, supermarkets were dominating sales of both local and imported wine. Beer gained access to supermarkets only in 1999. For a short time wine had a marketing advantage over other alcoholic drinks. The value of wine in the trolleys of supermarket shoppers is now worth more than any other single category of food or drink.

Thus, by 1960, the conditions were in place for the development of a quality wine industry in New Zealand. Legislation and cultural attitudes had shifted to allow the growth of wine sales in restaurants, wine shops, and at the cellar door. A group of young wine enthusiasts, many of them descendants of winemaking families, brought experience and new ideas to the business. And companies both large and small were beginning to show that vines and wines of quality could be grown in New Zealand soils and climates across a number of regions. After 1960, the country's wine production expanded rapidly as the industry went through a regional and varietal revolution.

3

Regional and Varietal Revolution

In the second half of the twentieth century the regional distribution and varietal mix of New Zealand winegrowing was transformed. From an initial base in Auckland and Hawke's Bay in the 1960s, substantial areas in vines have been planted in turn in Gisborne, Marlborough, the Wairarapa (Wellington), Central Otago and parts of Canterbury. The vine also has established a noticeable presence in the Auckland region at locations beyond its traditional base in West Auckland around Matakana and on Waiheke Island; in the Waikato at Te Kauwhata; and in Nelson.

Contemporaneously with this regional expansion, New Zealand winegrowers changed the varietal mix from hybrids and varieties suitable for fortified wine to the varieties of *Vitis vinifera* that flourished in the cooler and northern wine-producing regions of France. By the early twenty-first century, each New Zealand region was showing signs of developing its own specialisations in varieties of grapes and in the style of wines being produced.

In the 1960s and 1970s, very little was known about which varieties should be grown where in New Zealand, or the viticultural practices needed to produce grapes with the qualities to make table wines of distinction. Some individuals and organisations subsequently commissioned studies of the suitability of particular localities and regions for grape growing. Examples are those by Derek Milne (Martinborough area and Hawke's Bay), Wayne Thomas and the late John Marris (Marlborough), and the

Templars Hill, Mt Difficulty, Central Otago. *Matt Dicey*

Department of Scientific and Industrial Research (DSIR) and Ministry of Agriculture trials (Central Otago). But even these studies were noticeably silent or unreliable about which particular varieties to plant in different regions. They were often designed to convince people to invest in vine growing in these places rather than to assess growing conditions for particular varieties.

The varietal specialisation that has emerged in different New Zealand localities and regions has resulted mainly from trial and error by the enterprises planting the grapes and by the demands of the market. As the vine was planted in untried regions, few aspiring winegrowers examined all the available scientific evidence and maps and decided 'this is where this variety should be grown'. Rather, grape varieties considered suitable for the locality were planted and growers and winemakers demonstrated that they were able (or unable) to produce grapes with the desired qualities to make distinctive and appealing wines. Montana's success in Marlborough with Sauvignon Blanc is an excellent example.

Each of the regions successively colonised by the vine required new learning – with regard to soils of different structure and textures, drainage characteristics, moisture retention, and climates with different seasonal nuances. The pioneering family firms in localities such as Martinborough, Central Otago and parts of Canterbury were seldom sure when they first planted grapes whether they had chosen the right sites or whether they would be successful. In Central Otago, for example, three of the pioneering enterprises – Rippon Vineyards, Chard Farm and Gibbston Valley – have all made excellent still wine from Pinot Noir. The last two have now decided to extend their vineyards or source grapes from localities of Central Otago more recently colonised by the vine where growers from sub-regions such as the Bendigo Terraces have demonstrated their ability to ripen Pinot Noir more consistently.

The major New Zealand companies, alongside the small winemaking firms, have been crucial influences on the dispersion of viticulture in New Zealand. Not only did they invest in the regions, but through letting contracts to grape growers the major firms have helped transform how grapes are grown. For many grape growers, choice of varieties has since been strongly influenced by the advice, even insistence, of the buyers – the winemaking enterprises – which, informally and in written contracts, have specified their preferences. In the early stages of the development of the industry, when grapes were in short supply, almost any fruit were acceptable. Today, the growing of different grape varieties to meet a specified number of tonnes per hectare, often with sugar levels (brix) and acidity also specified by bands, is standard practice.

Many of these grape-growing families – especially in Gisborne, Hawke's Bay and Marlborough – were landowners with experience of growing other crops. Talking about what attracted his family into growing grapes, Phil Rose of Wairau River Wines said: 'We've been growing things all our lives really. It was just something different. Vines are

The country's leading winemakers gather at the 1970 Viticultural Association field day. The association's president, George Mazuran – a Croatian immigrant who had been growing grapes and lobbying government in New Zealand for more than 30 years – addresses the group. *Marti Friedlander, Auckland War Memorial Museum – Tāmaki Paenga Hira, PH-2008-4*

relatively easy things to grow once you understand the sort of philosophy of a vineyard.' The industry survivors now have more than 30 years of experience producing grapes for wine during times when the demands of the wine companies have been escalating. As corporate firms write ever more sophisticated contracts that require, for instance, low and precise yields of Pinot Noir for their premium wines, these grape growers have the understanding of canopy management to respond. They know the environment of the land they own. Many who entered as grape growers have since started their own wineries. Grape growing and winemaking families on their own holdings are equally as skilled – some would claim more skilled – in integrating the quality of grapes required to suit the style of wine they seek. Experience and learning on the ground by winemakers and grape growers have driven the varietal and regional revolutions in New Zealand.

Historical geography of the vine

The historical geography of the vine and wine in New Zealand is usefully viewed in a series of overlapping phases: the period of rural (and associated urban) settlement from the vine's first known planting in 1819 through to the 1930s; the period between about 1880 and 1920 when the temperance movement and restrictive legislation contributed to reducing the small area in vines; a period of steady growth from a small base during the 1920s and 1930s and rapid growth during the Second World War, followed by a decade of uncertainty, even crisis, as local markets evaporated when imported wines again became available; and the most recent phase, from the early 1960s, when the planting of vineyards recommenced at an unprecedented pace and has continued through the rest of the twentieth century and into the twenty-first, interrupted only by the vine-pull scheme of 1986. Changing societal and governmental attitudes, together with changing consumption patterns and changing marketing and distribution channels, have underpinned the latter developments, but this period of buoyant growth was founded on its past, and the period before 1960 reveals much about the culture–environment nexus of the vine and wine.

The vine arrived in New Zealand soon after the first settlement by Europeans. Samuel Marsden (who established the first Church of England mission in New Zealand) planted vines; and James Busby (the first British Resident) made the first wines in 1836. Dumont d'Urville, when he visited Busby in 1840, praised the wine made from these Bay of Islands grapes. It is quite possible that the vine had arrived earlier than this, because ships plied the Tasman from the late eighteenth century and vines were growing in Sydney Cove by the 1780s. In 1838 the writer and explorer J. S. Polack reported that in New Zealand vines were 'largely cultivated to the northwards of the River Thames' – that is, in Northland and South Auckland. Maori were quick to cultivate them and supply table grapes to the Auckland and other markets as they seized the opportunities provided by concentrated populations.

As in most New World countries, the vine was also disseminated with the Catholic missionaries. The Marist Brothers established a winery in 1855 at Meanee in Hawke's Bay (after grapes were first cultivated at Pakowhai), and later moved to Greenmeadows to become the Mission Vineyards. Sociologist and wine writer Jason Mabbett recounts plantings of vines by the Marist Brothers at Whangaroa (1839), Otaki (1850), Gisborne (1847) and on the Whanganui River, near Pipiriki. Wine was made from these grapes. During the second half of the nineteenth century and for the first two decades of the twentieth, when rural settlement spread rapidly, *Vitis vinifera*, like other crops of European origin, was planted in many parts of the country. Settlers experimented with various varieties as part of the mixed farming systems that they established. Most dairy farms, for instance, also had their own orchard until well into the twentieth century.

But the vine was not one of the perennial crops commonly found on all agricultural holdings of the predominantly Anglo-Celtic population. It usually appeared in one of two forms: as a family vineyard or vinehouse (glasshouse) in the British tradition, usually for table grapes; or on land owned or used by people from cultures with traditions of wine –

the 1840 Nanto-Bordelaise Company of Langlois in Akaroa, the Spaniard Joseph Soler in Wanganui (1869), Breidecker at New Plymouth, the Vidals of Hawke's Bay, Croats from the Dalmatian coast on the gumfields of Northland and in other parts of New Zealand.

Colonial commentators frequently tied the vine to non-British cultural groups. Mabbett quotes Petre (1842) who pointed out:

> One drawback upon the cultivation of the vine, the olive and the mulberry is that the English really know nothing about it. To cultivate them to any extent we shall require French and German cultivators, to whom the most liberal encouragement should be given.

Similar arguments were made in the regional press over the qualities of German settlers. The *Nelson Examiner*, commenting on the arrival of a shipload of settlers from Germany in the early 1840s, wrote: 'No immigrants are more valued than the Germans and we hail the intended cultivation of the vine by them with unfeigned pleasure.'

Vidal vineyards, Havelock North, Hawke's Bay, 1920s. Spanish immigrant Anthony Joseph Vidal established Vidal Estate in 1905. French, German, Croatian, Spanish, and other continental Europeans nourished a small tradition of winemaking in New Zealand through the years of restrictive liquor legislation, when most New Zealanders preferred beer. *Henry Norford Whitehead, Alexander Turnbull Library, Wellington, New Zealand, 1/1-004863-G*

Nevertheless, some settlers of British origin were important in establishing commercial vineyards in the nineteenth century. Most of them were wealthy landowners who preceded their planting by investigating winegrowing in Europe, California or Australia. Beetham planted vines in the Wairarapa in 1883. Tiffen's vineyard to the west of Napier in Hawke's Bay grew to almost 15 hectares by 1905 but declined when a prohibitionist became manager of the farm. Chambers planted a hectare of vines at Te Mata in 1892 and established a winery there. The Levets of Whakapirau (now Wellsford) were of more modest means, arriving in New Zealand as Albertland settlers in 1862. They established a vineyard and commercial winery near the Kaipara Harbour in the 1860s.

The Croatian-born, Italian-trained scientist Romeo Bragato provides a lively evaluation of the potential of the New Zealand industry at the end of the nineteenth century. His south-to-north journey from Central Otago reads something like the rural excursions of Arthur Young or even Robert Louis Stevenson into the continental Europe of the eighteenth and nineteenth centuries. His enthusiasm for the potential of New Zealand and its regions for vines is unbounded, and two characteristics of his observations are particularly relevant to the themes of this chapter: first, he was able to observe vines growing in almost every region of New Zealand; and second, the vines that he mentions are mainly *Vitis vinifera*.

Two of his other discoveries also provide a clue to the future. He identified *Phylloxera vastatrix*, the root-aphid that had devastated the European vineyards from the late 1860s, as well as other diseases that had earlier caused severe problems in Europe, notably öidium or powdery mildew. Nevertheless, most of the vines he observed were healthy and well cared for. Geographically, therefore, by the opening of the twentieth century *vinifera* grapes had been grown in most regions of New Zealand. Much of this regional experience was to wane or disappear in the next 60 years. Although Bragato's investigation of New Zealand's prospects for viticulture resulted in the establishment of the Te Kauwhata Viticultural Research Station in 1898 and his appointment as Government Viticulturist there in 1902, he left for Canada in 1909, disillusioned by his experience when he did not receive the support from the government that he had expected.

Larger social and cultural forces influenced changes to the area in vines between 1900 and 1950. The temperance movement had a powerful impact. Between 1880 and 1920, the state responded to the electorate by regulating to restrict the sale of alcohol, and particularly wine. Licensed wine shops were allowed, but over the whole country only four licences were granted. Sale of wine by single bottle from wineries was not permitted. Some restrictions were geographically specific. From 1895, certain electorates, including part of West Auckland, voted to go 'dry'. No alcohol could be sold in them even from their wineries. Such restrictions affected small wineries in particular because they found it difficult to get access to the many hotels controlled by the breweries.

Temperance combined with widespread prejudice against non-British citizens to cultivate a suspicion toward wine and its makers. Prime Minister W. F. Massey warned in 1914 of

> the manufacture and sale of what is called Austrian wine . . . a liquor that is sold in the district north of Auckland. I have never seen the stuff, but I believe it to be one of the vilest concoctions which can possibly be imagined. I do not know what its ingredients are, but I have come across people who have seen the effects of the use of Austrian wine as a beverage, and from what I have learned it is a degrading, demoralising and sometimes maddening drink . . .

Many Dalmatians had immigrated to New Zealand in reaction to the political turmoil in the Balkans and the incorporation of their province into the Austro-Hungarian Empire. These were the 'Austrians' that Massey is referring to. Their lot, and the attitude of some members of the Anglo-Celtic society toward them, was to deteriorate as the First World War progressed.

The nascent industry suffered as a result of the temperance movement and such suspicion towards non-British citizens, together with the penchant for beer among New Zealand's working class and the preference of social elites for imported wines. By the 1950s, New Zealand's annual wine consumption was less than 2 litres per head compared with France at 96 litres. Beer consumption in New Zealand was over 100 litres per head – third in the world after Belgium and Australia. At the same time, France was consuming less than 30 litres of beer per head. The New Zealand brewing interests exerted enormous economic and political power in distributing their products.

The First World War, the 1930s Depression and the Second World War began to change these conditions and set the environment for the rise of the modern wine industry. The experience of New Zealand troops serving in continental Europe, shortages of imported wines – indeed all alcohol during the Second World War – and the establishment of a series of wineries committed to earning a full-time living in the industry, all contributed. Modest increases in the area in vines began during the Depression but accelerated rapidly during the Second World War when alcohol of any description was in short supply. American troops stationed in New Zealand increased the demand. Wine consumption from New Zealand grapes increased rapidly, but it was almost all fortified wine, a style that was not playing to New Zealand's environmental strengths.

While the period from colonisation to 1960 represents the prehistory of the New Zealand wine industry, it is the regional and varietal revolutions since 1960 that have shaped its modern configuration.

Regional revolution

Strong growth in the area in vines has characterised the period from 1960 to 2010 and beyond (Figure 3.1). From a low base in 1960, the planting of vineyards quickened after 1975 before a flat period between 1982 and 1985. The government-sponsored vine-pull scheme of 1986 saw over 1500 hectares of vines removed. More vines were planted immediately, and after 1995 planting again accelerated. The growth showed little signs of slackening until the recession of 2008 slowed plantings in some regions, but most enterprises have recovered, and now many grape growers and wine enterprises are planning substantial increases in their vineyards. Accompanying the increase in area in vines has been substantial investment in wineries and associated plant by both large corporate and family firms.

The New Zealand industry that developed is highly oligopolistic. At the millennium, four firms – Montana, Corbans, Villa Maria and Nobilo – produced about 80 per cent of the wine. Almost 350 mainly family winemaking firms, and about 700 family-based grape growers, made up the rest of the industry. Over the last twenty years, takeovers and mergers have transformed the ownership structure of the largest firms. Montana bought Corbans and then in 2000 Pernod Ricard acquired Montana. In 2011, contract winemaker and exporter Indevin Partners New Zealand made use of the fermentation and storage tanks in Gisborne that had been underutilised as the New Zealand wine industry focused its attention on the rapid growth of the Central Otago, Wairarapa, Marlborough and Hawke's Bay regions.

In 1960, grape growing and winemaking were concentrated in Auckland and Hawke's Bay (Table 3.1). Together, these two regions grew 85 per cent of New Zealand's total area in vines. Since 1960, a series of regional growth spurts have transformed the distribution of vines in New Zealand. Four main stages are discernible. First, in a frequently neglected phase of the industry, an expansion took place in the Auckland region during the 1960s and early 1970s. Associated with this development was growth in the nearby Waikato region, dominated by the Te Kauwhata locality. Second, during the 1960s and

Table 3.1 The five regions with the largest area in vines (% of the national total)

1960		1970		1980		1990		2000		2010	
Auckland	44	Auckland	45	Gisborne	32	Marlborough	29	Marlborough	41	Marlborough	60
Hawke's Bay	41	Hawke's Bay	22	Hawke's Bay	31	Gisborne	29	Hawke's Bay	25	Hawke's Bay	15
Waikato	8	Gisborne	19	Marlborough	16	Hawke's Bay	27	Gisborne	16	Gisborne	7
Gisborne	5	Waikato	12	Auckland	12	Auckland	6	Canterbury	4	Canterbury	6
Northland	2	Northland	1	Waikato	2	Waikato	3	Auckland	4	Central Otago	5

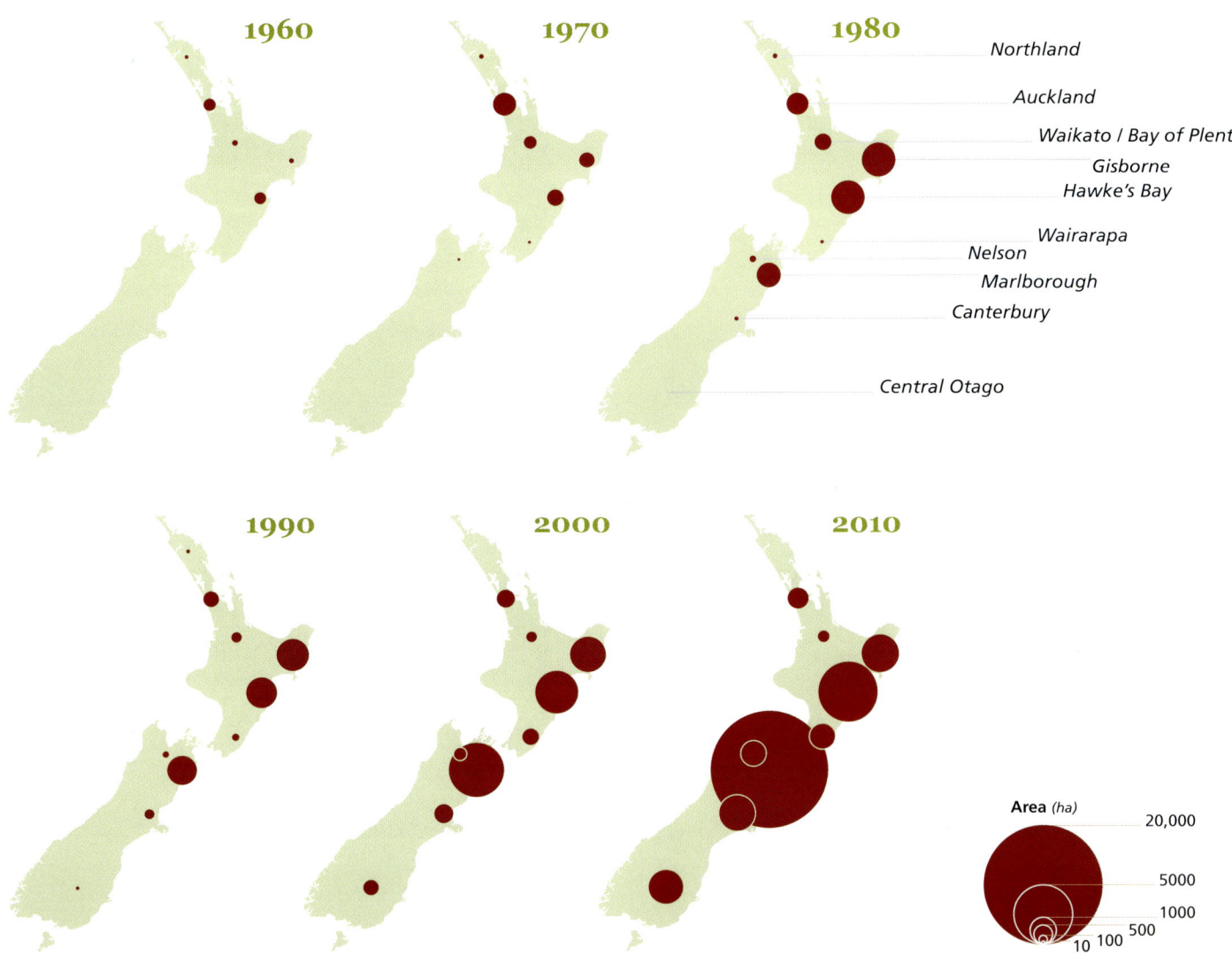

Figure 3.1 Regional dispersal of vines in New Zealand, 1960 to 2010

1970s, came the rise of Gisborne as a major winegrowing area. By 1980 it was growing more vines than any other region although only a single percentage point above Hawke's Bay. The third stage, the rise of Marlborough, began in 1973, but only in the 1980s did its area in vines begin to grow rapidly. Its growth rate accelerated in the 1990s until by 2000 it had 41 per cent of the country's vines. Fourth came the rise, mainly in the last decade, of other regions – notably Canterbury (especially Waipara), the Wairarapa, Nelson and Central Otago. Throughout the second half of the twentieth century, except for a brief

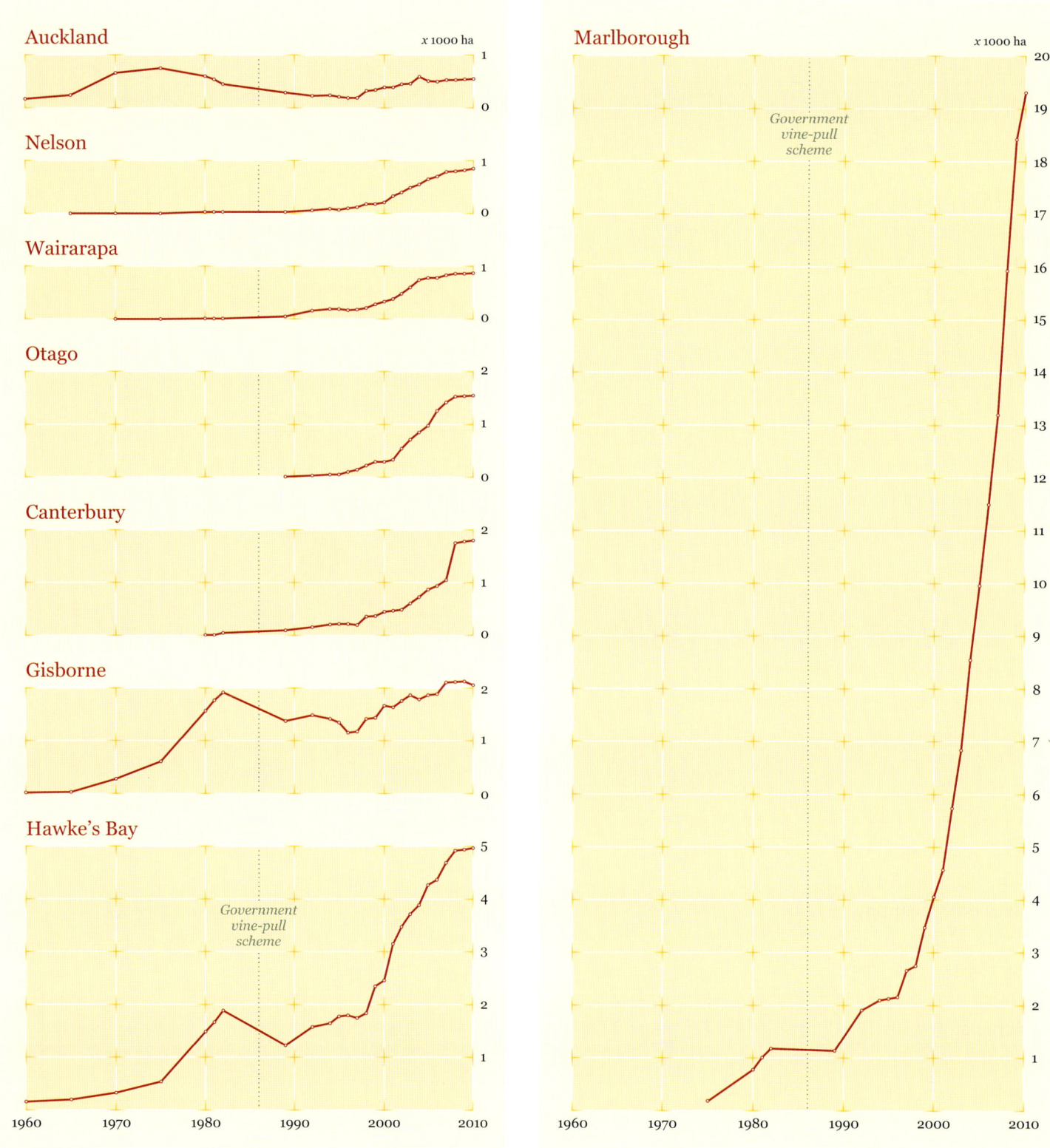

Figure 3.2 Area in vines in eight New Zealand regions, 1960 to 2010

period in 1990, Hawke's Bay has been one of the top two regions by area in vines and has played a distinctive and vital role in the New Zealand industry.

The expansion in vineyard area gained real momentum after 1965. Auckland was the region that grew most rapidly in the period 1965 to 1970. Three major firms – Corbans, Montana and Penfolds – began a rapid expansion of their vineyard area (Figure 3.3). Each had different motives for relocating or expanding. Corbans, the largest enterprise at the beginning of the expansion, was being pressured by urban encroachment close to its vineyards in Henderson, West Auckland. It could capitalise on this land's urban potential by selling some vineyards and buying and developing more suitable land cheaply within reasonable distance of its winery. Meanwhile, the Yukich brothers had become closely involved in their father's 5 hectares of grapes and small winery called Montana in the Waitakere Ranges. Working from a restricted site, they began a period of aggressive expansion of their business that accelerated when the American firm Seagram bought 40 per cent of Montana in 1973. By the end of the century, Montana would be making wine from about 3000 hectares of grapes. Finally, Penfolds of Australia entered the New Zealand industry by acquiring a large family vineyard and winery in Henderson owned by the Averill family.

From today's perspective and state of environmental knowledge, it seems surprising that in their first large plantings these three firms all chose sites on the outskirts of the Auckland metropolitan area. Within a decade all except Corbans' Merlot vineyard in Kumeu were out of production. Had this expansion taken place a decade or so later it is likely that the choice of sites, even within the Auckland region, would have been more sophisticated and the vineyards of higher quality. In the 1960s, however, knowledge of suitable varieties and clones, of canopy management, and the virus status of New Zealand vines was rudimentary. The South Auckland vineyard of Montana would have been much more successful had it been located in the eastern lee of the Hunua Ranges. The Penfolds vineyards near the west coast were within 10 kilometres of the very successful Rothesay vineyards of Collards in the Matua Valley that is much less exposed and receives noticeably lower rainfall on more versatile soils. Two of the Corbans vineyards in Kumeu were later sold and revitalised. Under different ownership and with better canopy management, they have produced some fine Merlot.

From 1970, a second period is characterised by the rise of Gisborne and Hawke's Bay. By 1980, both Gisborne and Hawke's Bay each had twice the area in vines of the Auckland region. Gisborne's growth resulted from Montana Wines continuing its aggressive expansion by letting contracts for landowners to grow grapes. Corbans and Penfolds were quick to respond by arranging contracts with other landholders in Gisborne. A series of well-established, but smaller, Auckland-based wine companies – such as Babich, Nobilo and Matua Valley – followed the larger companies and sourced grapes from these new regions.

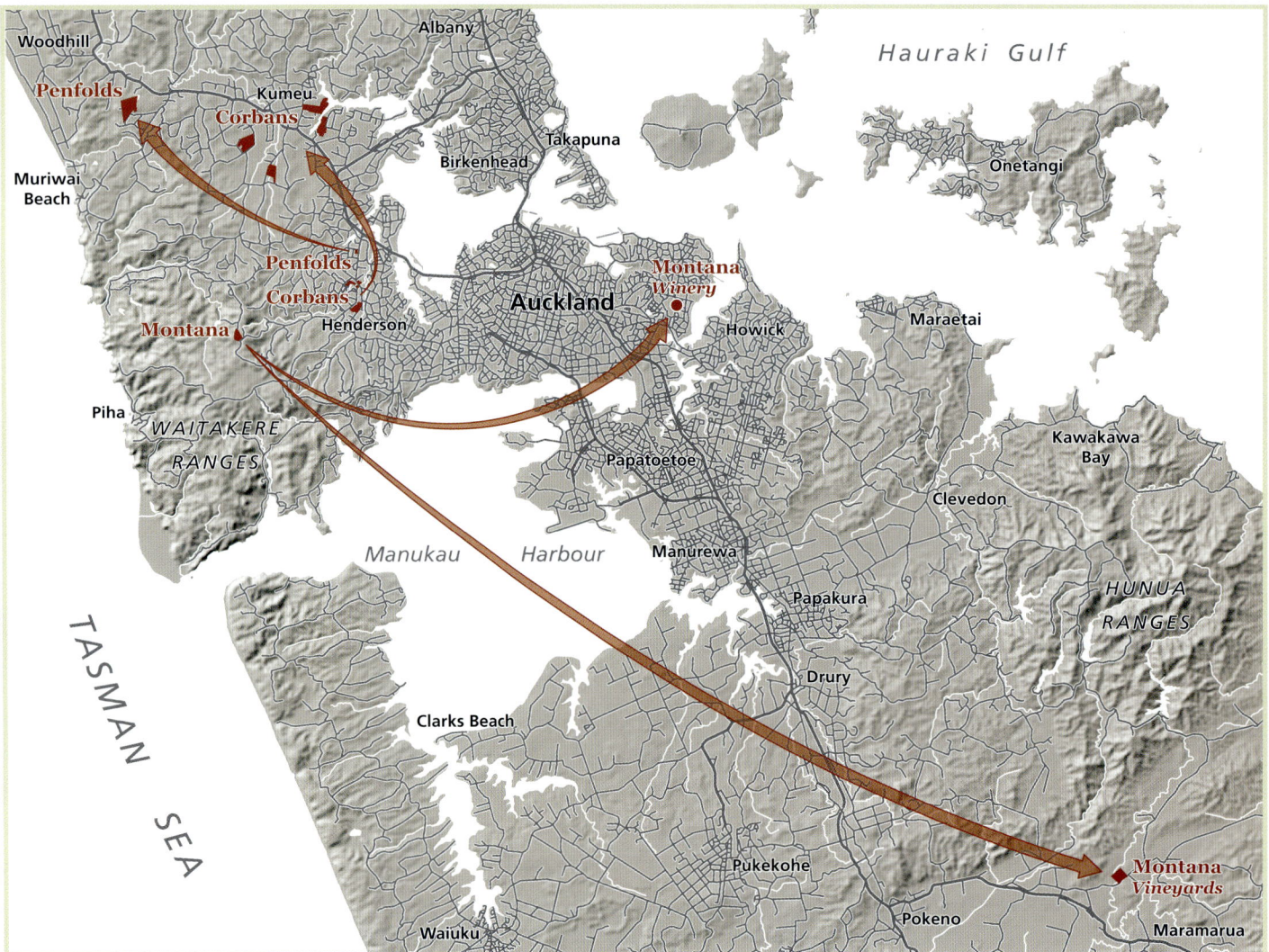

Figure 3.3 1960s dispersal of vineyards owned by Corbans, Montana, and Penfolds to urban peripheral land on the northwestern and southern fringe of Auckland

A similar sequence, with some different companies participating, occurred in Hawke's Bay. Existing local firms also influenced its growth by enlarging their holdings. McWilliam's Wines, the Australian company that began operating in New Zealand in 1947, continued to expand its Hawke's Bay vineyards in the 1960s and 1970s. Other firms that had been established earlier, such as McDonald's Wines and Glenvale Wines, also increased their vineyard area from the 1960s. During the same period a number of smaller firms also established there.

Growth in the North Island regions was soon rivalled by new developments in Marlborough, with Montana Wines again at the forefront. In the early 1970s, Frank

Yukich, the managing director of Montana, had decided that Marlborough was a region that offered strong environmental opportunities for grape growing in New Zealand. In this decision he was influenced by Wayne Thomas, formerly a government plant scientist, by now in charge of national viticulture for Montana. Some limited scientific evidence – more to convince the Montana board than to provide definitive judgement – supported these views.

Grapes were first planted there in the winter of 1973. Despite the heavy losses of young vines over the first summer, the quality of the grapes quickly established that Marlborough was a region of unusual potential. Between 1975 and 1980, Marlborough's area in vines increased more rapidly than anywhere else, and by 1990 it had a slightly

Throughout the 1960s, the Corban family continued to expand their footprint in West Auckland. In 1969, they bought 121 acres in Taupaki. Here the family (from left, Khaleel, Wadier, Assid, and Najib, and on right, David and Joe) bless the new plantings. *Marti Friedlander, Auckland War Memorial Museum – Tāmaki Paenga Hira, PH-2008-4*

Regional and Varietal Revolution

larger area in vines than any other region. As well as planting its own vines, Montana again let contracts to landowners in the region. The Marlborough bonanza had commenced. By 2000 it was growing over 40 per cent of New Zealand's grapes and by 2010 over 60 per cent.

Several economic and environmental advantages favoured the expansion in Marlborough. By viticultural standards, land prices there were low because the Wairau Plain was being converted from quite extensive sheep farming with some cropping and commercial seed production, and large areas of land were available. Marlborough's low annual rainfall, long growing season and mainly well-drained soils of low to moderate fertility suited many varieties of vines, although uncertain rainfall demanded irrigation, especially in their establishment phase. Most growers continued to irrigate, in difficult periods and with careful monitoring, even after the vines were established.

Although regional shifts were occurring, all major grape-growing regions – Gisborne, Hawke's Bay and Marlborough – grew rapidly in the late 1970s and early 1980s. For instance, in the five years between 1980 and 1985, both Gisborne and Hawke's Bay each added over 1000 hectares to their area in grapes – a rate of growth that surpassed that of Marlborough. The rapid expansion of the early 1980s had its detrimental effects. Intense competition for a share of the market saw prices for wine in New Zealand plummet in the mid-1980s. That drove a number of companies into receivership and led to several takeovers and mergers. In 1986 the government sponsored a vine-pull scheme as an economic remedy, providing a subsidy of $6,175 per hectare to remove vines. This response was quite uncharacteristic of the neo-liberal Labour government elected in 1984 and indicates the lobbying power of firms in the wine and liquor industry at that time. The total direct subsidy for the vine-pull scheme was almost NZ$10 million. Growers removed over 1500 hectares of vines, most of it from Gisborne (586 ha), Hawke's Bay (534 ha), the South Island (210 ha) and Auckland (162 ha).

In retrospect, the vine-pull scheme was an unexpected opportunity for the wine industry. By the mid-1980s, viticultural knowledge and practice in New Zealand had improved considerably. The scheme encouraged some wine companies and grape growers to change the varieties of grapes they were growing, to improve the virus status of their vines, to find a better combination of rootstock and variety, to modify their trellising systems and to plant the best available clones. Although for many wineries problems of cash flow necessitated the uprooting of vines, the majority of enterprises quickly re-established their area in grapes. Some grape growers took the opportunity to leave the industry, but the recovery of the area in vines in the major grape-growing regions demonstrated that by far the majority of growers remained. New grape growers and wineries more than replaced those which left. By 1995, Marlborough and Hawke's Bay both had more land in vines than ever before, and even Gisborne, where the largest area in vines had been pulled, had surpassed its 1985 total by the late 1990s.

The last two decades of the twentieth century saw the realisation of the third major stage of regional dispersion away from the two traditional regions of Auckland and Hawke's Bay. By 2000, Canterbury (mainly the Waipara area) had replaced Auckland as the fourth largest grape-growing region in the country and both Central Otago and the Wairarapa were growing fast. In these last two cases local landowners and purchasers whose scale is small have led the growth, with the major corporations and the medium-sized established wine companies slow to buy land or plant grapes. Canterbury, Central Otago and the Wairarapa each has a distinctive group of mainly local, pioneering firms (usually family enterprises) which both grow the grapes and make the wine. The many small vineyards in a region such as Central Otago have found innovative solutions to overcome their lack of scale. The Central Otago Wine Company, for instance, has made individual batches of wine under contract to the owners of small vineyards who market their own wine. Since the early 1990s, new capital has entered the industry in each of these regions and has increased the scale of operations.

Since 1980, the main vineyard regions have also experienced some revealing local readjustments. The forays into new localities have been influenced by both high prices for land in the core regions and a more sophisticated search for new vine environments with the potential to make fine wines. Existing enterprises, both intra- and extra-regional, are diversifying their production by buying land in regions with special qualities for particular varieties or in localities with a different potential from their existing site. New enterprises, often with substantial capital, sometimes from overseas, are seeking their own new and distinctive sites, often in localities where the vigour of vines is lower.

Numerous examples exist of these new areas being explored within traditional regions. In Marlborough the move into the Awatere Valley to the southwest of the region is a good example. In Hawke's Bay the planting of grapes on sites such as the upstream terraces of the Ngaruroro River or the rapid development during the 1990s of the Gimblett Road locality created another layer of local complexity. Even in the Auckland region, a new array of mainly small vineyards and wineries have appeared, this time about an hour's drive from the northeastern edge of the city, at Matakana east of Warkworth. Simultaneously, the area in grapes and the number of wineries have increased rapidly in the prestigious Auckland locality of Waiheke Island.

Alongside this regional growth and specialisation, a corporate geography has also developed to shape the wine industry. Auckland's position as the original home of many wineries has seen it develop into the industry's corporate centre. Early decisions by companies such as Montana and Corbans to relocate or extend their original winery in Auckland have proved to be locationally sound. In a small economy such as New Zealand, where the major local market is concentrated in Auckland, the suppliers of bottles are in Auckland, and Auckland is the main export port for wine, it makes sense to have processing, storage and bottling facilities there.

And such decisions have affected which facilities in the *filière* of the enterprise (the network which contributes to the production of fine wine) go to other regions. Montana and Corbans both had crushing plants, fermentation tanks and some storage facilities in Gisborne, Hawke's Bay and Marlborough. When the Villa Maria group (the third largest company) was created in the mid-1980s, in addition to its Auckland winery it had two in Hawke's Bay (now Vidal and Esk Valley). It makes wine in all three while maintaining its main bottling and distribution centre in Auckland, the home of the original Villa Maria. Some of the middle-sized wine enterprises transport grapes or partly finished wine to Auckland for finishing. By the beginning of the twenty-first century, increasing investment in wineries by medium-sized firms began to flow into the fastest-growing grape regions. Small family firms almost always have on-site wineries.

Varietal revolution

Vinifera varieties dominated the fledgling wine industry in nineteenth-century New Zealand. Much of the accumulated knowledge about growing these classical varieties disappeared during the first two decades of the twentieth century when the

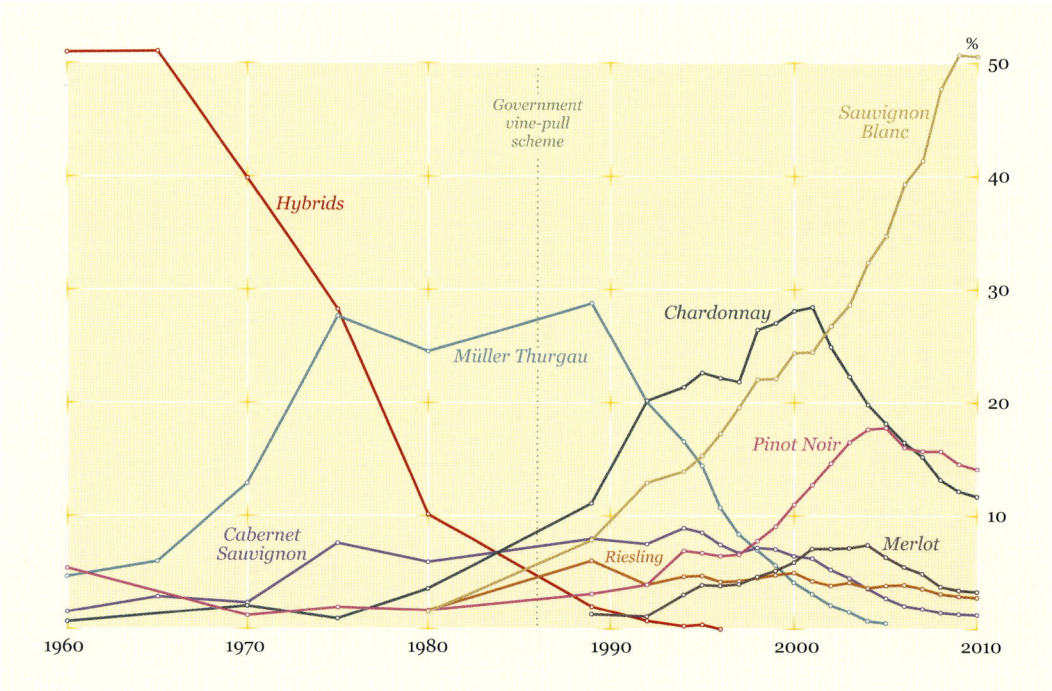

Figure 3.4 Vine varieties in New Zealand, 1960 to 2010

Table 3.2 The five principal grape varieties of New Zealand, 1960–2010 (% of the national total)

1960		1970		1980		1990		2000		2010	
Albany Surprise	15	Palomino	16	Müller Thurgau	38	Müller Thurgau	27	Chardonnay	28	Sauvignon Blanc	52
Baco 22A	11	Baco 22A	14	Palomino	10	Chardonnay	14	Sauvignon Blanc	24	Pinot Noir	15
Seibel 5455	7	Müller Thurgau	13	Cabernet Sauvignon	6	Sauvignon Blanc	9	Pinot Noir	11	Chardonnay	13
Chasselas	6	Chasselas	9	Chenin Blanc	6	Cabernet Sauvignon	8	Cabernet Sauvignon	7	Pinot Gris	5
Black Pinot	5	Seibel 5455	7	Gewürztraminer	5	Muscat	7	Merlot	7	Merlot	4

wine industry declined. The industry's period of modest growth from the 1920s was propelled by lesser varieties – first by the American *Vitis labrusca* varieties and then by the hybrid varieties. Romeo Bragato had imported American vines into New Zealand when he was charged with combating the phylloxera that he had discovered. He grafted *vinifera* varieties that would produce fine wine on to disease-resistant rootstock. But when he left New Zealand in 1909 and his grafting programme was abandoned, the *labrusca* vines were planted on their own roots.

The Concord sport, Albany Surprise, for a long period the most common New Zealand table grape, derived from these vines. From the mid-1850s, plant breeders in France experimented with crossing *Vitis labrusca* and other American vines with *Vitis vinifera*. They were attempting to breed vines bearing grapes with interesting characteristics, and to provide wine varieties more resistant to the fungus disease öidium that was seriously affecting the French vineyards. Some interesting hybrids resulted, especially from the plant breeder Seibel, but they all had a flavour derived from the *labrusca* parentage. It became known as 'foxy'. It was not surprising that the disease-resistant hybrids found their way to New Zealand. In the 1930s and 1940s, when vineyard area was beginning to expand, they were distributed from the Te Kauwhata Viticultural Research Station and planted widely.

The first reliable statistics, in 1960, show the varietal mix that had resulted from the plantings of the period from the 1920s (Table 3.2). Hybrids dominated. Almost 50 per cent of the vines in production in 1960 were hybrid grapes. Seibel 5455 was the dominant red hybrid, and Baco 22A the dominant white. Among the *vinifera* varieties, Palomino and Chasselas each had about 20 hectares, and the Riesling-Sylvaner cross (now called Müller Thürgau in New Zealand) just under 20 hectares. Palomino is used in Europe to make sherry in very warm climates; and Chasselas, a variety with low acid, is used mainly for bulk wines, usually in cool climates. Both have the advantage of being reasonably resistant to diseases and are heavy croppers. The Ministry of Agriculture vineyard survey of 1960 recorded just 3 hectares of Chardonnay being grown in New Zealand and 6 hectares of Cabernet Sauvignon, almost all of them in Hawke's Bay. Considering this unpromising base, the development, in the next 30 years, of an industry producing quality table wines from almost all of the best varieties is a notable achievement.

The hybrid varieties, especially the Seibel 5455 and 5437 together with Baco 22A, survived for some time. As late as 1980, with Palomino added, they made up a larger area of the national vineyard than all other varieties combined. During the initial expansion of vineyard area in the 1960s and 1970s the hybrids continued to be planted in substantial numbers. In 1975 there were almost 500 hectares of hybrids in production compared with 179 hectares of Cabernet Sauvignon and 52 hectares of Chardonnay. But it was the *vinifera* cross, Müller Thurgau, which dominated the planting of vines in the 1970s. By 1980 there were 1819 hectares of that grape growing in New Zealand – 737 in Hawke's Bay, 638 in Gisborne and 324 in Marlborough. No other variety reached 100 hectares in Marlborough and only 33 hectares of Sauvignon Blanc was planted there by 1980. The Riesling-Sylvaner cross known as Müller Thurgau was dominating even the exciting new regions (Table 3.3).

The dominance of Müller Thurgau during the 1970s is striking. It reflects the requirements of the New Zealand industry in that period. Müller Thurgau grows well over much of New Zealand and is relatively disease free. It yields well. It is not difficult to attain over 20 tonnes per hectare and have fruit of reasonable quality. In the early 1980s much of New Zealand wine was marketed in 4- to 6-litre cardboard casks and Riesling-Sylvaner was the dominant variety in these. As companies competed for market share and the demand for simple, fruity table wine was growing, the large producers could not afford to neglect it. Some companies, led by Nobilo, very successfully marketed their Müller Thurgau in bottles, a feat that they were later to repeat with their very successful 1990s promotion of the label White Cloud – initially Müller Thurgau and Muscat in another guise.

The rise of the classical vinifera *varieties*

Yet the evidence was there, in the plantings and in the wines, that the mainstays of the European industry – the *viniferas* – would also produce the best wines here and dominate the New Zealand industry. In the late 1950s and early 1960s, two winemakers in particular – Alex Corban and Denis Kasza (working with Tom McDonald) – began to experiment with and produce varietal wines from Cabernet Sauvignon and Chardonnay respectively, or Pinot Chardonnay as it was then called. The quality of the McDonald's Cabernet Sauvignon was readily apparent in the Bakano, marketed first in bottles and later casks, but it was fully confirmed when McWilliam's bottled it as the varietal Cabernet Sauvignon. All the wine commentators of the time, and the books on the industry since, applauded its quality and impact. The 1965 McWilliam's Cabernet Sauvignon is legendary. This potential was demonstrated in other regions with the excellent Cabernet Sauvignons and Pinot Noirs that were made by Nick Nobilo from Huapai, West Auckland grapes, especially the Cabernet and other blends of 1976. Glimpses of Romeo Bragato's enthusiastic reading of the potential for many regions of New Zealand to produce fine wines had begun to emerge.

The transformation of the varietal mix of the New Zealand industry had begun in the early 1980s but was hastened by the vine-pull scheme of 1986. Because it was newly established, by 1980 Marlborough already had a larger area in Chardonnay, Riesling, Sauvignon Blanc, Gewürztraminer, Cabernet Sauvignon, Pinotage and Pinot Noir than Hawke's Bay. Gisborne had the largest area in Chardonnay, Gewürztraminer and Pinot Noir of any region. The varietal mix at any date was strongly influenced, therefore, by the history and the stage of viticultural development of each region. Varieties removed by winemakers and grape growers during the vine-pull also gave a good indication of the direction of the industry. In descending order the varieties removed were Müller Thurgau (507 ha), Palomino (137 ha), Gewürztraminer (109 ha), Chenin Blanc (98 ha), Riesling (97 ha) and Cabernet Sauvignon (62 ha). The large area of Cabernet is surprising but was influenced by enterprises with cash-flow problems which needed the money to survive, as well as by adjustments in regions where this variety is difficult to ripen. The early dominance by variety was soon to change as new vineyards were planted in Hawke's Bay, new regions were developed, and the opportunities of replanting were realised.

Regional specialisation in varieties

By the 1990s, some regional specialisation in varieties was apparent in the larger regions (Table 3.3). In 1990, Müller Thurgau was still the dominant variety in Gisborne, Hawke's Bay and Marlborough, but the future was clear because Chardonnay was the second most-planted variety in two regions and the third in the rest of the country. By 2000, Sauvignon Blanc had streaked ahead in Marlborough but Chardonnay was the top variety in all three other regions. Gisborne trumpets itself as 'Chardonnay Capital' and the figures show that this is so. It also remains 'Bulk-wine Capital'. When the area in Müller Thurgau and the Muscat varieties (remnants of the 1960s and 1970s experience) are combined, they total almost the same area as Chardonnay. Hawke's Bay is the single major producing region where red varieties are dominant. Despite Chardonnay having the largest area, the combined area of the two Bordeaux varieties, Cabernet Sauvignon and Merlot, is higher than that of Chardonnay. Hawke's Bay's versatility is seen in the substantial area of Sauvignon Blanc being grown there.

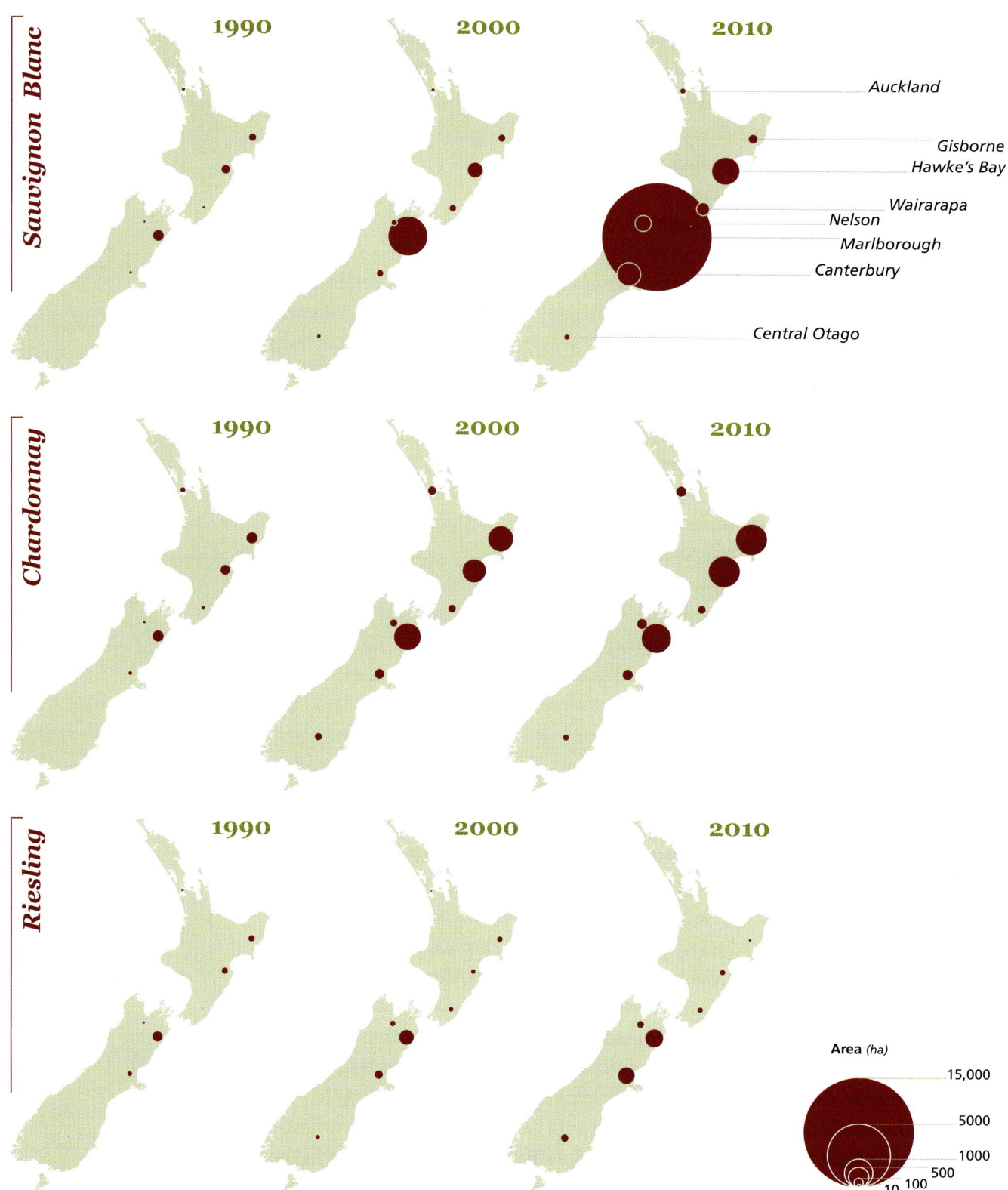

Figure 3.5 Regional dispersal of Sauvignon Blanc, Chardonnay, and Riesling, 1990, 2000, 2010

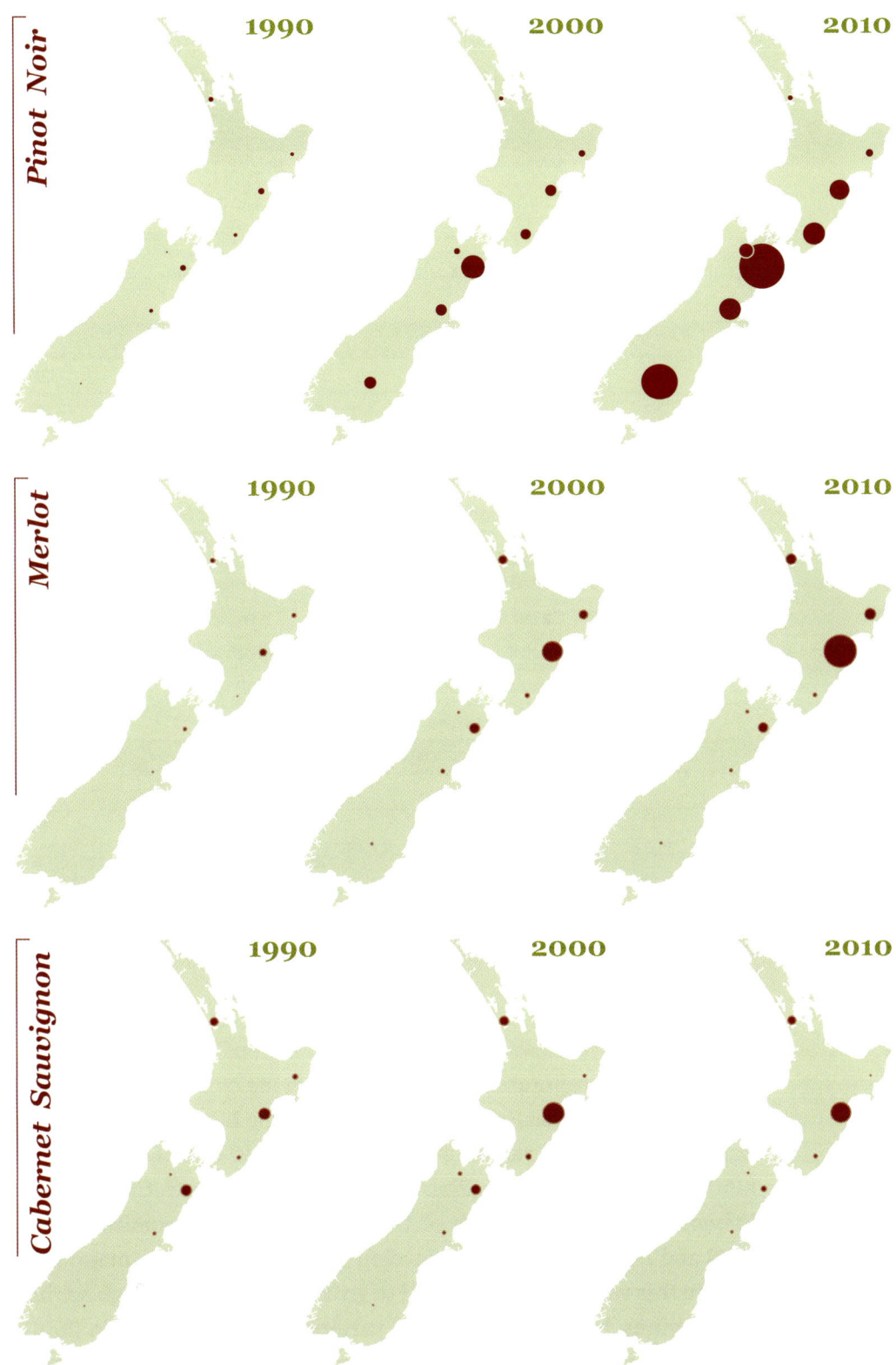

Figure 3.6 Regional dispersal of Pinot Noir, Merlot, and Cabernet Sauvignon, 1990, 2000, 2010

Table 3.3 The five dominant grape varieties for four regions (% of regional totals)

Auckland		Gisborne		Hawke's Bay		Marlborough	
1980							
Palomino	24	Müller Thurgau	41	Müller Thurgau	50	Müller Thurgau	42
Baco 22A	13	Chasselas	10	Chenin Blanc	9	Cabernet Sauvignon	12
Müller Thurgau	11	Palomino	8	Palomino	8	Gewürztraminer	11
Seibels	9	Gewürztraminer	7	Cabernet Sauvignon	6	Chardonnay	7
Cabernet Sauvignon	9	Chenin Blanc	7	Chasselas	5	Riesling	5
1990							
Cabernet Sauvignon	20	Müller Thurgau	32	Müller Thurgau	30	Müller Thurgau	29
Palomino	19	Muscats	11	Chardonnay	12	Chardonnay	18
Chardonnay	10	Chardonnay	10	Cabernet Sauvignon	12	Sauvignon Blanc	15
Pinot Noir	6	Reichensteiner	5	Chenin Blanc	8	Riesling	10
Merlot	6	Gewürztraminer	5	Sauvignon Blanc	7	Cabernet Sauvignon	8
2000							
Chardonnay	22	Chardonnay	48	Chardonnay	28	Sauvignon Blanc	47
Cabernet Sauvignon	20	Müller Thurgau	12	Cabernet Sauvignon	17	Chardonnay	22
Merlot	17	Muscats	9	Merlot	16	Pinot Noir	13
Cabernet Franc	8	Semillon	4	Sauvignon Blanc	11	Riesling	7
Pinotage	2	Merlot	4	Müller Thurgau	6	Semillon	3
2010							
Chardonnay	22	Chardonnay	52	Chardonnay	24	Sauvignon Blanc	76
Merlot	16	Pinot Gris	9	Merlot	21	Pinot Noir	10
Cabernet Sauvignon	11	Merlot	6	Sauvignon Blanc	18	Chardonnay	6
Syrah	8	Gewürztraminer	5	Cabernet Sauvignon	8	Pinot Gris	4
Pinot Gris	8	Muscats	5	Pinot Gris	7	Riesling	2

Marlborough, though, is Sauvignon country, with 47 per cent of its vineyard in this aromatic variety. New Zealand's reputation for making fine wine continues to be built unduly on the distinctive qualities that Sauvignon assumes in the Marlborough *terroir*. Marlborough is also the only major region where Pinot Noir is one of the top five varieties. In the 1990s, most Marlborough Pinot Noir was blended with Chardonnay in *Méthode Traditionnelle*. With the quality of the still Pinot Noirs coming out of Marlborough by 1998 and Montana's plans to develop Marlborough into a major still Pinot region, the area in this variety has continued to grow. Auckland, although having a much smaller area in vines, had a similar mix of varieties to Hawke's Bay in 2000. Thirty-seven per cent of its vines were in Cabernet Sauvignon and Merlot, reflecting the uniqueness of the Matakana and Waiheke Island environments and the skill of its grape growers and vinifiers in making quality Bordeaux-style reds, as well as the ability of the rest of the Auckland region to grow these varieties.

In 2000, each of the remaining regions of New Zealand had fewer than 1000 hectares of grapes although they were growing rapidly. For instance, as recently as 1980, Wairarapa (the locality of Martinborough) had only 7 hectares in vines, while Central Otago had fewer than 20 hectares. In 2000, Central Otago was growing over 220 hectares and the area in vines in the Wairarapa was over 300. As viticulture has diffused south, the varietal mix becomes distinctive (Table 3.4). Pinot Noir, in particular, but also Riesling and Pinot Gris, become proportionally much more important. By 2000 in Canterbury, Central Otago and Wairarapa, Pinot Noir and Chardonnay dominated.

In 2010, in both Central Otago and the Wairarapa, Pinot Noir was the most planted variety. It was Wairarapa that established New Zealand's reputation for making Pinot Noir still wines during the 1980s, with parts of Central Otago and a few examples of wine from Canterbury also showing their potential in the same decade. Central Otago has enhanced its reputation, and other regions, notably Nelson and Marlborough, have shown that they can compete in making Pinot Noirs of quality. Distinctive wines made from Riesling, Pinot Gris and Sauvignon Blanc also originate from all four regions and, like Marlborough, they also have the option of producing *Méthode Traditionnelle* from Chardonnay and Pinot Noir.

An ongoing revolution

This New Zealand story has contrasts, as well as parallels, with the French experience that inspired Dion and Gadille. The transformation of New Zealand viticulture and winemaking from an industry dependent on hybrid vines and fortified wines to one producing quality table wines has been extremely compressed. It took just 50 years. This transformation is impossible to compare with the long-term development of the French industry where the process extended from several hundred years BC and involved the gradual selection of vines that would yield grapes of quality in the cooler climates away from the Mediterranean. However, phylloxera and hybrid vines are key points of historical reference for both countries.

Identification of phylloxera in the late nineteenth century in New Zealand, and the availability of the American species and hybrid vines developed in France, and sold by the state in New Zealand, were important. These, combined with the absence of a culture of wine, and the presence of a temperance movement, all contributed to delay the development of a table wine industry for almost a century. In the interim, Croatian and other winemakers were responding to demand and to the population's prevailing

Table 3.4 The five dominant grape varieties for four regions, 1990–2010 (% of regional totals)

Canterbury		Central Otago		Nelson		Wairarapa	
1990							
Riesling	23	Pinot Noir	21	Chardonnay	18	Pinot Noir	27
Pinot Noir	19	Riesling	21	Riesling	16	Chardonnay	24
Chardonnay	14	Gewürztraminer	15	Sauvignon Blanc	13	Cabernet Sauvignon	18
Müller Thurgau	11	Sauvignon Blanc	15	Gewürztraminer	11	Sauvignon Blanc	15
Cabernet Sauvignon	9	Chardonnay	15	Cabernet Sauvignon	11	Gewürztraminer	3
2000							
Pinot Noir	27	Pinot Noir	49	Chardonnay	30	Pinot Noir	31
Chardonnay	25	Chardonnay	22	Sauvignon Blanc	23	Chardonnay	21
Riesling	18	Pinot Gris	10	Riesling	17	Sauvignon Blanc	16
Sauvignon Blanc	14	Riesling	8	Pinot Noir	17	Cabernet Sauvignon	8
Pinot Gris	4	Sauvignon Blanc	5	Cabernet Sauvignon	5	Riesling	8
2010							
Sauvignon Blanc	39	Pinot Noir	78	Sauvignon Blanc	39	Pinot Noir	53
Pinot Noir	32	Pinot Gris	9	Pinot Noir	23	Sauvignon Blanc	24
Riesling	19	Chardonnay	4	Chardonnay	14	Chardonnay	9
Pinot Gris	7	Riesling	4	Riesling	6	Pinot Gris	6
Chardonnay	7	Sauvignon Blanc	2	Pinot Gris	4	Riesling	4

attitude towards alcoholic drinks by maintaining a fortified wine industry. And some made remarkably good wine. The Australian story is similar although the dates are different and the ethnicity of the pioneering families very different. For a socio-political movement such as temperance to have such a powerful effect on the wine industry would seem highly unlikely in France, Italy or Germany.

The transformation of the New Zealand industry occurred in a lightly regulated environment compared with the Appellation d'Origine Contrôlée legal framework. Corporate and family firms planted different *vinifera* varieties in existing and new regions because they saw the potential of the industry in a range of natural environments. In this sense, the New Zealand industry has, despite the radical break in this tradition imposed by the temperance movement and the reaction to phylloxera, some similarities with the long empirical experience (under different conditions of transport and technology) that led to the strong regionalisation of varieties in France.

Such empirical experience of bringing out the best in varieties (and blends of varieties) in different environments was later written into the French appellation laws of 1935. New Zealand regions began to show their potential for different varieties as viticulturists and winemakers understood their new environments using advanced technical knowledge. Recently, more formal recognition of geographical indications in the New Zealand industry began with the submission of a list of localities and regions to the then European Community in 1981 and the voluntary phasing out of the use of French and other European names. After a period of debate within the New Zealand wine industry over the appropriate resolution at which names should initially be defined, rules were written in a generic manner for all rural industries as the Geographical Indications (Wines and Spirits) Registration Act 2006. This defines truth in labelling by regions and varieties. It has yet to be activated.

Although the transformation of the geography of New Zealand winegrowing has been unusually rapid, its potential remains unrealised. The matching of varieties to sites and the blending of different varieties to make distinctive local wines are still tentative. Some of the regions have scarcely two decades of experience of growing particular varieties, not always virus free and not always with the best, or right, mix of clones. With a variety such as Pinot Noir, for example, the recent evidence demonstrates that fine wines are being made from it in a number of regions. With appropriate vineyard management for different sites, more experience of vine phenology, more understanding of its vinification, and more years of different weathers, New Zealand is now in the fortunate position of having a number of different styles of Pinot Noir emerging from many *terroirs*.

Experimenting with producing distinctive wines by judicious blending of different varieties has hardly begun in New Zealand. The last decade has seen major advances in blends of Merlot and Cabernet Sauvignon or Merlot and Malbec, or Merlot, Malbec and Cabernet Franc. But each region, or rather each locality, may require its own particular blending to achieve its potential. Some fine late-harvest dessert wines have been produced in New Zealand, notably from Riesling but also from Sauvignon Blanc and Gewürztraminer. Blending of different white varieties, including different blends for different *terroirs,* may produce an outstanding dessert wine. Who would be bold enough to suggest that each variety and clone of *Vitis vinifera*, when transferred to the New Zealand environment, may not perform differently in its new homes, and blended with another or others, be even more special?

4

Natural Environments in Human Terms

The serendipity that was to associate the country New Zealand and the region Marlborough with Sauvignon Blanc was commercially cemented at a London wine tasting in 1984. In his 2006 memoir *Wine: A Life Uncorked*, Hugh Johnson, the doyen of British wine writers and the original author of the best wine atlas ever produced, captures the occasion colourfully.

> The top floor of the 17-storey New Zealand House in London, near Trafalgar Square and commanding one of the best panoramas in town, qualified definitively as wine country in June 1984. Twenty or so wine journalists assembled, their expectations not, I suspect, as high as the venue, to taste the new vintage of New Zealand wines. A buzz soon started. Five or six of the wines were Sauvignon Blancs. This was Sauvignon with the volume turned up. I remember the surge of scent, the snap on the tongue, the hundred-amp shock through the system. Like Sauvignon or hate it, here it was in primary colours. Some tastes, I thought, are simply better at low volume.

Now we know that this is New Zealand's potential, perhaps for any grape variety. Her latitude corresponds to the places in the northern hemisphere where fine wines were born. Her volcanic soils can be embarrassingly fertile. In many places warm days are followed by cool nights; the recipe for concentrated fruit flavours. Whether the wine was calculated

Picking Syrah at Te Mata's Bullnose vineyard in Hawke's Bay. *Murray Lloyd Photography*

to demonstrate all this with the most pungent grape variety I somehow doubt, but there was no doubt about the impact. A new wine idiom had arrived. It could recruit drinkers who had scarcely noticed wine before, and it has.

Johnson's memory of the taste cannot be doubted. Yet the speculations in his second paragraph are flattering but flawed. New Zealand does not, even with the 'perhaps' inserted, have similar potential for any grape variety. Varieties such as Grenache, Mourvèdre and Carignan, that for centuries have dominated the hot climates of the Mediterranean regions of France, are difficult to ripen in New Zealand. New Zealand's latitude does not correspond to the places in the northern hemisphere where fine wines were born (Figure 4.1). Very little wine is produced from vines grown on volcanic soils in New Zealand, and the Sauvignon Blanc wine was certainly not 'calculated to demonstrate all this'. Its intense fruit flavours resulted from a complex interaction of the variety with the climate and soils and culture of the place where these grapes were grown – the very essence of the French word *terroir*.

Johnson is on the right track about New Zealand climates when he states that in many places warm days are followed by cool nights, the recipe for concentrated fruit flavours, although even this claim is difficult to verify when the minimum temperatures after the onset of ripening are compared between Burgundy and the Pinot Noir regions of New Zealand. In winegrowing terms, New Zealand is on the climatic edge. But its marginality has little to do directly with latitude and everything to do with the country's narrow shape, terrain, and the maritime climate which results. New Zealand is able to ripen only some varieties of *Vitis vinifera* – those that originated in the cooler climates and prestigious appellations of middle and northern France. And in some years many of the regions developed by New Zealand winegrowers struggle to ripen even those.

As the Romans planted the Mediterranean varieties of *Vitis vinifera* in the Rhone-Saône Valley, and towards Bordeaux on the west coast, these precocious vines crossed with the indigenous grape varieties of Gaul. Those crosses of *Vitis vinifera* that ripened in the cooler climates of northern France and on the maritime west coast, as well as producing grapes and wines with desirable flavours, were nurtured, propagated and reproduced, often by layering them, using canes from mature vines. Over hundreds of years, the varieties that proved successful gradually became dominant in different localities and regions until during the first third of the twentieth century they were prescribed for each region in the Appellation d'Origine Contrôlée (AOC) laws.

With no restrictions on which varieties are planted where in New Zealand, we have seen that varietal specialisation by region is emerging. Two questions are relevant. Where in France are the varieties grown that now dominate the New Zealand industry? What can we learn about natural environmental influences on the localisation of the vine in New Zealand by comparing them with France, especially their climates? This leads to an exploration of the way in which New Zealand grape growers have drawn on science and experience to wrestle with the complexities of a variable environment.

French varieties in their cool climates

The regional distribution of the six French varieties that dominate production in New Zealand helps make sense of the relationship between varieties and climate. Sauvignon Blanc is the main white grape in the upper Loire Valley in the hinterland of Sancerre and Pouilly, and also in Bordeaux where it is commonly blended with Semillon in both the dry Graves and the sweet Sauternes. Pinot Noir, considered by many to be the finest red wine grape, is also versatile. It is the main red variety of eastern France, notably in Burgundy, and is planted over 300 kilometres (about three degrees of latitude) from Champagne in the north to Les Maranges in southern Burgundy. Chardonnay is the principal white variety of Burgundy, from Chablis in the département of Yonne to the Mâconnais, also a north–south distance approaching 300 kilometres. By being the second most important variety in Champagne, Chardonnay also extends its latitudinal range and, with Pinot Noir and Pinot Meunier, provides complexity in blends of Champagne as well as in the Blanc de Blancs – Champagnes made from varieties with both white skins and flesh. Pinot Gris, the fourth most-planted variety in New Zealand, and Riesling the sixth, are both Alsatian varieties. Merlot, the fifth most important in New Zealand, has increasingly become the mainstay of the red wine industry of Bordeaux at the expense of Cabernet Sauvignon. The same trend has happened in Hawke's Bay.

The dominant varieties in New Zealand, therefore, are among those that in the French appellation system are referred to as being *locaux, loyaux, et constants* in the regions where they are authorised. They are the varieties that occupy one or more of six regions that extend over this broad sweep of French territory from the Atlantic coast of Bordeaux, through the upper reaches of the Loire at Sancerre, into Burgundy in central France, and to Alsace and Champagne in the northeast of the country. Although the distances are considerable, these are among the French regions that are categorised as having cool climates and have reputations for producing fine wines. Each of them has its own climate, but as a group they have strong similarities. Their climatic similarity is one reason many wine writers and publicists attempt to differentiate the wine regions and sub-regions of France by the individuality of their soils.

When making still wine in the prestigious French appellations, Chardonnay, Pinot Noir, Pinot Gris and Riesling are seldom blended with other varieties, although opportunities such as *Bourgogne passe tous grains* must be noted. In this regional appellation of Burgundy, the Gamay is blended with Pinot Noir. When it comes to

Figure 4.1 New Zealand superimposed on Europe and North Africa with isotherms for mean temperature in the warmest month of 16°C, 19°C (New Zealand) and 19°C, 22°C (France). New Zealand's key winegrowing regions (except Central Otago) are nearer to the equator than the wine regions of France, but they are all significantly cooler.

regulating winegrowing in France, the political is never far from the natural. Blending two or more varieties in an appellation is one means of more fully capturing the natural environment because the different varieties express its different qualities.

In the mid-1960s an Australian scientist, James Prescott, attempted to establish the polar limits of the vine by comparing France and Australia. He used the mean temperature of the warmest month as the indicator of the thermal regime of the two countries, preferring it to the degree-day (discussed later) because it was more immediately comprehensible and correlated very closely with the degree-day. He concluded that in France the isotherm of 18.7°C was the best estimate for the polar limit of the vine.

I take a similar approach in Figure 4.1 where the temperatures of the French and New Zealand winegrowing regions are compared. The 20°C isotherm of the warmest month just clips the northern tip of New Zealand and the 19°C one includes parts of Northland and coastal Bay of Plenty as well as the vine-growing regions of the Gisborne Plain and coastal Hawke's Bay. Nowhere south of there does the 18°C isotherm appear. On the Prescott criterion, much of New Zealand would be considered too cool to mature grapes.

Nevertheless, vines are being grown very successfully in these regions and some of the most flavourful grapes and most expensive wines in the country are produced from fruit grown in the Wairarapa region northeast of Wellington, in parts of Canterbury and in Central Otago in the South Island. The explanation lies in the limitations of Prescott's method. But we can definitely pronounce that New Zealand is a cool-climate region for the vine – how cool, I will discuss later in the chapter.

New Zealand vines in their climates and soils

Viewed from the vine's perspective it is limiting, although often necessary, to separate climate from soils when trying to understand why vines are cultivated by people in particular localities and regions. Grapevines have their roots in the soil and their leaves in the atmosphere. The plant reacts to stimuli from its total environment as it proceeds each year towards its biological imperative of producing fruit and seeds that will ripen, be eaten by birds and other animals, and reproduce the parent plant.

In the spirit of this integrated or eco-physiological approach, I begin by associating the regional pattern of vineyards in New Zealand with the precipitation they receive annually and the broad categories of terrain and soils they occupy, by using a map of the location of Quaternary sediments. Maps of the thermal environment of the vine (various measures of temperature and hours of sunshine) are then used to tease out the components of cool climates in the localities and regions of New Zealand. Using

Figures 4.2, 4.3, 4.4 The New Zealand vineyard mapped alongside Quaternary sediments and precipitation

the evidence of the last two decades, it is now possible to identify the particular characteristics of the climate in the regions where different varieties of vines have become localised. Without the benefit of such hindsight, New Zealand grape growers and winemakers had to learn these lessons by trial and error.

Do the New Zealand regions colonised by the vine since 1960 have some common natural attributes for viticulture? The answer is a loud 'yes'. All of them have temperatures during the growing season that are among the hottest in the country, their soils are made up mainly of coarser materials with gravels predominating, they have low annual rainfall, they are less humid than the rest of the country, and they mainly occupy land that is relatively flat, although always with hills nearby that are

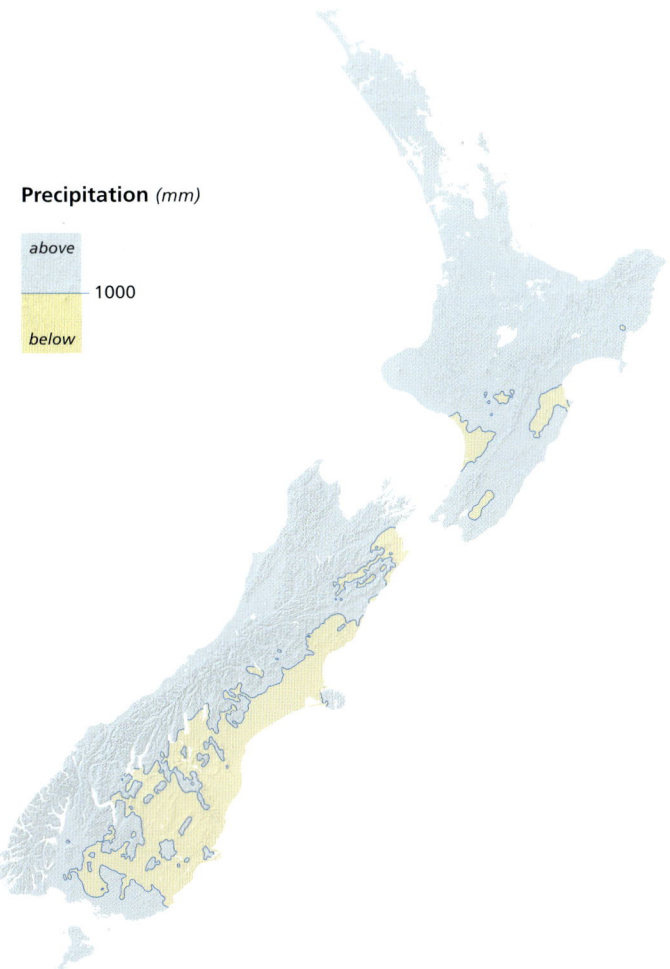

Precipitation *(mm)*

above
1000
below

increasingly being planted in vines. To demonstrate these associations I first use three maps (Figures 4.2, 4.3 and 4.4). Figure 4.3 shows the distribution of vines in 2010. Flanking it are two indicators of the natural environment – those parts of the country receiving less than 1000 millimetres of precipitation annually and the location of the Quaternary sediments.

Ninety per cent of the land in wine grapes receives less than 1000 millimetres of precipitation annually. Only three of the regions growing vines – Auckland, Gisborne and Nelson – receive more than 1000 millimetres. Two parts of those – a very small part of the Gisborne Plain and probably small parts of Waiheke Island in the Auckland region – also squeeze under the 1000-millimetre isohyet (the line on a chart connecting areas of equal rainfall). In some winegrowing regions, annual precipitation is noticeably lower. Part of coastal Hawke's Bay, the Wairau Plain, and much of the Canterbury Plains receive under 800 millimetres of rain annually, while much of Central Otago receives under 400 millimetres. Low rainfall, especially when it comes with low humidity, is an economic advantage for viticulture because it means lower probabilities of many diseases and reduced costs for disease control, although these benefits are offset by the necessity to irrigate, especially when the vines are young.

The map of Quaternary sediments is a surrogate for aspects of the surface materials that shaped the terrain of many wine regions and were gradually transformed into soils. In both islands almost all vines are grown on these Quaternary sediments. They were mainly deposited in the last million years, beginning during the most recent ice ages. In the South Island the soils were shaped by terrestrial deposition of materials eroded mainly from the Southern Alps and subsidiary ranges by glaciers and rivers. These deposits formed the Canterbury Plains, the largest area of gently sloping land in the country, as well as smaller plains like the Waimea and Wairau in Nelson and Marlborough respectively. Similar work by glaciers and rivers over time formed the valleys and terraces of Central Otago.

In the eastern lower North Island, from Hawke's Bay to the Wairarapa, the sediments are mainly marine in origin, including limestone, siltstone and sandstone. In both islands these Quaternary sediments have since been transformed by both the erosion and the deposition from the major rivers draining them. Much of their terrain now consists of gently sloping terraces and former flood plains, often with gravelly soils that can be hundreds of metres deep.

When these two criteria – precipitation under 1000 millimetres and the Quaternary sediments – are combined, large areas of land are filtered out. In the North Island, the fine alluvial soils of the Hauraki Plains and Waikato, and the volcanic and alluvial soils of Taranaki and the Manawatu, do not meet both criteria. Nor do the alluvial soils of the West Coast and Southland in the South Island. The competitive advantage of these regions, partly derived from the higher rainfall and soils of higher natural fertility, sees them practising intensive grassland farming, mainly dairying and fattening sheep and cattle and growing various crops. The vine does not get a look in and nor should it.

Three maps of New Zealand unravel the calculation of 'mean temperature of the warmest month' that was used by Prescott (Figure 4.5). It is quickly apparent from this group of climate stations in wine regions that the pattern of maximum temperatures is very similar across the North and South Islands. The continental effect of the Southern Alps and associated ranges explains these higher temperatures at more southern latitudes in the interior and towards the east coast of the South Island. Lower minimum temperatures at night decrease the mean temperatures in the South Island. If these minima were higher in the South Island (more similar to the North Island), several parts of it would see even the 19°C isotherm appearing. It seems, on the surface, that the heat accumulation must be greater than shown by this measure and is partly

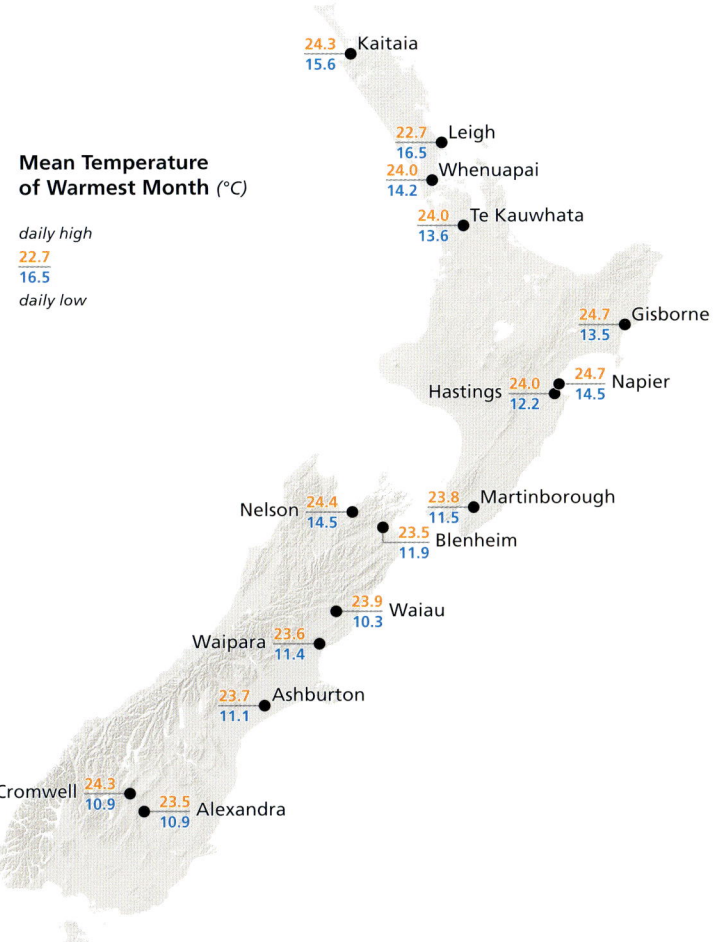

Figure 4.5 Mean temperature of the warmest month

explained by day length. Various scientists have included day length and other variables to improve such measures. Nevertheless, the best evidence that the climate is suitable is the performance of the varieties of vines being grown.

Another measure of temperature – number of days during the year with temperatures over 25°C – identifies very effectively the major localities growing vines (Figure 4.6). It also demonstrates that the conditions during the daylight hours, when the vine is actively photosynthesising, are the most important for achieving physiologically ripe grapes. Leaving aside the humid Hauraki Plains and Waikato, where intensive pastoral farming on fine alluvial soils takes first choice of the land, the temperature map identifies the main localities where viticulture is currently concentrated. In the North Island these are the Gisborne Plain and adjacent land along

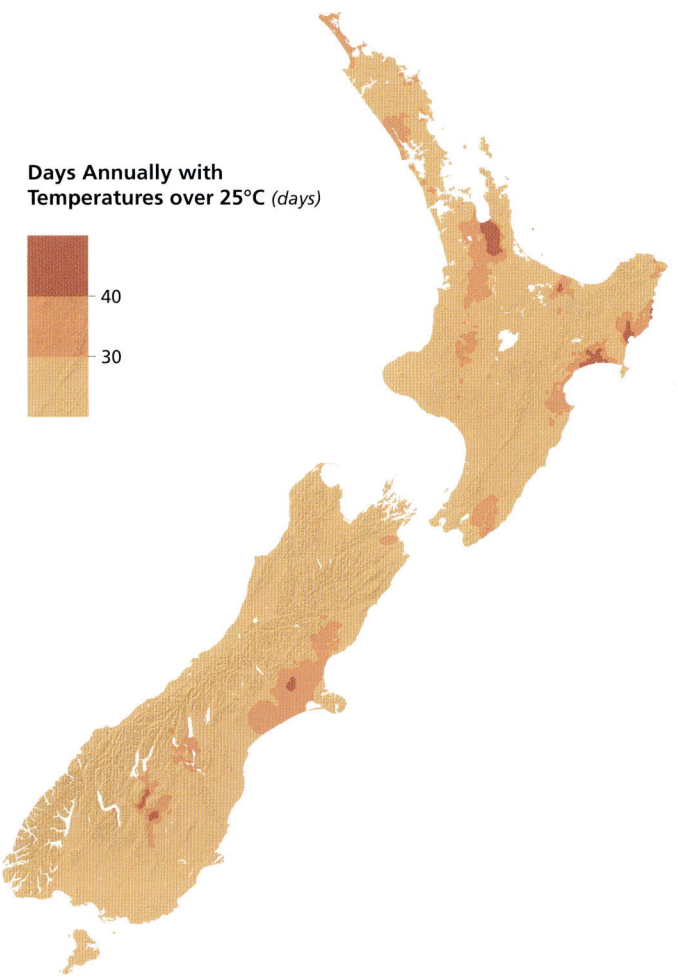

Figure 4.6 Average annual number of days over 25°C

the coast including Tolaga Bay, the coastal plains and river terraces around the bight of Hawke Bay, and part of the Wairarapa. In the South Island, conditions for viticulture are concentrated on the Wairau Plain, a broad strip of the eastern area of Canterbury from inland and north of Waipara to mid-Canterbury, and the plains of the Mackenzie country and Central Otago. These last two localities are the 'continental' part of the South Island because the protection of the highest parts of the Southern Alps to their west modifies their climates to make them resemble those of the interior of continents.

The descending air masses on the leeward side of the mountain ranges are also responsible for the nor'westers of the Canterbury Plains (Föhn winds) that dry as they descend and suck the moisture from the soil and plants, making irrigation essential for grapes to thrive in these desiccating conditions. Although much of the Canterbury

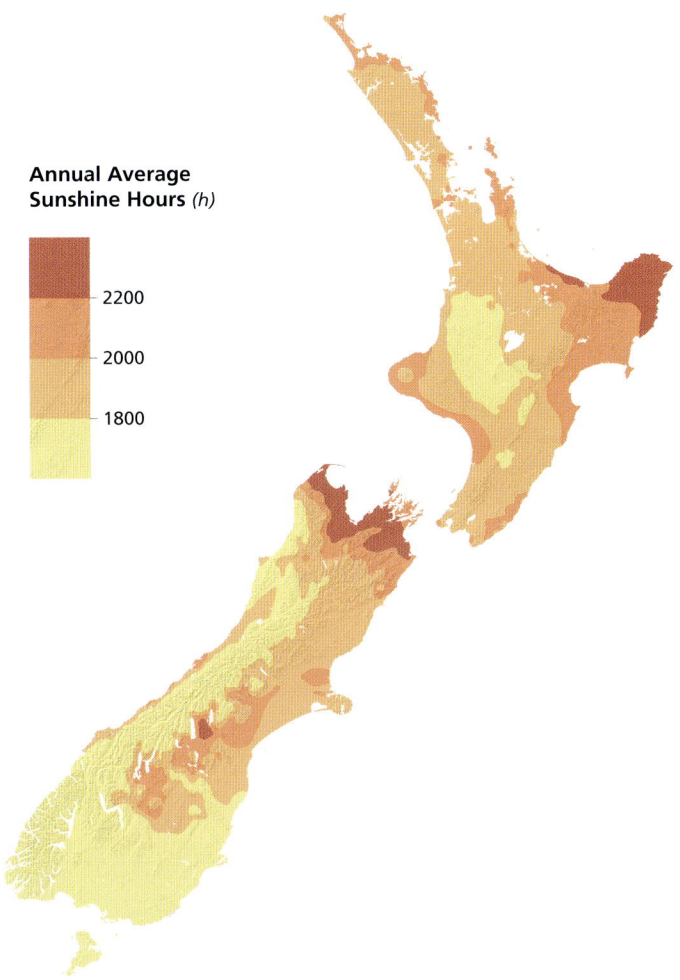

Figure 4.7 Average annual number of sunshine hours

Plains appears to have the potential for viticulture, such conditions make choosing appropriate sites essential. In addition, competition from other systems of agriculture, such as dairying on irrigated land, has resulted in increased land values in Canterbury.

The map of annual hours of bright sunshine adds further insights into the atmospheric conditions of regions where grapes are now grown (Figure 4.7). The isoline of over 2000 hours of sunshine annually includes the areas where over 90 per cent of New Zealand grapes for wine are planted. It encompasses the large regions, Hawke's Bay and Marlborough, but also Gisborne, Nelson, Waipara and Central Otago. It also distinguishes the middle and upper Waitaki Valley, Mackenzie Basin (where grapes have been planted) and other parts of south and central Canterbury as potential areas for vines. In the South Island, Nelson and Marlborough stand out from the rest

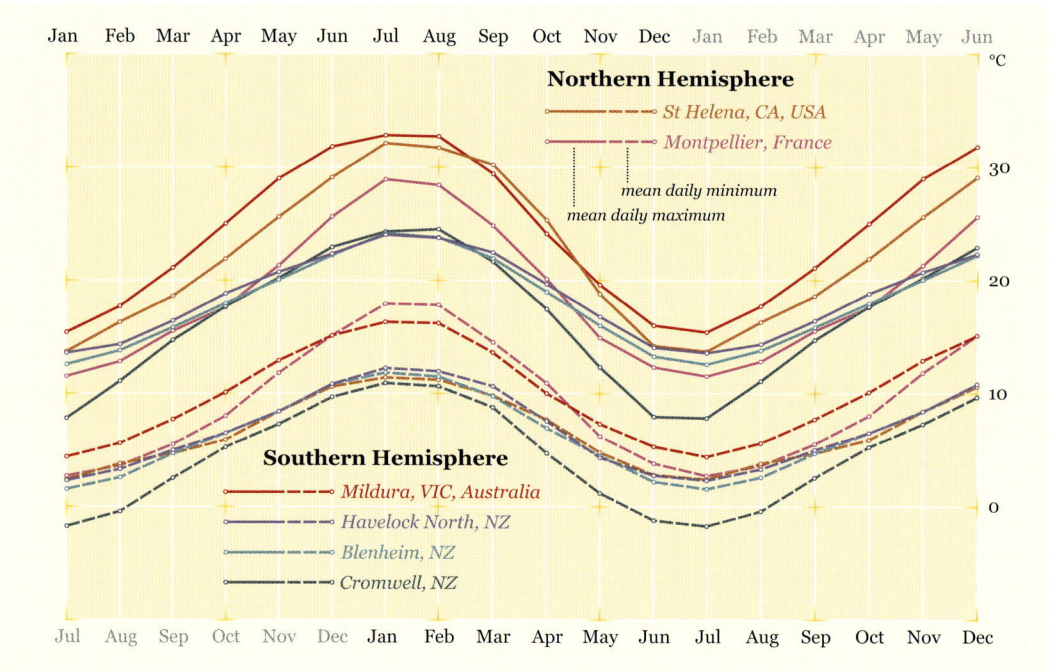

Figure 4.8 Mean daily maximum and mean daily minimum temperature normals for three New Zealand and three international climate stations

because both have substantial areas with more than 2200 hours of sunshine annually. In Nelson's case, these higher sunshine hours partly offset its noticeably higher annual precipitation and humidity compared with Marlborough. As with most climatic measures, hours of sunshine also show a definite west to east gradient.

Comparison of temperature curves of the French 'cool climate' wine regions with the New Zealand regions reveals one important difference (Figure 4.8). New Zealand temperature curves are noticeably flatter in all parts of the country but especially in the North Island. The steeper French curves means that annual temperature ranges are greater in France than in New Zealand. Some French regions, such as Bordeaux, have both higher temperatures in summer and lower temperatures in winter. These same generalisations apply to the growing season for the vine, usually defined as April to October in the northern hemisphere and October to April in the southern.

Winters are much warmer in most parts of New Zealand with the result that temperature curves are much flatter. In other words, annual ranges of temperature are noticeably lower in New Zealand. Again, this results from the influence of maritime conditions on the climate and weather of the country. Air masses crossing New Zealand are always influenced by their passage over water. This tends to suppress the extremes, cooling the air masses in summer and warming them in winter. Middle-latitude France and Mediterranean Europe are exposed to the continental influences of both Africa and Eurasia and have noticeably hotter summers and colder winters.

Damian Martin, a New Zealander who completed his doctoral work under Professor Gérard Seguin in Bordeaux, and former CEO of the Marlborough enterprise ARA, expresses clearly why a climate that is both cool and dry extends the window for picking until the berries have reached optimum ripeness:

> One of the advantages of cool, dry climates is that it becomes easier to impose a moderate water deficit than in a hot climate.... The optimum ripeness window on an individual berry may last only for a very short period of time.... Because cooler climates extend the optimum ripeness window they are more likely to enable the production of great wines.

Martin's argument can be taken further. The flatter temperature curve in the wine regions of New Zealand encourages a more 'gentle' sequence of growth of the vine with sufficient hot spells to stimulate the ripening of the berries. In such thermal conditions it becomes even more important that the final period of ripening is not compromised by too much precipitation or periods of humidity.

It is not surprising that the east coast of the North Island, where the probability of low pressure systems from the east in the late summer and early autumn is quite high, is not as favoured for winegrowing as it might otherwise be. The Gisborne region is the most susceptible. These lows are sometimes remnant tropical cyclones that have been downgraded to intense lows and may compromise a vintage. Occasionally, as was the case with Cyclone Bola in 1988, full-blooded tropical cyclones can virtually wipe out a vintage. Fortunately, they occur infrequently.

As the vine was initially being dispersed to untried regions, few aspiring winegrowers examined all such maps and decided 'this is where this variety should be grown'. Rather, grape varieties thought to be suitable for the locality were planted there, and growers and winemakers demonstrated that they were able (or unable) to produce grapes with the desired qualities to make distinctive and appealing wines. Sauvignon Blanc in Marlborough is the best example. In 2009, on the occasion celebrating 30 years of its production, Gerry Gregg, Montana's Marlborough winery manager in 1979, recalled how the arrival of the first Sauvignon fruit at the winery was something never to be forgotten:

> When we got it into the winery, we didn't know what to do with it. It was so pungent and strong.... The first big shipment that went to the UK in 1982 sold straight away.

No other variety grown in New Zealand expresses such a distinctive signature.

Managing a variable climate

Although the average conditions described in these maps are a useful indication of where different varieties of grapes might be grown, they are not sufficient to understand the complexity of the way that grape growers must interact with their natural environment if they are to be successful. The weather of the growing season is different each year. In addition, the growing conditions of one year are carried forward to the vine's behaviour in the next year through the accumulation of proteins and other elements in the trunk, branches and roots of the vine, and in the fertility of next year's buds. These circumstances make it necessary to manage the vine's growth each year to attempt to achieve the optimal size of crop for the quality of wine being produced.

This management is a difficult task because it must be done without knowing what the weather is going to be in any single year. Pruning to a number of buds, known from accumulated empirical experience to produce the desired crop, is the main way most viticulturists manage crop levels. But weather conditions before and during flowering and setting of the berries, or hail afterwards, can have huge effects on the size of the crop, as can the temperature during the growing season in ripening it. So too does rain when bunches are almost ripe. The plant quickly absorbs moisture and pumps it into the berries. They swell and may split which makes them prone to mildews and botrytis. In general, therefore, many viticulturists producing quality wines prune to set a larger than necessary number of bunches and *vendange en vert* (literally, 'harvest in the green') by cutting off bunches towards veraison (the onset of ripening) if the vines seem unlikely to be able to ripen their crop.

The degree-day is one way to assess such variability. The measure was originally developed, based on average monthly temperature statistics, to express the suitability of different climates to grow various crops. It became popular in the United States as a measure for distinguishing different thermal environments for the vine, especially in California, where in the mid-twentieth century viticulture was expanding into new areas. It proved useful there because variations in temperature from one region to another, or even within the same region, such as northern California, are considerable. Aspiring grape growers were able to judge which varieties of grapes they might grow in their region or sub-region because the degree-day distinguished the full range of growing conditions from the cool (coastal California north of San Francisco) to the moderately hot (Napa Valley) to the extremely hot (Central Valley).

Calculation of degree-days assumes that the vine starts actively growing when temperatures are above 10°C. For each month of the growing season (October to April in the southern hemisphere and April to October in the northern) temperatures above 10°C are summed. The normal calculation begins with the average temperature of the month, subtracts 10 from it, and multiplies the remainder by the number of days in the month. The degree-day is therefore superficially attractive as a measure because it is simple to calculate and gives the impression of energy accumulating over the growing season.

The measure has several deficiencies, however, the main one being that minimum temperatures during the night, when the vine is not photosynthesising, can unduly influence the result. Such underestimation was one of the main reasons some scientists were overly sceptical about the prospects for viticulture in Central Otago. Many scientists, but initially James Prescott, have also pointed out that degree-days correlate closely with even simpler measures such as the average temperature of the warmest month discussed earlier. This similarity results because the high point of the regular annual temperature curve predicts other points on the curve very accurately. Despite these limitations, and largely because of its simplicity and familiarity, many enterprises continue to use the degree-day to summarise thermal conditions in New Zealand and elsewhere. It is their common currency for discussing temperatures in different years.

The degree-day is, therefore, a useful measure to illustrate the variability in atmospheric conditions that viticulturists face from year to year in all regions of New Zealand. Two maps, one of average degree-days calculated over a 30-year period (1975 to 2005) and a second of degree-days in the 1997/98 growing season, show the magnitude of the differences (Figures 4.9, 4.10). The 1998 vintage is used as an example because in most New Zealand regions it is the warmest season on record since grapes became an important crop. Grape growers and wine enterprises struggled with decisions about when they should pick. In Marlborough, where Sauvignon Blanc was by then clearly the most important variety, the decision was especially difficult. Winegrowers wanted to retain the acidity, vibrancy and vitality that characterise the aromas and flavours of Sauvignon from this region, but were also wary of picking too early.

In this 1997/98 growing season the differences in degree-days from the average were substantial. All grape-growing regions except Central Otago had passed their average expectations by more than 200 degree-days. In Marlborough's case this meant up to 25 per cent more solar energy than normal. In a 'normal' year it would expect a total approaching 1200 degree-days, whereas by vintage 1998 some sites in the Wairau and Awatere valleys received between 1400 and 1500 degree-days. (Even Cabernet Sauvignon might have ripened effortlessly in Marlborough and Martinborough in that season.) Marlborough winegrowers were unsure whether to pick or leave their grapes on the vine. Some delayed and regretted the decision because the grapes did become overripe and began deteriorating. A few growers picked part of their crop quite early and the rest later – probably the best solution considering the uncertainty in achieving the balance in sugar levels, acidity and flavours they were seeking. 'We'd do it a damn sight better if we had a similar season next year!' commented Peter Babich laconically three months after the 1998 vintage. Empirical experience counts.

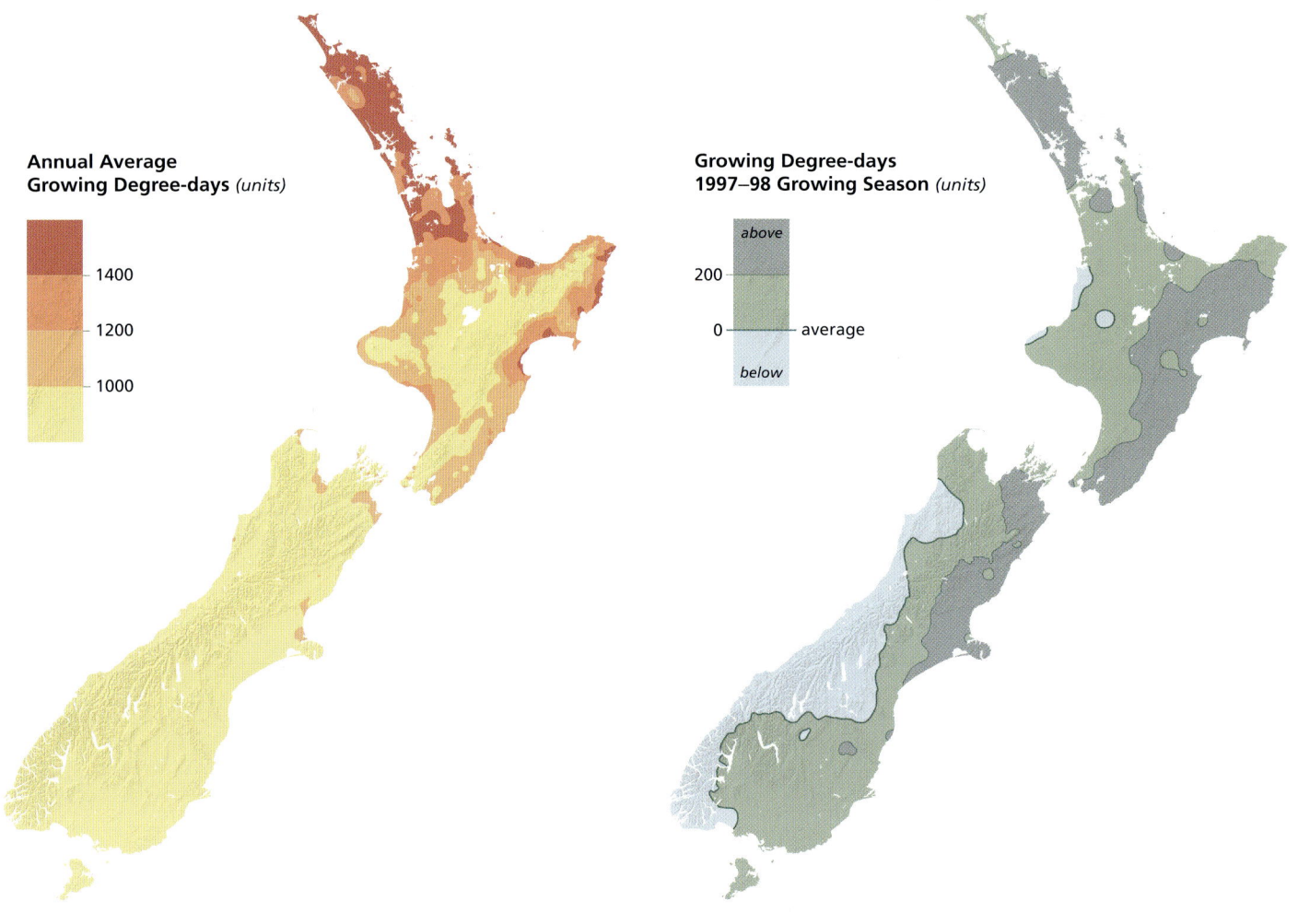

Figure 4.9 Average annual growing degree-days over 10ºC
Figure 4.10 Additional annual growing degree-days over 10ºC in the 1997–98 growing season

Viticultural imperatives in cool climates

Too cold can be as troublesome as too hot. Given New Zealand's cool climate, getting the grapes physiologically ripe with aromas and flavours that express the variety and where it is being grown is the primary viticultural imperative. Viticulturists achieve ripeness by managing the architecture of the vine and level of the crop through pruning and rubbing off unwanted buds and by managing the canopy to maximise photosynthesis. Successfully achieving these objectives assumes that nutrient levels and the moisture regime in the soils and vine are also effectively monitored and managed.

The second imperative is to avoid catastrophic events that drastically reduce yield.

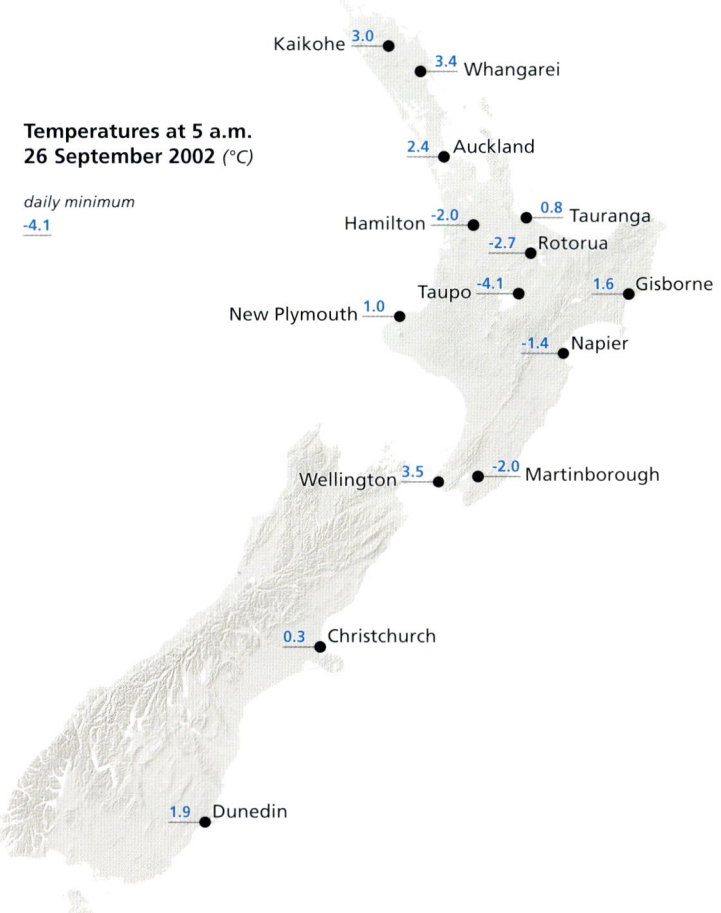

Figure 4.11 New Zealand temperatures at 5 a.m. on 26 September 2002. The plunge in temperature damaged a number of New Zealand vineyards.

Frost after the leaf buds have burst in spring is the best example. Hail at almost any time in the growing season is another. The vine is especially vulnerable to hail when shoots and leaves are young and when fruit are ripening. In deciding precisely where to plant grapes the probability of such catastrophic events needs to be considered alongside the seasonal temperatures and rainfall conditions that influence the vine's ability to ripen its fruit.

Some of the variability in growing conditions can, of course, be ameliorated. Irrigation is the main means of overcoming deficits in soil moisture but it remains a controversial viticultural practice. France allows irrigation under the AOC laws but only for vines under three years of age. Its argument is that after vines become

Central Otago vineyards use water sprinklers (above left), pot burners (above right), and wind machines (opposite) to fight frost. *Felton Road (above left); Alan Kwok Lun Cheung (above right and opposite)*

established their roots must be encouraged to explore more deeply to tap additional reserves of nutrients and moisture especially in dry periods. But there is a simpler explanation. Few, if any, of their appellation wine regions need to irrigate because they seldom experience strong moisture deficits during the growing season. In France the legislation is also embedded in the conflict between the Midi and the prestigious appellations. After phylloxera, much of the Midi profited from being the first region back into production. In the last two decades of the nineteenth century it produced at high yields and grapes grown there were bought by producers from prestigious regions such as Bordeaux and Burgundy and passed off as their own.

Temperature is much more difficult to influence through vineyard practices than lack of moisture. Choosing a northerly aspect on sloping land and aligning the rows north and south on flatter land ensures that each side of the row is exposed to solar radiation and evens out the temperature in the canopy. Placing reflective material immediately under the vines increases the temperature in the row. Managing the canopy by plucking leaves in the fruit zone at veraison to expose the bunches to direct sunlight also hastens ripening. All of these techniques are practised in parts of New Zealand but it must be remembered that generally cool conditions in late summer and autumn are an advantage for growing vines. The window of opportunity for picking grapes that are physiologically ripe is longer because grapes tend to ripen more slowly than in warmer climates.

Given the potential of spring frost to kill buds and reduce or even destroy the crop, it is not surprising that within most viticultural regions participants in the industry have established networks of weather stations to monitor temperature and warn growers when severe early-morning frosts are imminent. When a frost warning goes out, enterprises jump into action. Their response depends on the nature of the frost and the protection systems they favour. If the frost is caused by a temperature inversion

(warmer air trapped above a layer of cold air) helicopters are quickly airborne. Provided the cool layer is not too deep, they are often able to force the warm air down and mix it with the cold, thus avoiding damage to the buds or leaves of the vines. The terrestrial wind machines nestled in the frost-prone hollows of many viticultural regions work in a similar way. They set up a turbulence that disturbs the cool air ponding there. Viticulturists grumpy from disturbed sleep are common in the late spring.

Some vineyards, like Delegat's 300 hectares on the left bank of the Ngaruroro River in Hawke's Bay, have installed overhead sprinklers in addition to their drip irrigation. When frosts seem likely, the pumps are switched on by 4 a.m. to ensure that their two small reservoirs remain full while the vineyard sprinklers are spinning. By coating the vulnerable buds, shoots and young leaves in fine layers of ice, they are protected from frosts of several degrees below zero. The large enterprise ARA, on the west bank of the Waihopai in Marlborough, achieves a similar result more economically with overhead sprinklers that are used for both irrigation and frost protection.

Scientific knowledge and canopy management

As well as innovative technology, science has played a distinctive role in the transformation of New Zealand's vineyards. Lacking the long European empirical experience, grape growers and winemakers sought, and have been provided with, local viticultural research. They have also advanced this knowledge themselves. Whereas in the French industry the quality and reputation of wines provide a certainty that their viticulture is working, New Zealand growers have benefited from theoretical and empirical research that has improved their understanding of their new environments. The research on canopy management of the mid- to late 1980s was especially important in empowering

Lack of competition between vines in these widely spaced rows in the Hawke's Bay encouraged thick hedges, shaded grapes, and slow ripening.
Marti Friedlander, Auckland War Memorial Museum – Tāmaki Paenga Hira, PH-2008-4

grape growers to understand quality viticulture and use these principles to advance it. Successful experiments that reduce the vigour of vines by inter-row planting of suitable cover crops, while simultaneously reducing pest problems, is promising. So is work on the biological control of diseases such as *Botrytis cinerea*. Winemaking knowledge, which tends to be less regionally specific, has been augmented by formal training, local sharing of knowledge in the close-knit wine communities, and regular (often annual) experience in other countries.

Between 1960 and 1980, three aspects of viticulture were limiting New Zealand's ability to produce the best-quality fruit to make fine table wines. First, the *vinifera* stock were heavily virus infected. Second, suitable clones for New Zealand conditions were not available for all varieties. Third, knowledge of methods of canopy management was limited. All three deficiencies were progressively ameliorated during the next three decades so that New Zealand's potential for growing grapes to make fine wine was realised.

Canopy management is the shorthand phrase for the trellising of the vine and the training and trimming of its leaves to maximise its ability to photosynthesise and produce grapes of optimum quality for making wines of high quality. The scientific programme that was carried out during the 1980s to advance canopy management in New Zealand viticulture was particularly important. One individual, Richard Smart, was especially influential. An Australian plant physiologist and microclimatologist with a PhD from Cornell, one of his scientific interests was the trellising system for the vine and the way that this influenced its microclimate and ability to ripen its fruit. In viticultural studies the microclimate is usually defined as the climate within the canopy – the atmospheric conditions that directly influence the vine's leaves, fruit and roots. Smart and other scientists had modelled the effects of temperature and sunlight on berries and the photosynthesis of leaves, the influence of orientation of rows, and the impact of the width of the vine 'hedge' on the ripening of grapes. The architecture of the pruned vine affects the arrangement of the leaves and their ability to photosynthesise effectively. Smart demonstrated that when the hedge of vines was thick the interior leaves functioned at less than 5 per cent of their potential. Mildews were also difficult to control in the interior leaves. Grape growers were converted to the thin canopies that he advocated.

Smart went one stage further by designing and experimenting with different trellising systems, several of which proved to be highly efficient. When he returned to Australia to become an international viticultural consultant, he was disappointed that these efficient trellising systems had not been taken up more widely as had the Scott-Henry system in Oregon and internationally. Nevertheless, his influence on New Zealand viticulture was profound. In field days, seminars and conferences his knowledge and enthusiasm for effective canopy management was infectious and was transferred to the new generation of viticulturists. Regardless of the trellising system being used, grape growers and winemakers became acutely aware of the principles underlying the management of the canopy. Cumulatively, Smart's work demonstrated that in the cool climates of New Zealand it was possible to ripen the chosen varieties of *Vitis vinifera* in most seasons.

These scientific results are not surprising given the practices that have been evolved empirically in regions such as Burgundy. There, as in many of the prestigious regions of France, *vignerons* achieve low vigour by having the vines closely spaced (1 m by 90 cm) and practising a regular programme of leaf plucking and vine trimming. Smart's work established the science behind these practices and was widely publicised and discussed both locally and internationally. His greatest influence was not in the wholesale adoption of a particular type of supporting trellis but in raising the general level of understanding of the importance of balancing grape crop with vine vigour – something that can be achieved in a variety of ways on a variety of trellising systems. There is no doubt that New Zealand grape growers are much more aware of the importance of the ratio of leaf area to crop and are now adept at producing fruit of optimal quality for making wine from grapes grown in different environments.

Natural environments in cultural terms

By tying environmental characteristics such as slopes, soils or geology to the quality of wines, oversimplified explanations of successful wine regions underestimate the critical

During the 1967 field day at the Te Kauwhata Viticultural Research Station, Dr Jack Perle instructs winegrowers on yeast varieties. *Dick Scott Collection, Auckland War Memorial Museum – Tāmaki Paenga Hira, PH-2008-4*

role of people. With two French colleagues from the Institut National de la Recherche Agronomique in Dijon, I was driving to an interview on the Heretaunga Plains near Gimblett Road in Hawke's Bay. Alongside me in the front seat was Jean-Baptiste Traversac, a graduate in biochemistry from Montpellier and in viticulture and oenology from Bordeaux, two of the eminent French tertiary institutions in wine studies. Suddenly, a question from Jean-Baptiste: 'Warren, why are these vines on flat land?' My response, struggling a bit with the French, was: 'Why shouldn't they be, Jean-Baptiste? They are receiving all of the solar energy they need to ripen their crop, the vines are in balance, the soils are free draining . . .' Jean-Baptiste was insistent and the discussion became quite intense. After several minutes, in a brief lull in the debate, from the back seat Philippe Perrier-Cornet, an economist with a liberal bent, diffused the tension. 'But Warren,' he said, 'you must remember that in France the vines are Catholic – they must suffer!'

The vehemence of my French friend in defending the association of vines and hills shows the extent to which such environmental determinism (in this case, sloping terrain on the location of vines) has penetrated the teaching of French viticulture and oenology. The vines are on the hills, the wine from them is of high quality, so the hills must be the cause. Such simple association of environment with quality denigrates the centuries of day-to-day observation, experimentation and effort that went into

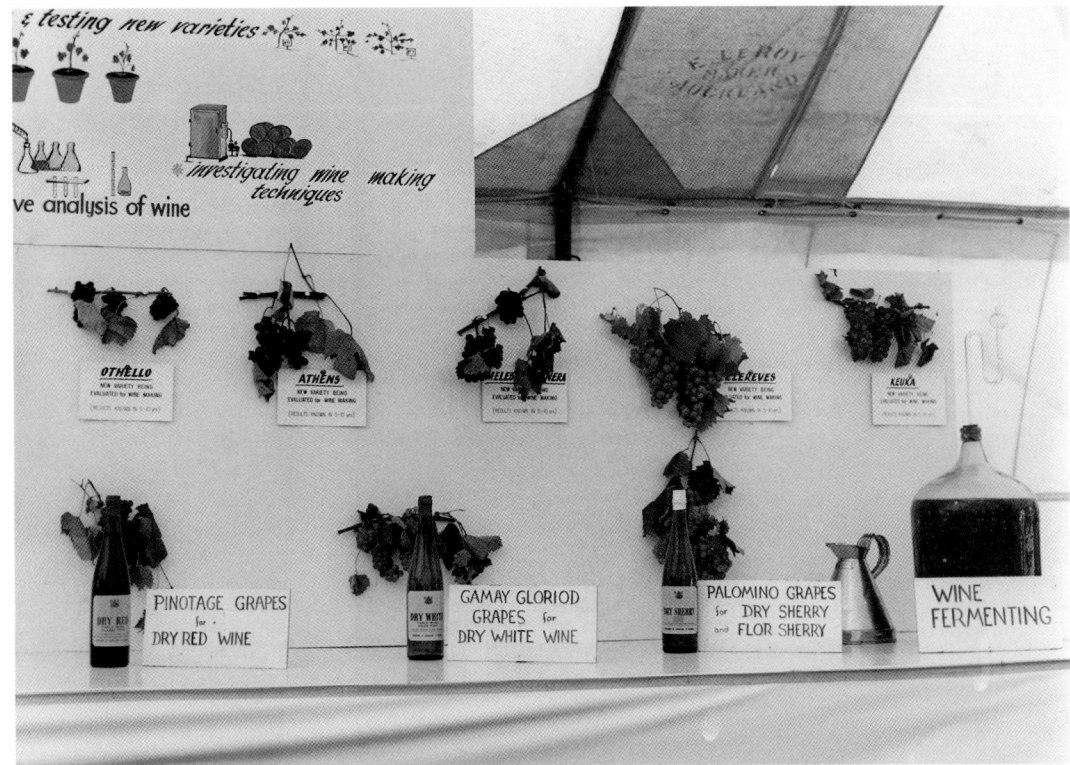

The grape varieties recommended at the 1967 field day bear almost no resemblance to the *vinifera* varieties grown in New Zealand today. Othello, Athens, and Keuka are no longer grown, while Pinotage, Gamay, and Palomino are rare. *Dick Scott Collection, Auckland War Memorial Museum – Tāmaki Paenga Hira, PH-2008-4*

understanding how to realise the potential of these natural attributes. The Burgundian people may have been God's people, some in the guise of monks of the Cistercian order, but the struggle and effort, the hard work and skill, was theirs. The slopes of Burgundy give some natural advantages, like better drainage and higher solar energy (when they face the right direction), and cool-air drainage that affords some protection against late-spring frosts. But in localities where soils are free draining anyway and additional energy is not necessary to ripen the variety, and spring frosts are not a problem, these conditions become irrelevant. When Philippe Perrier-Cornet says that the vine must suffer, he is expressing a cultural view as much as a scientific understanding.

The complexity of interactions in the physical environment is given added dimensions by the capacity of humans to modify these interactions to their own ends. The *vignoble* (vineyard) of Burgundy, for instance, is a managed not a natural landscape. Its hydrology has been transformed. The vineyards are a maze of ad hoc and planned drainage systems that have altered the original pattern. Stream banks are concreted and water flow managed. Disused quarries are evident from Chambertin to Meursault and beyond, with vines now nestled in their remade surfaces. Even the soil, the gift of God, is opened, re-engineered and rewrapped. It is increasingly common for vineyards to be reconstituted when they are being replanted. Huge earthmoving and

Natural Environments in Human Terms

Hoar frost on the vines at Akarua's Cairnmuir Road vineyard in Central Otago.
Akarua Winery, Central Otago

rock-crushing machines alter the soil profile and even the subsoil to make areas freer draining and easier to work.

Environmental learning in the dispersion of the vine

It is tempting to interpret the dispersion of the vine in New Zealand in the second half of the twentieth century solely through the soils and climates of the evolving regions. At a macro scale, several aspects of the New Zealand climate, soils and relief are pertinent. Both islands are characterised by strong west to east gradients in rainfall, but their intensity varies with local conditions and at various resolutions. Their pattern is more straightforward and intense in the South Island where the Southern Alps are responsible for a marked rain-shadow effect and rainfall gradient from west to east. In less than 100 kilometres between the Alps and Central Otago, annual precipitation falls from several metres to under 300 millimetres – a figure less than half that of the prestigious grape-growing areas of France such as Burgundy and Bordeaux.

In the North Island the patterns are more complex because two or three ranges of hills or mountains usually intervene from west to east to provide successive rain shadows and slight 'continental' effects. Waiheke Island, Hawke's Bay and the Wairarapa all receive lower rainfall than areas to the west of them. The last two have annual precipitations of under 1000 millimetres, while much of Canterbury receives under 750 millimetres. Gisborne receives higher annual rainfall partly because in some seasons it is influenced by remnant tropical cyclones in the late summer months.

In very broad terms, we have seen the dispersal of the vine to regions where climatic conditions are more favourable – regions with lower precipitation in the crucial parts of the growing season, higher daily temperatures after veraison, and higher sunshine hours during the ripening period. The southern regions have greater risk from late-spring frosts and the possibility that in some seasons it will be difficult, maybe even impossible, to ripen grapes to a level to make still wines of real quality. If that happens, all of these southern regions at least have the possibility of directing their Chardonnay and Pinot Noir grapes to sparkling wines, where the level of sugar at harvest is not so demanding. Soils of the expanding regions are generally free draining, with Gisborne an obvious partial exception.

Yet such simple spatial association of natural environment with activity belies the role of people in the process and a host of micro-effects. Consider the complexity of the relationship between weather and varieties of *Vitis vinifera*. Like the prestigious regions of France, all of New Zealand is close to the polar limit for ripening many varieties of grapes. The problem of weather variability is better expressed in probabilistic terms. Empirical experience over many seasons is required before it is clear whether a variety will ripen to a satisfactory balance of sugar and acidity in a sufficient number of years to produce grapes with the flavour characteristics to make wines of real quality. In a sense, grape growing for wine is not about finding sites with the 'ideal' climates but about finding sites where the probability of a sufficient number of outstanding years, or very good, or even good years is high. In addition, the probability of 'wipeouts' – from late-spring frosts, or rampant fungal diseases from regular rain and high humidity after veraison – must be low. The task of the wine enterprise is to make outstanding wine out of the best seasons and the best possible wine from the worst seasons.

Moreover, any analysis of the weather record needs to be made for specific varieties, or indeed different clones each with their own phenology. Each variety (or clone) has bud burst at a different time, flowers at a different time, undergoes veraison at a different time and reaches physiological ripeness at a different time. And each event in this phenological sequence influences the next. The weather of any single year also affects the vine's performance in the following year, notably in the fertility of the buds. Yield, one of the key variables that the viticulturist is trying to influence, is affected. The weather sequences of particular years are seldom if ever exactly repeated in another. And the viticulturist/winemaker has only 40 or so vintages in which to perfect their art, or 80 or so if blessed with the constitution to be a flying winemaker between the southern and northern hemispheres into their sixties. Herein lies the joy and frustration of growing grapes and making wine.

5

Gisborne or Poverty Bay?

I saw this wee ad in the paper. It said 'Wanted to buy – grapes'. So I got on the phone very nervously . . . it was Montana up in Auckland in the Waitakeres. Frank Yukich answered very gruffly, 'Yup, whaddya want?' 'I've got some grapes for sale, sir.' 'Where are you?' 'Gisborne.' He said, 'Well, it's a long way, you know. We don't want just a few boxes – we want 300 to 400 pounds at least. How much have you got?' 'I've got 40 ton.'
– ROGER McLERNON

When James Cook named Poverty Bay because he had been unable to procure provisions from local Maori, he ensured that in the twentieth century most grape growers and winemakers would call their region Gisborne. In fact, Cook was misleading future settlers, because some of the soils on the flood plain of the Waipaoa River are among the most fertile and versatile in New Zealand. Perversely, it may even have been effective to have used Poverty Bay, playing on the common association of fine wines with meagre environments, despite the region being anything but meagre. Moreover, many successful winemaking firms in New Zealand have mined the word 'bay' in their names or brands – Cloudy Bay, Destiny Bay, Koura Bay, Lazy Bay, Oyster Bay, Pegasus Bay, Tasman Bay, and even the ersatz Monkey Bay coined when Brian Vicieli was CEO of Nobilo.

Gewürztraminer grapes ready for picking at Nick Nobilo's Vinoptima Estate in Gisborne. *Vinoptima Estate*

In fact, Nick Nobilo was one of the few bold enough to christen their Chardonnay Poverty Bay and to convince British Airways to serve it on their European routes. Montana has also had much success with its strong Gisborne Chardonnay brand, winning international accolades and awards with it. So too have smaller enterprises such as Coopers Creek for their austere, unoaked Gisborne Chardonnay that won Elite Gold in the 2009 Air New Zealand Wine Awards. Gisborne winegrowers were even bolder by branding their region 'Chardonnay Capital' when the United States-led 'ABC' (Anything But Chardonnay) set was undermining this elegant variety.

Gisborne holds a special place in New Zealand winegrowing. In the two decades between 1970 and 1990, grapes from Gisborne helped transform the New Zealand wine industry from one based on fortified (alcohol added) sweet wines made from hybrid grapes to one based on the production of table wines made from varieties of *Vitis vinifera*. For these two decades, Müller Thurgau, one cross of Riesling and Sylvaner, was queen of Gisborne. But Gisborne remained an essential source of grapes in the transformation of New Zealand winegrowing for much longer. Indeed, it took until the 1995 vintage for Marlborough regularly to produce more grapes than Gisborne and until 2004 for Hawke's Bay to do the same. Gisborne's contribution to the evolution of New Zealand winegrowing is incontrovertible.

Enterprises from Auckland rather than the nearby Hawke's Bay initiated the growth of Gisborne as a winegrowing region. In the early 1960s, Corbans, Montana and Penfolds all increased their area in vines by establishing vineyards mainly within the Auckland region. Smaller, mainly Dalmatian, family enterprises did the same, but usually close to their existing cellars and dwellings. The new vineyards met an immediate need for grapes but most had relatively short lives. Some sites, such as Montana's at Mangatangi (west of the Hunua Ranges), proved unsuitable because the soils were heavy, the climate humid and the vines too vigorous, especially when the *vinifera* varieties began to replace the hybrids, and new, more suitable environments for the vine had been discovered.

In targeting Gisborne as a source of grapes, Montana and Corbans were joined by a group of smaller Auckland enterprises such as Babich, Delegat's, Matua Valley, Nobilo, Penfolds and Selaks. Only Corbans immediately purchased bare land and planted grapes on it. All of the others (including Corbans) arranged formal and informal contracts with Gisborne landowners to grow grapes for them. The Auckland enterprises provided the technical advice and often cuttings. Most of these vines were not grafted but on their own roots.

Farmers on the Gisborne Plain, who were already skilled in growing a variety of crops, were quick to respond. So were accountants, iwi organisations, lawyers and environmental consultants, who also saw tax advantages in growing grapes. Many growers initially treated grapes like any other crop. As the supply of grapes was short,

Antonio (Tony) Zame began making wine at his Capri Vineyards on Hapara Road, Gisborne, in the 1930s. By the 1950s, Zame was growing 30 tons of grapes a year and buying in another 30 to produce a variety of wines, sherries, and liqueurs. *Marti Friedlander, Auckland War Memorial Museum – Tāmaki Paenga Hira, PH-2008-4*

and they were being paid by weight, they aimed for high yields. On most of the soils of the Poverty Bay flats they obtained those yields without irrigation. Ten tonnes to the acre, the equivalent to about 24 tonnes to the hectare, was common.

During the period from 1965 through to the early 1980s the area planted in grapes in Gisborne grew more quickly than in any other region – slightly faster even than Hawke's Bay where winegrowing had been established for much longer. By the time of the vine-pull scheme of 1986, Gisborne had a similar area in vines to Hawke's Bay, about 2000 hectares, despite it having started from a much smaller base. Gisborne growers extracted a total of 586 hectares in the 1986 vine pull, of which Müller Thurgau made

Gisborne or Poverty Bay?

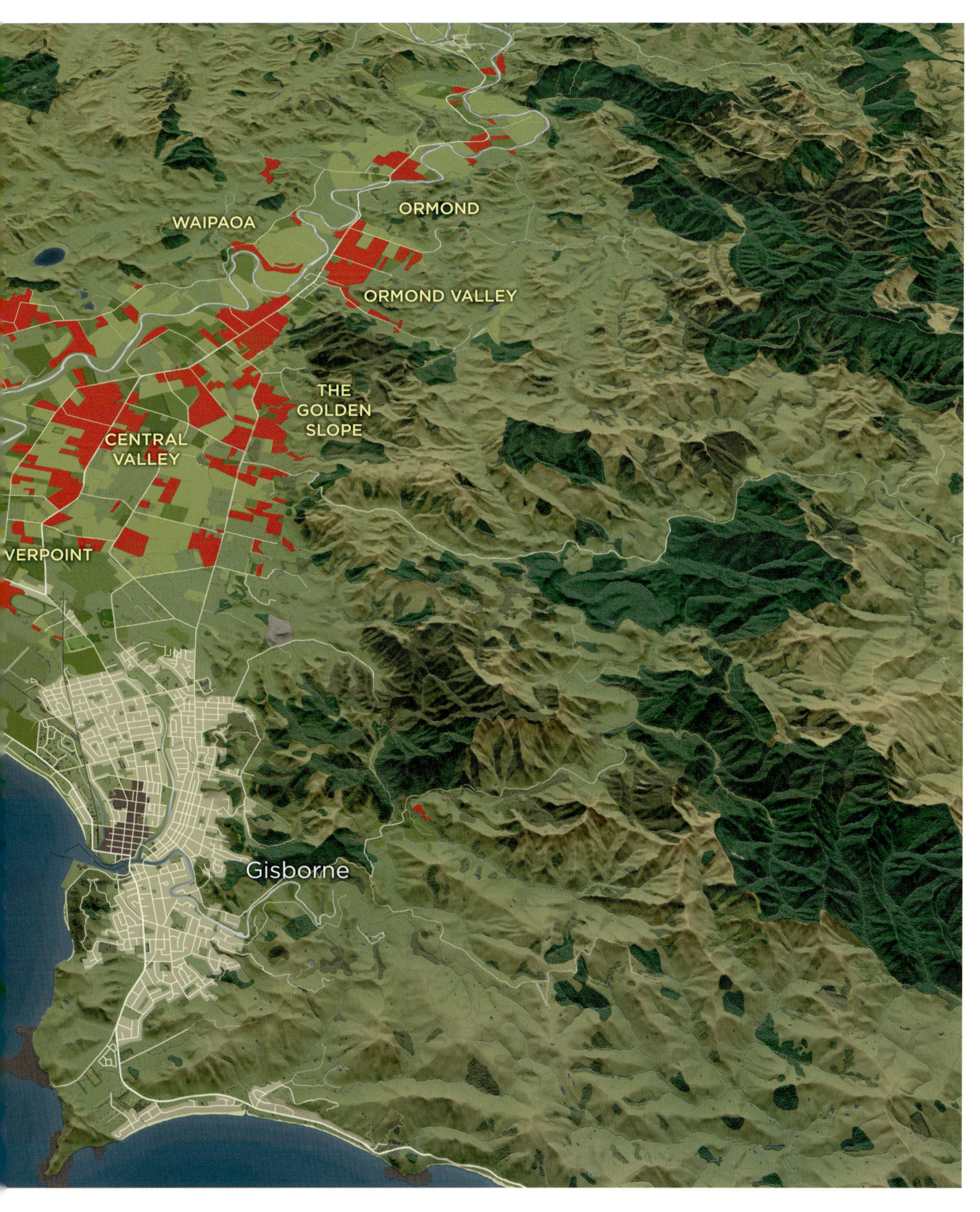

Friedrich Wohnsiedler was forced out of his Gisborne butchery in 1914 by a crowd of anti-German locals. He headed into the Poverty Bay countryside and, under the Waiherere Wines label, pioneered commercial winemaking in the region. *Dick Scott Collection, Auckland War Memorial Museum – Tāmaki Paenga Hira, PH-2008-4 (above); Marti Friedlander (above right)*

up 216 hectares. Between 1990 and 1995, the total area in vines in Gisborne remained relatively stable before dropping to under 1200 hectares in 1996–97. This decrease resulted from the removal of much of the remaining area planted in high-yielding varieties, especially Müller Thurgau. Since 1996–97 the area in vines has steadily increased as more Chardonnay has been planted. Increased demand for Pinot Gris in the twenty-first century has seen it quickly become Gisborne's second most-planted variety, but with only 185 hectares in the ground, it is well behind the 1084 hectares of Chardonnay.

Unfortunately, the early period of high yields per hectare has branded Gisborne as a bulk producer of grapes for wine of moderate quality, a reputation that it has not deserved for at least the last decade. This reputation for high yields derives partly from

Montana using Gisborne to source their Pinot Noir and especially Chardonnay grapes as the base for their sparkling brand Lindauer. These varieties are picked early in the autumn at very high yield and low sugar (brix) compared with still wines, thus avoiding the autumn rains and high humidity that in some seasons are a problem.

Partly because they must respond to an environment that naturally favours high yields for many varieties, Gisborne's grape growers are among the most sophisticated in the country. Many have embraced techniques to limit this abundance while also meeting the increasingly strict requirements of their corporate clients. Gisborne's climate sometimes makes downy and powdery mildew difficult to control, while botrytis can also be a problem. Autumn rains, before the grapes are physiologically ripe, sometimes demand early picking.

The experienced winegrowers of the region have adapted well to these environmental necessities. Just as the remaining winegrowers of the Auckland region have modified their methods to limit the impact of higher humidity, so too have those of Gisborne where such problems are less severe. These generally strong relationships were severely tested when in mid-2009 Pernod Ricard NZ stunned the Gisborne winegrowing community by announcing that it was negotiating to terminate contracts with many Gisborne growers. The international company Constellation Brands and the New Zealand enterprise Mud House had also begun to buy their growers out of contracts.

The early success of Gisborne extended beyond grape growing under contract. Local entrepreneurs bought land, or used what they owned, to establish vineyards with the idea of making their own wine. Three Gisborne families – the Irwins (1975), James and Annie Millton (1984) and the Thorpes (late 1980s) – established winemaking enterprises that were to have an extended influence on the region and on New Zealand winegrowing more generally. Gradually, more independent wineries have been added, but the number has remained small compared with Hawke's Bay and Marlborough.

Why Gisborne?

A small winegrowing industry already existed in Poverty Bay in the late 1950s, with the Chitty, Wohnsiedler and Zame holdings being the largest, although the total area in wine grapes was under 20 hectares. These winemaking enterprises had demonstrated that they could produce grapes of quality from both *vinifera* and hybrid vines on the Gisborne Plain, even though the *vinifera* grapes were being used to make sweet ports, sherries and flavoured liqueurs. At the time, horticultural holdings on the plain also produced grapes for sale as fresh fruit. When short of fruit, in the early years, the wine producers were quite prepared to purchase these Albany Surprise table grapes for their ferments.

By the 1950s, stopbanking by the Poverty Bay Catchment Board had reduced the frequency and extent of flooding on the Gisborne Plain, making even more potential horticultural land available. In 1952, Wattie's of Hawke's Bay established a canning and freezing factory in Gisborne primarily for sweet corn. Farmers widened their experience by extending the range of vegetables and fruit they grew. But in the mid-twentieth century, Gisborne's southern neighbour Hawke's Bay remained clearly New Zealand's largest and most important centre for pip- and stone-fruit orchards, as well as for growing vegetables for processing. Competition for land there was much more intense than in Gisborne and as a result land values were noticeably higher in Hawke's Bay – an advantage for Gisborne grape growing when aspiring *vignerons* began buying land.

Grapes were a natural choice for larger-scale production on the 20,000 hectares of the Gisborne Plain. The climate of the region, although not dissimilar to parts of Auckland in its high humidity during summer and autumn months, has the advantages of higher sunshine hours and lower rainfall. The coastal, southeasterly part of the Poverty Bay flats receives under 800 millimetres of annual rainfall, although this increases to over 1000 millimetres closer to the surrounding hills. The gentle relief of most of the Waipaoa flood plain encouraged mechanised viticulture and harvesting. Few similar opportunities existed closer to Auckland. Parts of the Bay of Plenty have a suitable climate, although rainfall is higher there, but the area of land with subdued relief is more restricted. By the 1970s, landowners in the Bay of Plenty were more interested in growing kiwifruit and their land prices were climbing rapidly while the Muldoon National government allowed tax relief for professionals investing in rural industries.

One characteristic of the Poverty Bay climate was to prove more troublesome to grape growing than initially recognised. Former tropical cyclones, revitalised as intense middle-latitude cyclones, sometimes drift down the east coast of the North Island and bring heavy rain, strong winds and flooding, especially to the protruding East Cape and Gisborne region. They occur irregularly but most commonly in March to April at the time when grapes are ripening and are vulnerable to mildews in warm, moist conditions. Occasionally, these intense low-pressure systems strike the region directly. Such catastrophic events tend to have a disproportionate influence on subsequent behaviour. This was the case with former tropical cyclone Bola when it devastated the vineyards of Gisborne in 1988. The Poverty Bay harvest was severely affected. Grapes were spoiling on the vine because the de-stemming and crushing equipment could not keep up with the harvested fruit.

After the event, Montana's production manager, Peter Hubscher, insisted on having duplicate crushing facilities installed on the site of their winery and bottling plant in Glen Innes, Auckland as insurance against such events, although they have since been used infrequently. The probabilities of another remnant tropical cyclone striking the Gisborne Plain have been incorporated into the broader strategies of the major companies even to the extent of Montana reducing its commitment to Gisborne grape growers in the winter of 2009.

The soils of the Gisborne Plain

Gisborne winegrowers are privileged with the best soil maps of any horticultural locality in New Zealand. Alan Pullar was a highly respected scientist working for the Soil Bureau of the DSIR in the 1950s and 1960s, and his maps at a scale of 1:15,800 were sufficiently detailed from his meticulous field surveys that they guide almost everyone buying or cultivating land on the Gisborne Plain. Grape growers, drivers of harvesters, real estate agents and growers of all crops swear by them. Dig a soil profile on one side of a line dividing two soil types on the map and then move 10 metres to the other side, dig another, and the profile will be different.

Alan Pullar's soil maps of the Gisborne Plain identified subtle variations in the fertile soils of the flood plain. Winegrowers have preferred to establish vineyards on the Matawhero silt-loams and avoided heavier, less free-draining clay soils and areas with high water tables. Nevertheless, there are fine Gisborne vineyards on the Kaiti clay-loam soils around Patutahi.

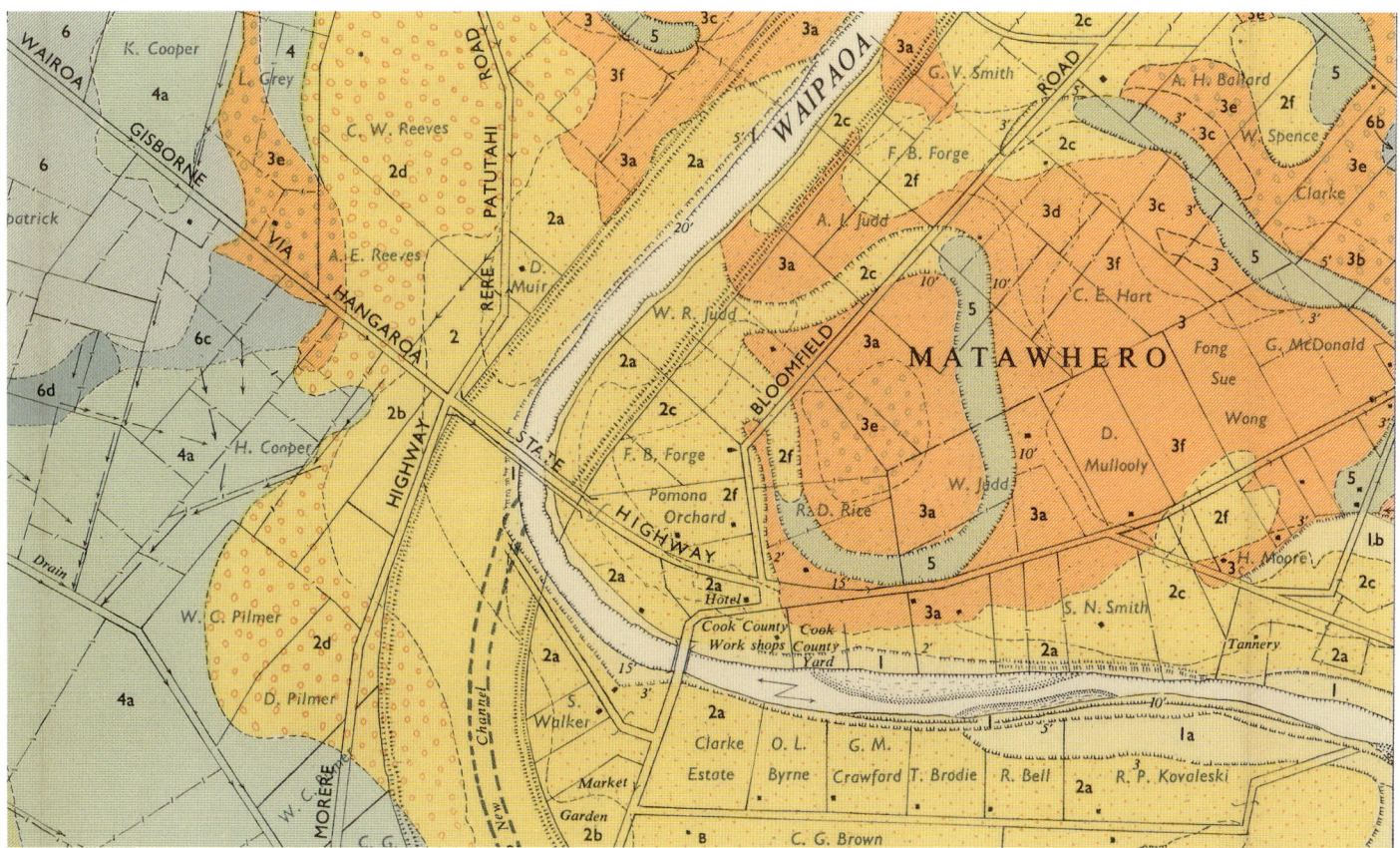

Gisborne or Poverty Bay?

The flood plain of the Waipaoa River is made up of soils derived mainly from finer sediments than those of either Hawke's Bay or Marlborough. Its headwaters are in the Ruakumara Range and include the notorious Tarndale slip near Mangatu. The Waipaoa's suspended sediment load is much higher than that of most New Zealand rivers because it is eroding mainly fine-grained and soft sedimentary rocks, especially mudstones and siltstones. Until stopbanking and other flood-control measures reduced the frequency of floods in the mid-twentieth century, these fine sediments were the parent materials for many of the soils of the Gisborne Plain. But as the flood plain developed, the physical properties of the soils were highly variable spatially. In addition, before European settlement, much of the plain comprised wetlands, and

Figure 5.1 Gisborne and the Poverty Bay flats. The Manutuke, Matawhero, and Patutahi triangle.

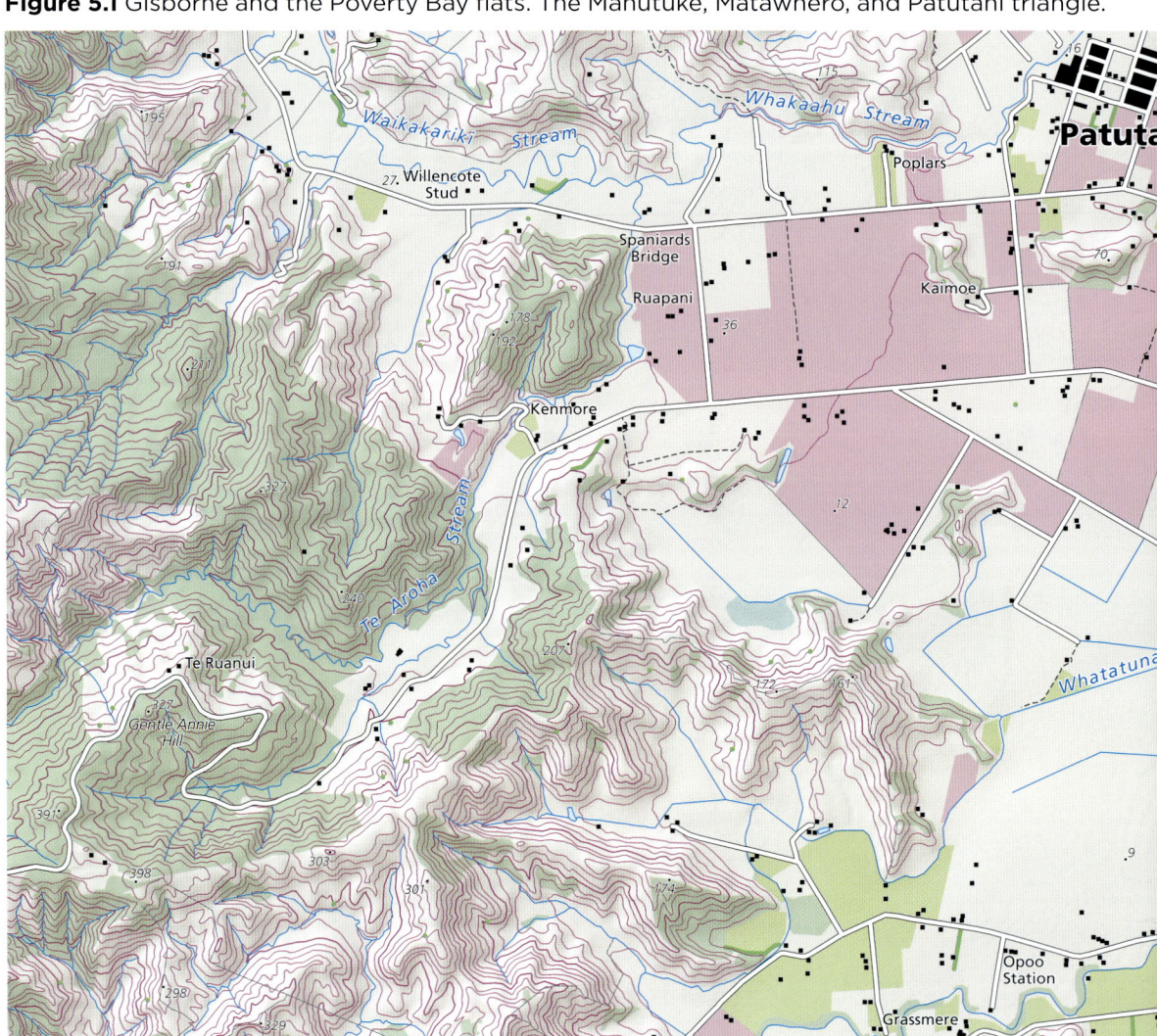

in parts of these lowlands the water table is close to the surface. Pullar's maps and soil descriptions provide an accurate guide to this detailed variability, and when combined with the experience of local landowners in growing many crops – especially different varieties of grapes – the qualities of different soils, including what varieties and clones of grapes performed well on them, gradually became a form of codified knowledge.

The soils of the Poverty Bay flats have two distinctive characteristics compared with many recent alluvial soils of New Zealand. They are slightly alkaline and some are low in organic matter. The alkalinity (low to medium pH – 5.8 to 6.2) originates from the calcareous bedrocks of the Waipaoa's catchment; the low organic matter, from the youth of most of the soils. The Waipaoa group of soils, in particular, has both

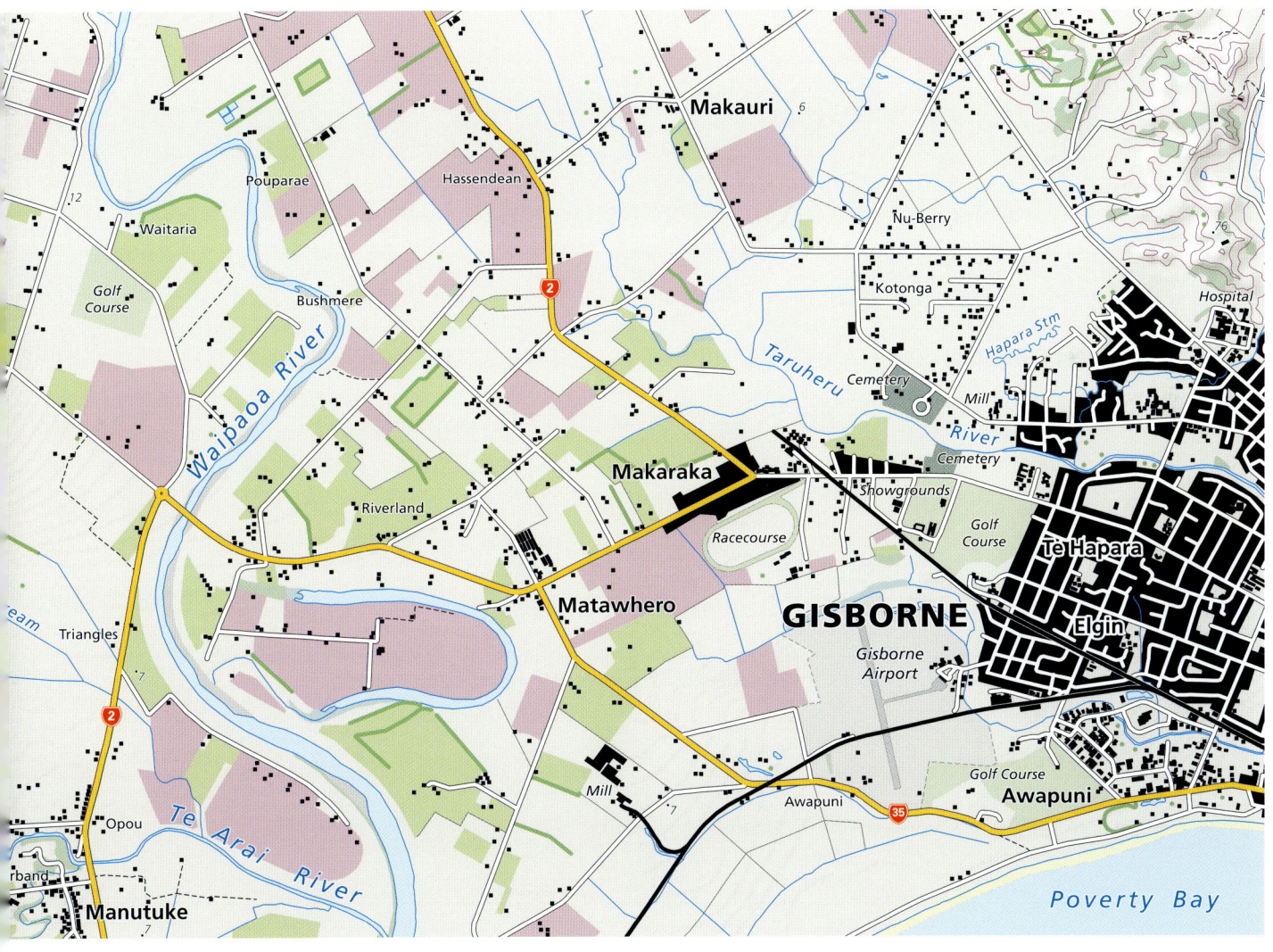

Gisborne or Poverty Bay?

Nick Nobilo's Vinoptima produces Gewürztraminer from deep, rich, alluvial clay soils in inland Poverty Bay. The pumpkins growing through the fence next door tell a tale of fertility.
Vinoptima Estate (right); Warren Moran (far right)

characteristics. They are extremely young, most being deposited since 1930 when accelerated erosion in the headwaters resulted in regular flooding at an average of more than one flood a year for the following 20 years before flood control was in place. The deposited materials aggraded the Gisborne Plain with layers of sediment. These regular floods restricted vegetation growth so that organic matter and nitrogen in the soils was initially low.

But with the fine sediments also came lime (calcium carbonate). Pullar suggests that with every 8 centimetres of silt deposited came about 25 tonnes of lime per hectare. The high calcium of the Waipaoa soils means that they take up water in winter and dry out in summer. Vines are able to perform in this regime especially if the reduction in soil moisture occurs slowly. Indeed it may be an advantage if, as the season advances and ripening of grapes proceeds, the vines access deeper soil moisture and nutrients. Managing the available nitrogen in the vineyard and in the wine is important, but possible here, given that in many soils it started out low. Now that flooding is better controlled, cover cropping and other organic practices are common and grape growers are managing the nitrogen status of these soils.

Other soils of the flood plain are older and deeper with better-developed topsoils largely because they have been inundated less frequently and have been consistently growing crops for longer. These include the five phases of the Matawhero soils and the seven phases of the Waiherere soils that Pullar identified. In addition, he recognised a separate group of soils (with nine categories within it) that he called 'gleyed recent soils'. These are sticky, clay-based soils. Most needed artificial drainage before they were suitable for cropping or intensive grazing. The Poverty Bay flats present, therefore, a more subtle diversity of soils than many other winegrowing regions of New Zealand.

Enterprises in the New Zealand filière: *wine producers and grape growers*

The intense competition between Montana and Corbans that enlivened New Zealand winegrowing during the last four decades of the twentieth century was sparked in Auckland, lit in Gisborne in the late 1960s, before jumping Cook Strait to Marlborough in 1973. By far the most important stimulus to growing grapes in Gisborne was the decision by Montana, followed closely by Corbans and other Auckland wine enterprises, to expand aggressively there by letting contracts to local grape growers. Gisborne was the first region where the two companies were in direct competition for grapes, although Frank Yukich had already begun to use his West Auckland connections to buy grapes from anyone who would sell them. But things moved quickly and by 1973 Yukich had extended Montana's interest to the South Island and Corbans again followed. Despite Montana planting rapidly in Marlborough, Gisborne continued to have a larger area in vines. Not until the early 1990s did Marlborough's vineyard reach 2000 hectares, an area that Gisborne and Hawke's Bay had both attained in the early 1980s.

The form that the New Zealand wine *filière* would take for the next half-century emerged in Gisborne in the late 1960s. The rapid growth of New Zealand winegrowing required considerable capital for both vineyards and cellars. Wine companies offloaded some viticultural costs and responsibilities by offering contracts to landowners interested in growing grapes, but as mentioned above, Corbans was the only Auckland wine enterprise to buy land in Gisborne and plant grapes on it. This family – almost communal – company continued to act as it always had, assessing land carefully and proceeding cautiously, even planting a small experimental vineyard with a wide range of varieties on each site that it purchased. In 1969, Corbans purchased a total of 121 acres on the Poverty Bay flats (almost 50 hectares) – 76 acres on Riverpoint Road near Matawhero and 45 acres off Bond Road in Ormond.

No other Auckland companies seeking grapes in Gisborne bought land there in the 1970s and 1980s. Montana under Frank Yukich was more interested in buying the last third-share of the Wohnsiedler winery in Waiherere as an initial base for their activities in Gisborne, although it did include a vineyard that was later replanted. In an interview in 2006, Yukich commented on the difficulties they faced in Gisborne in the late 1960s and early 1970s:

> We had around about 30 to 40 growers . . . when the grapes started coming in the price wasn't high enough and . . . everybody was saying that there wasn't enough money in it. We went through a very difficult period. Grape growers also began to challenge the way in which the prices for grapes were being set.

Describing an exchange in 1975 after he returned from South Africa, Denis Irwin recalls these times from the grower's point of view:

> Yes, the contract was with Montana. I was one of the first people to take Frank [Yukich] on, in terms of price. He had a meeting here at the Gisborne racecourse. Frank got up and he said, 'Okay, boys, you've all seen your contract, you've all seen the price this year and sorry about the drop but we did our best.' So, of course, I stood up and said, 'Point of order Mr Chairman. According to the terms of my contract, price is supposed to be negotiated between the company and the grower – there were certainly no negotiations as far as I was concerned.'

Having a representative group of growers collectively bargain with representatives of the companies initially solved such issues. But the differences smouldered for over a decade until the Commerce Commission ruled in 1991 that the rights of individual growers to do their own bargaining had to be respected.

Other, mainly Dalmatian-owned, enterprises from Auckland such as Babich, Matua Valley, Nobilo and Selaks also set about competing for grapes in Gisborne but bought no land. Because most were smaller, often with the family members advising growers and negotiating over price for grapes, the most successful were able to establish close working relationships with their growers. Some made a point of identifying the names of their grape growers on the labels. Names such as Judd, Tietjen and Witters began to be recognised by discerning consumers. Another wave of planting occurred in Gisborne when Frank Yukich bought Penfolds in 1977 because he sought new grape growers and lured some away from other companies.

Gisborne was also one site where the brewing companies and wine and spirits wholesale and retail outlets took a renewed commercial interest in wine producers. They were seeking to colonise the *filière* by taking a financial interest in selected producers who supplied them with wine. For almost 50 years the Wohnsiedler family's wine business in Gisborne had been marketing its port and sherry to hotels via the licensed trade. In 1960 it was in need of capital to continue in production. The Wellington regional distribution company W. and R. Smallbone Ltd took a one-third interest in Wohnsiedler's Waiherere Wines, and Campbell and Ehrenfried took another third. By 1972, New Zealand Wines and Spirits had bought Smallbone and owned half of Campbell and Ehrenfried, with New Zealand Breweries (Lion) owning the other half. Montana bought the remaining third of the Wohnsiedler enterprise. Such convoluted transactions occurred because Campbell and Ehrenfried had earlier financed Montana in its rapid expansion, and in the revised form of New Zealand Wines and Spirits was later to squeeze Frank Yukich into a position where he had to sell Penfolds.

The sudden inclusion of a new group of protagonists – grape growers – in the *filière* had repercussions for the regional organisation of the wine companies and the power structure within the winegrowing of the region. Wine enterprises had to develop organisational structures that encouraged their growers to produce grapes of quality. These had to be transformed into distinctive wines that appealed to the spectrum of the New Zealand wine-buying public. Its taste was beginning to become more sophisticated but opportunities existed for a range of table wines of different qualities and price points, some in bottles and some in 'bag-in-box' – plastic bags of several litres inside cardboard casks.

The larger companies appointed viticulturists in each grape-growing region. They were the private-sector equivalent of farm advisory officers of the Ministry of Agriculture, and in some cases the same people. Montana, for instance, appointed Warwick Bruce in Gisborne and Gary Wood (formerly of the Ministry) in Hawke's Bay. Bruce describes his role:

> In 1971, I moved down to Gisborne.... My role as field officer was to regularly visit the growers and advise them on aspects of the viticulture... then in the lead-up to vintage, to field test the grapes and arrange for the harvest and trucking to the winery. I think we had 20 to 25 growers at that stage.

Having skilled staff in the winery able to handle the detailed scheduling was just as important, especially during vintage. For over 40 years Roger McLernon managed the day-to-day operation of the Montana winery in Gisborne, until his retirement in 2008. Life during the vintage became temporarily a little less hectic for him especially after Montana had acquired both the Penfolds winery in 1986 and in 2000 the Corbans. These Gisborne fermentation and storage facilities are the site where much of the base wine for Montana's very successful sparkling wines, notably Lindauer, has been produced.

However, when Montana acquired Corbans in 2000, the merged company's policy of buying more land in Gisborne changed. Instead of being a buyer of land, Montana became a seller. Here was the opportunity to reassess its Gisborne vineyard land in the light of its experience in Marlborough and more recently in Hawke's Bay. In the early 2000s it offered to sell land to a selection of its Gisborne growers on very favourable terms. A number of them, including John Clarke, the chairman of Gisborne Winegrowers, took up the offer.

Grape growers and grape varieties on the Poverty Bay flats

The vineyards of any winegrowing enterprise evolve as more suitable varieties are discovered, new clones emerge, or the demographics of wine drinkers change and people favour different wines. Philip Gregan, CEO of New Zealand Winegrowers, talks about the influence of 'legacy' on the mix of grape varieties grown in different regions of New Zealand. He is referring to the varieties and clones of grapes that were available and popular when the region was first planted but have subsequently been pulled out and the vineyard replanted with other varieties. Some parcels of the previously popular varieties almost always remain from the period when different dynamics were driving the taste of consumers.

Nowhere is this legacy influence stronger than in Gisborne. It was the first of the 'new' regions to supply the emerging table wine production of the late 1960s. In addition, it was the first region where Auckland wineries recruited grape growers in large numbers to supply them. Farmers, booksellers, accountants, iwi, lawyers, teachers, hydrology consultants and 10-acre block holders responded enthusiastically and planted grapes. Their impact was well documented. The Ministry of Agriculture published five surveys of New Zealand viticulture at five-yearly intervals from 1960

Table 5.1 Regional production of wine grapes in 1975

Region	Area in vines (ha)	% grapes produced by Growers	Wineries	% Vinifera	Hybrid	Tonnes per ha*
Northland	22	<1	>99	35	65	8
Auckland	750	18	82	53	47	11
Waikato	247	13	87	71	29	8
Poverty Bay	612	84	16	81	19	9
Hawke's Bay	537	22	78	80	20	14
Marlborough	175	-	-	>99	<1	-
NZ Total	**2168**	**35**	**65**	**72**	**28**	**11**

Note Bay of Plenty had 1 hectare in grapes, Taranaki–Wellington 2, and Nelson 6.
* The tonnes per hectare is an underestimate because a proportion of grapes in each region were not bearing as the vines had recently been planted.

to 1980. Frank Berrysmith, its Horticultural Advisory Officer (Viticulture), authored those of 1960 and 1970 which appeared in the *New Zealand Journal of Agriculture*, but the 1975 account, published as a booklet, is especially useful because it distinguishes grapes being grown for wine from grapes grown in glasshouses and outdoors to be consumed as fresh fruit. It also separates and tabulates grapes grown by landowners to sell to wineries and grapes grown by the wine enterprises themselves (Table 5.1).

The 1975 report captures the growth of the industry two years after grapes had been planted in Marlborough. Between 1965 and 1970, the area of vines in Poverty Bay grew from 27 to 278 hectares. By 1975 it had reached 612 hectares and was the fastest-growing vineyard region in New Zealand. Auckland still had 750 hectares planted but had reached its peak and was about to decline. Hawke's Bay's vineyard had started to increase, but with only 537 hectares of grapes had been passed by Gisborne. While Marlborough is present in the table, the rows and columns for its production are blank because the grapes are not yet bearing, although the report does document (in remarkable detail) that 175 hectares of grapes have been planted in the emerging region. Its vineyard then consisted of 323,542 *vinifera* vines and only 76 hybrid vines (*vinifera* x *labrusca* crosses). At 1850 vines per hectare, the planting is at conventional spacing for the time. It reflects the width of tractors and other machinery available in New Zealand rather than judgements of yield per hectare or per vine.

By the mid-1970s the regional pattern of the ratio of *vinifera* to hybrid grapes shows a strong north-to-south trend. Only in Northland and Auckland are hybrid varieties close to or above 50 per cent of the vineyard. Further south, the *vinifera* varieties are more than 70 per cent of the vineyard in all regions – even in the Waikato where vines planted in the Te Kauwhata Viticultural Research Station influence the result. Thirty-five per cent of Northland's vines were *viniferas*, 53 per cent in Auckland, 71 per cent in the Waikato (Mangatangi and Te Kauwhata), 81 per cent in Gisborne (referred to as Poverty Bay in the original table), and 80 per cent in Hawke's Bay. Marlborough's 99 per cent of *vinifera* vines is a remarkable adjustment in a very short time. A few years earlier, companies had been recommending that Gisborne growers plant a proportion of their vineyard in hybrid vines. By 1975 the national total was *viniferas* 72 per cent and hybrids 28 per cent. The days of planting hybrid grapes were over despite their resistance to disease in the more humid climates of the North Island and their variable resistance to phylloxera.

In the fifteen years since New Zealand winegrowing had begun to stir, some inklings of its future are apparent. Gisborne (Poverty Bay) stands out as having the highest proportion of grapes being produced by growers rather than wineries. In 1975 the 98 grape growers of Poverty Bay produced 84 per cent of the grapes made into wine. The next highest proportion was in Hawke's Bay where 22 per cent of the grapes made into wine came from grape growers. By 1980 the number of grape growers in Gisborne had nearly doubled to 190 and Hawke's Bay numbers had also increased rapidly to 120 and even Marlborough recorded 44 growers. Gisborne grape growers produced 34 per cent of all grapes made into wine in New Zealand.

Andrew Ewart, Horticultural Advisory Officer for the Ministry of Agriculture and Fisheries, Gisborne, published a short article titled 'Grape Varieties in Poverty Bay' in the *New Zealand Journal of Agriculture* in late 1974. Two years after Montana's first Gisborne vintage, and one year after Corbans', he takes the theme of Gisborne's role in the 'tremendous expansion of the New Zealand industry' by analysing the ten most commonly planted varieties in the light of 'the increased call for grapes of high quality'. His discussion shows how the most common Gisborne varieties were viewed in the mid-1970s. It also reveals almost inadvertently, in his advice to growers, how they had adapted their management practices to the environmental conditions where they were growing these grapes.

Riesling-Sylvaner (not yet called Müller Thurgau) was the most planted variety in the region because it is an early grape, 'harvested before the unsettled autumn weather', and 'yields well, approximately 10 tons to the acre'. Ewart also noted that its main problem is 'its inability to cope with wet weather' and added that 'to avoid this deterioration viticulturalists have picked this grape at an early stage of maturity'. The paradox is that Riesling-Sylvaner 'does not have much characteristic flavour and needs to be fully mature if this is to be obtained'. Golden Chasselas yields were at a similar level and it 'has a definite place in the district despite it being aptly described as "a bag full of sweet water"'. It was not ideally suited for varietal wines. He saw Chasselas as 'quite suitable for standard white wine and sherry production', although after leaving the grapes on the vine for two months after the commercial harvest had finished the Manutuke Research Station's Chasselas was 'in good condition at 21.4 brix and 6.4 grams/litre tartaric acid'.

The white hybrid Baco 22A, at the time one of the stalwart varieties of the Auckland region, was seen as having 'two saving graces, it yields well – 11 tons to the acre – and it hangs well . . . the berries and bunches being robust enough to leave on the vine until well into the autumn'. But he also pointed out that when harvest was delayed until 7 May 1974 at the Manutuke Research Station the sugar level reached 25.2 brix and 7.7 grams per litre of tartaric acid. He noted the distinct trend away from what he called 'hybrid-type wines to *vinifera* or European-styled wine, a trend similarly reflected in the varieties planted in Poverty Bay'.

While very enthusiastic about Cabernet Sauvignon, as growers in most regions were at that time – 'a first-class grape . . . capable of making excellent red wines' – Ewart also recognised the associated problem of late maturity when 'in poor weather it is difficult to ripen this variety'. Between 1975 and 1995, Cabernet Sauvignon consistently represented over 15 per cent of the New Zealand vineyard before dropping to about

7 per cent in the next decade as many wineries and growers experienced difficulty in ripening it. The area in two other red varieties, Pinot Noir and Merlot, increased more rapidly until by 2000 each represented a higher proportion of the national vineyard than Cabernet.

Ewart's constant reference to the need for high yields, of both hybrid and *vinifera* species, is at odds with the main message to grape growers that comes through strongly in his conclusion: 'Although there will still be a demand for hybrid grapes ... if New Zealand is to increase the export of wines these will need to be of top-quality *vinifera* varieties.' He was right, of course, but one acknowledgement was missing. Chasselas, Palomino and Riesling-Sylvaner (Müller Thurgau) are all *vinifera* varieties. In Gisborne at the time they were producing about 25 tonne of grapes to the hectare. To make table wine with body, texture, flavour and mouth weight – in other words, Ewart's 'top-quality' – yields needed to be reduced to 10 tonnes per hectare or lower. Yet high yields are almost lauded in the text. This is not surprising because many Gisborne growers in the 1970s and early 1980s were aiming for high yields and achieving them. Demand for grapes was outstripping supply. Grape growers' incomes depended on the tonnes per hectare that they could harvest, and the buyers – the enterprises making the wine – were much less demanding of quality than they were to become in the 1990s. So were the consumers at that time, many of whom had only recently been introduced to table wines.

Publications, field days with growers, and advice of horticultural advisory officers like Andrew Ewart meant that existing or aspiring grape growers were not short of valuable information and debate. Locals such as Bill Irwin joined the cacophony of knowledgeable growers while the larger wine companies recruited field officers who were resident in the region and available to their grape growers. Andrew Ewart is remarkably sanguine about Gisborne's high yields in the early 1970s. Yet, as a member of a government agency responsible for advising growers, he had to be wary. In his writing he seems to be weaving a delicate path between encouraging grape growers to reconsider the varieties they were growing while not alienating them by overemphasising the need to lower their yields, and their income. If such high yields had continued, New Zealand would have been destined to make much wine of moderate quality.

Winemaker initiatives and scientific developments

Two developments in winemaking and viticulture helped change the attitudes within the industry and among the wine-buying public. From the mid-1970s a series of young Auckland winemakers began meeting every fortnight to taste their wines against imported wines of quality. They recognised the need for lower yields and ripe grapes if similar standards of quality were to be achieved. Results from competitions, such as the Easter Show and Air New Zealand wine awards, were beginning to reinforce the association between lower yields and the quality of wines from *vinifera* varieties.

The arrival of microclimatologist and viticulturist Richard Smart in New Zealand in 1984 was the second development. Having already published a series of seminal papers on the microclimates and photosynthesis of *Vitis vinifera,* he instigated a systematic programme of research on trellising systems for the vine and the management of its canopy. For fruit of a particular variety to reach physiological ripeness, crop levels and leaf canopies needed to be in balance. To be disease free and function effectively, canopies must be thin with air flowing freely through them.

Trimming excessive foliage and leaf plucking to expose the bunches were essential components of managing the vines to achieve ripe fruit and develop its aromas and flavours. Smart also developed a set of innovative trellising systems, none of which, despite the quality of the science underlying their design, were widely adopted. The simpler vertical shoot positioning became the preferred pruning system.

Varietal transformation in Gisborne, 1980–2010

In the last 30 years, many grape growers in Gisborne have changed their varieties several times, sometimes in a rather measured way as demand for different varieties and wines becomes apparent. Growers must protect their income during the three years it takes vines to come into full production. When the demand for grapes is increasing, and wine enterprises are encouraging landowners to increase their area in vines, planting new varieties or top-grafting existing vines are both possible. In times of overproduction or falling demand for some varieties, decisions become more complicated. These individual commercial decisions of grape-growing families underlie the set of changes evident in Table 5.2.

By 1980, Gisborne was well established as a producer of a polyglot of grape varieties – mainly high-yielding. The top three varieties – Müller Thurgau, Chasselas and Palomino – made up 60 per cent of the region's vineyard. Immediately following them were three classical *vinifera* varieties – Gewürztraminer, Chenin Blanc and Chardonnay – each with over 100 hectares planted and together making up over 20 per cent of the Gisborne vineyard. Their presence proclaimed an interesting future for Poverty Bay. Which variety would dominate was not clear, although Chardonnay's versatility in different environments made it a likely contender.

A decade later in 1990, the vine pull of 1986 had seen almost 200 hectares of Müller Thurgau removed in Gisborne, but with 457 hectares remaining (including some new plantings) it still occupied more than twice the area of any other variety. The rapid rise of the Muscats reflected their distinctive aromas, high yields and versatility in

Table 5.2 Evolution of grape varieties in the Gisborne region, 1980–2010

1980			1990				2000				2010			
Variety	Ha	%	Variety	Ha	%	T/Ha	Variety	Ha	%	T/Ha	Variety	Ha	%	T/Ha
MT	638	41	MT	457	32	19	Ch	813	49	11	Ch	1084	53	11
Chs	161	10	Mu	203	14	23	MT	195	12	16	**PG**	185	9	13
Pa	132	9	Ch	162	11	12	Mu	151	9	20	Me	117	6	8
G	113	7	**R**	90	6	18	S	75	5	14	G	106	5	8
CB	102	7	G	76	5	9	**Me**	70	4	8	Mu	99	5	14
Ch	102	7	**S**	75	5	12	R	61	4	19	SB	79	4	15
Mu	58	4	**SB**	61	4	15	SB	59	4	16	PN	76	4	11
B	51	3	CB	58	4	17	G	40	2	6	**V**	74	4	17
Ga	32	2	Chs	48	3	17	CB	40	2	12	R	62	3	9
Pi	31	2	**RR**	46	3	12	**PN**	39	2	14	S	61	3	11
O	152	10	O	145	10	–	O	138	8	–	O	140	6	–
Total	1572	100		1421	100	17		1681	100	13		2083	100	11

New varieties each decade are in **bold**. B = Baco 22A, CB = Chenin Blanc, Ch = Chardonnay, Chs = Chasselas, G = Gewürztraminer, Ga = Gamay, Me = Merlot, MT = Müller Thürgau, Mu = Muscats, O = other, Pa = Palomino, PG = Pinot Gris, Pi = Pinotage, PN = Pinot Noir, R = Reichensteiner, RR = Rhine Riesling, S = Semillon, SB = Sauvignon Blanc, V = Viognier.
The Ministry of Agriculture publication of 1980 does not include the data to calculate yield per hectare.

enhancing the flavours of blended wines. The increase in Muscats, together with Chardonnay climbing to third place with 162 hectares planted, had restored most of the area in vines removed in the vine pull.

The region's vineyard was back to over 1400 hectares but many varieties were still being cropped at very high levels. The yield of Muscats in 1990 was 23 tonnes per hectare, Müller Thurgau 19 tonnes per hectare, and Reichensteiner (a complex cross of varieties, with Müller Thurgau one parent) 18 tonnes. In particular vintages of the early 1990s a few varieties averaged as much as 30 tonnes to the hectare, or a startling 225 hectolitres of wine per hectare. Yields of Chardonnay at 12 tonnes per hectare and Gewürztraminer at 9 tonnes per hectare in 1990 were at more appropriate levels to attain the intensity of flavours necessary to make table wines of quality, although still, in Chardonnay's case, more than twice as high as the Grand Cru vineyards of Burgundy. By 1990, Semillon, Sauvignon Blanc and Rhine Riesling were among the top ten varieties. Palomino, Baco 22A, Gamay and Pinotage had dropped out.

At the millennium Chardonnay had leapt to almost half of the region's vineyard. With the declining Müller Thurgau and Muscats added, these three made up 70 per cent of the area of Gisborne's vineyard. Two red varieties, Merlot and Pinot Noir, were now amongst the top ten, although most of the Pinot Noir was being vinified as a white wine for Montana's base wine for the Lindauer brand of sparkling wine.

By 2010, Chardonnay was 53 per cent of the Gisborne vineyard. Pinot Gris, with 185 hectares planted, had climbed rapidly to second and had the distinction of being among the four most-planted varieties in the history of Gisborne's grape growing. In the search for a red variety suitable for Gisborne's conditions and the public's palate, Merlot had reached third place, Gewürztraminer regained fourth and the versatile Muscats still had over 99 hectares in production. Like Marlborough, Gisborne had a single dominant variety and four varieties with over 100 hectares. The only other time Gisborne had achieved this feat was in 1980, but only Gewürztraminer had been common to the top five varieties in both years. The top four varieties – Chardonnay, Pinot Gris, Merlot and Gewürztraminer – now comprise over 70 per cent of the Gisborne vineyard. Andrew Ewart's wish for 'top-quality' varieties in Poverty Bay had been realised just 34 years after he made his call.

Gewürztraminer has had a constant presence in Gisborne, with 113 hectares in 1980, hanging in at 76 hectares after the vine pull of 1986, before falling to 40 hectares in 2000 and climbing back to 106 hectares by 2010. Its yields in Gisborne have always been moderate, although it also retains the reputation of being difficult to grow. Its Gisborne story has more chapters to come. Pinot Gris had jumped to prominence in less than a decade with 175 hectares planted by 2008. In the previous decade, wine made from Pinot Gris, or in its Italian style Pinot Grigio, had become very trendy, especially in the United States and Canada but also more widely.

The recent popularity of Pinot Gris amongst Gisborne's grape growers has much to do with demand influencing the price companies are prepared to pay for it. In Gisborne, buyers pay noticeably more for Pinot Gris than other varieties, although its price, as well as that of most varieties, is higher in all other regions. The average price for all Gisborne varieties at the 2008 vintage was NZ$1,130 per tonne. Pinot Gris grown in Gisborne averaged $1,810 per tonne compared with $1,961 in Hawke's Bay, $2,268 in Marlborough and $2,910 in Central Otago. Chardonnay (Mendoza and Clone 15) averaged $1,159 per tonne in Gisborne, $1,672 in Hawke's Bay, $2,845 in Marlborough and $3,000 in Waipara. Yields per hectare and the availability and quality of grapes in the different regions influences these prices. Yields are lower in most of these South Island regions while the higher costs of production, especially for expensive irrigation schemes in regions like Central Otago, increases production costs. These are partly offset by lower costs for disease control.

Harvesting Pinot Gris at Ashwood Estate's vineyard in the Matawhero area.
Strike Photography

Grape growers, vine varieties, and wine enterprises

Does the New Zealand organisation of the *filière* (which is the same as in many 'New World' wine countries) make a difference to the varieties planted, especially in a country where they are not specified in law? The answer from Gisborne grape growers is a definite 'yes'. Because there are very few local wineries in Gisborne, the demands of the wine companies have always influenced the varieties of grapes chosen by growers. Reid Fletcher, one of the large Gisborne growers and esteemed contributor to New Zealand grape growing, planted his first vines in 1974 and succinctly expresses the corporate influences on his enterprise:

> I'm a contract grower and I've made a profession of being a contract grower and I aim to be a very good contract grower. I don't aim to be a petite winery owner producing a small amount of one very good wine. That's the varietal mix I've got . . . that's what the companies have influenced.

By the beginning of the twenty-first century the Fletcher family's decisions on their varietal mix reflects what the companies would pay for different varieties as well as the history of the region and the impact of phylloxera on vine health. Müller Thurgau had been reduced to about 10 per cent of their vineyard and the hybrids had been pulled out. Reid describes the transformation:

Gisborne or Poverty Bay?

> Prior to 1980 everything was on its own roots. We changed everything onto grafted plants . . . just pulled out and put in new plants. We've now got 4.3 hectares of Breidecker, 5.9 of Semillon, 4.2 of Clone 15 Chardonnay. And then in the home block we've got 4.8 hectares of Müller Thurgau, 5 of Merlot, 5.2 of Mendoza Chardonnay, 4 of Early White Muscat, 4.1 of Clone 15 and some Clone 7 Chardonnay, 5 of Chenin Blanc and 2.5 of Semillon.

Of these varieties, only the Breidecker, Early White Muscat and Müller Thurgau, and perhaps Chenin Blanc, would be unlikely to be planted today.

These tens and hundreds of decisions by grape growers in Poverty Bay, being made now and in the past, have resulted in the distinctive mix of varieties of this region. Reid Fletcher also recognises the risks that they face if their relationships break down with the companies they supply:

> I want to look at some security of market as well. And local growers say 'you're a good grape grower, you have no trouble dealing with companies'. But actually it's not quite like that because if I ever fall out with Corbans, I have a hell of a lot of tonnes of grapes to put on the spot market. It's not like a grape grower with 10 acres who can shop around. I can't really with that tonnage.

This caution is based on experience in the tough and vitriolic times of the wine price wars in the mid-1980s when some Auckland-based wine enterprises broke their contracts with their growers in Gisborne and Hawke's Bay.

With over 30 years of experience of growing grapes behind him, Reid Fletcher also has clear ideas on where the future lies as far as Gisborne's grape varieties are concerned:

> Yeah, I definitely think that the four varieties that show the most promise in Gisborne are Chardonnay first, then I think Gewürztraminer has a big future in Gisborne; I think Semillon has a big future and I think of the red varieties Merlot may have a future.

At the same time he recognises that despite his experience they are still learning about the behaviour of different varieties under the conditions of any particular season:

> Some of the other crops, we're not sure what the balance is and it's like that this year in the Chenin. Last year we got 13 tonnes to the acre of not high-quality grapes in the Chenin Blanc, so this year we did a massive shoot thinning and changed the pruning system to a certain extent and I think we've dropped the yield to about 4 tonne to the acre. So it's going to be a financial loss this year. But that's just experience, because if we go somewhere halfway in between we'll get a consistent yield each year. And after about 20 years we should have a database of what that is!

In 2010, the Gisborne region had five varieties with over 99 hectares planted – the same number as Marlborough, despite Marlborough having 19,295 hectares of grapes compared with Gisborne's 2083. Gisborne's five principal varieties were Chardonnay 1084 hectares, Pinot Gris 185 hectares, Merlot 117 hectares, Gewürztraminer 106 hectares and the Muscats 99 hectares. Pinot Noir occupied 76 hectares in Gisborne with 60 hectares of this being used for sparkling wine. Sauvignon Blanc with 79 hectares and Semillon 61 hectares were the next most important white varieties.

In Gisborne, Chardonnay is almost as dominant as Sauvignon Blanc is in Marlborough. With over 1084 hectares planted, Chardonnay comprises 53 per cent of Gisborne's vineyard and dominates all other varieties. Pinot Gris, the second most popular variety, makes up 9 per cent of the Gisborne vineyard. The recent increase in the area in Pinot Gris in Gisborne is all about supply and demand and regional variability in price. At $1,810 per tonne, the average price of Pinot Gris grown in Gisborne is almost $700 per tonne more than the average price for all grapes grown in the region, which at $1,130 per tonne in 2008 was the lowest of any region in New Zealand.

The Auckland firms sourcing their grapes from Gisborne were beneficiaries of the knowledge their grape growers accumulated about the sugar, acid levels, tannins and flavour profiles of different varieties of grapes, but the winemakers in the companies had an even more comprehensive understanding of such qualities and their influence on the final wines. In each region this knowledge soon became more complicated as the varieties and clones began to proliferate and companies accumulated understanding of the micro-environments of the different regions and localities where they were planting.

Grape growers and corporate organisations

In 1968, Roger McLernon was among the first grape growers in Gisborne to be offered a contract by Montana. As McLernon recounts, the same week that Frank Yukich talked to him,

> he chartered a plane and flew down with Rolph Porter. I got given a 33-year contract – a bob a pound and a refrigerated truck and a cheque before the grapes left the place. And I suddenly came of age and actually made some money.

In typical Yukich fashion, Frank went one stage further, probably because he had already decided on his strategy for Gisborne.

Roger McLernon was working for Wohnsiedler at their Waiherere winery at the time, although he did not initially mention this to Yukich. The table grapes he had sold were Albany Surprise and Seneca from a vineyard planted by his father. When they met in Roger's lunch hour the next day Yukich told him:

> 'If you put your backside up and your head down for two more years, you can come to Montana and be the manager.' I wasn't the manager, I was the assistant manager for approximately eight months, and I've been the winery manager ever since in Gisborne.

McLernon's own assessment of Frank Yukich is also revealing:

> I think people have to understand who Frank Yukich was – he was one of New Zealand's pioneers. He was a workaholic. He was energetic, he was arrogant, he was everything that made a good entrepreneur. The moment he saw the potential down here, he was planning, and I've still got the original plans of the winery. It was going to be out at Makaraka by the racecourse. Council wouldn't hear of it and drove us in here into the industrial area and we were in production by 1971. That was our first season.

Corbans quickly followed Montana into Gisborne, with their large winery being completed in time for the 1972 vintage. According to wine historian Dick Scott, Frank Yukich had offered Corbans 'the joint use' of Montana's Gisborne plant but 'for many considerations – and pride was not the least of them – the proposal was rejected'. While admiring his entrepreneurial talents, many people involved in the wine industry, including some of his Croatian colleagues, were wary of Frank Yukich. This characteristic had been evident when, in the early 1960s, he called a meeting in Oratia, West Auckland to suggest that a group of them form a co-operative. Those attending were less than enthusiastic so Frank and Mate Yukich went their own way.

During the 1970s and early 1980s, as was later to happen in Marlborough, Corbans was in direct competition with Montana in Gisborne, but often a short step behind. Nevertheless, the sympathy of grape growers often seemed to be with Corbans – probably because Montana was increasingly outspoken about grape prices in New Zealand being too high. These differences culminated in 1991 with Montana taking a claim to the Commerce Commission that grape growers were acting illegally and fixing prices by using a price they had already agreed on collectively. Individual growers had to have the opportunity to negotiate their own prices for grapes.

Corbans Wines Ltd in Gisborne

The 1970s were telling years for Corbans. It began the decade as clearly the largest and most successful independently owned wine enterprise in New Zealand and ended it

Corbans' Cottage Block vineyard, planted during the 1980s in Mendoza Chardonnay. *Warren Moran*

associated with Dominion Breweries as part of the Brierley stable of companies. Several decisions of policy by Corbans, together with changes to the ownership structure of the production and distribution of beer, spirits and wine, contributed to the family losing control of their enterprise to Rothmans by 1979.

Although Corbans owned three wine shops, their policy was not to increase the number. Instead they distributed their wines through what was known at the time as 'the wholesale trade'. These were regionally owned and based beer, wine and spirits merchants that supplied hotels but were also major retail outlets. The private company Corbans Wines Ltd was formed in 1963. In 1964, as Dick Scott recounts, ten of these regionally based merchants were invited to take up a 19 per cent shareholding in Corbans and representatives of three of them were invited to join its board. The geography of these ten merchants encompassed the main regions and cities of New Zealand and seemed a sensible approach to the company maintaining their wholesale and retail distribution.

By 1972 the regionally based wine and spirit companies were themselves being reorganised. Douglas Myers was bringing together New Zealand Wines and Spirits Co. Ltd (NZW&S), a company owned 50/50 by Campbell and Ehrenfried and New Zealand Breweries. In the process, NZW&S acquired W. and R. Smallbone of Wellington as well as two of Corbans' regional merchants. These developments weakened Corbans' distribution network. One commercial battlefield for the Montana–Corbans skirmish was in Gisborne.

Gisborne or Poverty Bay?

While avoiding what seemed to be the main threat – control by the brewing-related companies – Corbans had become vulnerable to takeover through the heavy load of debt that it carried. Because of its rapid expansion, partly in response to competition from Montana, Corbans had a voracious appetite for capital during the 1960s and 1970s. From the mid-1960s the company invested heavily in their Henderson, West Auckland production, processing, bottling and distribution centre as well as substantially increasing their area in vines.

Corbans' first move to purchase more vineyard land was, naturally enough, northwards. Joe Corban, vineyard manager, with his uncle Najib, vineyard director, searched exhaustively for likely sites. They acquired parcels in three locations successively more distant from their winery – one in Whenuapai near Brighams Creek (named the Riverlea vineyard of Riverlea Riesling fame), several in Kumeu mainly in Cemetery Road, and a further one in Taupaki. These totalled 390 acres – a quite different proposition from the original 30 acres of the Great North Road vineyard in Henderson. With most of the new vineyards being on heavy soils, they had to be ripped, drained and cultivated before being planted, a practice Corbans had mastered in the heavy clay soils of their Great North Road and Valley Road vineyards in Henderson. All the new Auckland vineyards were within 20 kilometres of the Henderson winery. This distance was neighbourly compared with Corbans' next vineyard purchases which were over 600 kilometres away in Gisborne. The capital it needed to purchase land on the Poverty Bay flats further increased the company's debt load.

Both Corbans and Montana began sourcing grapes from Gisborne in the late 1960s. Montana first let contracts in Gisborne in 1968, while Corbans quickly followed suit. These contracts were initially simple documents, as Roger McLernon's experience affirms. Frank and Mate Yukich decided on a 33-year tenure to attract grape growers by providing continuity. Corbans quickly bought land, but Montana under Frank and Mate Yukich relied entirely on grape growers. This decision captures the character of the two enterprises. Corbans was the well-established communal family firm. Owning land on which they planted their own vines was an imperative – 'a stake in the country', as Dick Scott titled his 2002 book on the family. Frank Yukich was more commercially astute – the challenger with a limited reputation, few assets and, unlike Corbans, no internal, multi-family bureaucracy.

The prospect of a new crop attracted 180 people to a Gisborne growers' field day in 1969 where Joe Corban (viticulturist), resplendent in white shirt, tie and dark jacket, spoke to the prospective growers, and Alex (winemaker) displayed the engraved spade used to plant the first vines. Corbans had bought 76 acres on Riverpoint Road (not far from the Irwin family vineyards) and a further 45 acres at Bond Road, Ormond.

Enterprises in the Gisborne story

Matawhero Wines

A local bookseller, Bill Irwin, with his son Denis, bought land and imported clones of Chardonnay and other varieties to begin growing grapes before establishing Matawhero Wines with its first vintage in 1975. The free-spirited Denis Irwin became an influential figure in New Zealand winemaking – first by quickly revealing his own talent to make stylish Chardonnays and Gewürztraminers that towered over the one-dimensional Müller Thurgau wines of the time, and second by becoming something of a guru to aspirant winemakers of similar disposition. Some of the most influential winemakers of the late twentieth century and into the twenty-first, such as Alan Limmer of Stonecroft, Alwyn Corban of Ngatarawa and Hätsch Kalberer of Fromm, were strongly influenced by Denis, as was Kim Salonius of Eskdale.

According to Denis, his father 'always had a hankering to get onto the land and so . . . after many hours of driving round the flats, studying the water tables . . . and getting the first book of Pullar's maps', he finally found the land he wanted in Riverpoint Road. 'The property was probably well beyond his [physical] means in the sense that he was 55 when he took it on and it had about 80-odd acres.' However, intellectually, the task was not beyond Bill Irwin. An avid reader, he settled down to finding out all he could about grape varieties suitable for the Gisborne environment. 'He got to be a sort of textbook specialist of grapes in the country,' recounts Denis. 'Any book on grapes and wines at that stage that was going, he was into. So he was writing to all sorts of people. He was writing to Geisenheim [Grape Breeding Institute], to [its grape breeder] Helmut Becker. He was writing to Australia, and to the DSIR.' Regular, deep and animated discussions about suitable vine varieties and viticultural practices also took place with the then Department of Agriculture's horticultural advisory officer in Gisborne, Paul Cullen. The first vines were planted in Riverpoint Road in 1968 – 20 acres of Müller Thurgau with the contract to supply the grapes to Montana. Soon after, Chasselas and Riesling (or Rhine Riesling as it was called) were added to the mix. By the early 1970s the cash flow from selling grapes was beginning to improve.

Meanwhile, in 1969 and 1970, before leaving on his OE, Denis worked for Mate Yukich at Montana's Mangatangi vineyard (Mate was the viticultural force behind the flamboyant Frank, and knowing both brothers well made Denis very skilled when it came to negotiating firmly over grape prices when he returned to New Zealand). By 1971, he had managed to save enough to buy a one-way ticket to Cape Town. As the vintage approached, he hitch-hiked his way to Stellenbosch where he met Spatz Sperling who owned 'a lovely little winery called Delheim' and invited him for lunch. As they walked up towards the house Denis saw some young vines and

Denis Irwin's Matawhero Gewürztraminers of the 1970s helped establish an international reputation for New Zealand wine. *Strike Photography*

just automatically bent down to take off the laterals and wind the vine up the string. And he said, 'What the hell are you doing?' And I said, 'I'm just teaching the vine how to grow!' So of course he was quite impressed with that and he eventually got me a job.

It was here that Denis learned all about how to run a cellar, but probably more importantly, 'this was the first time in my life that I'd actually tasted wine of any consequence'. He tasted many more styles during his next stop in the Rhine Valley, Germany, where he first worked in a small vineyard before being employed in the huge ZBW (Zentralkellerei Badischer Winzergenossenschaften), a German co-operative that produces and sells Kaiserstuhl-Tuniberg wines.

At home, Bill Irwin had recognised that the varieties and clones available in New Zealand were unlikely to result in wines of the style and quality that they were seeking. By the early 1970s his letter writing and discussions internationally and with government scientists were beginning to bear fruit. He had selected a number of the varieties and clones that were to become the foundation of the Irwin vineyard, notably UCD7 (University of California, Davis) Cabernet Sauvignon and UCD4 Gewürztraminer. By now, these and several others were out of quarantine, a number virus free, and established in the Irwin vineyard. As well as planting their own vineyard, Bill separated the various varieties and clones in a number of rows and made the wood available to the industry. His selection and importing continued for a second round in the late 1970s, concentrating on clones of Merlot, Malbec and Pinot Noir, which added to the library of New Zealand varieties.

Denis Irwin returned from his OE in 1973, made his first what he calls 'sort of homemade wine' in 1974, and by 1975 was on his own. Andrew Ewart, another Gisborne Department of Agriculture employee, helped him with the chemistry. The Irwin Gewürztraminers, Chardonnays and Cabernet Sauvignons captured consumers and wine judges alike. Two years after making his first commercial wine, his 1977 Gewürztraminer was fourth in that class at the World Wine Show in Paris, and his 1980 Chardonnay was ninth in New York out of the top 100 New World Chardonnays. His Gewürztraminers were unquestionably one of the wines that caught the attention of national and international consumers and wine writers. His own description of what he was trying to achieve is in marked contrast to the aroma-wheel and fruit-flavour descriptions that typify current wine assessment: 'I want to be making long, elegant-style wines, with fibre. Backbone and fibre is what I'm looking for.' And he was also definite about the direction in which he wanted to take his customers:

> We were appealing to those people who were experienced in European styles of wine. That was really what I was basically leading the palate to – especially with the Chardonnays.

Denis Irwin made his first forays into international marketing with a tasting in Los Angeles in 1979 and Japan and Hong Kong in 1980 and 1981. Although he discovered strong interest in his wines, he found it difficult to establish reliable distributors, largely because he was not producing the volume they required. With the New Zealand market tightening in the mid-1980s he made the decision to develop his Australian market through Melbourne rather than Sydney. This venture developed much more impetus than originally intended when he discovered Gisborne, Victoria and bought 200 acres of land there with the idea of trading on having vine and wine enterprises in both countries. He also purchased a hotel in Melbourne, the Rose of Australia, as a means of improving the cash flow of his businesses and as one avenue for his distribution. It listed 300 wines for sale by the glass, and Denis became quite an identity in the Melbourne wine and food scene.

While in Australia, Denis was fortunate to have the talented Hätsch Kalberer (later at the Fromm winery, Marlborough) as the Matawhero winemaker. Bill Irwin had died in 1985. Denis returned to Gisborne, New Zealand and Matawhero for the 1989 vintage. Extracting himself from his Australian investments had taken effort and time but he had come out of the experience debt free. But Matawhero Wines was not in good financial health. Putting his Australian restaurant experience to use, he started Scottie's Bar and Grill in a former bank building to provide the cash flow to get the wine business back on its feet. However, in 1994, Denis and his wife had a serious accident driving home to Gisborne from Hawke's Bay in a hailstorm. They both recovered from the accident and Denis worked again in the vineyard and winery, but in attempting to move the vineyard to being organic and reducing spraying he struggled to control the fungus diseases. New owners, the Searle family, took over the winery and in 2009 announced that they were rebuilding the Matawhero brand.

Denis remains nostalgic for the early years of the winery when the oldest vines were almost a decade old, the varieties that were to make his reputation were producing promising fruit, and he was a talented, articulate and colourful winemaker and innovative marketer of Matawhero Wines:

> The raw enthusiasm of life when I didn't have any pressure.... I had my father looking after the running of the finances, and we had staff in the vineyard ... and it was coping.... It was only just a hobby. I mean, I'd come over in the weekends.... By 1977 we were serious. We had this building here up and I was 37. But it was always serious, it was always extremely serious. Anyway, we were getting right, and then I had this bloody car accident.

In the late 1970s and the early 1980s, Denis Irwin was the Elvis Presley of the rock-star winemakers. It is unlikely that any other New Zealand winemaker will again quite command the respect that he held in that period. He approached winemaking as an art and was untarnished by the practices associated with making fortified wines of the previous era. He made exciting wines and was unquestionably cool, even in the language of that time. When the surf was up on Waikanae Beach, the cellar door went unattended. Wine buffs and winemakers alike sought his Gewürztraminers, Chardonnays and Cabernets. He was in the table wine tradition of Alex Corban, Denis Kasza, Bob Knappstein, Joe Babich and his contemporary, Nick Nobilo, who made New Zealand's first outstanding Pinot Noir from grapes grown in Huapai in the immaculate West Auckland vintage of 1976.

Doug and Delwyn Bell, winegrowers, Ormond Road

When Corbans and Montana let contracts in the late 1960s, grape growers came from many directions carrying many skills. Doug and Delwyn Bell have been grape growing in Gisborne since 1983, prior to which he was a design engineer in Auckland and she was a travel agent. Initially, the couple knew nothing about grape growing, but both came from dairy farming backgrounds and were adamant that they wanted nothing to do with cows. Doug's parents had just sold their dairy farm in Auckland and were looking to purchase a vineyard in Gisborne and put a manager on the property. When they suggested that perhaps Doug and his wife would like to buy one of the 10-acre titles in the vineyard and run the whole operation as one unit they agreed and soon found themselves caring for '22 acres of net canopy of grapes (about 25 acres of land in total), in two varieties, Müller Thurgau and Flora'. They spent about a month learning from George Evans, the previous owner, who 'showed us just basically how to mow and how to trim and we saw that first vintage'.

However, 1983 was not an auspicious year to begin any horticultural enterprise while carrying high debt alongside aspirations to extend the vineyard. The neo-liberal reforms of the fourth Labour government were imminent, followed by global economic difficulties and high, fluctuating interest rates from 1987. Moreover, the two varieties on the property were for bulk wine still being grown at high yields and bought by the wine companies at low prices per tonne. Their contract was initially with Penfolds, owned by Frank Yukich at the time, but in 1986 Montana bought Penfolds. As Doug points out, 'we tried to develop a good working relationship with our wine company because they had viticultural staff who were assisting us in terms of learning about the industry'. Decisions over price were not individually negotiated:

> A small group of elected members of the grape growers committee basically went to Montana, Corbans and Penfolds and all sat down around a table... and negotiated a price for the different varieties so there was a price by variety and a price per brix [sugar] level.

After the 1991 Commerce Commission ruling on collective bargaining, that system changed and so did their vineyard.

They approached Penfolds for advice who recommended replanting the Müller Thurgau and Flora on grafted, phylloxera-resistant rootstock. That decision was the first step in vineyard renovation and extension that has continued to the present. In the late 1980s, Doug's parents bought another 10 acres of land. The family decided to plant this in Clone 6 Chardonnay – one of the first in the district. At the same time, they decided to change companies to Corbans, 'and they were keen on us trying a new variety and we were also keen to do something a little bit wide of the normal as it were!' The variety was from Geisenheim – GM 312-53. Doug and Delwyn were attracted to it because 'it's extremely disease resistant. It basically doesn't have any problem with powdery, downy, or botrytis.' It has these characteristics because it is a hybrid grape – 'a Riesling-Seibel cross'. Their next move was to replant the Flora block with Mendoza Chardonnay, at the time one of the most popular Chardonnay clones in Gisborne and New Zealand. Then, in 2000, they took up a small interest in a 25-acre vineyard with members of Delywn's family. It had four varieties each between 6 and 7 acres – Chardonnay, Reichensteiner, Sauvignon Blanc and Semillon. Within three years a manager was running this vineyard and Delwyn and Doug were back to replanting their home vineyard.

In September 2000 the Commerce Commission gave Montana the green flag to purchase Corbans. Shortly afterwards, Delwyn and Doug decided to change their allegiance and supply Coopers Creek who were actively seeking experienced Gisborne growers prepared to produce a range of less common, more trendy even, varieties to their specifications. With more than seventeen years' experience as winegrowers the Bells were well prepared for this opportunity. The current configuration of their vineyard demonstrates the rapidity of the changes they have made to their varietal mix in the last decade. It now consists of three different clones of the Rhone Valley variety Viognier making up a total of 8 hectares. To this have been added 3 hectares of Arneis, the Italian Piedmont white variety colloquially called 'little rascal' in its homeland because it is considered difficult to grow. They have also planted 2 hectares of the Portuguese variety Albariño in 2009 and another 2 hectares in 2010. They are experimenting with almost 1 hectare of the Rhone Valley and traditional Languedoc-Rousillon variety Marsanne. It, too, is contracted to Coopers Creek. The Bells may be signalling a revitalised mix of grape varieties for Gisborne.

All of these newer varieties are widely spaced (3.5 metres apart in the row) with the rows the standard 2.9 metres apart. Doug summarises this spacing as complying with Richard Smart's 'big vine theory'. The vines are spur pruned, partly to reduce labour costs. Doug also believes spur pruning better enables them to control the vigour of the vines and have their vegetative growth in balance with the vines' ability to ripen the crop. Coopers Creek are seeking low yields of 6 to 7 tonnes per hectare. To achieve crops at this level requires more work in the vineyard but the price per tonne of grapes is much higher. The Bells are at ease with this trade-off because their objective is to grow grapes of the highest quality. They are quite prepared to make the extra effort, and indeed prefer producing grapes with the flavours and acid-sugar balance to make such wines, provided they are rewarded for it.

The remainder of the Bell vineyard is predominantly planted in Chardonnay – 4 hectares of Mendoza and almost three of the new 131 clone. These grapes are managed differently. They are pruned in the more common system of vertical shoot positioning with the aim being to produce Chardonnay crops of about 12 tonnes per hectare. These grapes are contracted to Constellation Brands. The price per tonne for these Chardonnay grapes is, of course, much lower than for the varieties they are growing for Coopers Creek. In most years, though, the income per hectare works out at being higher for the varieties planted specifically for Coopers Creek.

In 1983 when they first planted grapes, the Bells relied heavily on advice from the viticultural advisors of the companies buying their grapes. While they continue to benefit from such advice, they are now in a much stronger position to assess the yields that they might reasonably be expected to achieve, compared with the cost of the viticultural practices required to meet them. Doug admits to being 'a bit of a gambler' and is prepared to take risks provided the possibility is there for a higher net income per hectare. When in the 1990s Corbans introduced a system of higher payments per tonne for grapes that reached higher sugar levels and were free of botrytis the Bells were strongly in favour of it. Supplying a smaller company, such as Coopers Creek, that is committed to producing distinctive wines at high prices from different but proven varieties, also appeals to them.

What appears to be a rather gradual move towards the classical *vinifera* varieties by the Bells must be seen in terms of the complexity of the decisions in a developing industry that initially relied on grapes being grown at high yields. All grape growers, and especially Gisborne ones, many of whom have had a lifetime career in the industry, have to consider the changing demands of the company who are requiring a gamut of grapes for a gamut of wines. For the grower, price per tonne has to be considered against the yields that they can achieve compared with the qualities that the company seeks for each level of wine, and especially those qualities that they are able to measure. From the 1990s, the large wine companies increasingly attempted to quantify the qualities they required in the grapes for different wines in their portfolio. Companies confronted such issues in the 1990s after the Commerce Commission's determination over collective bargaining by grape growers. Montana, as the dominant company for much of the period, often appeared to be playing a political game by taking opportunities in the press to talk down grape prices.

Doug's skills in toolmaking and engineering have also been invaluable to keeping costs down in the grape-growing business: 'We've built a trimmer and a mower – a four-head rotary mower which is the correct width for our rows, and a trimmer that trims both sides and the top so that I can trim a row in one pass.' But his pièce de résistance is that 'we've changed our crop sprayer to a new German tangential head-type sprayer, very low water volumes, and as a result of that have halved our chemical usage'. With James Millton and Chris Parker, Doug has held the technical and research portfolio of Gisborne Winegrowers. This spray research was conducted with Paul Miller, an Australian consultant, and they hope to reduce the chemicals even further. The principle is 'that the droplets are so fine there is no run-off and we can attach a lot less chemical to the canopy'.

Gisborne grape growers have made an incommensurable contribution to the principles and practice of the deinvigoration of grapevines. Vigorous vines result in thick canopies with many of the leaves in the interior of the hedge not photosynthesising effectively. Fruit tend not to ripen well. *Vignerons* in some regions of France and other European countries reduce vigour by having up to 10,000 vines per hectare competing against one another. In Gisborne, on the alluvial soils of the Poverty Bay flats, high yields were an advantage in the 1970s and into the 1980s when grapes were in limited supply. But it soon became obvious that vines needed to be less vigorous if quality was to

Overleaf: Millton's Clos de Ste Anne vineyards where planting began in 1981 to assess the potential of hillside vineyards in Gisborne. *Millton Vineyards & Winery*

Gisborne or Poverty Bay? 117

improve, especially because many soils on the flats retain moisture well and the water table is in places close to the surface. Gisborne grape growers opted for deinvigorating vines through selected rootstock and planting a variety of cover crops between the rows. Those like the Bells may be right up with the world's best practice. As Doug puts it: 'There's unique characteristics in each area and you manage your environment to make the best of what you have available.'

The Thorpe family's rural enterprises

When in 1969, at the age of 58, Jack Thorpe retired, he and his wife Joyce set up a family trust with their eight children as beneficiaries. Its main assets were horticultural properties Jack intended to develop using capital accumulated while a major shareholder and production manager of Columbine Hosiery. During the next five years the family trust accumulated five properties totalling over 400 acres on the Gisborne Plain. By the mid-1970s the Thorpe family trust's orchards and vineyards were approaching full production. They included about 150 acres in kiwifruit, 80 acres in persimmons, as well as 50 acres of grapes. The remaining 120 acres were at various times in mandarins, navel oranges and nashi pears. While all the Thorpe children have had some connection with the land, four – Bill, Geoff, and twins John and Richard – became deeply enmeshed in land-based production. Geoff, the initiator of Riversun Nursery, has influenced viticulture in all regions of New Zealand. Their enterprises also demonstrate how grapes are just one of the crops competing for use of the versatile Poverty Bay flats.

Buying, planting, spraying, pruning, maintaining and marketing the trust's 170 hectares of intensively planted perennials required a tight organisation. 'My father ran the properties on a daily basis,' says Bill Thorpe, 'and we had foremen who were there running them hour by hour. Dad was a good organiser and liked to be involved, and I ran the accounting and the financial side at night, because I was full time at Columbine.' In 1980, brother Richard became involved in the management of the trust's horticultural properties. However, in 1984, when expenditure on horticultural development could no longer be deducted against income from other sources, the trust came under pressure financially. Bill also suggests that at that time it 'was probably carrying more debt than it should have been. And then Dad retired, in about 1985, and started to become quite nervous about the exposure that we had.'

Initially, grapes were treated as just one of the crops in the Thorpe family's portfolio. They signed a long-term contract with Corbans in the early 1970s, and as Bill recounts, 'we got quite good at growing very big crops of Müller Thurgau. You know, 10, 11, 12 tonne to the acre and 5, 6, 7 tonne [of] Pinot Noir. In retrospect, I guess we ran a reasonably efficient grape-growing activity.' In the vine pull of 1986 they replaced their Müller Thurgau with Clone 6 Chardonnay. Grapes were not high on the list of the most profitable crops grown by the trust, and by 1988 some of the beneficiaries began to express concern that it was not producing 'anything very flash in the way of net revenue'. Over a three-year period the family came to an agreement to progressively realise capital. Given the intense competition for land at the time, prices were favourable. Some of the transactions were within the family. Richard took the whole of the persimmon area and John got all the grape-producing land. The rest – three kiwifruit properties and the navel orange property – were sold.

Winemaker and restaurateur John Thorpe (Landfall wine label and later Gisborne Wine Company) became owner of the 50-acre vineyard in Manutuke growing Chardonnay and Pinot Noir. With local lawyer Ross Revington he started the Whitecliffs winery in a converted maize crib producing primarily Gewürztraminer and Chardonnay and some Müller Thurgau from his refurbished vineyard and a small one owned by Revington. The name Whitecliffs was challenged legally by a Hawke's Bay enterprise and became Thorpe Brothers' Wines with Landfall as a brand. Selling grapes to Corbans continued to be one source of income until John sold the Manutuke vineyard in the late 1980s.

Bill Thorpe remembers John and his father coming to see him in 1991 and asking, 'What chance do you think there is of setting up a more commercially focused wine marketing company?' Bill was surprised by his own decision to become involved, especially when wearing his management accountant's hat: 'I've got to say, it was slightly misguided, particularly when it came to producing things like Müller Thurgau, because the margins, for a small winery, just do not stack up.' But he tempered this doubt by recognising that he already had a basic involvement in growing, packing and marketing fresh fruit and produce, and saw this new venture as a 'possibility of turning grapes into higher value'. And Müller Thurgau was not their main target.

Bill set up Longbush Wines and increased the working capital to expand John's winery and equipment because at that stage it was producing only about 1500 cases of wine. Longbush contracted John, who as the Gisborne Wine Company produced the wine for it. 'We buy the grapes, we buy the barrels, John basically provides the winemaking expertise and the infrastructure.' Bill took the view that Longbush should build its volume quickly and for five years they incremented their production by about 2000 cases per year until by 1997 the winery produced 18,000 cases of which 14,000 cases (126,000 litres) were Longbush. Part way through this growth, Bill, as owner of Longbush, decided to represent their own brand nationally and employed a small staff rather than using agents.

By the beginning of the twenty-first century Longbush was buying most of its grapes from six growers. Vineyards in Gisborne were their main source but they also bought

Cabernet Franc from Hawke's Bay and Sauvignon Blanc from Marlborough. Their Chardonnay grapes came from several vineyards on what locals now call the 'Golden Slopes', including, in some years, the Tietjen and Witters vineyards. 'Golden Slopes' is a tongue-in-cheek take on the Côte d'Or, the name of the French département and wine region of Burgundy. Bill summarises the locality's qualities succinctly: 'facing the afternoon sun, inland enough to get away from the sea breeze, well drained, quite light soil type, sort of limestone underlay'. In the 1970s and 1980s the qualities of the Chardonnay fruit from the Tietjen and Witters vineyards were already sufficiently celebrated that Auckland wine companies were pleased to identify the name of the grape grower on their wine label, while Bill Thorpe suggests that Longbush popularised the name Golden Slopes in their publicity. Geordie Witters, on Gisborne's Back Ormond Road, has since registered his grape-growing and tourist enterprise as 'The Golden Slope Ltd' and captured that intellectual property.

Towards the end of the twentieth century several subtropical crops grown in Gisborne could outbid grapes for use of the land. Mandarins were generating gross returns of NZ$60,000 to $65,000 per hectare. Persimmons were close behind. Grapes could not match these returns and attracted additional costs for pruning, canopy management and disease control. It took some time for landowners to realise that vines could thrive, and require less intensive care, if grown on some of the less fertile soils of the Poverty Bay flats. Yet, at the beginning of the twenty-first century, Bill Thorpe found himself questioning his continued involvement in the wine business:

Between Bill Thorpe's Longbush Wines (far left) and brother John Thorpe's Gisborne Wine Company (left), the Thorpe family grew a significant wine enterprise out of their business and horticultural expertise.
Strike Photography

'I've got to say that when John withdrew, I really thought hard about do I want to keep going as well.' He was frank in admitting that Longbush had 'made very little money out of making wine', while recognising that he had become involved in it because he 'saw it as a possibility of turning grapes into higher value' in a similar way to his achievements marketing other crops. Moreover, with Longbush and Thorpe Brothers' Wines, they had already put 'a huge investment into developing our brand, developing our reputation, developing our infrastructure'.

Having already taken some difficult decisions to keep production costs to a minimum, while not compromising the quality of grapes purchased in Gisborne, Hawke's Bay and Marlborough, he decided to make maximum use of the distribution network for wine that he had set up. Longbush already stored and distributed their wine from Auckland, Wellington and Christchurch in an arrangement with a transportation company. Bill decided to accept the approach of the large Chilean winery MontGras to be their New Zealand representative and distribute these wines through the same network as their own. However, in 2004, Bill reluctantly decided to close Longbush Wines down. In the early years of the twenty-first century, a small-scale producer without their own established vineyards, who was both buying grapes in competition with larger companies and attempting to compete with them in the supermarkets, found it very difficult to thrive.

Meanwhile, younger brother Geoff Thorpe had founded Gisborne's Riversun Nursery in 1982. In that year, New Zealand had 5900 hectares in vines. Gisborne, with 1920 hectares, was the largest regional vineyard. The vine pull of 1986 saw the national vineyard fall to 4390 hectares by 1989. This same year, Riversun won its first Marlborough contracts to produce grafted vines. With Marlborough (and other regions) now expanding rapidly, opportunities abounded for specialised enterprises to supply grape growers and wine companies with certified cultivars. Riversun was one of the nurseries to grasp this opportunity. By 1998, Riversun was grafting more than one million vines annually. At a density of 2000 vines per hectare, this enabled it to provided sufficient grafted cuttings for 500 hectares of new vineyards – about one third of the total vines being planted each year of the late 1990s. Nurseries were finding it difficult to keep up with the demand.

In 1999, Riversun launched a subsidiary, Linnaeus, with the objective of providing a virus-testing and diagnostic programme concentrating on viticulture and avocados. They wished to ensure that its propagation practices produced plant materials 'of high health and known virus status'. In addition to its skilled viticultural team led by Nick Hoskins, in 2000 Geoff employed molecular biologist Dr Rod Bonfiglioli who, as technical director, quickly became involved in developing a certification system for grafted grapevines and set up a sophisticated diagnostic laboratory. Bonfiglioli used his extensive experience and scientific contacts in Europe and Latin America to join Geoff Thorpe in a new round of importation of cultivars to suit New Zealand conditions. Over 100 new varieties, clones and rootstocks were brought into the country.

When, in 2008, Bonfiglioli set up his own consultancy business he designed an ambitious and innovative research programme in conjunction with the scientific committee of New Zealand Winegrowers. It involved mapping the diffusion of one of New Zealand's debilitating viruses (Grapevine Leafroll-associated Virus Type 3) in the red-grape varieties of Gimblett Gravels, Hawke's Bay and in Martinborough. These locality studies were to be followed by a planned removal and replanting of infected vines and act as a model for other parts of New Zealand. Although Rod Bonfiglioli died in May 2009, his virus project continues. The commercial objectives initiated at Riversun are having spin-offs for New Zealand winegrowing at large.

Millton Vineyards

For James and Annie Millton, coming back from their OE to Gisborne grape growing of the late 1970s must have been a rude shock. Their story encapsulates the tensions faced by farmers on the Poverty Bay flats as they transformed themselves into grape growers when their immediate predecessors were pastoral farmers or smallholders.

Annie Millton (née Clark) is the great-granddaughter of the owner of one of the largest sheep and beef runs on the East Coast of the North Island. Her great-grandfather

At Riversun Nursery, every year Geoff Thorpe produces more than a million grafted cuttings for vineyards around New Zealand.
Wayne Crosby, Riversun

John Clark arrived in New Zealand in 1875 from Scotland and by the early twentieth century had at various times developed or farmed the Ngatapa block, the Opou Station, Te Arai Station and Waipaoa Station, and been Chairman of Cook County. By the mid-twentieth century Annie's father John William Clark and mother Dorothy were living on and farming Opou Station. At the time, it carried over 9000 sheep and over 1000 cattle. Like many owners with some land on the Gisborne Plain, John had diversified into grapes in the late 1960s as a grower for the large Auckland wine companies. James Millton is a West Coaster brought up near the Franz Josef Glacier. Together, James and Annie operate Millton Vineyards on land carved off from the Ngatapa block and the Opou Station on the Gisborne Plain and surrounding hills.

After James Millton left school he acted on his early wish to get involved with wine by accepting a position as a cadet with Montana in the mid-1970s that included an introduction to the viticulture, winemaking and marketing sides of the company. Following this three-year stint, he travelled to Europe and did vintages in Burgundy and Germany. Having completed her diploma in horticulture at Lincoln College, Annie was in England extending her practical experience as a florist in London. She also did a vintage in Burgundy at Chorey-les-Beaune, across the Route Nationale 74 from Aloxe-Corton, and two vintages in Germany. Add these experiences to the vintage they both did in the Barossa before leaving for Europe and their commitment to learning about the vine and wine is clear.

Gisborne or Poverty Bay?

Back in New Zealand in 1979, James and Annie began discussions about where they would establish their enterprise. They were sufficiently serious about the potential of Central Otago to have a close look at it around the time that it was stuttering into existence and the New Zealand wine community had been debating its potential. 'But in the end,' says Annie, 'it came back to staying here. So we then set down a few conditions. We had to be assured of being able to get the varieties right because there was no point establishing a winery if you still had Chasselas and the Seibels!' Consequently, they took over, tidied and replanted the family vineyard prior to establishing their winery on the Te Arai River near Manutuke in 1984.

Ameliorating the existing Opua Station varieties included establishing a small nursery for rootstock and grafting vines. The commitment of James to more sustainable vineyard practices was reinforced by his distaste for the spraying regime of the time. Most spraying schedules in Gisborne were similar to the pattern established on traditional West Auckland vineyards. Whether it was needed or not, fungicides, and sometimes insecticides, were sprayed on a regular fourteen-day cycle often influenced very strongly by the supplier of the materials. Spraying herbicides was also standard practice. James began experimenting with reducing spraying and eliminating many accepted practices and replacing them with biodynamic ones. Weed control became mechanical and cover crops were later added. Even botrytis sprays at flowering were limited.

Chenin Blanc was one of the varieties that the large companies had recommended growing in Gisborne at high yields as a base for white table wines usually sold in bag-in-box packaging. James and Annie had kept the Chenin Blanc vines and in 1984 made a late-harvest wine (a wine with residual sweetness). James rates his 1985 late-harvest Chenin even better and they have experimented with the same style of wines from Riesling. The Milltons are playing a similar role in Gisborne as the Hogan family of Te Whare Ra in Marlborough and also Alan McCorkindale, formerly of Corbans, now in Waipara, while Nick Nobilo has now reinforced the Gisborne reputation for 'stickies' with his stylish Vinoptima, made from Gewürztraminer. The New Zealand wine-buying public were (and remain) rather wary of any wines with residual sweetness. After all, they had only recently been converted to drier wines that replaced the sweet ports, sherries and liqueurs of the mid-twentieth century industry. But the late-harvest wines are totally different. Their sugar, aromas and flavours come entirely from the grapes.

Gisborne would be low on the list of potential regions for anyone establishing a biodynamic vineyard in the early twenty-first century. Yet James and Annie Millton have managed to adapt their practices to meet the demanding BioGro certification. Their prescience and persistence have seen them well ahead of the pack as New Zealand Winegrowers intensify efforts towards all participants committing to their unified programme of sustainable winegrowing. James has mastered the more humid, less continental climate and alluvial and hill soils, and has done it while maintaining

his registration as a biodynamic grower. Until the last decade, botrytis had never been seen in Central Otago, while here on the Gisborne Plain fungus diseases are the main environmental threats for vines.

Winemaking at James and Annie Millton's winery.
Millton Vineyards & Winery

James Millton's powers of observation, and knowledge of his varied sites, run deep. This ability to relate the vine's sequences of growth and the characteristics of its fruit to the Gisborne environment is based on decades of careful observation combined with encouraging the diversity and balance of plant and animal life that enables his vines to thrive. He enriches his own experiences by keeping in close touch with the New Zealand biodynamic community, combined with regular trips to work in Europe on enterprises that practise biodynamics. At its heart is the timing of interventions in the vineyard in relation to the vine's seasonal patterns of growth from bud burst through to pruning. His efforts with Pinot Noir are an example.

Most of the Pinot Noir grown in the Gisborne region was for Montana's sparkling wines. As in Champagne, the grapes are picked at high yields and before they reach physiological ripeness. James and Annie produce Pinot Noir from different clones that are pruned to give much lower yields and have the aromas and flavours to make a still wine. Grapes are kept on the vine until they have an acceptable acid-sugar balance and colour, and the tannins have had the opportunity to evolve. These components combine in the barrel fermentations and maturation to give the complex flavours in the finished wine. Their Pinot Noir vineyard is planted on a hilly, well-exposed site in Manutuke on calcareous base rock and the resultant wines belie the assumption that still Pinot Noir of quality cannot be made from grapes grown in the Gisborne region. Their Chenin Blanc – which has remained one of Millton's signature varieties even though only 50 hectares of it is grown in New Zealand – has also achieved a consistency that sees it regularly ranked among the best in the country.

Gisborne or Poverty Bay?

Because of their deep knowledge and demonstration through practice of their dedication to organic and biodynamic practices, Millton Vineyards were invited to become a member of the 'Family of Twelve' – a co-operative of twelve of New Zealand's premium wineries, several of whose members are convinced both philosophically and pragmatically of the future of organic and biodynamic production. Tapping into the consumers who believe in the necessity for all land-based production to become more sustainable offers hard-nosed commercial advantages to those like the Milltons with a long-standing commitment to biodynamic winegrowing.

Vinoptima

Nick Nobilo was also bitten by the Gisborne and Gewürztraminer bug. In the early 1960s, like many second-generation Dalmatian winemakers, he joined his parents' small wine and orcharding business on Station Road, Huapai. Nick, the middle Nobilo son, had been a very promising rugby player in the Henderson High School First XV but was also very serious about wine. When Nick mused about continuing with his rugby, his father Nicola, the future of the family business in view, gave him clear options: 'You play-a the rugby or you make-a the wine, not both!' Nick chose the wine. Within a decade his two brothers – Steve running the marketing, and Mark the viticulture – were also involved in the rapidly expanding family firm.

Encouraged by his father, Nick had begun renovating their existing Huapai vineyards, as well as buying more land locally, aggressively planting both with classical varieties. He included Gewürztraminer as one of the preferred varieties but

> we got very poor yields. The first year we picked half a tonne per acre, the second year three quarters of a tonne, the third year another half a tonne and the old man said, 'We'll go bankrupt', and then we pulled them out and back in went the old Baco 22A. But not before I'd had the chance to make some commercial wines from them.

Such yields did not cut it compared with the 10 tonnes to the acre from the hybrid Baco 22A. Nick's father gently insisted that the Gewürztraminer had to come out. It did, but the variety's quality on the West Auckland clay-loams was not forgotten.

When Nick joined the other Auckland enterprises in negotiating contracts with Gisborne growers he encouraged Dave Thomas to plant Gewürztraminer, this time with carefully selected clones. The vines needed nurturing, and their fruit gentle treatment, but the resultant wine captured Nick's palate. It confirmed his faith in the variety and the flavours its fruit delivered. That commitment to Gewürztraminer smouldered for almost three decades while as CEO he saw the capital structure and

Nick Nobilo's Gewürztraminer grapes at Vinoptima Estate. *Vinoptima Estate*

principal investors in the Nobilo enterprise change several times. When the Australian firm BRL Hardy finally bought Nobilo in 2000, Nick made the bold move of launching his own wine enterprise in Gisborne by establishing a boutique winery and christening it Vinoptima. He chose the region, Gisborne, the variety Gewürztraminer, the site on the Makaraka heavy silt-loam and the Makauri clay-loam east of Ormond on Ngakoroa Road, and partly funded the new vineyards by encouraging a local iwi organisation as partners in the enterprise.

His choice rested heavily on his experience of the quality of the grapes he had bought from Dave Thomas and of the wine he was able to make from them. He set modestly ambitious targets. His publicity brochure states that he is 'dedicated to producing the world's best Gewürztraminer', and he means it. Reviews of the wine suggest that he is already on the way to achieving this objective. Wine reviewer Neal Martin gave Vinoptima Gewürztraminers the highest average score, over the 2004 to 2008 vintages, of all wines he tasted during his 2008 visit to New Zealand. At over NZ$50 for a 375-ml bottle, the wine is probably underpriced for its quality, and certainly much less expensive than other wines of similar style and quality such as those of Sauternes. The immaculate, ultra-modern winery he built in Gisborne is designed to vinify Gewürztraminer in small batches, with Nick doing most of the work.

Nick Nobilo's long association with Gisborne and knowledge of the qualities of the grapes from different sites there allowed him to make sophisticated judgements on the

Gisborne *agro-terroir*. While his site is nestled towards the hills on two of the favoured soils for viticulture on the Poverty Bay flats, other similar ones abound. In 2010 the 109 hectares of Gewürztraminer in Gisborne made up barely 5 per cent of the region's vines, of which Vinoptima had 10 hectares. The world market for hand-crafted wines similar to Vinoptima, from a clean, green Gisborne, is certain to become much larger.

'There might be something we're doing right here…'

Gisborne makes much of being part of the first region of New Zealand to see the sun. That it was also the first region to see the growing of grapes on a large scale has indelibly marked its economy, landscape and the organisation of winegrowing in New Zealand. In Gisborne's abundant environment landowners were quick to respond to offers of contracts to grow grapes for Auckland firms. By 1980, 126 grape growers were supplying 84 per cent of the grapes harvested from almost 1600 hectares of vines. Gisborne was the largest regional vineyard in the country. The Gisborne experience established the fundamental form of the wine *filière* in New Zealand. It consists of landowners growing grapes, usually under contract to firms of various sizes, who buy the grapes and use them, and some they grow themselves, to produce wine.

In Gisborne's case, the structure of the wine *filière* is distinctive in several ways. The large wineries established in Lytton Road are fermentation and storage facilities rather than full wineries. For much of its Gisborne life, Montana's winery had no cellar door where the public could purchase wine, although winery manager Roger McLernon did later establish one for some years. Without a sales area, their winery had a similar atmosphere to some of the impersonal bodegas of the Rioja region of Spain. Like them, it was a processing plant for grapes. The wine was bottled, dressed and distributed from Auckland. Much was also retailed from Auckland in cardboard casks. Very few small wineries were established in Gisborne. By 1980, only five wineries were recorded as 'growing their own grapes used for winemaking'. This confirms that Gisborne was then, and indeed remains, the region with the smallest number of wineries relative to its area in grapes of any winegrowing region in New Zealand.

Gisborne was the first staging post in the regional dispersal of winegrowing that began in the late 1960s and continued into the twenty-first century. Montana's move to Marlborough in 1973 shifted attention away from Gisborne and had impacts that are clear in a close reading of the regional statistics. After the vine pull of 1986, Gisborne's area in vines continued to decrease until 1997 before beginning to increase slowly again. In comparison, the area in vines was increasing again in both Hawke's Bay and Marlborough by 1990. The large companies had shifted their attention to Marlborough, and grape growers there, as well as in Hawke's Bay, were responding.

With this regional shift in production, the varieties of grapes being grown were also changing. In the five years between 1975 and 1980 the proportion of *vinifera* vines in the national vineyard shifted from 72 per cent to 91 per cent. The attraction of hybrid grapes was over, even in more humid regions such as Gisborne, where they had offered resistance to diseases and some cost savings. New hybrids such as Reichensteiner had only a short time in the spotlight. Consumers and enterprises now had their sights firmly fixed on a narrow range of *vinifera* grapes and varietal wines.

When large companies developed a presence in, and knowledge of, two or more regions the opportunity to substitute grapes grown in one region for those grown in another increased considerably. For wines of low to moderate price, the large companies could continue to buy inexpensive Gisborne grapes of lesser varieties to be blended with the new *viniferas* in wines sold at lower price points. But Gisborne growers were also able to respond to demand for new varieties because irrigation was not necessary and most varieties they planted yielded well. As is evident from the interviews with the Bell and Fletcher families, the enterprises purchasing their grapes strongly influence the varieties being planted by growers.

When takeovers and mergers among large winegrowing enterprises quickened, the number of large enterprises that had previously bought grapes from Gisborne winegrowers decreased. Conversely, the increased scale of Pernod Ricard NZ Ltd (Montana) saw the area of its own vineyards increase in several regions, notably in Gisborne. In the early 2000s, Montana's ratio of company to grower vineyards was 30:70. At that time, its influential and outspoken CEO Peter Hubscher was expressing the wish to increase their own vineyards in Gisborne until the ratio was about 50:50. Their takeover of Corbans accomplished this target in one fell swoop, even allowing Montana to sell some vineyards.

Given its history in the region and nationally, it should have come as no surprise when Pernod Ricard NZ Ltd announced in June 2009 that it was entering into discussions with its contract grape growers in Poverty Bay to reduce further their area of vines under contract. The specific reason given for this renegotiation was that demand for its Lindauer brand of effervescent wines and for Chardonnay was weaker than expected.

Each of the small enterprises analysed in this chapter provides insights into the distinctive features of Gisborne winegrowing. Longbush attests that winegrowing offers no easy path to prosperity in Gisborne, or elsewhere. Despite Bill Thorpe's commercial success in all aspects of other horticultures in Poverty Bay, it took considerable time, effort and acumen for Thorpe Brothers' Wines and the Longbush label to make progress. But it could not be sustained. James and Annie Millton's commitment to growing varieties such as Chenin Blanc and Pinot Noir biodynamically in Gisborne must at times have been daunting. Having some of the varieties in the ground gave them a slight head start, as did the possibility of extending their vineyard on to the well-exposed hills of the Clark family property. This extension enabled them to capitalise on Gisborne's hot summers and extended autumns in the best years. Their experience of growing organically, then biodynamically, made them a natural choice for the Family of Twelve.

Nick Nobilo had some unfinished business after BRL Hardy of Australia bought the family business in 2000. He had begun his career in the 1960s extending his parents' Huapai vineyard and contracting grape growers in Gisborne. When he 'retired' he was again prepared to commit to the garnet-coloured Gewürztraminer of Gisborne. Few others could match his depth of experience, viticultural knowledge and winemaking skills, coupled with entrepreneurial drive, commercial nous and access to capital. The international reviews of his wine and his marketing initiatives suggest that he just might be successful in helping to reposition Gisborne in the market.

Denis Irwin had demonstrated in the 1970s that Gewürztraminer had a special affinity with Gisborne's environment, even when vinified more conventionally. Any enterprise that was able to sell 80 per cent of its production by mail order, as Matawhero did between 1975 and 1982, must have been doing something right, even if the competition then was less intense. Denis Irwin, like Nick Nobilo, ranks among the winemaking stars of his time.

The best Gisborne wine news of 2009 was the relaunch of the Matawhero brand by the Searle family with Kim Crawford as vinifier. Having conquered the mass market with his personalised brand, Crawford is now in a position to explore making more artisanal wines – an aspiration that he expressed shortly after news of the sale of that brand to Vincor (now Constellation Brands) was announced. Again, Gisborne's wine reputation should benefit. Skills and capital accumulated from the first generation of successful wine firms are being recycled back into Gisborne winegrowing.

Wine awards are always a dicey business. Gisborne grape growers and wine enterprises, both large and small, have won their share. Probably the most surprising for the region's grape growers, and those of New Zealand as a whole, was Gisborne's Amor-Bendall winning the trophy for the top Sauvignon Blanc in the prestigious Air New Zealand Wine Awards of 2004. The fruit for this wine did not come from Marlborough but from 3.4-metre trellises growing Sauvignon Blanc for grafting in the Riversun Nursery of Geoff Thorpe on the Poverty Bay flats. This result raises two questions. First, it demands some exploration of the physiological processes and canopy management that have provided such excellent fruit from such an unusual source. Second, this *terroir*-shattering result needs to be assessed against the environment of the particular season, the site, and the clone of these vines. Doug and Delwyn Bell's preference for using Richard Smart's 'big vine theory' may have a special place on the Poverty Bay flats.

The incident that Doug Bell recounts concerning the visit of one of Kendall-Jackson Vineyard Estates' research scientists, Daniel Roberts, to Gisborne and the Tietjen vineyard is particularly revealing about meagre or prolific environments and the vine:

He was interested to have a look at some of our soil types and so we took him to some soil pits between some rows on Paul Tietjen's vineyard. And he walked up to the soil pit and he said he couldn't believe that we would even plant this ground – he said that this is just such lovely country that they wouldn't entertain the idea. And we went to another grower who Corbans had asked to plant this particular area and had a soil that they thought was yielding good flavours, and even before he went to the hole he said they were mad, that he shouldn't even entertain the idea of planting here – for goodness' sake get some sites on the hill or something, get it out of this ground because it was like a swamp. A week after he left, the London Wine Awards were released where Gisborne's Saints Chardonnay got the best white wine in the world. So we did have the cheek to email Daniel with the results and say well, hey, there might be something we're doing right here!

Many of Kendall-Jackson's vineyards are perched on the coastal hills of Central California. Sprawled across these hills on thin and stony soils that are separated by patches of remnant forest, where deer are hunted, and interconnected by steep tracks, they are some of the most difficult slopes to cultivate and tend of the winegrowing localities of California. Under that state's environmental legislation, it is unlikely that cultivation would be permitted there today.

The same week I visited these Kendall-Jackson vineyards the conference field excursion included a visit to the renowned Franciscan vineyards of the former Robert Mondavi enterprise, now owned by Constellation Brands. The viticulturist had done us proud. A rectangular soil profile 2 metres deep had been dug alongside the Cabernet Sauvignon vines on the flat floor of the Napa Valley. The dark brown, friable topsoil was at least a metre and a half deep with very little change in colour. The roots of the vines penetrated the full depth and more. Here was a soil profile much more like those on the Poverty Bay flats than those of Kendall-Jackson's coastal vineyards. These vines on the floor of the Napa Valley were pruned and tended to suppress their vigour.

A five-year-old Robert Mondavi Cabernet Sauvignon from this Napa vineyard was served with lunch. In the sales outlet it retailed for US$128 and its quality justified its price. One of my colleagues at the conference, who considers *terroir* begins and ends with geology, flatly refused to believe that the wine drunk with lunch could possibly have come from the flat and fertile Franciscan vineyard we had seen in the morning. Yet, as the Gisborne winegrowing region has proven, friable, fertile soils need not necessarily be anathema to making fine wines provided the vines are managed wisely and yields are restricted through canopy management so that their fruit develop the rich and multi-layered flavours that carry over to the final wines.

6

Hawke's Bay

The Hawke's Bay Province is, in my opinion, the most suitable for vine-growing I have visited in New Zealand. It possesses thousands of acres which, by reason of the nature of the soil, natural drainage, and sufficiency of heat, will produce grapes of both table and wine making varieties in rich abundance. – ROMEO BRAGATO

At the turn of the twentieth century, Romeo Bragato was fulsome in his praise of the viticultural potential of many regions of New Zealand, perhaps too fulsome. Yet he was quite unequivocal that Hawke's Bay was the best that he visited, although it must be remembered that he did not assess Marlborough. Despite Bragato's enthusiasm, the Hawke's Bay region has had a chequered history of grape growing and winemaking.

Three interrelated circumstances are responsible. First, the four local companies producing 90 per cent of this region's wine in the mid-twentieth century – Glenvale Wines, McDonald's, McWilliam's and Vidal – were closely connected to New Zealand's brewing companies and even more dependent on making fortified wine than those in the Auckland region. They had to change their mindset and commercial strategies to get fully involved in the production of table wine. Second, competition for land on Hawke's Bay's Heretaunga and associated plains has always been more intense than in any other rural region of similar size in New Zealand. Vines did not automatically have first choice of land here as they did in Marlborough. In Hawke's Bay, grapevines had to

Elephant Hill Wine Estate in Te Awanga, Hawke's Bay, looking from the coast up toward Havelock North and Te Mata Peak. *Bruce Jenkins Photography*

Crab Farm Winery sits among a number of new and old enterprises in the Esk Valley, Hawke's Bay.
Richard Brimer

pay their way in competition with many other fruit and vegetable crops (Figure 6.5). Some wealthy landholders were even prepared to withhold land from the market rather than see it go into vines. Third, because Hawke's Bay had a small but established wine industry when New Zealand winegrowing expanded, the region faced all the difficulties of rapid growth.

Conflicts between grape growers and wine companies were sometimes vitriolic in Hawke's Bay as protocols for winegrowing were established. In particular, the vine extraction scheme of 1986 affected Hawke's Bay severely. It took until 1998 for its vineyard to reach the size that it first attained in the early 1980s. Since 1998 its area in vines has almost doubled in size to over 5000 hectares as the region has begun to realise the potential that Bragato recognised.

This chapter begins by discussing the distinctiveness of the Hawke's Bay experience compared with Marlborough and Gisborne. The vine varieties, climates and soils of Hawke's Bay are then interpreted with a view to assessing whether Bragato's assertion is credible. As in Marlborough, the spatial pattern of growth in the Hawke's Bay vineyard is revealing (Figure 6.4). After initial plantings not far from the coast by 1960 (from the lower Esk Valley in the north to Te Awanga in the south), vines became scattered across the Heretaunga Plains during the 1980s, before finding two niches where they became dominant: the first on the gravel soils of former riverbeds and the stony terraces of mainly two rivers – the Ngaruroro and the Tutaekuri – and the other on clay soils, often overlain by loess. This sequence is interpreted through the actions and commentary of participants in the Hawke's Bay industry, both local family firms and the large corporate enterprises who at first let contracts to Hawke's Bay grape growers before buying land and planting vines on land more tightly under their own control.

Vines without many wineries

Growth of the area of vines in Hawke's Bay has fluctuated greatly. It grew slowly but steadily until 1975 when the rate of growth quickened for a decade as both grape growers and local wine firms planted mainly Müller Thurgau. By 1980, Hawke's Bay vineyards were growing 737 hectares of this variety, or almost exactly half of this regional vineyard. The vine pull of 1986 resulted in 534 hectares of vines being removed in Hawke's Bay, only 50 hectares less than Gisborne. From 1990, steady growth recommenced from a lower base as winegrowers renewed and extended the regional vineyard by planting *vinifera* varieties. From the late 1990s the rate of growth quickened once again when the major companies refocused on Hawke's Bay as opportunities for buying quality viticultural land in Marlborough became fewer. During this decade many new winegrowing enterprises decided to invest in Hawke's Bay, a substantial number of them bringing capital from outside New Zealand.

Between 1960 and the mid-1980s, therefore, Hawke's Bay and Gisborne were the beneficiaries of the first phase of rapid growth in New Zealand winegrowing. By the early 1980s these two regions shared 65 per cent of the New Zealand vineyard in about equal proportions. Marlborough had just 20 per cent, with the remaining 15 per cent across other regions. But the major Auckland companies chose to invest in modern vinification facilities in Gisborne and Marlborough rather than in Hawke's Bay. The sole Auckland wine company to acquire a Hawke's Bay winery in the 1970s was Villa Maria. In 1976, George Fistonich purchased the Vidal winery in Hastings and made it the focus of his Hawke's Bay and Gisborne vinification. To keep Villa Maria in the public eye, he also opened New Zealand's first vineyard restaurant on the same site.

In contrast, by 1972 both Montana and Corbans had built large, modern processing and storage facilities in Gisborne. Montana had also completed its Marlborough winery by 1977, even though they planted their first grapes there only in 1973. Hawke's Bay was denied such state-of-the-art wineries until 1988 when Montana surreptitiously purchased the former McDonald Winery, by then owned by Corbans but not being

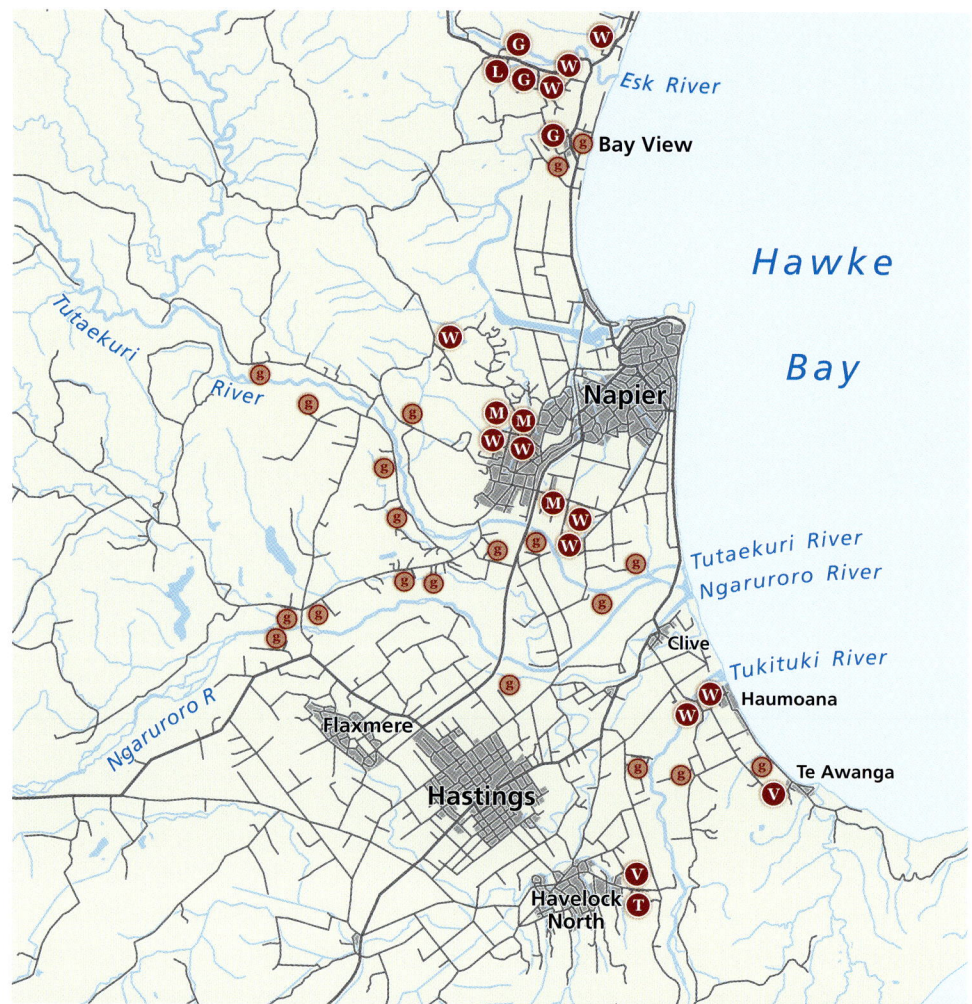

Figure 6.1 Vineyards of wine producers and grape growers, 1981.
Key G: Glenvale; L: Van der Linden; W: McWilliam's; M: Mission; V: Vidals; T: Te Mata; g: grape growers.

used. Montana invested over $15 million as it gradually extended and converted it into an important centre of red-wine production, notably for the Bordeaux blends.

Between 1975 and 1985 much of the rapid increase in the area in vines in Hawke's Bay came from existing landowners, especially orchardists and growers of vegetables for processing, who decided to plant grapes, under informal or formal contracts, mainly with Auckland companies such as Babich, Corbans, Delegat's, Matua Valley, Montana, Nobilo, Penfolds and Villa Maria, as well as local enterprises, especially McWilliam's. A few pastoral farmers, including some former town-supply dairy farmers, also planted grapes, while other landowners began to consider ways to enter the industry.

These new grape growers had much to learn about growing grapes for table wine. However, being mainly families with horticultural knowledge, they learned quickly. Most of them initially grew Müller Thurgau and aimed for high yields – often at least 10 tonnes to the acre (24 tonnes to the hectare) – to gain maximum revenue. Müller Thurgau was, of course, ascendant by 1980 with 1819 hectares of it planted in New Zealand, whereas Chardonnay and Cabernet Sauvignon, the two *vinifera* varieties with the largest share of the national vineyard at the time, had only about 750 hectares between them. In these early years of the modern wine industry, contracts between grape growers and wine companies gradually evolved as both parties negotiated their way.

One crucial difference distinguished Hawke's Bay from Gisborne in this period. From the late 1970s to the mid-1980s a group of family enterprises, intent on making table wine from their own *vinifera* vineyards, entered Hawke's Bay winegrowing. They wanted nothing to do with the practices of some of the earlier Hawke's Bay winemaking fraternity, including the infamous 'black snake' – the black hose that snaked across the cellar floor and added water to the juice or wine in the tanks, often in large quantities.

In one sense, Chris Pask was the earliest into winegrowing of this group, but while he was growing grapes and aerial topdressing, John Buck was learning the wine trade and culture of wine in the United Kingdom and France, while Kim Salonius, having enrolled in a Master's degree in medieval history in Germany, was working in the vineyards and cellars of Alsace. Alan Limmer was completing a double major in chemistry and soil science at Waikato University followed by a Master's and PhD in soil science. Meanwhile, Alwyn Corban was completing his formal training with a BSc majoring in mathematics but also doing chemistry and physics at the University of Auckland, followed by a diploma in food technology at Massey University and a Master's in oenology at the University of California, Davis. New Zealand's 'knowledge economy' started much earlier than some would have us believe.

Together with some of the existing Hawke's Bay enterprises – notably McWilliam's Wines, Mission Vineyards, Vidal and later Esk Valley under Villa Maria – these winegrowers demonstrated that Hawke's Bay could make table wines of excellent quality. They established a reputation for wines produced in this region that attracted a much larger group of new entrants during the 1990s, and by the 2000s, firms funded from overseas capital.

Grape varieties

Hawke's Bay is the most versatile of all New Zealand's grape-growing regions. Although it grows only about one quarter of Marlborough's total area in vines, it has nine varieties each with over 100 hectares planted. Marlborough has five. This difference derives

Table 6.1 Varietal change in the Hawke's Bay region, 1960–2010 (hectares)

VARIETIES	1960	1965	1970	1975	1980	1990	1995	2000	2005	2010
Baco 22A, 1, 2-11	43	20	20	21	16	2	-	-	-	-
Seibels 5455, 5643, 5437	53	37	41	72	54	7	-	-	-	-
Palomino	16	15	65	126	121	36	28	-	-	-
Chasselas	17	20	60	49	75	27	37	12	-	-
Müller Thurgau	12	15	40	133	737	400	294	149	39	15
Chardonnay	-	-	-	12	26	161	484	679	1057	1165
Chenin Blanc	-	-	-	-	127	105	87	94	31	15
Sauvignon Blanc	-	-	-	-	23	97	253	276	502	910
Pinot Gris	-	-	-	-	-	5	5	12	86	355
Pinot Noir	-	?	?	11	6	36	88	118	333	379
Cabernet Sauvignon	5	12	17	43	93	154	315	419	432	388
Cabernet Franc	?	?	?	?	?	16	50	58	124	107
Malbec	-	-	-	-	-	<1	8	37	113	105
Merlot	-	-	-	-	10	43	193	384	1114	1020
Syrah	-	-	-	-	-	-	16	31	159	204
Total HB listed (ha)	**146**	**90**	**226**	**461**	**1306**	**1063**	**1821**	**2257**	**3990**	**4663**
Other varieties			101	76	184	252	268	186	260	330
Total hectares	**148**	**198**	**327**	**537**	**1490**	**1315**	**2089**	**2443**	**4250**	**4993**

mainly from Hawke's Bay's ability to grow and ripen (in most years) the red varieties of Bordeaux – Merlot, Cabernet Sauvignon, Cabernet Franc and Malbec. These four varieties make up over one third of the Hawke's Bay vineyard with Merlot and Cabernet Sauvignon dominant. By 2000, the area planted in Merlot in Hawke's Bay had begun to approach the amount planted in Cabernet Sauvignon. Since, the preference for Merlot over Cabernet Sauvignon has progressively increased until its area is almost three times larger (Table 6.1). In Hawke's Bay, Merlot ripens a few weeks earlier and more evenly than Cabernet Sauvignon.

Hawke's Bay also asserts its versatility through the willingness of many of its experienced viticulturists and vinifiers to experiment with varieties originating from Mediterranean Europe such as the lower Rhone Valley, Languedoc, and parts of Italy and Spain. Such regions have longer and hotter growing seasons than most of New Zealand, especially the South Island, whereas in Hawke's Bay winegrowers have demonstrated that some *vinifera* varieties from these hotter European regions will ripen with acceptable regularity.

In the last decade of the twentieth century, the northern Rhone variety Syrah showed its potential in Hawke's Bay. When made in a lighter, more refined style than the full-bodied Australian Shiraz, it rapidly developed a strong reputation both locally and internationally. Enterprises such as Stonecroft, Te Mata, Trinity Hill, Vidal and others have revealed Syrah's qualities, and it seems highly likely to become a more important variety in the regions. Other red varieties such as Tempranillo (Trinity Hill), Gamay Noir (Te Mata), Zinfandel (Stonecroft) and several Italian varieties are also being grown successfully. These have shown the possibility of extending the range of varieties in Hawke's Bay.

Among the white varieties, Hawke's Bay has a larger area planted in Chardonnay than any other region, but only by a small margin over Gisborne and Marlborough, all three each growing a little over 1000 hectares. Rather surprisingly, Sauvignon Blanc, one mainstay of Bordeaux white-wine production, has only recently began to show signs that it will reach 1000 hectares in Hawke's Bay. Sauvignon develops aromas and characteristics here quite different from those found in Marlborough wines. With the price of land at a premium in Marlborough, large companies such as Delegat's, Nobilo (Constellation Brands) and Pernod Ricard NZ have planted extensive areas in both red and white varieties on the gravel terraces of the Ngaruroro River. The area in Pinot Gris has also increased rapidly until over 355 hectares had been planted by 2010. As recently as 2000, just 12 hectares were being grown.

Such versatility has its drawbacks. It is difficult to give each of the wide range of red varieties suited to the varied sites in Hawke's Bay the attention it deserves. Hawke's Bay producers have yet to demonstrate their ability to make Pinot Noir of distinction as consistently as the more southern wine regions of New Zealand. Large companies, notably Montana (Pernod Ricard), have instead used Hawke's Bay as a source of Pinot Noir for sparkling wines using different clones grown at higher yields. It is difficult to name many outstanding still Pinot Noirs being produced from grapes grown in Hawke's Bay, although wineries in parts of Central Hawke's Bay look like changing that.

Asked why he thought Hawke's Bay had not yet produced many Pinot Noirs of distinction, a very successful Marlborough producer of Pinot Noir suggested, 'Perhaps they haven't tried hard enough.' He was implying that Hawke's Bay wine companies had a surfeit of choice. Pinot may have not received the attention it deserves because other varieties have taken higher priority. The more conventional answer is that Hawke's Bay is too hot, or that the diurnal range of temperature is insufficient to produce the delicate flavours characteristic of the variety. As is increasingly becoming apparent, however, Hawke's Bay has many lightly explored sites further inland, and especially south of the Heretaunga Plains, with the natural environments to produce fine Pinot Noir.

The natural environment

Was Bragato right in his favourable assessment of Hawke's Bay's natural environment for the vine? From a climatic perspective, the answer has to be 'yes'. The region's varietal versatility is the most convincing evidence. It is able to ripen a wider range of grape varieties than any other region in New Zealand. Growers can achieve this because Hawke's Bay has both a longer and hotter growing season than most parts of New Zealand, although still remaining within the cool-climate spectrum. This attribute combines with an annual rainfall of under 1000 millimetres (much of the Heretaunga Plains receives under 800 mm) and low humidity. Other parts of the North Island are as hot in summer, some even persistently hotter, but none combine the long, hot growing season with relatively low humidity and low rainfall (Figure 6.2).

Hawke's Bay's distinctive climate for the vine does distinguish it from other regions of New Zealand. Over the growing season it accumulates more degree-days than any other of the main New Zealand winegrowing regions. Parts of coastal Hawke's Bay from north of Napier to south of Hastings and extending almost 20 kilometres inland receive on average 1400 degree-days annually. It is not surprising therefore, that Hawke's Bay, together with Auckland and Northland, are the only wine regions of New Zealand

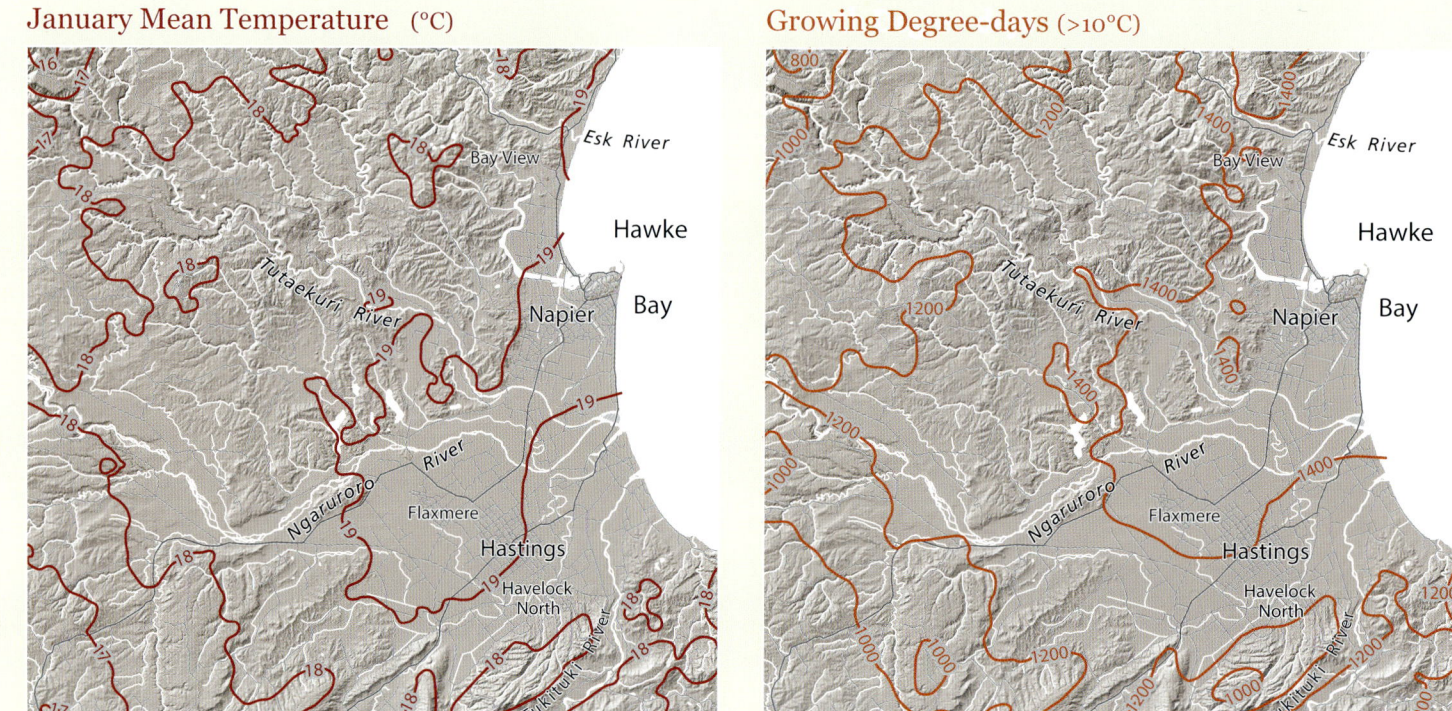

where Merlot and Cabernet Sauvignon are overrepresented compared with other varieties. Other regions have difficulty in ripening such varieties that require a longer growing season and hotter summer conditions than most of New Zealand can provide, other than in the warmest seasons. Despite his attraction to the variety, and success with his Celèbre blend of Cabernet, Clive Paton of Atarangi, Martinborough could not achieve ripeness in sufficient seasons for him to maintain his Cabernet Sauvignon in production.

Interacting with these atmospheric qualities is a wide range of soils with a reasonably high proportion of them free draining. The detailed pattern of soils is very complicated on the Heretaunga and associated plains, river terraces and rolling hills of Hawke's Bay, but four broad categories of surface materials that relate to the geomorphology of the region can be identified.

The first category, which comprises a strip of land roughly parallel to the shoreline but varying in width from hundreds of metres to over a kilometre, consists of former beach gravels in a matrix of sand with sandy loams on the surface. The second category is fine alluvium. It covers much of the Heretaunga Plains and was originally wetlands before being extensively drained from the mid-nineteenth century. These fertile soils are now largely protected from flooding by the stopbanks along the main rivers of the

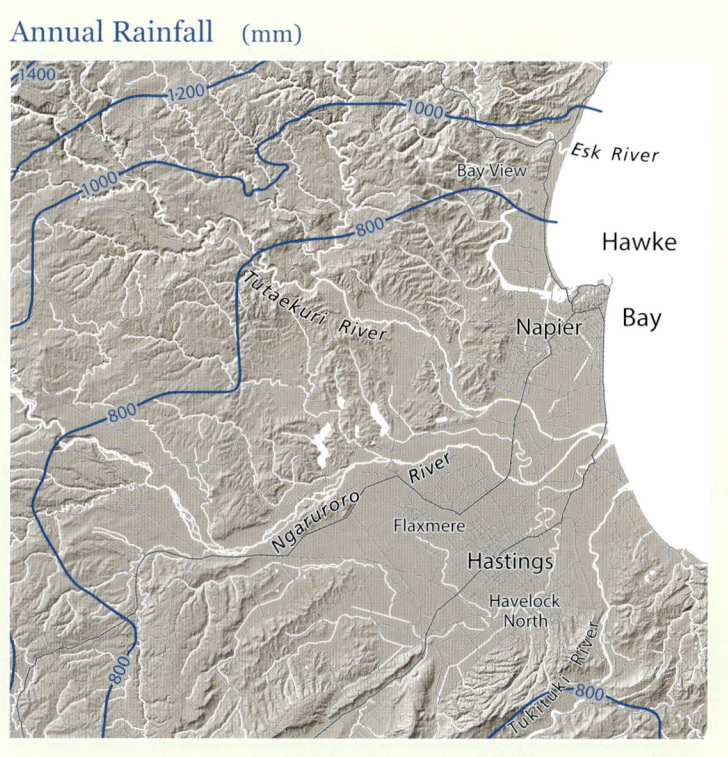

Figure 6.2 Natural environmental conditions of Hawke's Bay vineyards

Hawke's Bay

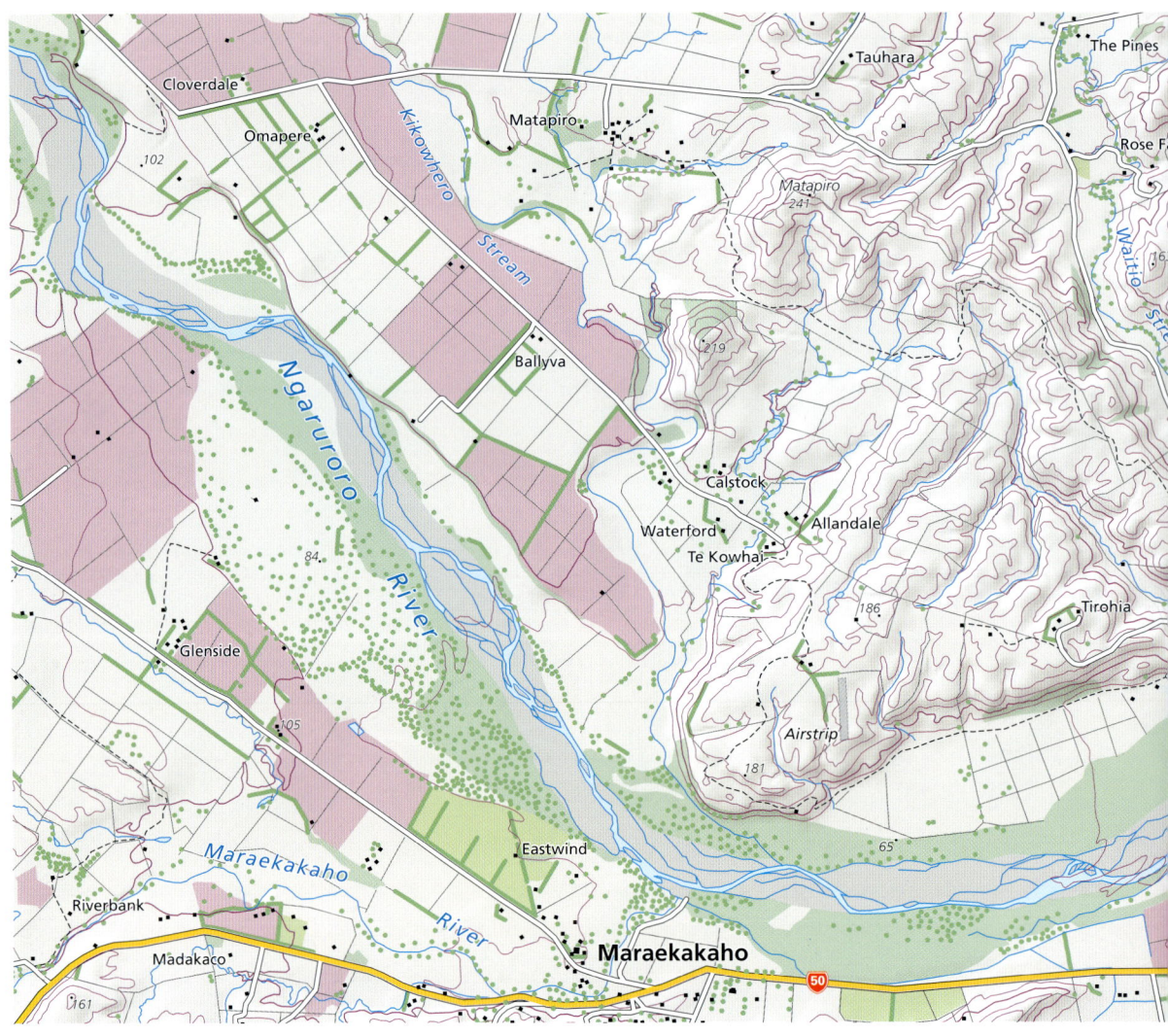

Figure 6.3 Vineyards of the Ngaruroro Terraces, Bridge Pa, and Gimblett Gravels

plains. The third category, an increasingly important site for viticulture, is the gravel terraces of the main rivers that are extensive at elevations of about 60 metres above sea level. Former gravelly riverbeds on lower land have similar soils. In the fourth category, the hills that make up most of the region have either clays or limestone underlying them. Loess is the surface material on much of these hills, and it often forms a discrete topsoil, especially over some of the limestones.

The plains were formed through deposition by the colourfully named rivers that drain them – the Esk, Tutaekuri, Ngaruroro, Clive and Tukituki. As a result, underlying much of them are gravels derived from greywacke, the basement rock of New Zealand.

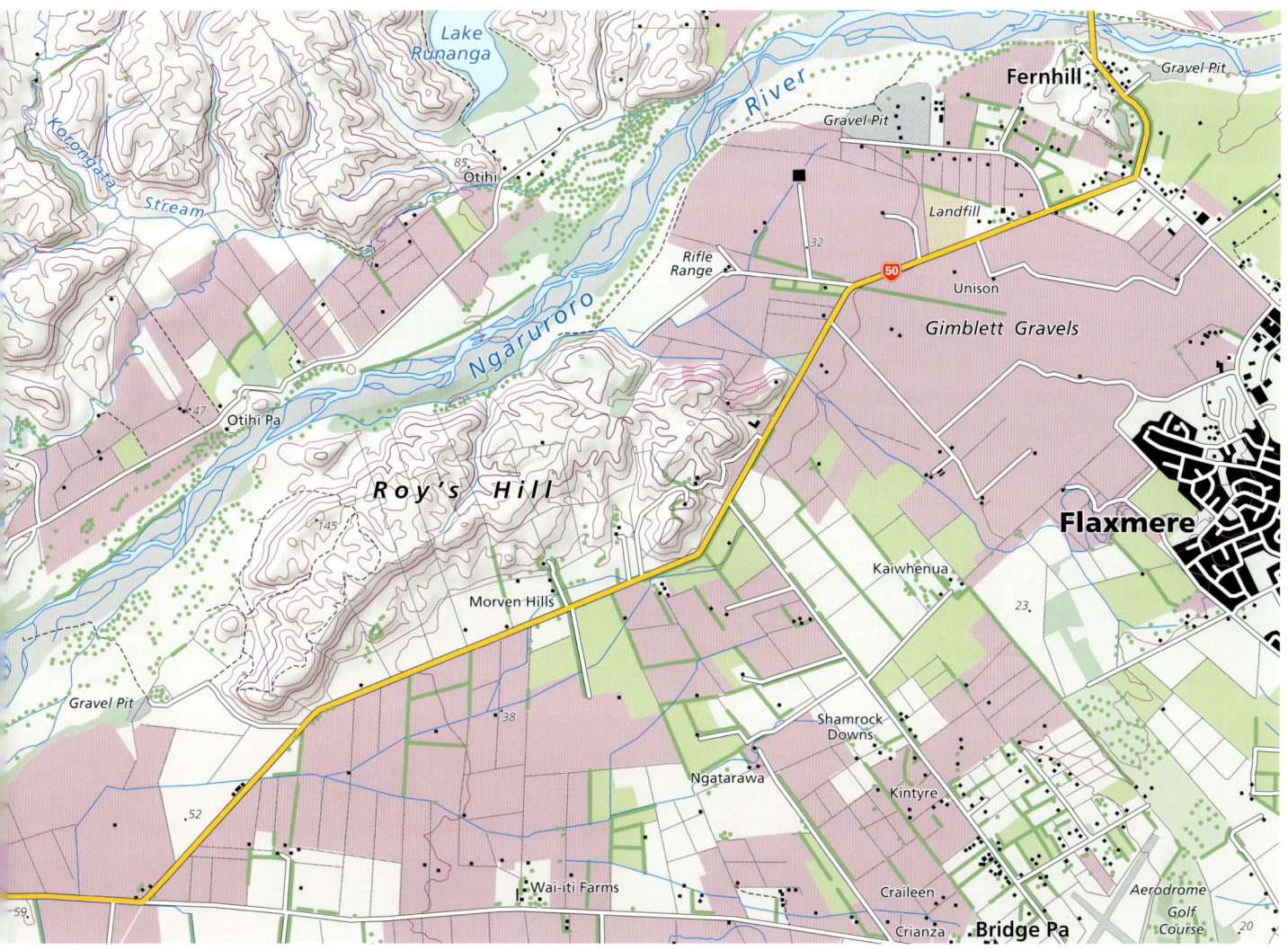

At lower elevations, where rivers have changed their course, these former riverbeds are exposed, as is the case with the Gimblett Gravels. Overlaying these gravels and interspersed among them is a wide range of finer sandy and silty materials deposited by the rivers as they have flooded and meandered across the plains and formed wetlands mainly closer to the coast, most of which have been drained.

These soils vary greatly in their stage of development but most are youthful and their composition is complicated by recent geological events. Deposits of ash from the volcanic eruptions of the central North Island have fallen in the headwaters of the rivers and on the lowlands. Loess from the period of the Pleistocene glaciations when vegetation was sparse is still present on much of the Hawke's Bay hill country but elsewhere it has been eroded, re-sorted, redeposited and reconsolidated as was the volcanic ash.

Upstream from where these rivers emerge from the hills are extensive suites of terraces at different elevations, notably along the Ngaruroro River (Figure 6.3) but also the Tutaekuri and the Tukituki. Where the Ngaruroro comes out of the hills at Maraekakaho, for instance, its bed is about 60 metres above sea level and the extensive terraces above it on either side of the river are between 100 and 140 metres above sea level. Fifteen kilometres further upstream, the riverbed is at about 160 metres and the highest parts of the terraces approaching 200 metres above sea level. Tributaries of the Ngaruroro also have suites of terraces associated with them, especially on its southern or right bank. These are at even higher elevations, almost all being above 200 metres.

From a viticultural point of view the presence of soils with a well-developed profile underlain by clay on the gently sloping hills of Hawke's Bay is also an advantage. Such clay soils, like many limestones, have the ability to retain moisture, enabling its slow release during summer and autumn. This tendency encourages the berries to develop flavour and colour from their deeply penetrating roots as the growing season proceeds.

The mainly younger gravel terraces of the rivers also provide soils suitable for viticulture, most of them being well drained. Some viticulturists would suggest too well drained, making irrigation essential. In addition, many of these clays and gravels have hard pans at varying depths beneath the surface. Some winegrowers favour ripping these soils to a depth of about a metre to allow the roots to penetrate more deeply. Others prefer to be more cautious because, on some soils, freeing the roots allows them to reach more fertile horizons and encourages the vines to become too vigorous. The gravels and the clays do allow the grapes to develop different flavours and aromas, giving winegrowers the opportunity to produce a range of different wines. Hawke's Bay, therefore, has the two main types of soils – clays (Saint-Émilion) and gravels (Graves) – which are also the foundation of the Bordeaux industry.

Vineyard dispersal, 1960–2010

Four maps – 1960, 1980, 1990 and 2010 – reveal a definite sequence in the evolution of the Hawke's Bay vineyards (Figure 6.4), especially when their changing distribution is related to the soils and climate of the region. The sequence also reflects the role of different forms of enterprise that were beginning to participate in the wine *filière*, especially grape growers from the early 1970s and, from the early 1980s, an increase in winegrowing enterprises owned by families. Beginning in the 1990s, but intensifying after 2000, the large corporate wine firms, some with access to capital and bold expansion plans from their new international owners, became particularly influential on the size and the location of new vineyards.

Gimblett Gravels soil profile. *Gimblett Gravels Winegrowers Association*

In 1960, most vineyards were on soils of moderate to low fertility. During the 1970s and into the 1980s, most new plantings were on the more fertile, fine and deep alluvial soils on the Heretaunga Plains where vines grew more vigorously and yields were high. Most landowners who became grape growers were on these soils. From the mid- to late 1980s, vines began to disperse again to sites where soils were less fertile and yields lower. These sites were the former riverbeds of the Ngaruroro in the Ngatarawa Triangle and the land west of Flaxmere that became known as Gimblett Gravels. Until the late 1980s, the large terraces further upstream along the Ngaruroro and Tutaekuri rivers saw few vines but in the last fifteen years these have been planted.

Alwyn Corban of Ngatarawa Wines Ltd captures the changing site selection from the finer alluvial soils to the gravels when he recounts: 'Lots of the vineyards then [in the 1980s] were planted in quite heavy soil and were green much of the year with strong vegetative growth.' Lurking beneath the surface of what appears to be a simple process are complex sets of learning about the vine environments of different regions of New Zealand including the accumulated experience of enterprises that had earlier faced similar decisions in Gisborne and Marlborough.

Three nodes of vines are evident in 1960 – Eskdale-Bay View, Greenmeadows and Te Awanga-Te Mata. The choice of these early sites was fortuitous as they all have soils of low to moderate fertility. In the lower Esk Valley are sandy loams with some patches of alluvium; in Greenmeadows, topsoils developed on clays; while much of the Te Mata locality of Havelock North has mainly loess over clays. In all cases, the

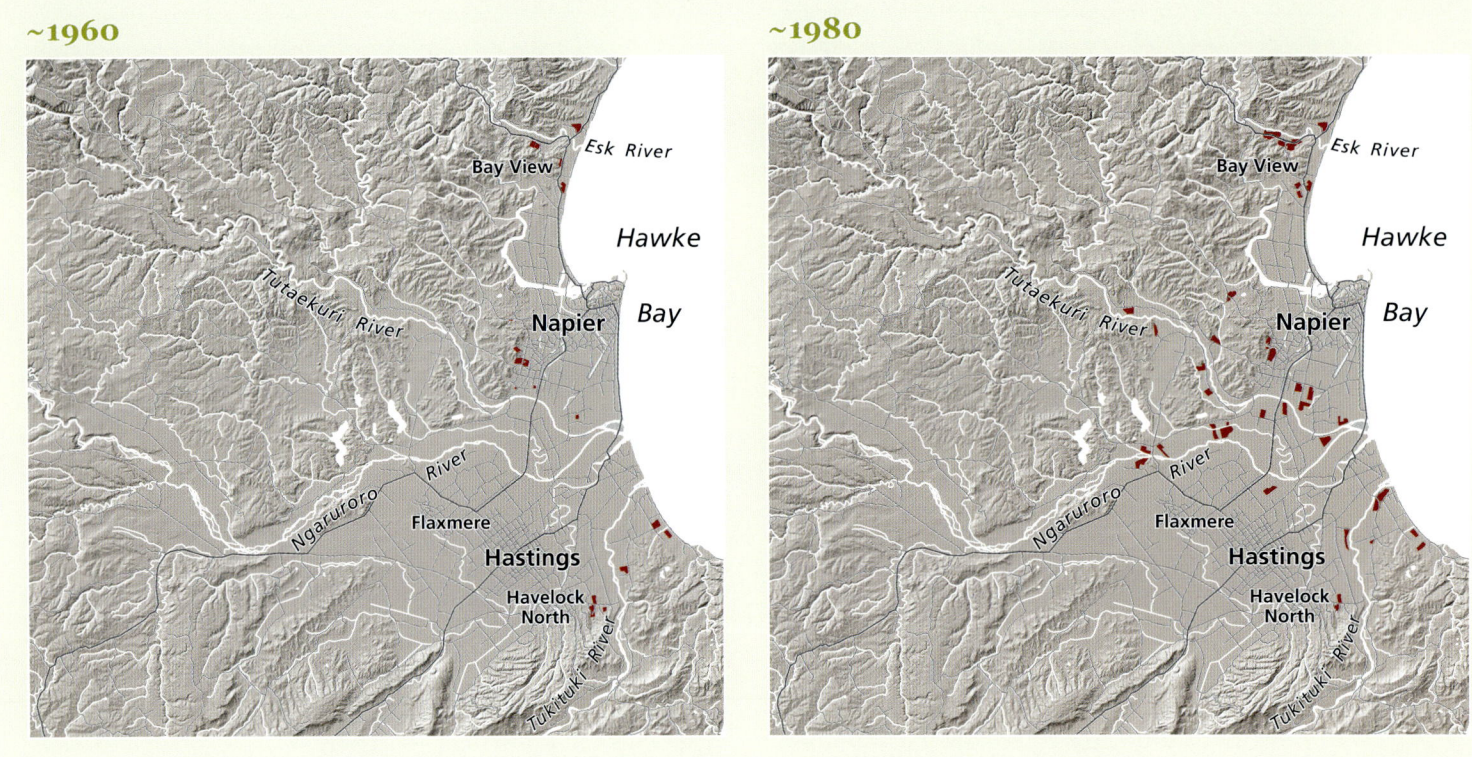

Figure 6.4 Hawke's Bay's area in vines, 1960, 1980, 1990, 2010

suitability of these localities for vines is attested by their long, continuous period in production and the qualities of the wines produced from them, although the vineyards of Greenmeadows have now largely succumbed to the urban spread of Taradale and Napier. Two wineries, Mission Vineyards and the Church Road winery of Montana (Pernod Ricard), were later to benefit from their newly urbanised location in Taradale by being close to their local and tourist markets.

By 1980, vineyards had begun to disperse away from these original nodes and occupy land along the lower parts of the valleys of the Tutaekuri and the Ngaruroro. Planting also intensified around the three 1960 nodes, but initially few vineyards were planted on the alluvial soils of the Heretaunga Plains. McWilliam's had three substantial vineyards in the Esk Valley by 1980, but it also dominated the Taradale-Meanee area where Mission was also well established. Two large vineyards which McWilliam's had planted on the right bank of the Tukituki River near the coast are still in production.

These new plantings did give a clue to the future environments that the vine would inhabit. Along the Ngaruroro River, vines had reached Fernhill and Omahu where Matt Love had planted on either side of the river. Further downstream on its left bank, Nigel

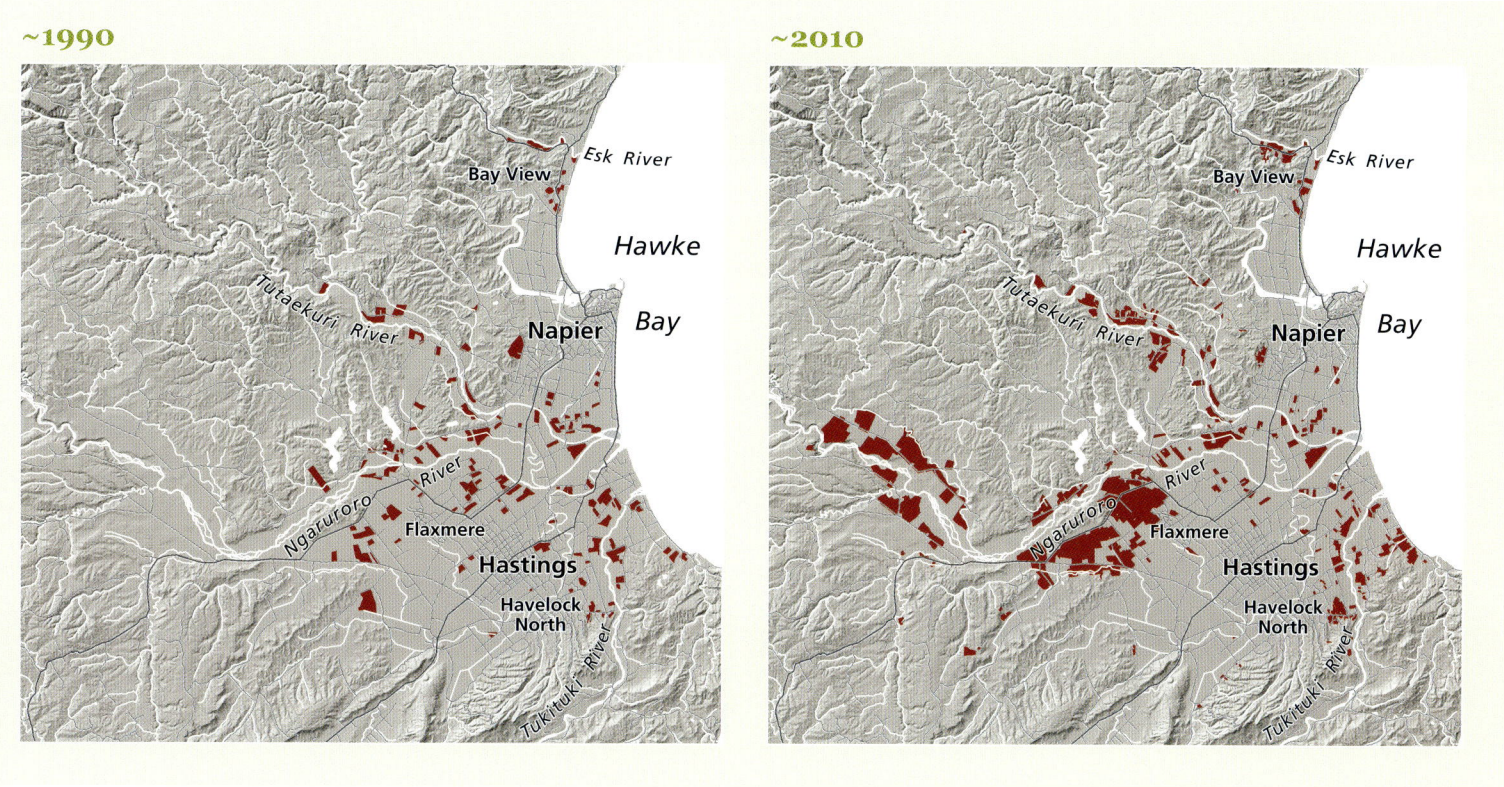

~1990   ~2010

and Mark Read had planted. Towards Dartmore, on the left bank of the Tutaekuri, Ron Smith had planted vines and signalled the emergence of a later migration of vineyards to the terraces formed by all three main rivers. By 1980, therefore, grape growers owned the majority of the vineyards of Hawke's Bay, some of which were on the fertile parts of the Heretaunga Plains where high yields of Müller Thurgau were possible.

The distribution of vines is quite different by 1990. Despite the vine-pull scheme of 1986, small parcels are now scattered relatively evenly over the alluvial parts of the Heretaunga Plains. They are small because grape growers and relatively small wine companies are still growing most of the vines in Hawke's Bay. Vines have also appeared on the parts of the plains that are less suitable for orcharding and cropping because the soils require irrigation or are more difficult to cultivate. Grapes are now discernible on the gravels of Mere Road and off Gimblett Road and in the Ngatarawa Triangle, as it has become known. Both areas have stony and sandy soils where grapes are less vigorous. During the 1980s, tongues of vines also became denser along the lower Tukituki and the left bank of the lower Ngaruroro west of Taradale.

In 2010, vines occupied much larger, continuous chunks of land. Wine companies have been moving towards growing a higher proportion of their own grapes, many aiming to have at least 50 per cent or more of their vineyard directly under their own control, although often under complicated ownership structures. They have chosen to expand on large sites where they could capture the economies of scale of large parcels of vines on relatively flat land, much as had happened in Marlborough. The extensive terraces on the left (northeastern) bank of the Ngaruroro were an obvious opportunity. Pernod Ricard and Delegat's acquired land there. Nobilo (Constellation Brands) bought land on the Ngaruroro's right bank east of Gimblett Gravels. Earlier, Craggy Range, Villa Maria and others had been quick to take up the opportunity to buy land offered by Milburn Cement (Fraser Shingle) off Gimblett Road after it was unsuccessful in its plans to strip-mine these gravels. The vine landscape of Hawke's Bay was transformed.

Interpreting the changes

Hawke's Bay has had a noticeable presence of vines longer than any other region in New Zealand. Indeed, the vine may have occupied a much larger area of land had not Hawke's Bay also been the nation's most versatile and productive horticultural region. It has the natural attributes to grow almost all middle-latitude fruits and vegetables. The region continues to produce most of New Zealand's pip and stone fruits and much of its vegetables for canning and freezing. Heinz Wattie's sources products for local production and for export to Europe, Asia and the Pacific rim from Hawke's Bay. Its major processing plants are here. In the last two decades, strong export markets for squash and other cucurbits have also been developed.

Competition for land is, therefore, intense on the Heretaunga Plains and other pockets of easily cultivable land in the region, and consequently land prices are high. When landowners began to increase their area in vines from the mid-1970s, this 'crop' had to compete for space with others. In the technical jargon of the economic geographers and economists, the economic rent (roughly equating with net income per hectare) is higher for intensively farmed crops such as asparagus or even peas than for grapes for wine. Fortunately, grapes are able to thrive on land of lower fertility where their roots are able to explore more deeply for nutrients and moisture than annual crops. Alternatively, the nutrients can be 'fertigated' in the drip irrigation that also sustains the vines during the growing season. Low to moderate yields are indeed a prerequisite for producing grapes with the qualities to make fine wines. A comparison of the distribution of orchards with the distribution of vines in the early twenty-first century is thus revealing (Figure 6.5). Orchards have replaced large areas of vines on the more fertile, alluvial soils of the Heretaunga Plains.

Moreover, as in Marlborough, the owners of Hawke's Bay hill-country sheep stations, flush from the boom years of the peak wool prices of the 1950s and into the

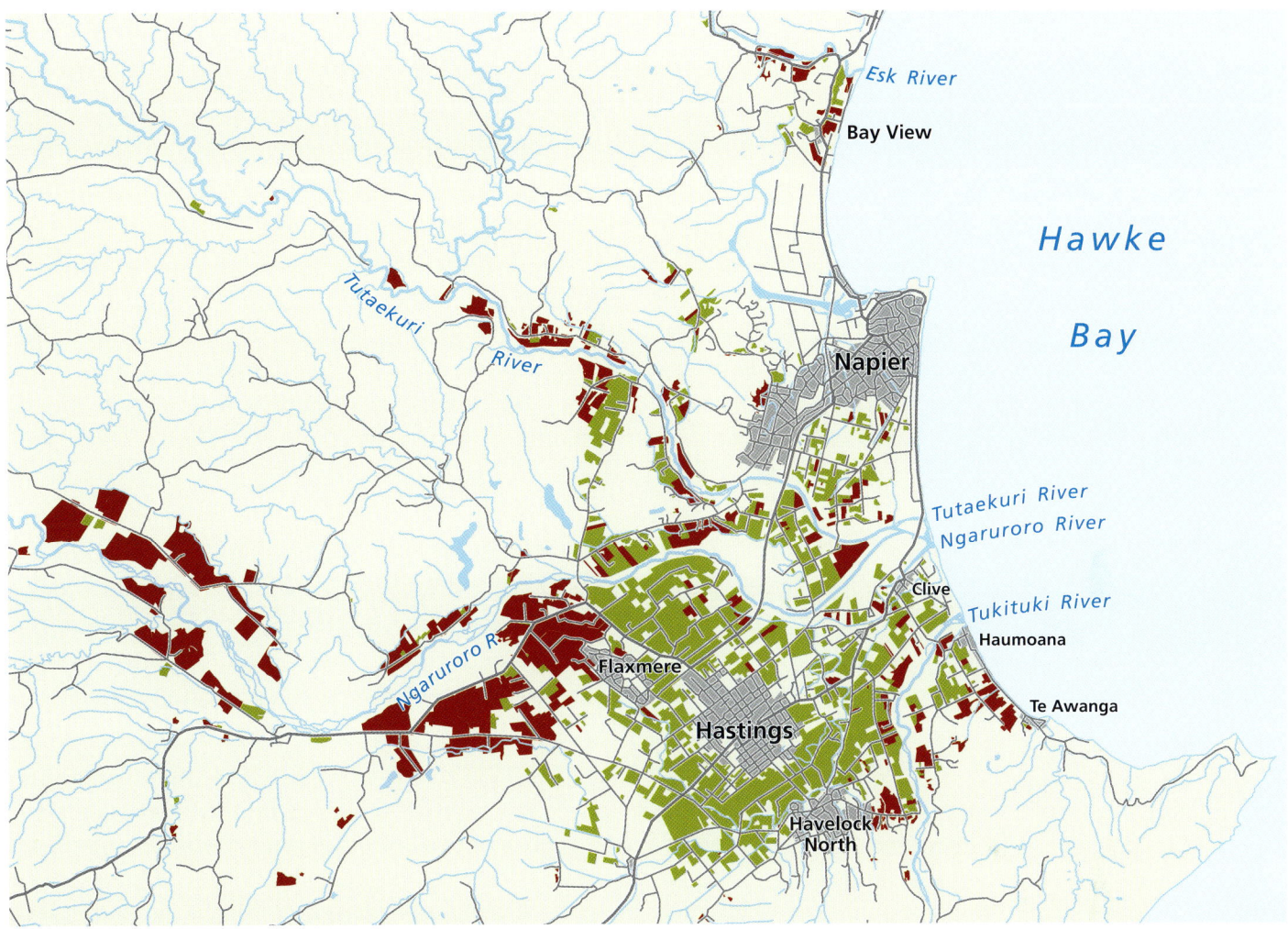

Figure 6.5 Hawke's Bay's vineyards (red) and orchards (green), 2002

1960s, were not going to accede lightly to this new crop invading their lowland pastures, especially when they were likely to be restricted in spraying chemicals within 5 miles (8 km) of any vines. They fattened their lambs on these pastures, although the lambs had to be 'off to the works' by the end of November before they lost condition as the early summer droughts set in. Deeper-rooted perennial crops such as *Vitis vinifera*, genetically programmed to handle the summer droughts of the Mediterranean climate, were better able to handle such conditions, although it took some time for winegrowers to realise this. Indeed, with irrigation, grapes also thrived on gravelly soils except, they thought, the driest, such as those of Flaxmere. State housing occupied it but left the Gimblett Gravels (between Flaxmere and the Ngaruroro River) to shingle mining, the drag strip, and deerstalkers' huts.

Until the 1990s, none of the suites of terraces on the Ngaruroro had vines on them. Morton Estate, influenced by microclimatologist Richard Smart, was the first enterprise to plant a vineyard – Riverlands – on the lower terraces of the Ngaruroro in 1988; Kemblefield followed; both on the accessible right bank, upstream from Maraekakaho. Few people foresaw the much more extensive plantings that were to occur after 2000 across the river on the left or northern bank of the Ngaruroro along the Matapiro Road in the vicinity of Crownthorpe by the large companies such as Montana (Pernod Ricard) and Delegat's.

In contrast, Nobilo (Constellation Brands) chose sites for their expansion closer to the Ngatarawa Triangle on older soils. On the terraces of the Tutaekuri River, Sacred Hill was the first to plant vines in the late 1980s. Te Mata followed in 1993 when it purchased the Woodthorpe Station of the horse-racing Lowry family. This was their third viticultural site. They had earlier planted their Bullnose vineyard in 1988.

The move to the gravelly soils of these terraces and on the plains must be seen in the light of the Marlborough experience of many of these companies. Over a 25-year period from 1973, viticulturists had learned to grow varieties of *Vitis vinifera* on similar soils in Marlborough's Wairau Plain and later in the Awatere Valley. Here, in Hawke's Bay, these terraces have the advantage of a greater variation in elevation further upstream. This presented the possibility of matching vine varieties to subtly different atmospheric environments, although winegrowers in Hawke's Bay have become very wary of frost damage as a result of several severe late-spring frosts in the late twentieth and early twenty-first centuries. The larger producers calculate such risk in relation to expenditure on frost protection in models of their internal rate of return. Some, such as Delegat's, have installed comprehensive water storage and distribution methods through overhead spray lines to ameliorate frosty conditions. In their case these are in addition to their drip systems for irrigation and nutrients at ground level.

When it is suggested that there are other suites of terraces about 200 metres above sea level higher up the Ngaruroro and with good air drainage, informed viticulturists of the region are quick to respond negatively. Yet, on these higher terraces, frost should be no more of a problem than on the lower terraces already occupied. In Central Otago, by comparison, vines are already planted above 400 metres in several localities.

A new era of winegrowing

Hawke's Bay had nine significant wine-producing enterprises when the New Zealand wine industry began to evolve rapidly in the 1960s. The four largest firms – Glenvale, McDonald's, McWilliam's and Vidal – produced about 90 per cent of Hawke's Bay wines. The five small ones – Brookfields Vineyards, Lombardi Wines, Mission Vineyards,

St George Estate and Te Mata Vineyards (not yet owned by the Buck family) – produced the remaining 10 per cent.

Among the large companies, McWilliam's initially had a strong influence on convincing New Zealand consumers that distinctive table wines of quality could be made from Cabernet Sauvignon and Chardonnay grapes grown in Hawke's Bay. It was able to do this because more than 60 per cent of Hawke's Bay varieties at the time were old *vinifera* vines on their own roots. Phylloxera had not yet infested the region's vines. McWilliam's Cabernet Sauvignon, made first in 1965, and often attributed to Tom McDonald, assumed mythical status among New Zealand wine enthusiasts. Chardonnays produced by McWilliam's in the early 1970s under the guidance of Bob Knappstein were similarly acclaimed.

Paradoxically, as well as awakening the New Zealand public to the qualities of wine from classical varieties, McWilliam's also convinced some talented winemakers that they wanted nothing to do with the general practices that were common in many New Zealand cellars at the time. Kim Salonius was one. He describes his distaste of such winemaking when, after travelling to Germany to enrol in a postgraduate degree, he was seduced into winegrowing by doing a vintage in Baden Würtenburg. A native of Peterborough, Ontario, he followed his Germanic sojourn with vintages in Canada's Niagara Peninsula, and Australia's McLaren Vale and Barossa Valley.

Salonius was 'absolutely convinced that New Zealand could produce good wine. I mean the climate – from top to bottom, you've got to find some place that is ideal. And so I was putting together skills, I thought, to run a very small winery.' After settling in Hawke's Bay, he worked the 1973 vintage as a cellar hand for McWilliam's Wines:

> I was just an ordinary summer hand, watching and picking up as much as I could. And I learnt a lot about New Zealand conditions, especially tons and tons of sugar and making wine out of sugar, and water, and dry skins. What a shocking scandal that was! Never mind. I just started looking for land.

Kim's memory of the quality of the early 1970s Cabernet Sauvignons made at McWilliam's is equally clear:

> I thought they were very, very interesting, good – very different from Australian Cabernets. I think it was a '71 that they were ageing in bottles at the time. And yes, it was very good, but he [Tom McDonald] didn't make it really. I mean, Denis Kasza made the wine – and Denis had a lot of skill.

Peter Hubscher was also working for McWilliam's around the same time. However, he applied for a job at Montana because he 'was frustrated with McWilliam's. I didn't agree

Competition for land led winegrowers into the hills and terraces of the Ngaruroro, Tutaekuri, and Tukituki rivers. Sacred Hill (above) and Te Mata (opposite) started growing grapes high upriver on the Tutaekuri Terraces. *Sacred Hill Vineyards (above); Tim Whittaker Photography (opposite)*

with where they were going or what they were doing. And, though I was heir apparent to McDonald, I didn't want to inherit a sherry factory that was based on sugar and water.'

Kim and Trish Salonius belonged to a small group of winegrowers who established their family-based enterprises in Hawke's Bay in the late 1970s and early 1980s. In order of their first significant vintage in Hawke's Bay, these five enterprises are Eskdale Winegrowers (1977), Te Mata Estate Winery (1979), Ngatarawa Wines (1981), Stonecroft Wines (1984) and CJ Pask Winery Ltd (1985). They included individuals with a range of experience from practising viticulture and making wine on three continents (Kim Salonius), to deep understanding of the European culture and marketing of wine (John Buck), to international training in viticulture and oenology (Alwyn Corban), to sophisticated soil science (Alan Limmer), to rich empirical knowledge of Hawke's Bay and boldness and acuity in developing an enterprise (Chris Pask). Not only were they clear about the styles of wine they wanted to produce, but they all showed confidence in Hawke's Bay as the place they wanted to develop their enterprise, even though the main

mentor for two of them, Denis Irwin, was growing grapes in Gisborne. Their influence continues to the present with most still running their own enterprises, although in some cases the second generation is now managing the day-to-day operations.

To this group can be added the Mission Estate Winery, because winemaker Brother John and his successor Paul Mooney shared their philosophy and associated with them, as did Vidal under its reincarnation as part of the Villa Maria group. By the mid-1980s, all were asserting the qualities of Hawke's Bay to make distinctive wines.

These smaller, mainly family wineries, established in the 1970s and 1980s, were important in setting the tone for a new era of winegrowing in Hawke's Bay. They quickly established a reputation for quality red wine, initially based on the Bordeaux grape varieties, and quality white wine, notably Chardonnay and Gewürztraminer. But it is possible to find examples of excellent wines made from a very wide range of varieties in Hawke's Bay. Grape growers and winemakers who started in these decades have the advantage of a longer experience with the nuances of their sites than in many other

McWilliam's Bakano, a blended dry red, and Cresta Doré, a sparkling wine, head to market. *Auckland War Memorial Museum – Tāmaki Paenga Hira, PH-2008-4*

regions. Moreover, their vines are older. It is not surprising that for a variety such as Chardonnay, wines from Hawke's Bay tend to dominate the wine awards and other competitions in New Zealand.

Enterprises in the Hawke's Bay story

Eskdale Winegrowers Ltd

Kim Salonius found his sandy loam soils at Eskdale in the Esk Valley where he and his wife Trish established their boutique enterprise. The house and winery are tucked away inconspicuously in the trees on the edge of the hills. They planted vines on the flats in 1973 and 1974, with their first tiny vintage in 1976 and a larger one in 1977.

They had bought 20 acres of land but most of the time they have had only about 12 acres in grapes. Kim was intent on keeping the enterprise to a size where he could manage both the viticulture and winemaking with minimal additional labour.

He continues to make highly distinctive wines in the European artisanal tradition. For him, this involves minimum interference with the grapes that arrive at the cellar door combined with continuous innovation in his vineyard including changing varieties and clones when necessary. Malbec is one of the varieties that he has favoured in the last decade or so, but his Cabernet Sauvignon and Chardonnay have been consistently interesting and complex wines.

As the millennium approached, the wine industry was rightly proud of coining the name 'New Zealand Winegrowers' for the combined organisation representing enterprises growing grapes (the New Zealand Grape Growers Council) and enterprises making wine (the Wine Institute of New Zealand). In the Esk Valley, Kim had beaten them to the punch. The Salonius enterprise has always had the viticulturist and vinifier wearing the same hat.

Alwyn Corban considers Kim Salonius one of the largely unsung heroes of Hawke's Bay winegrowing in the 1970s:

> Well, at that time Kim was probably at the cutting edge of the industry. He had varietals, Chardonnay, Cabernet, Pinot Noir, just table wine. And I used to go up there weekends and talk with him, work with him a bit and used to say, well you know, 'I'd like to start a small winery', that sort of thing. And in the end he said, 'Well, Gary Glazebrook comes out and says the same as what you do, so perhaps you two should talk to each other.' So Kim introduced us.

Alan Limmer adds his own colour to the story as he identifies the essence of the relationship that underpinned the establishment of Ngatarawa Wines:

> Alwyn was wanting to get out on his own. He had no money. Kim knew Gary Glazebrook well and knew he had money, so Kim said, 'Why don't you go and see a guy called Alwyn Corban. He works for McWilliam's, he's a good winemaker, but he's got no money!'

A graduate in medieval history, Kim Salonius built a cellar door of arched brick doorways, old timber and stained glass. When I visited the winery, a bell tower had been built and only awaited chimes from New York for the sounds of the winery to ring out over the Esk Valley.

Ngatarawa Wines Ltd

Joint enterprises between a winemaker/viticulturist and landowners take many forms in New Zealand. Alwyn Corban and Gary Glazebrook did meet, and in 1981 entered into a formal business association that lasted until 1999. It began as a legal partnership with

Ngatarawa in the Bridge Pa triangle. *Tim Whittaker*

formal reviews at seven-year intervals. At the first of these in 1988, both parties agreed to form a company, each owning 50 per cent, giving them the option later to distribute their shareholding to their beneficiaries. Brian Corban, Alwyn's cousin, became a director at this time, as did Gary Glazebrook's daughter.

The Glazebrooks brought to the enterprise the distinctive racing stables that had been started by Gary's father and 40 acres of their land in what became known as the Ngatarawa Triangle. From the early 1980s, the 'red metal' soils that cover part of this area became among the most sought after localities for vines. These distinctive soils were also the result of the Ngaruroro changing its course. Here, in contrast to Gimblett Gravels, a better-developed topsoil overlies the deep and layered gravels of the former riverbed although it is also prone to wind erosion. The Glazebrook family planted another 20 acres of grapes on their adjoining land and leased it back to the company for a set period. The stables became the façade and administration block for the winery, an immediately recognisable symbol.

Ngatarawa's soil (far left) is a contrast to the Gimblett Gravels only a few kilometres away. Peter Gough and Alwyn Corban survey the vineyard (left). *Gary Glazebrook (far left); Ngatarawa Wines Collection (left)*

Alwyn Corban brought his scientific knowledge, winemaking skills and experience to the venture. He is definite about the value of his education, especially the topping off at Davis where his strong scientific background allowed him to give his full attention to the oenological theory and practice:

> It was an understanding of wine which I wouldn't have had, had I been in New Zealand. You know – what you did with your mates and the tastings you had – that really developed your views on the wines you wanted to make, and quality levels and all that sort of stuff.

Alwyn is also forthright about the learning that was required to get the enterprise operating smoothly. From the beginning their wine was well received. Their original intent was to produce all of their own grapes on their own estate, but their decision to increase production coincided with some difficult viticultural years, especially the hailstorms of 1994 that followed a cool growing season in 1993. Both events reduced their yield. They began buying in grapes, but with supply short and prices high it proved difficult. Colleagues in the industry (James Millton, Peter Hubscher) helped by directing small quantities of grapes their way.

Hawke's Bay

> We were always buying fruit in. But we never developed relationships with growers because in the back of our mind was that, well, we are going to be estate grown. It wasn't really till '94 that we made the decision that we would always have some fruit we hadn't grown ourselves, and we should be developing better relationships with growers instead of buying it on the spot market, or whatever. And since then there's been a lot of growth in the winery and that's all been through outside fruit, contract growers, which is the reverse of the industry trend really.

The company's critical decision was to purchase a proportion of their grapes on a regular basis. To do this they had to strengthen their relationships with their ten growers and influence their viticulture to ensure they received grapes with the qualities they required:

> If it was reds, we wanted them to use Scott-Henry [trellising] as a training system so that they'd open up the canopy, get that fruit exposure and then also do some thinning at veraison. Not specifically to reduce the crop but so that we evened up the crop and its maturity, so when we harvested it we're not getting a range of flavours from green through very ripe.

To help achieve such developments, Peter Gough was employed to manage the vineyards as well as participate in the winemaking. When the Glazebrooks decided to sell their shareholding in 1999, Brian Corban bought their 50 per cent, ensuring that the Corban name quietly lives on.

Stonecroft Wines

Alan Limmer had been captured by wine while doing isotope chemistry using a mass spectrometer for his PhD on soil nitrogen at Waikato University. He shared the same lab and similar techniques with John Dunbar who, when he established ways of detecting water in wine in the early 1980s, helped eliminate 'the black snake'. Being students of chemistry, they also had to try their hand at making wine at the Te Kauwhata Viticultural Research Station. It often sparkled. After doing a holiday vintage with Kim Salonius in 1983, Alan returned to Te Kauwhata in 1984 to do a vintage there with Rainer Eschenbruch and Tom van Dam as preparation for making wine from his own vineyard. While at Te Kauwhata, he helped Richard Smart assess the national varietal collection and took cuttings from the Syrah vines in a virus trial initiated by government plant scientist Wayne Thomas. He bulked them up on his own property. These later became the basis of Stonecroft's very successful Syrah production in the late 1980s.

Alan Limmer, like Chris Pask a pioneer of Gimblett Gravels, planted his first vines in Mere Road in 1983, although he continued to run a soil consultancy business until 1990.

A PhD chemist and soil scientist, Stonecroft's Alan Limmer pumps over the tank. *Stonecroft Wines Ltd*

He and his wife Glennice had bought a 10-acre property and house in 1982 opposite the quarry of Fraser Shingle. At the time the only grapes he knew of in the area were a parcel on Mere Road, although Chris Pask had begun accumulating land fronting Gimblett Road from 1980 and planting it in the early 1980s.

Alan's search for land was wide and deep. By the time he bought the land, he had dug to the water table in Mere Road and decided that with 8 to 12 metres of gravel beneath them the vines would be unlikely to reach it. His consultancy work had led him to conclude that many growers during the horticultural euphoria of the 1970s had chosen the wrong crop for the land they owned. He was determined to find a soil–climate milieu where the vines would manage their own vigour with him managing their water supply:

> I've dealt with a heap of orchards and vineyards and kiwifruit places that were basically unsuccessful because you could see that they had soil-related problems for what they were trying to do. They were in the wrong place. I knew that what I was looking for was about the most free-draining piece of land – but then you had the climatic factors over the top of that.

From his Esk Valley perspective, Kim Salonius approved of Limmer's choice of site:

Hawke's Bay

> I enjoy very much where I live – the view is wonderful, the valley's great, the river over there is terrific and I spend a lot of time there. But if I had a choice or a magic wand I would choose that soil west of Hastings.

Alan took his first cuttings from Matawhero Wines in Gisborne and grafted them himself:

> I've spent a lot of time with Kim Salonius and with Denis Irwin drinking Matawhero Traminer and those were absolutely bloody stunning. They were the benchmark wines I think – so I had to plant Traminer. The first things we planted were Chardonnay, Cabernet and Gewürztraminer. What Bill Irwin brought back, the Mendoza Chardonnay, was probably the best thing going… UCD7 Cabernet that was virus free, and the Traminer was UCD4.

He added Sauvignon Blanc in 1984, after Glenvale won a gold medal using grapes from other vines in Mere Road, and began planting his Syrah vines in the same year. His Syrah became flavour of the year by 1989. By 1993, faced with the alternative of staying small on the Salonius model, or increasing scale to a size where he could employ labour, he decided to expand. He turned down the chance to buy more land on the Gimblett Gravels, by then being marketed aggressively, and instead bought 15 acres on adjacent Roys Hill, in a subtly different natural environment where he has extended his Syrah and other varieties:

> I thought if I want to survive in this and do well I've got to be competitive at an international level which means I have to understand the standards that they're up to – and I have to be able to make a living at those prices.

With this extra land Stonecroft reached a scale where the capacity of the cellar had to be increased while at the same time effort had to be put into international marketing. Both happened. The cellar can handle over 100 tonnes of grapes. Nicholas and John Buck of Te Mata helped Limmer open up excellent marketing opportunities in England, and his neighbour, John Hancock of Trinity Hill, did the same in Australia. He increased his prices in all markets, often at the insistence of his distributors.

Despite, or perhaps because of, his specialised scientific training, Alan Limmer remains an intuitive viticulturist and vinifier in the Denis Irwin and Kim Salonius mould. When a visitor from the University of California, Davis was coming to visit he became concerned at the simplicity of his scientific equipment:

> And I thought, he's going to expect to see a wine lab – all I've got would fit in a shoebox – the only thing I ever really measure is sulphurs to try to keep them within a certain allowance.

Limmer understands the complexity of the interactions between vine and wine in their 'natural' environments, uses his science and experience in establishing what he should do, and simply gets on with it.

Te Mata Estate Winery Ltd

John Buck entered winegrowing through the front door of marketing. After studying accounting at Victoria University for a BCom, he immersed himself in all facets of the wine trade for the next decade of his career – first at Hughes & Cossar in Khyber Pass, Auckland in 1962 before he was apprenticed until 1965 at Stowells of Chelsea in London (the wine division of Whitbread), rotating through different mentors including Masters of Wine courses and most of a year in France. On returning to New Zealand in 1966 he was in partnership with Graham Kerr in wine and food promotion in Wellington for nearly three years, before starting Avalon Wines and Spirits with two friends. Contemporaneously, he owned two wine shops, one jointly with a friend.

From the beginning of his commercial ventures, John's accountant and friend Michael Morris has been involved. Michael and his wife June became minority shareholders with John and Wendy Buck when an agreement was signed to purchase Te Mata Vineyards in 1974 with possession of the winery in 1978. Sale of the Buck wine shops provided the capital to get the new commercial venture under way, after which John worked for Douglas Myers who was setting up New Zealand Wines and Spirits in Auckland. He commuted from Havelock North until 1980 when he worked full time in the Te Mata Wine Estate. Vineyards were renovated, the buildings put on the triage table – the sound ones rebuilt, the others demolished.

Hawke's Bay had not been John Buck's sole focus in the search for a vineyard site. He 'flirted', as he says, with Auckland, where his friends Bill and Ross Spence live, even looked at Waiheke Island, and had several visits to the emerging Marlborough region but decided that 'for the style of wine I was interested in, it was clearly too cool' – an assumption that has been proven to be correct. His interests lie in the Bordeaux blends and Chardonnay, a coming together of the two most renowned still wine regions of France – Bordeaux and Burgundy.

Te Mata branded their two Bordeaux blends Coleraine and Awatea. Both were first made in 1982 and sold in 1984. Initially they were both single-vineyard wines, but as their new vineyards – Bullnose in the Ngatarawa Triangle and Woodthorpe on the terraces of the Tutaekuri (Figure 6.7) – came into production they have selected their fruit more widely. Elston, their premium Chardonnay, was first made in 1985.

Bullnose was bought in 1988, with the first crop in 1992, and Woodthorpe in 1993, with the first crop in 1997. Each has a different shareholding. Capital from Wendy's

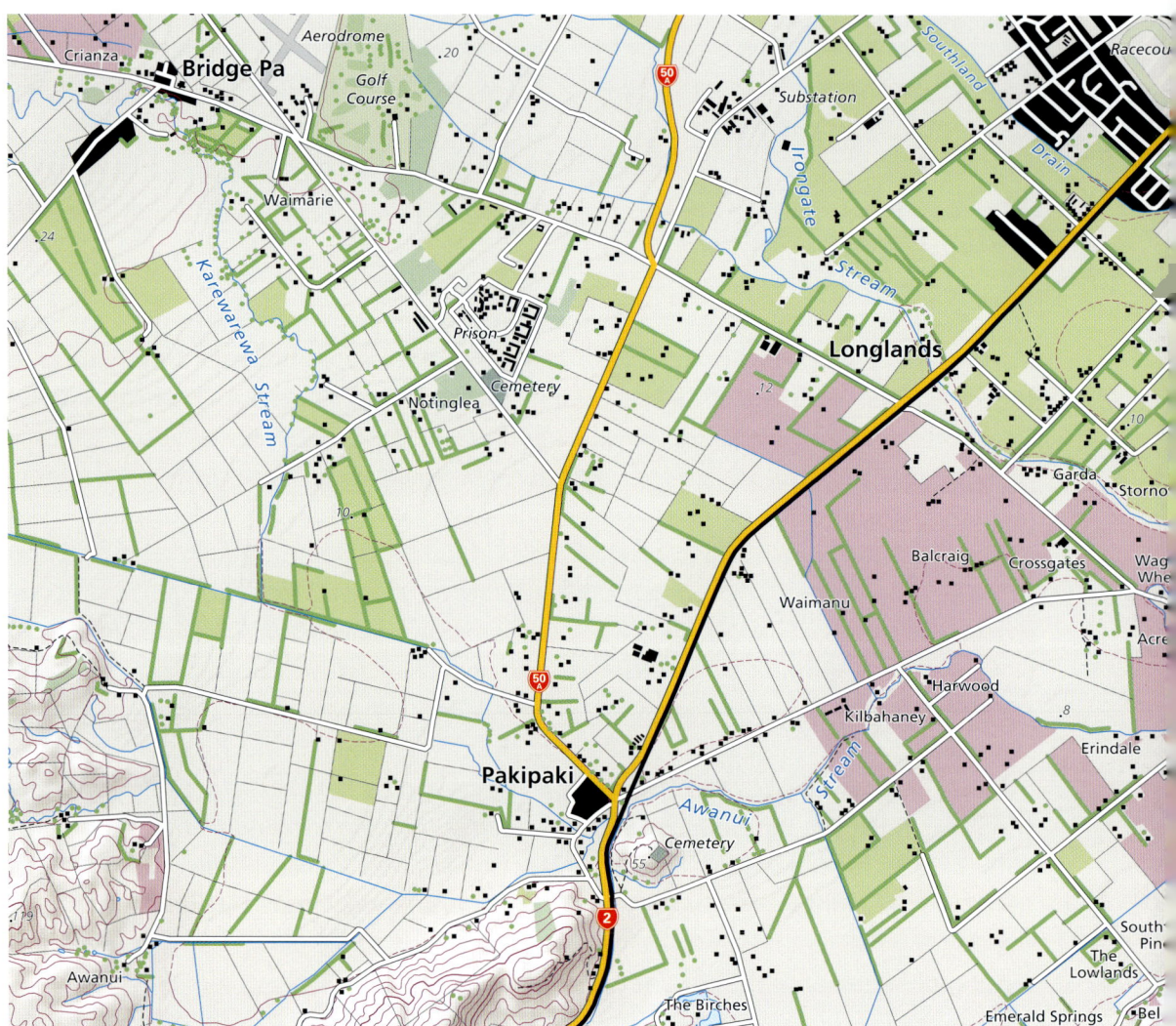

Figure 6.6 Vineyards of the Havelock hills

family is involved in Woodthorpe, although it was refinanced in the early twenty-first century. The name Bullnose is linked to the surnames of two of the vineyard's main shareholders, Michael Morris and skilled winemaker Peter Cowley – a car produced by the English company Morris Cowley was nicknamed 'Bullnose' due to its distinctive radiator. Te Mata has also sold grapes from the Woodthorpe vineyards to Montana.

John and Wendy Buck's efforts with Te Mata Estate are a good example of some of the paths to success in wine enterprises. They purchased a site with excellent potential and a winery that had been established in the nineteenth century. This allowed them to extend the story of the history of their business. They carefully and gradually renovated the

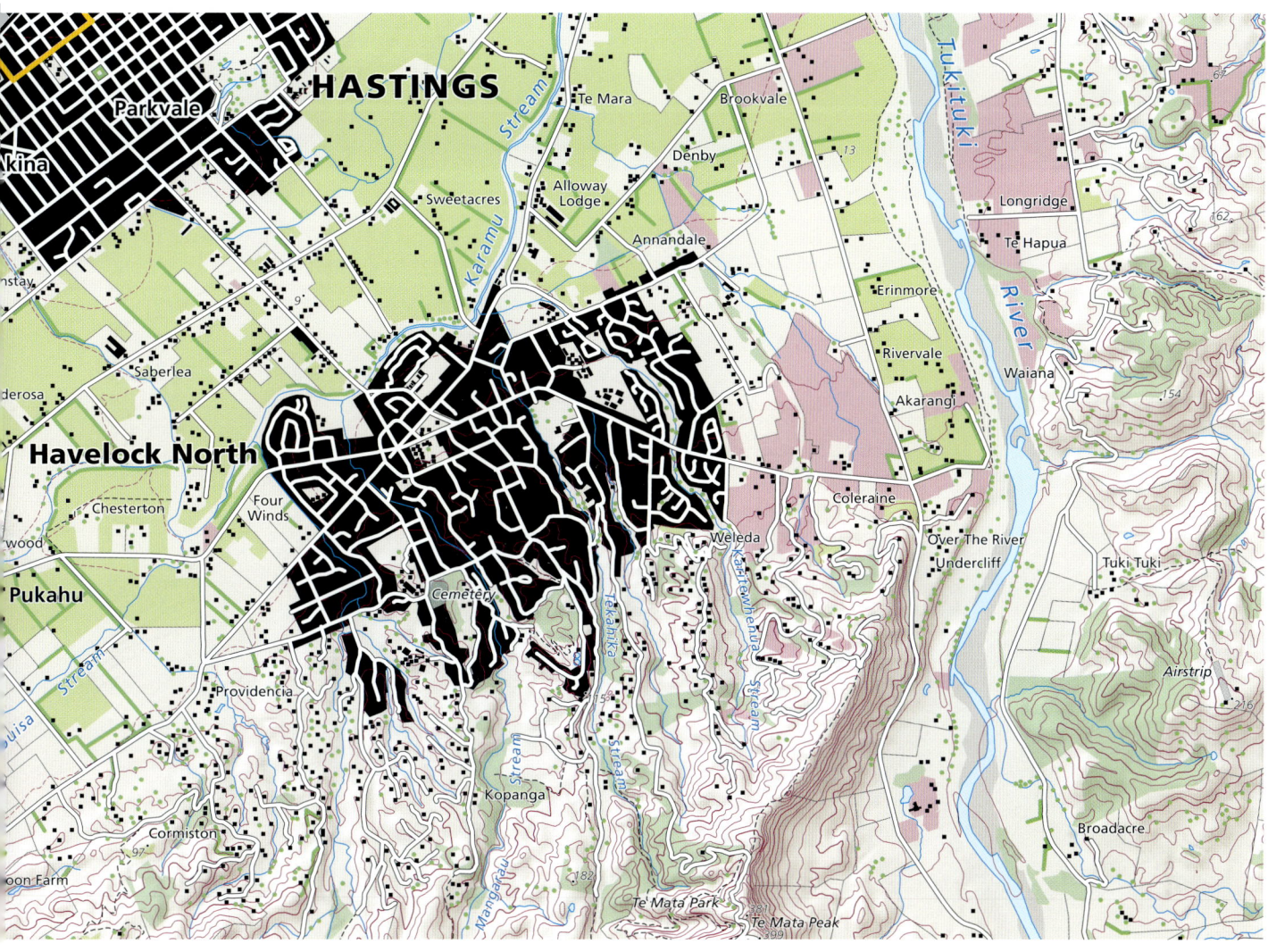

winery and its surroundings to the highest standard in a functional but elegant manner with a welcoming entrance and sales area. Their major red wines – Coleraine and Awatea – were soon at the top of the price range for Cabernet blends and made in a consistent style, as was their Elston Chardonnay. They quickly developed a strong following and a substantial mail-order trade as well as export markets. When the Bucks built their home they had it designed by Ian Athfield, a former neighbour in Wellington and one of New Zealand's most distinctive architects, and set it among their Coleraine vines.

Te Mata Estate could not have achieved its reputation as a company making world-class wine without John Buck's earlier experience in the international and local wine trade, especially his period working in England. It provided him with a close knowledge of the most complex wine market in the world, where companies have an

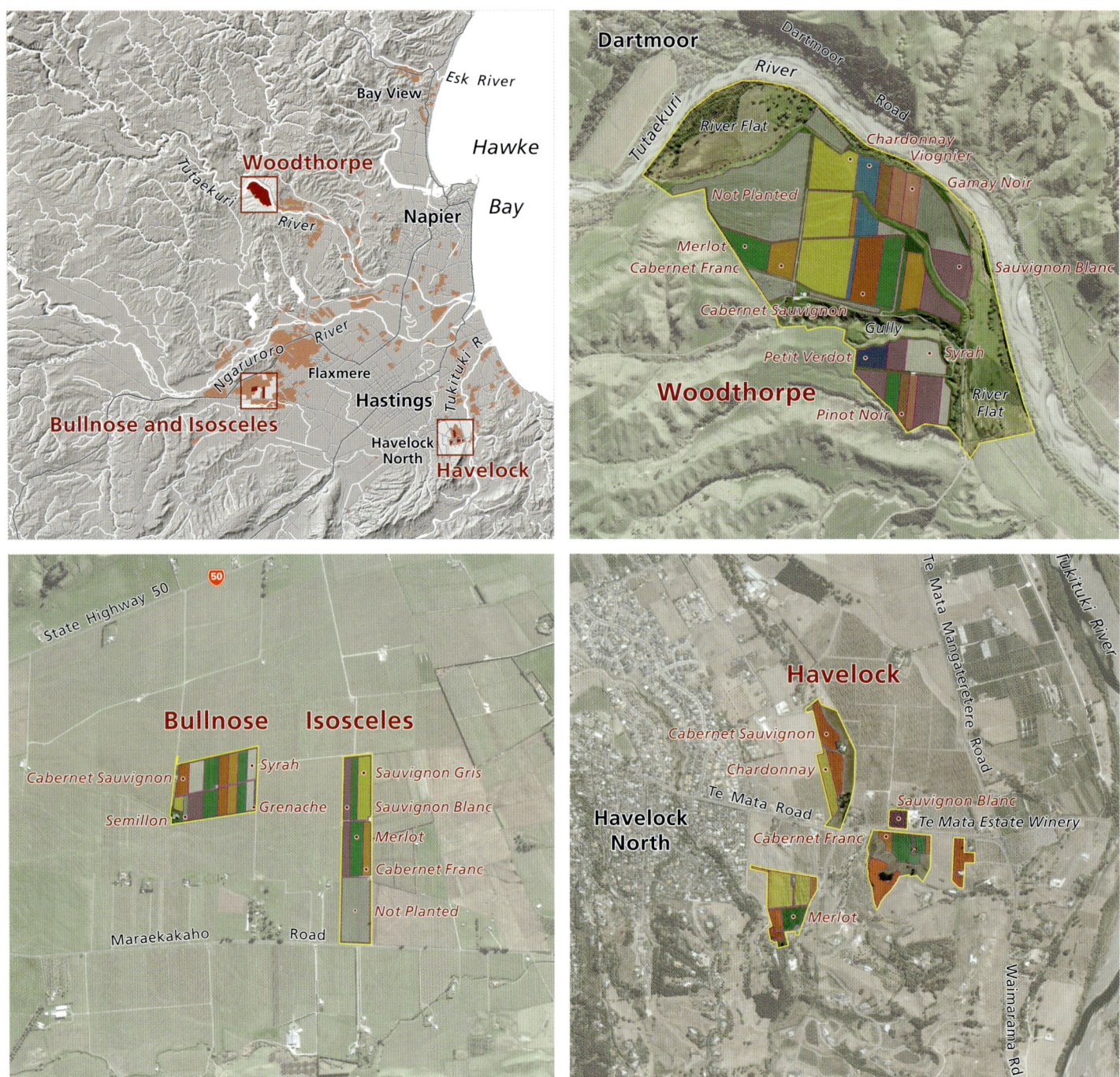

Figure 6.7 Te Mata Estate expanded its landholdings from its base in Havelock North out to the edges of Hawke's Bay winegrowing land in the 1980s and 1990s – establishing the Woodthorpe Terraces vineyard up the Tutaekuri River and Bullnose and Isoceles on the Ngaruroro. Alongside geographical diversification, Te Mata experimented with new varieties. While the Coleraine vineyard in Havelock North is dominated by Cabernet Sauvignon, Chardonnay, and Merlot, the new vineyards are more diverse and include admired but relatively rare varieties, such as Grenache, Viognier, Petit Verdot, and Gamay Noir.

intimate association with European producers and *négociants,* so it is not surprising that Te Mata's aspirations and models are French.

International wine events confirm the standing of Te Mata as among the elite New Zealand wine enterprises. British wine writers selected it for their annual vertical wine tasting in 2007 to 2008. Over the seventeen-year sequence, its two Bordeaux blends, Coleraine and Awatea, proved their longevity by being effusively praised and differentiated by the tasters. In 2008 the Robert Parker representative, Neal Martin, on his first visit to New Zealand, scored the 2005 and 2006 Coleraine at 93 and 94 respectively and the 2006 and 2007 Elston Chardonnays at 91. These accolades did not come about by chance.

CJ Pask Winery Ltd

Chris Pask entered winegrowing in a quite different way. His knowledge is richly empirical. As a topdressing pilot running his own company he knew the nooks and crannies of Hawke's Bay's land well, almost as well as the landowners, and used this knowledge to buy 94 acres in Korokipo Road. He first planted grapes there in 1971 and developed a successful business. He sold his last plane in 1989.

In the meantime, he had reoriented his grape-growing business. After a decade of growing on his Korokipo Road site he was well aware of its shortcomings:

> A lot of the land we planted on had to be tile drained – water was very close to the surface, the land was heavy and didn't grow red wine successfully, and it seemed to me logical that the old riverbed country of the Ngaruroro down at Gimblett Road would do a far better job of ripening red grapes.

In 1980 he began buying land on Gimblett Road and planted his first vines there in 1981. By 1998 he had accumulated over 100 hectares made up of parcels bought from private landowners as well as the Hastings City Council.

After persistent offers from Montana, and Peter Hubscher who knew the land from buying grapes from him, Chris sold the Korokipo block. As he explains:

> Peter Hubscher was very, very fair to deal with, gave me a really good solid, honest price and he was very good at letting me stay there for another year to get myself settled here and that was a very good relationship.

In the late 1980s, Montana were seriously considering their future in Hawke's Bay while increasing the proportion of grapes they grew in-house. Their wider portfolio of wines could find a place for the higher yields of some varieties from the Korokipo land.

Looking down onto Te Mata Estate's Coleraine block and the Tukituki River flats over the iconic Buck house designed by Ian Athfield.
Toby Buck

From the beginning, Chris Pask was impressed by the Merlot and Cabernet fruit coming off the silty, sandy and gravelly soils of the Gimblett Road property:

> The Gimblett Road land is typically shy bearing but very good quality. You don't get such big berries as you do on the heavy clay land, thank God, so the wine quality is very good there.... But by 1990 I soon found a little learning is a very dangerous thing – if it wasn't for people like Alwyn Corban and Kate [Radburnd] when she was at Vidal giving me advice and helping me with some tests and all that sort of thing, we would have had some disasters!

Despite these doubts, the fruit from the young vines soon showed its qualities, the first commercially produced wines being judged New Zealand's best red several years running by *Cuisine* magazine in the mid-1980s. By the 1991 vintage, Kate Radburnd was employed as the first professionally trained winemaker at CJ Pask. She knew the grapes she would be working with because Vidal had bought grapes from these Pask vineyards:

> One of the biggest reasons I moved here was that every year Chris's vineyard produced the best Chardonnay and the best reds that we received at the winery. And I had worked with Chris's fruit in '87, '88, '89 and '90 before coming here in '91.

Her commitment and skill in winemaking, as well as the increased scale of the winery, saw Chris Pask, influenced by Kate, widen the expertise of the group by employing Michael Collins as vineyard manager. Increased sophistication in the winery and in the vineyard was a characteristic of Hawke's Bay winegrowing in the 1990s.

Michael Collins became responsible for the viticulture of CJ Pask in 1996. At Roseworthy (the agricultural college now part of the University of Adelaide) in the early 1990s, as a mature student, he chose the viticultural option because he believed that great wines were expressions of their site and he wanted to understand that more fully. His experience at Penfolds in the Coonawarra and at Vidal convinced him further that 'all the big changes and all the big influences in quality and future development in wine must surely come from the vineyard'.

After discussion with the existing staff he defined his task as adjusting the mix of different varieties in the vineyard on the basis of the last decade's experience of growing on these Gimblett Road sites, and improving the quality of the fruit so that premium wines could be produced from it:

> Right from the start, Kate felt, and I agreed with her, that Chardonnay was the white and Merlot the red that performed best out here. So the reserve Chardonnay and the reserve Merlot blocks were the ones I went into. And our newer plantings, which were on good

CJ Pask's Syrah and Sauvignon Blanc blocks on the Gimblett Gravels.
Richard Brimer

rootstocks and pretty good clonal material, obviously deserved to be dealt to well, rather than some of the old material which had a limited lifespan.

More of the vineyard was changed to the Scott-Henry trellising system already being used on some of their Chardonnay blocks, and a much more aggressive approach to influencing crop levels of different varieties was adopted through canopy management and, where possible, finer control of irrigation by adjusting it to suit the considerable variability in the moisture-holding capacity of the soils on their land. Collins concedes that 'it's always going to be a limiting factor here that the soil profiles are so variable within blocks – but with our new plantings we're trying to sculpture our blocks much more to our soil profiles and altering the irrigation to get control on those blocks'.

The CJ Pask experience with renovating a decade-old vineyard has been repeated many times in all regions of New Zealand. Cuttings on their own roots have to be replaced. Choice of clones for particular sites is difficult. So is matching rootstocks. Most importantly, the only real way to test the initial decision of matching plants to a site is growing the grapes and making wine from them. Even then, consumer tastes change and new varieties have to be introduced. Chris Pask's approach to lifting his business to another level so that it can continue to compete on local and international

Hawke's Bay

markets is to employ experts like Kate Radburnd and Michael Collins – 'because I'm not expert enough to do it myself'. He appreciates that the success of the enterprise comes from the skills of his staff.

Vidal, Esk Valley and Villa Maria

George Fistonich bought Vidal in 1976 and the Esk Valley winery and vineyards of Glenvale Wines in 1986. These acquisitions have paid dividends for Villa Maria in Hawke's Bay and nationally, despite the difficulties the enterprise experienced during the intense competition for market share of the mid- to late 1980s. Among the larger wine companies, Villa Maria has had the longest continuous presence in the region without change of ownership. Until 1986 it owned no vineyards there but processed the grapes from its growers in Hawke's Bay, and from Gisborne, at Vidal Estate. The Esk Valley winery of the Bird brothers of Glenvale helped to build Villa Maria's reputation for making high-quality, single-vineyard red wines using grapes from its Terraces Vineyard, although only a small proportion of the wines vinified there came from that vineyard. With these two medium-sized wineries Villa Maria has been able to process the increasing quantities of grapes grown in Hawke's Bay but also those grown in Gisborne where, like many major Auckland companies, they had let contracts to grow mainly Müller Thurgau in the 1960s and 1970s.

Villa Maria is one of the companies that went out of its way to have good relationships with its grape growers. Such associations have reciprocal advantages. Growers who were ill at ease with legally complicated contracts were attracted to Villa Maria, as was the case with Chris Pask. George Fistonich ensures that his winemakers from the group's three entities compete for the grapes they vinify. This stimulates them to know the grape growers and in turn encourage the growers to improve their viticulture. Through doing so, growers are able to obtain higher prices for their grapes.

Kate Radburnd grew up in Australia and did her oenology degree at Roseworthy in Adelaide. After being interviewed there by George Fistonich the 21-year-old accepted the job as assistant winemaker at Vidal:

> It was a mixture of cellar work, lab work, plus of course there's the overview of Villa as well – we were involved in all Villa's wine tasting, planning, management. From day one at Vidal, we were making Sauvignon, Chardonnay, Merlot, Cabernet, Pinot – although we had lots of Müller as well. My first vintage was '84 and we were making all those wines then.

Rod McDonald, who followed Kate at Vidal as assistant winemaker, captures the emphasis on bulk wine and large fermentations that persisted into the 1990s:

We had six 140,000-litre silos on site at that stage – and they each take about 180 to 200 tonne of fruit. We had one of Gisborne Sauvignon Blanc, one of Gisborne Müller Thurgau, one of Hawke's Bay Müller Thurgau and one of Hawke's Bay Chenin Blanc. The change [since then] is incredible – next vintage, we're probably not taking any Gisborne fruit. All the tanks we've bought in the last five years have been less than 10,000 litres except for one. But we have about 1400 barrels here. When I started in 1994 we had 130.

In 2002, George Fistonich grasped the opportunity to get access to a large parcel of land on the Gimblett Gravels. Steve Smith, who had formerly been responsible for relations with Villa Maria's grape growers, had identified the possibility when Milburn Cement (Fraser Shingle) had decided to sell. At the time, Steve was assembling the viticultural land for Craggy Range, the Peabody family's new enterprise. When working for Villa Maria, he had also been involved in the development of Seddon Vineyards and Terra Vitae in the Awatere Valley so was in a strong position to judge the characteristics of the Gimblett Road site. Like Kate Radburnd, both George Fistonich and Steve Smith knew the qualities of the fruit that they had earlier bought from Chris Pask, although the parcels of land they were buying were on more gravelly soils.

Montana (Pernod Ricard NZ Ltd)

The three large companies of Hawke's Bay – Glenvale, McWilliam's and McDonald's (which merged with McWilliam's in 1974) – were not aggressive initiators in the rapid transformation into producing table wines during the 1970s and 1980s. Individuals such as Tom McDonald remained important figures in the New Zealand industry and McWilliam's in particular produced some striking Cabernet Sauvignons and Chardonnays, but these companies were nowhere near as influential as might be expected from their initial scale and especially the access to markets they had secured through close association with the beer and liquor marketing channels. It was the rapidly expanding companies based in Auckland – Villa Maria and Montana – that took advantage of the surplus wineries that became available in Hawke's Bay. Contemporaneously, the distribution of beer, spirits and wines in New Zealand was being transformed and these existing and emerging enterprises were beginning to take financial positions in the major wine companies.

During the 1970s and early 1980s, Montana and Corbans had emerged as the two largest wine companies. As a duopoly they were competing strongly, because they needed New Zealand retail and wholesale outlets for their increasing wine production. Montana had entered into an agreement with Campbell and Ehrenfried, while Corbans had involved a selection of regionally based wine and spirits wholesalers by offering them shareholdings in their family company. In the maelstrom of takeovers and mergers beginning in the mid-1980s, McWilliam's, the last of the large Hawke's Bay companies to remain independent, merged in 1984 with Cooks Wines, the Auckland and Te Kauwhata enterprise of David Lucas. In turn, this new entity merged with Corbans Wines Ltd in 1987, itself having already had its family shareholding diluted by inviting the participation of various liquor merchants in a private company before being bought by Rothmans then Brierley who also controlled Dominion Breweries, one of New Zealand's two main brewing companies at the time. Corbans remained under brewery control until it was sold to Montana in 2000.

More than any other company, Montana's geography reveals the influence of decisions taken at one time on its subsequent regional presence and organisation. During the 1960s and into the 1970s, in addition to its own plantings, Montana purchased almost all of its grapes from Gisborne and Marlborough growers as well as buying grapes very aggressively on the emerging spot market. Its Titirangi winery had been built in the 1960s followed by the functional Gisborne winery in 1971 and 1972. Montana also moved from Titirangi to its new administrative headquarters and bottling plant in East Tamaki in 1975. With the purchase of over 2900 acres of land in Marlborough in 1973 and the completion of a winery on the edge of Blenheim by 1977, Montana was heavily committed financially and ambivalent about committing to production facilities in a new region until the right opportunity arose.

It arrived in 1986. After being squeezed out of Montana in 1977, Frank Yukich had bought Penfolds Wines and for several years competed aggressively with Montana before running into difficulties over alleged additives in Penfolds' wines. Lion Breweries bought a controlling interest in Penfolds from him in 1981. During the tight trading conditions for wine in the mid-1980s, Lion offered Penfolds to Montana, by now emerging as a promising enterprise within Corporate Investments Ltd. Montana bought Penfolds in 1986. As Peter Hubscher, winemaker at Montana from 1973, then production manager for most of the 1980s before becoming managing director in 1991, explains:

> When we took over Penfolds we inherited quite a few red-grape contracts in Hawke's Bay. And that really started us going there. But it was really to produce good red labels. If we wanted to have a Bordeaux presence of any magnitude, then Marlborough wasn't the place to look to develop that.

Montana put considerable investment into building the quality of its red wines from Hawke's Bay during the 1990s in technical collaboration with Cordier, the Bordeaux *négociant*, who advised it on aspects of its viticulture and winemaking. In 1988, Montana bought 250 hectares of land in Hawke's Bay – some in vines, some not – and began converting it to the varieties and clones it was seeking. One of its important decisions was the type of soils on which to expand its Cabernet Sauvignon, Merlot, Cabernet Franc and Malbec varieties.

Like Bordeaux, Hawke's Bay is favoured by having some local environments where clay soils predominate and others where alluvial gravel soils are dominant. Cordier, its Bordeaux experience to the forefront, argued strongly for concentrating on the clay-based soils of Te Mata and other localities with similar soils. They supported their position using the principle of the *bilan hydrique* (literally 'water balance sheet') – the association of grape maturity with a gradual decline in the availability of soil moisture in clay soils during the summer and early autumn that brings concentration of flavours to the berries. Empirical evidence of the Te Mata soils being able to achieve this in many seasons came from the Cabernet blends that had been produced over a long period by Te Mata Estate and other companies.

Despite some of Montana's viticulturists arguing for planting some of their vines on gravel soils – at the time, and subsequently, some wines of very high quality have been produced from the Bordeaux varieties grown on the Gimblett Gravels – the Cordier point of view prevailed and the Montana vineyard purchases were concentrated on the clays.

The old McDonald winery site was also purchased in 1988 and has since become the winery for Montana's Bordeaux blends including its icon wine, Tom, named after Tom McDonald, the original owner and an important figure, along with Denis Kasza, in the emergence of Hawke's Bay as a producer of quality red wines.

New wineries and more vineyards

The processing capacity of Hawke's Bay took off in the 1990s and has continued to increase rapidly into the twenty-first century. Twenty-two enterprises began producing in the 1990s. They included Alpha Domus, Gunn Estate, Kemblefield Estate Winery, Kim Crawford Wines, Craggy Range, Matariki Wines, Sileni Estates, Te Awa Farm and Trinity Hill. In the first decade of the new millennium a further 30 wineries were registered. One characteristic stands out from this clutch of new wineries. Entrepreneurs who have been highly successful in developing and profiting from other businesses have established some of the largest of them. Such enterprises have shown confidence in the Hawke's Bay region and its wine industry by deciding to commit substantial capital. Two of them, Sileni and Craggy Range, are contrasting examples in the way they are organised and in their philosophies. Both are what New Zealand Winegrowers classifies as medium wineries because they produce over 200,000 litres of wine annually but less than 4,000,000.

Sileni Estates Ltd

As CEO and owner of Sileni Estates Ltd, Graeme Avery is responsible for strategic planning and export market development. Because Sileni was established when New Zealand winegrowing was maturing, he was able to assemble an impressive list of technical staff with experience both here and internationally. Grant Edmonds, formerly chief winemaker for Villa Maria, who had also worked from their Esk Valley Estate in Hawke's Bay, was Sileni's first chief winemaker and had already developed his own Redmetal label when he joined Avery 'to create Sileni Estates from the ground up' in 1997. He has long experience of vinifying Merlot, while senior winemaker Rachel Garnham has a special interest in Chardonnay.

The qualifications and experience of the viticultural staff is equally impressive. Group viticulturist Stephen Bradley had previously worked for HortResearch (now Plant & Food Research) in Hawke's Bay, Delegat's in both Marlborough and Hawke's Bay, and Constellation Brands in Marlborough. Although based in Marlborough, where he is able to ensure that the Sauvignon Blanc crop is up to standard, he also regularly visits Sileni's three main Hawke's Bay vineyards. This trio of vineyards – Plateau in Maraekakaho, Triangle around the winery, and Parkhill in Haumoana – are on some of the favoured free-draining soils of moderate fertility in Hawke's Bay including the former beach gravels at Haumoana.

Even for an enterprise that, from the beginning, emphasised its vision to grow first-class grapes, make first-class wines and sell them internationally, the Sileni list of international distributors is impressive. Thirty countries are covered with the only continents lightly represented being Latin America (Brazil only) and Africa. Maintaining strong commercial relationships with this wide sweep of Asian, European and North American markets is no small task – even more so when they have to be built from scratch by a new and ambitious wine producer. In Roman mythology, the Sileni were the demigods of Bacchus the god of wine – and whether the company brand will become one of the strongest among New Zealand's medium-sized wine enterprises is firmly in the lap of those gods.

Craggy Range

Craggy Range has a different approach to management again. When the company was established, its owner, Terry Peabody, opted for employing a CEO with deep experience in New Zealand viticulture as well as knowledge of winemaking and the organisation of the industry. Steve Smith had worked as a technician with Richard Smart before running the contract vineyards of Villa Maria for George Fistonich. In these positions

Craggy Range on the banks of the Tukituki River. *Craggy Range*

he had the opportunity to accumulate an intimate understanding of many sites in most wine regions of the country that he could put to good use in choosing the vineyard land to be purchased, and other vineyards from which to source grapes. He grafted his winemaking knowledge to this rootstock.

Smith has firmly nailed his flag, and that of the company, to the *terroir* mast. His *terroir* is soils, soils and more soils, backed up by allusions to the climatic character of Gimblett Gravels being especially warm because it is at the same latitude as Madrid. (The climate of Hawke's Bay and the Martinborough hinterland is, however, nothing like Madrid's.) 'Terroir' is also the name given to the company's restaurant. Craggy Range was conceived as an enterprise with its winery nestled under the Craggy Range, east of Te Mata Peak, and with access to 100 hectares of vineyards on the Gimblett Gravels in Hawke's Bay. Its second main vineyard is close to Martinborough in the Wellington region on the northern side of Te Muna Road. It thus encompasses the two North Island regions with the strongest reputations for the Bordeaux blends and Pinot Noir respectively.

The Craggy Range philosophy is 'to select and source the very best vineyards in the country, plant these with only the vines that are perfectly suited to that terroir, [and] bottle them all as single estate wines' – summed up in the marketing phrase 'single vineyard, single minded'. The task seems difficult, if not impossible, especially as someone else may already own the very best vineyards and may not wish to sell their grapes. Nevertheless, if Steve Smith is again able to develop close relationships with enterprises already growing grapes (whether grape growers, wine companies with their own grapes, or grape growers who aspire to also make wine) he may well be able to develop a unique portfolio of single-vineyard wines by sourcing grapes from specially chosen sites.

Culture and viticulture

Setting up such enterprises as Sileni and Craggy Range would have been much more difficult without the groundwork of the first wave of the pioneering table wine enterprises of Hawke's Bay and elsewhere in New Zealand. These pioneers developed their own enterprises from scratch with few local models to draw on while contemporaneously experimenting in the vineyard, cellar, and national and international markets. They initially had the advantage of a rapidly growing New Zealand market consisting of people seduced into wine drinking by the approachable Müller Thurgaus of the 1970s and 1980s. Soon, wine aficionados sought new grape varieties and local wines with more subtlety, depth and style. Many first found them in the varietal wines and Bordeaux blends of Hawke's Bay. At the same time, Marlborough was gearing up to attract new, local and international wine drinkers to its Sauvignon Blanc that was to dominate planting in vineyards, and consumption of New Zealand wine, locally and internationally into the twenty-first century.

The wine industry has a reputation for testing the skills of entrepreneurs who enter it from other avenues. The reasons are less frequently explored but are undoubtedly related to the importance of understanding the culture of wine as well as viticultural and winemaking practices as they influence the qualities of the grapes that are expressed in the final wines. A culture that incorporates the very essence of the place where the grapes and wine are produced gives an authenticity to the wine that is difficult to replicate and takes time to acquire. Having all of the technical parts right may not be sufficient in itself. Enterprises such as Sileni and Craggy Range will be interesting to observe as they, and their vines, reach adolescence and maturity. During times when the world economy is in disarray they, like all wine enterprises, will be tested.

Gimblett Gravels

The evolution of the Gimblett Gravels area in Hawke's Bay illustrates the complex set of interactions among the natural attributes of places and the strategic efforts by producers to capitalise on these attributes to make their own places even more renowned. Like many of New Zealand's eastern coastal lowlands, the Heretaunga Plains has its share of gravels derived from greywacke. The gravels around Gimblett Road were deposited mainly by the Ngaruroro River over tens of thousands of years. When it changed course late in the nineteenth century, these gravels became a dry, relatively infertile plain in which orchardists and market gardeners were little interested. The Limmer family enterprise, Stonecroft, was the only winery sited on it until Fraser Shingle made its move.

Fraser Shingle, a division of Milburn New Zealand Ltd, planned to strip mine the Gimblett Gravels for shingle for roading and concrete. Alan Limmer fought their plans, initially alone but gradually gathering support, notably from John Buck, chairman of the Wine Institute of New Zealand at the time, and soon joined by the institute and its legal advisors. In the New Zealand planning legislation and case law of the 1980s, protecting agricultural land in the district schemes of New Zealand local authorities was largely confined to those parcels with the qualities to produce food. Coarse, dry gravels appeared to have little potential for producing food crops, so the legal arguments in this dispute traversed new ground. Fraser Shingle finally lost the case – an outcome that contributed to the resolve of New Zealand Winegrowers to protect their rights in similar circumstances such as the encroachment of urban activities onto viticultural land.

Paradoxically, the saving of the gravels increased the demand for these soils. The qualities that such soils can bring to wine had become more widely recognised, partly from the Marlborough experience in growing vines on a wide range of stony soils. In addition, the stony, coastal soils of the Esk Valley and the Te Awanga area of Hawke's Bay as well as the gravel terraces associated with the rivers of the region were producing interesting wines. Steve Smith of Craggy Range and George Fistonich of Villa Maria along with firms such as Babich, Delegat's, CJ Pask and others acquired substantial areas of land in the locality of Gimblett Gravels. It has since become the largest area planted continuously in grapes in the North Island and a key source for the varieties contributing to the Bordeaux blends.

Stimulated by Steve Smith's enthusiasm, and supported by the marketing manager of CJ Pask at the time, the group set about increasing the profile of Gimblett Gravels and consolidating its reputation for producing fine wines, especially those from the Bordeaux varieties. They initially wished to establish a geographical indication within the legislation that was developing internationally, including in New Zealand. The group's legal definition of the locality used the physical boundary of the gravels – an extremely difficult, if not impossible, distinction to make, and essentially an ownership and political decision, rather than one based on wider criteria. Unlike the French appellation system, and similar legislation on geographic indications, it included no limitations on production levels, or the varieties of vines to be grown.

In a compromise solution the producers within the boundary of the Gimblett Gravels, in discussion with New Zealand Winegrowers, decided to adopt the name as a trademark rather than as a geographical indication. Membership was voluntary and initially included a subscription for participation in publicity and promotional events. It evolved into levies on grapes using the special 'Gimblett Gravels' label that the members devised. As Jim Hamilton, one of the most experienced viticulturists in the country and a Hawke's Bay resident as well as vineyard owner and manager, said at the time of the legal battle over this unique area: 'It's such an incredible shame to dig a bloody big hole and ruin it forever.' Without the efforts of Alan Limmer and New Zealand Winegrowers, Fraser Shingle would have dug that hole.

Central (or Southern?) Hawke's Bay

In the last decade the potential of land in Central Hawke's Bay, south of the Heretaunga Plains, has been demonstrated with wines of distinction being made from a variety of sites. Among the most promising are the loess-covered hills with limestone underlying them that occur intermittently from the hills immediately south of the Heretaunga Plains right through to the Wairarapa. Rosie Butler and her husband Roger Tynan have established a successful vineyard and winery on Butler family land about 10 kilometres west of Waipawa. It adjoins a limestone quarry and is on well-developed soils overlying limestone.

From this small enterprise, evocatively named Lime Rock, Rosie, formerly a winemaker for Montana and with considerable experience in Australia, has made distinctive wines. The Sauvignon Blanc from this vineyard has characteristics reminiscent of Marlborough rather than Hawke's Bay. These probably relate to the greater range of temperature in Central Hawke's Bay than on the Heretaunga Plains where maritime influences penetrate further inland. Their Pinot Noir is more similar to those of the Wairarapa than many originating from Hawke's Bay, while their Riesling combines richness and austerity on the palate. The bouquet of this wine promises and delivers much. These wines suggest that Central Hawke's Bay has different environmental nuances from the vineyards further north. Roger and Rosie are still learning about them.

Lime Rock is not the first vineyard to grow grapes in this geographically rather awkwardly named region. During the 1980s, both Gary and Malcolm Johansen planted vines near Takapau and the late Sir Richard Harrison planted an experimental block of vines on his farm further to the west. This encouraged John and Jo Ashworth to plant Pinot Noir, Pinot Gris, Riesling and Gewürztraminer on their Takapau sheep and beef farm, with the result that John became more interested in the vines than pastoral farming. Just south of Waipukurau, on the Pukekora Hill, Max, Anabelle and Kate

With a climate closer to Marlborough or Wairarapa, Lime Rock has developed distinctive wines in Central Hawke's Bay. *Lime Rock Wines Ltd*

Norman have established a hillside vineyard of Pinot Noir, Merlot and Chardonnay on the site of a former sanatorium. At Ongaonga to the west more Normans (Kate and Roland) are operating the Tukipo River Estate, initially supplying Sileni Estate with Chardonnay and Pinot Noir.

The successful wines are not confined to those on limestone. At Porangahau close to the east coast of Central Hawke's Bay, the Mouats have established a substantial vineyard on their Mangaorapa Station. Part of their farm has a soil derived from argillite that is free draining but with good moisture retention. Pinot Noir and Sauvignon Blanc grapes from here have established an excellent reputation. The 2600-hectare station has 175 hectares of argillite soils and it looks as though more of these may be developed for viticulture and financed through sale of some of the remaining land.

For more than a decade, two of the most respected and experienced winemakers in Hawke's Bay – John Hancock and Alan Limmer – have been enthusiastic about the potential of Central Hawke's Bay. Limmer says:

> I have seen some outstanding Chenin Blanc, Pinot Noir and Riesling among some of their experimental wines. Absolutely first rate – examples you would rarely encounter within New Zealand. So the proof is in the pudding, so to speak.

In one sense it is unproductive to think of Hawke's Bay and the Wairarapa as separate wine regions, even though their cores are over 200 kilometres apart. They are analogous

Hawke's Bay   183

because both are in the lea of ranges to their west and sheltered from the prevailing west-to-east weather systems responsible for most of New Zealand's rainfall. Both regions also have pockets of land that are protected from easterly maritime conditions. Parts of Central (really Southern) Hawke's Bay have climatic conditions that are very similar to the Wairarapa further south.

It may be more appropriate to consider Hawke's Bay and the Wairarapa as two viticultural nodes with a huge number of sites (totalling thousands of hectares) between them, each with distinctive natural environments. Many outstanding wines will emerge from well-chosen sites within such localities. Micro-environments in this eastern belt are sufficiently distinctive from the rest of the North Island to suggest that selected sites will produce distinctive wines. After all, the villages and communes of Chablis and Givry are more than 300 kilometres apart, but they are both included in the region of Burgundy.

Competition and consolidation

Hawke's Bay is one of the most sophisticated horticultural and pastoral farming regions of New Zealand. Traditionally, many of its hill-country sheep and beef farmers owned, leased or rented land on the Heretaunga Plains and other lowlands between Napier and Hastings and further inland. Here, they fattened their lambs and finished their cattle. Advances in pastoral farming on Hawke's Bay's hill country have transformed the carrying capacity of these farms to the extent that they now finish a much higher proportion of their sheep and cattle on their own properties. Aerial topdressing and other scientific developments in pasture management have allowed them to increase the carrying capacity of their properties and reduced the need to sell their stock prematurely if the season is difficult or find grazing to 'finish' them on the lowlands. It has become less common to see sheep grazing on the vineyards of the region during the winter months.

Vineyards are now a prominent feature of the Hawke's Bay landscape, and competition between vineyards, orchards and other horticultural crops is intense. By 2002, the location of vines showed a distinctive pattern, especially when their distribution is compared with the pip- and stone-fruit orchards of the plains (Figure 6.5). Orchards take first choice of the land and cluster on the clay and alluvial soils that form a halo-like effect around the urban settlements of Havelock North, Hastings and Flaxmere. In contrast, vineyards have found their linear niche along the four rivers of the region and on pockets of land along the Bay View and Te Awanga coastlines. More than 80 per cent of Hawke's Bay's vines are planted on the gently sloping terraces adjoining four of its rivers – from north to south: the Esk, Tutaekuri, Ngaruroro and Tukituki.

In 1988, Peter Hubscher, CEO of Montana, bought land and planted 250 hectares in the red varieties of Bordeaux on the Heretaunga and associated plains. Montana stayed off the Gimblett Gravels, settling instead for the clay-based soils that their French advisor Cordier recommended for the Bordeaux blends. This initiative saw Montana (now Pernod Ricard) successfully consolidate their red-wine production to the large parcels of land on the terraces of the upper Ngaruroro River. Jim Delegat, of Delegat's Wine Estate, on the other hand, bought land on the Gimblett Gravels as well as developing vineyards in other localities of Hawke's Bay such as the higher gravelly terraces of the Ngaruroro River where Chardonnay and Pinot Noir were planted. By the end of 2012, Delegat's owned 440 hectares of vines in Hawke's Bay, including three parcels of land on the Gimblett Gravels.

When the Gimblett Gravels vineyards and winery of Matariki Wines were placed in receivership in late 2012, Delegat's purchased the 61 hectares of vineyards and winery assets for NZ$8.5 million early the following year. With the winery included, this transaction values the Matariki vineyards at about NZ$140,000 per hectare. The predominantly Merlot and Syrah vines adjoin the existing Delegat's vineyards and complement those grown by this enterprise.

The details of the transaction demonstrate the value of mature vineyards to an efficient enterprise such as Delegat's. By acquiring Matariki's vineyard, Delegat's Wine Estate consolidated their very strong position in Hawke's Bay, bringing their holdings to 500 hectares, or 10 per cent of Hawke's Bay's total vineyard. Delegat's did not purchase the brands owned by Matariki but will bottle the wine made from these vineyards under the company's established labels. As one of New Zealand's largest and most successful companies with annual sales of wine exceeding 4,000,000 litres, Delegat's Wine Estate Ltd is well represented in Hawke's Bay.

For almost all of the 1980s and 1990s, the Hawke's Bay vineyard was less than 2000 hectares in area. It reached its lowest point of 1200 hectares in 1989, three years after the 1986 vine-pull scheme. Its vineyard grew steadily over the 1990s to attain its pre-vine-pull area of almost 1900 hectares by 1999. *Vinifera* varieties, including some Müller Thurgau, were responsible for this growth. From the millennium, the pace quickened, and the area of the Hawke's Bay vineyard increased by more than 3000 hectares in a decade to reach 5046 hectares by 2011. This robust recovery reflects the demand for the distinctive mix of grape varieties that are being grown successfully in Hawke's Bay and the resilience of the region's rural economy. The continuing interest of some of New Zealand's largest and most successful wine enterprises in consolidating their presence in Hawke's Bay suggests that this region's winegrowing will continue to prosper.

7

Marlborough

'To the Blenheim vineyards,' said Mr Justice Beattie yesterday afternoon. 'Raise your glasses to the Blenheim vineyards.'
'Sandy, you heard the Judge's toast. He said "to the Blenheim vineyards". You get hold of Montana's public relations man and make the name stick. Cloudy Bay vineyards is a terrible name. Blenheim vineyards it is.' – MAYOR OF BLENHEIM, MR S. P. HARLING, QUOTED IN THE *MARLBOROUGH EXPRESS*, 25 AUGUST 1973

That Frank Yukich used the words 'Cloudy Bay' for the name of Montana's legal entity that in 1973 bought 2900 acres of Marlborough farmland in ten days has been forgotten by all but the most fervent followers of New Zealand winegrowing. None of the vendors had any idea that vines were to be planted on the land they sold to Montana. In 1985, David Hohnen, the owner of the West Australian wine company Cape Mentelle, embraced the name of Blenheim's coastal waters and called his Marlborough winery Cloudy Bay. He designed a label and created such a successful brand that it later enticed one of the world's trendsetters in luxury goods – LVMH (Louis Vuitton Moët and Hennessy) – to buy the enterprise for its stable in 2003.

All grapes going into Cloudy Bay's Sauvignon Blanc, Pinot Noir, Riesling, Gewürztraminer and *Méthode Traditionnelle* are grown in Marlborough. What is it about this environment that gives its grapes and wines, especially Sauvignon Blanc, qualities

Hunter's Wines, Marlborough. *Hunter's Wines*

that attract international winegrowers and consumers? Even the viticulturists and winemakers, those closest to the daily and seasonal development of the vine and wine, as well as the scientists, find that question difficult to answer. This chapter explores the application of human effort in Marlborough's natural environments to tease out the complex interactions between the two.

The Wairau and Awatere valleys

On a clear day when your plane lands at Wellington airport from Christchurch or Auckland it is easy to imagine that the North and South Islands were joined as recently as two million years ago. They overlap. Picton and Nelson are at the same latitude as Wellington, while Motueka is north of Martinborough, and Cape Palliser, the southernmost tip of the North Island, is well south of Blenheim. Because the rugged southern tip of the North Island protrudes so far south it provides some shelter to the Wairau Valley from easterly weather conditions (Figure 7. 1). Even more importantly, the Richmond Range protects the Wairau Valley from the north and west, and the Inland and Seaward Kaikouras protect it from the south. Weather systems from the west also often funnel through Cook Strait, so it is not surprising that the Wairau Valley has low precipitation compared with most of New Zealand and that most years Blenheim vies with Nelson for the highest annual sunshine hours. Their location gives the valleys of the Wairau and Awatere distinctive atmospheric environments for the vine.

The Wairau River has its headwaters in the Spenser Mountains and St Arnaud Range. When you cross from St Arnaud at the base of the Rainbow Springs ski field into the headwaters of the Wairau River the origins of the downstream plains become obvious. The tumbling mountain streams surging across tussock pastures have names like Stony Creek and the Wash. They are charged with smooth, flat and rounded pebbles and boulders that strew the already braided beds and fill the narrow valley. On its course to the sea at Cloudy Bay the Wairau flows only slightly north of east, hugging the Richmond Range that separates Blenheim from Nelson. On its northern bank the flood plain is narrow and the tributaries are short. This is one fork of the Alpine Fault that reappears in the North Island.

When the Waihopai joins the Wairau from the south, about 10 kilometres west of Renwick and 30 kilometres from the east coast of Cloudy Bay, the valley widens. These southern rivers – the Waihopai, the Omaka with its tributaries Mill Stream and the Fairhall River, together with the Taylor River, that gathers in several streams before joining the Opawa – are much longer than those on the north bank. They have formed a series of almost flat valleys subsidiary to the Wairau, face north and are separated by low ridges rising to between 100 and 200 metres. These ridges have mainly clay soils, often

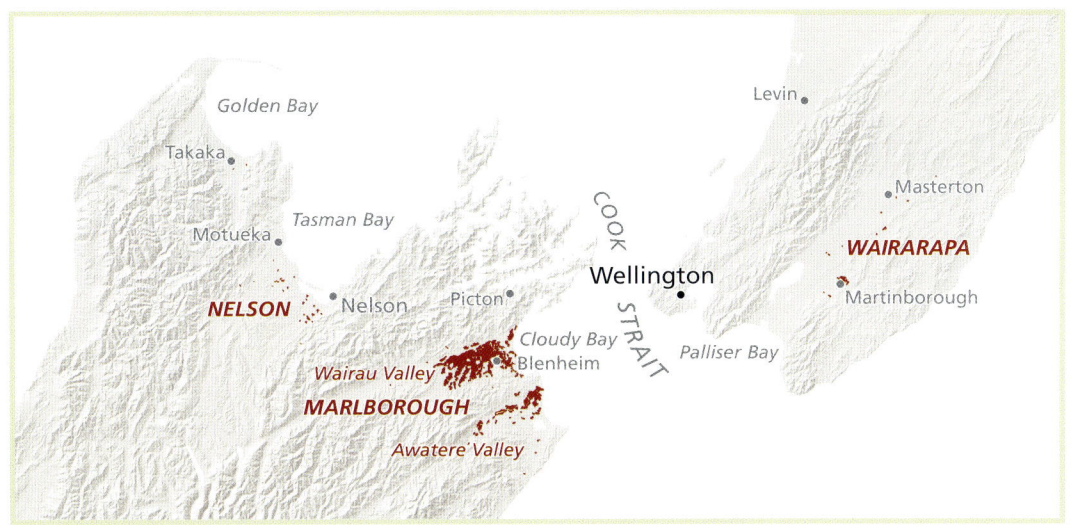

Figure 7.1 Marlborough, Nelson, and Wairarapa vineyard regions in their North and South Island settings

overlain by loess. The valleys between them are a very complex mix of silts, gravels and clay with clay-loam soils. On the terrain of these valleys and the flattish plain between them and the Wairau River, an intensification of land use has been played out. It is as dramatic as has occurred at any time, anywhere in New Zealand. During the last four decades the species *Vitis vinifera* has taken over this Wairau Plain as well as the terraces and rolling hills flanking the Awatere River to the south.

The pattern of streams and rivers of the Wairau Plain, and especially of the Southern Valleys, gives clues to their origins and the soils that have formed here (Figure 7.2). Today, smaller watercourses wander across the flat valleys and plain as if not quite knowing in which direction to flow. Without artificial drainage their courses would be even more complicated. Their current pattern is just one instant in a long history of changing sea level, periods of glaciation and glacial melt, and changes in the types of rocks being eroded in the headwaters of rivers and transported during many sequences of deposition and erosion. Rivers and streams have changed course; parts of the plains have been lakes when fine sediments have been deposited and later exposed. The presence of loess – materials fine enough to be blown by wind then deposited – makes the range of parent materials and their presence in the current soils even more complicated. It is not surprising that these soils and their deeper surface stratigraphy change rapidly, even over small distances.

As recently as 1863 the whole of the Wairau flood plain was covered in floodwater. When the Wairau and Waihopai are in full spring flood, more than 5000 cubic metres of water per second rush past Conders Bend. Before the flood-control works of the 1960s

Figure 7.2 (overleaf) Vineyards alongside natural and built drainage of the Wairau Plain

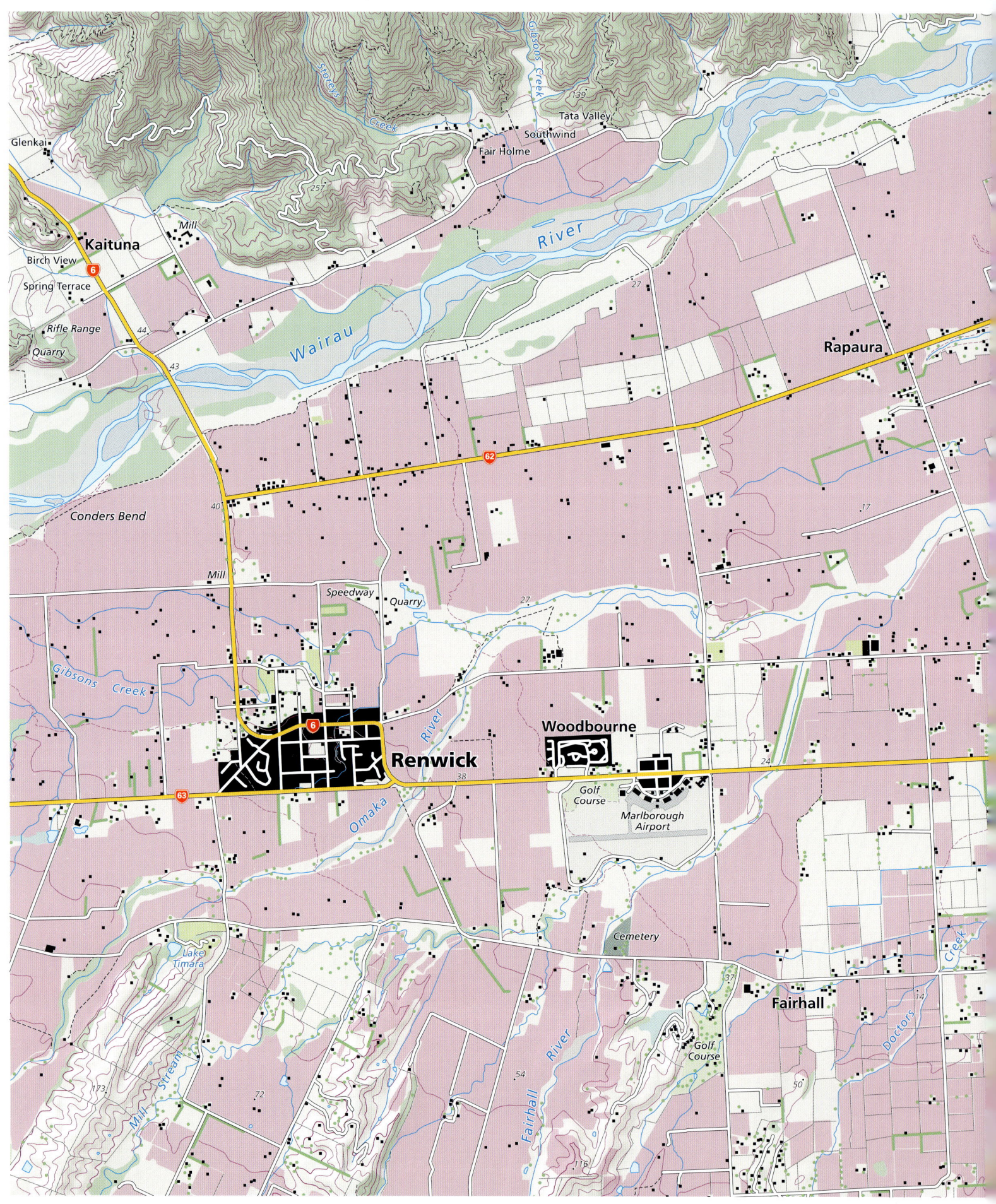

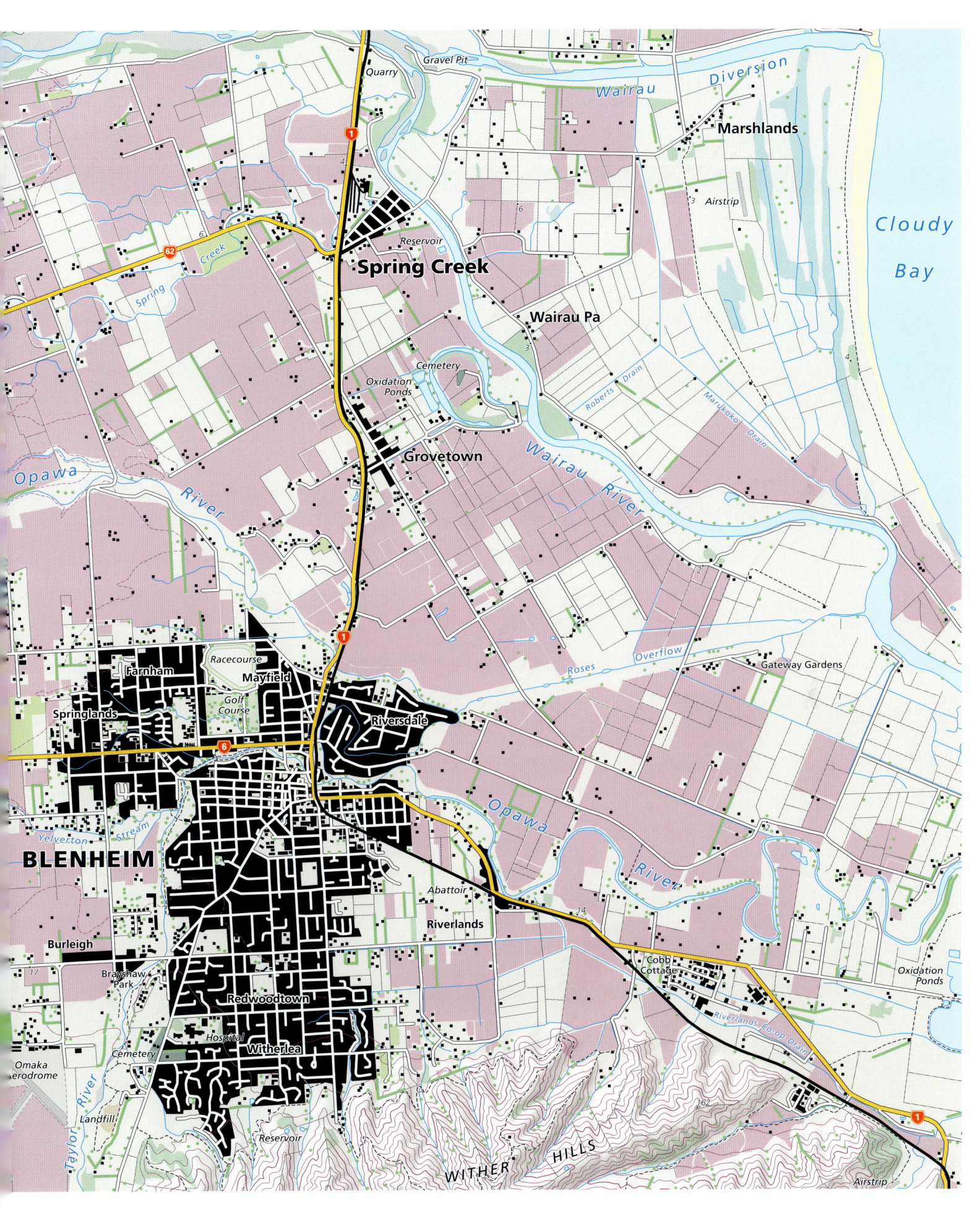

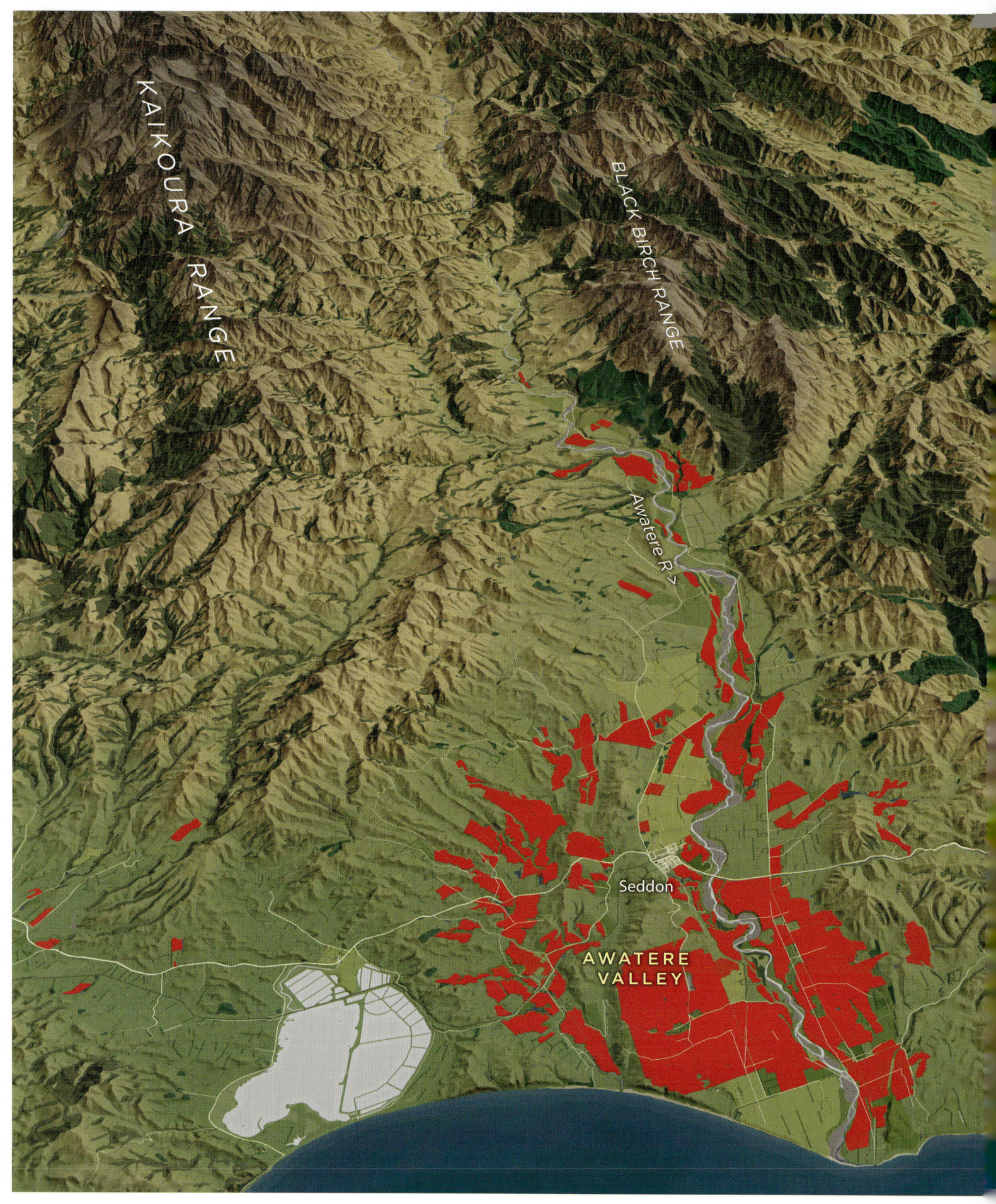

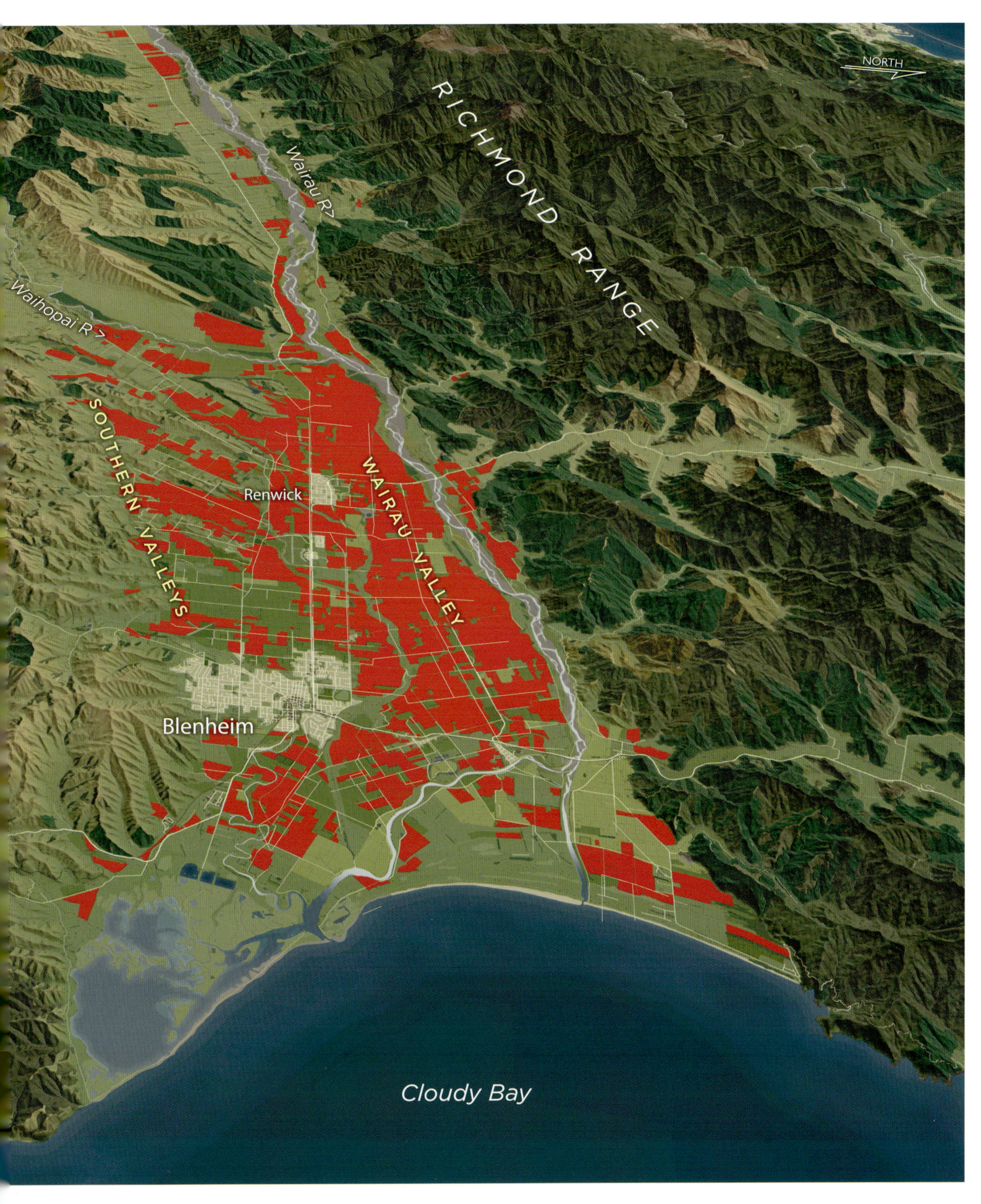

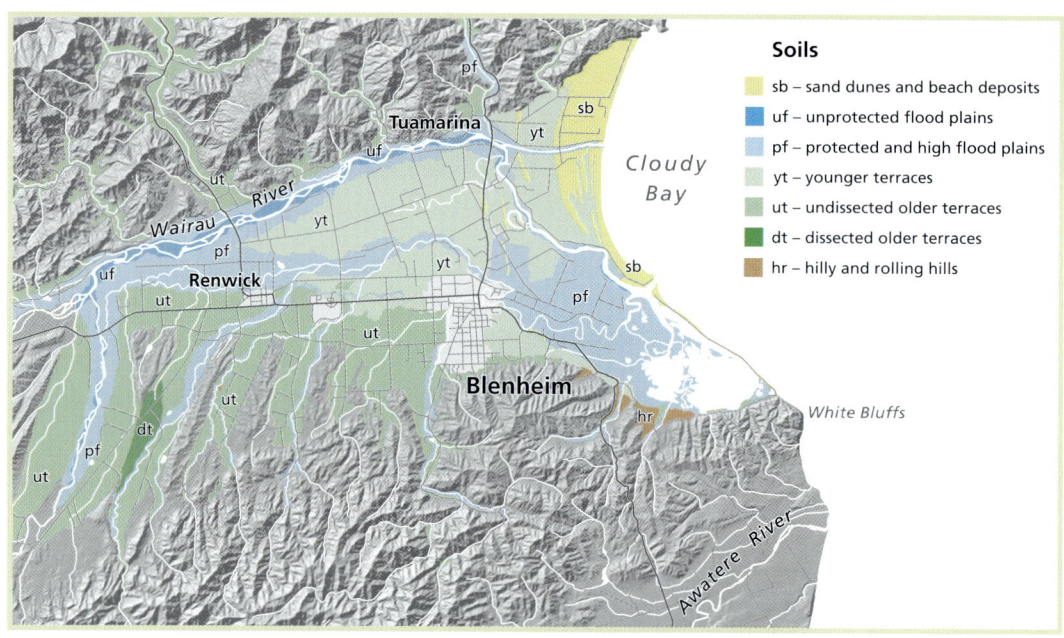

Figure 7.3 Soils of the Wairau Plain

were completed, this water spilled out from the Wairau and along the shallow floodway of the Opawa River and over the plain. In the waning of the most recent glaciation, about 20,000 years ago, the volume of water would have been much greater and the gradient of the river steeper because sea level was lower and the Cloudy Bay shoreline 40 kilometres or more further east.

Coarse gravels from this period of aggradation are more than 300 metres deep, underlying the younger alluvia that are the parent materials of the soils of the Wairau Plain. These soils can be best understood as deriving from the fans of the main rivers – the Wairau from the west and the Waihopai, Omaka, Fairhall and Taylor from the south. From Blenheim for about 5 kilometres towards Cloudy Bay are swamp deposits to the north and lagoon deposits to the south. Beach deposits in a crescent-like shape are also about 5 kilometres wide at the line of the Wairau diversion which runs from State Highway 1 at Tuamarina direct to Cloudy Bay.

All soils of the Wairau Plain are, therefore, derived from post-glacial alluvium or beach deposits. They are young. The oldest are those of the undissected higher terraces of the Southern Valleys where dates on the Taylor fan have them at less than 4000 years. The soils of the higher flood plains parallel to the Wairau, Waihopai and other rivers are more recent and mainly gravelly (Figure 7.3). The large, delta-like area of younger terraces from Renwick to the beach deposits is mainly younger than 1000 years. In general, the alluvial sediments in the soils of these younger terraces become finer closer to the sea. This is especially the case where the recent natural course of the Wairau turns sharply towards the southeast near Spring Creek. Within each of these broad categories up to fourteen soils have been identified and described, but even these do not capture the complexity of soils found on some single vineyards of just 50 hectares.

The Yukich gamble?

Inside the cover of a manila folder dated July 1973 are listed the nine properties that John Marris helped Frank Yukich buy for Montana over ten days and nights (Table 7.1). The third protagonist – and a very influential one – was Wayne Thomas. Formerly a government plant scientist in the Department of Scientific and Industrial Research in Auckland, he was now in charge of national viticulture for Montana. Thomas assembled the evidence that convinced Yukich that Marlborough was the place for Montana to expand its vineyard. Frank Yukich had already toyed with buying in Hawke's Bay, but land was too expensive there, especially when local owners got wind of his intentions.

Their reconnaissance on the ground in Marlborough was clandestine and hasty – far from the meticulous field analysis that might be expected for such a major investment. As John Marris described it:

> There was Frank Yukich in the car, there was Mate Yukich in the car, there was Wayne Thomas in the car and myself, and we just roared all over the place. We went right out to Seaview. The trees looked too bent over there, a bit windy, and they tended to move away from the Awatere back to the Wairau Plains.

Table 7.1 Vineyard land identified by John Marris for Montana wines, 1973

Vendor	Acres	Purchase price	$ per acre	Commission
E. & G. Gardiner	170	107,500	632	2,575
D. & A. Giles	621	176,000	283	3,260
Mrs M. Gill	243	139,725	575	2,897
D. P. Newman	219	109,900	502	2,599
M. J. O'Connor	464	195,000	420	3,450
D. & M. Waldron	463	232,000	501	3,820
J. M. Walsh Estate	338	202,800	598	3,528
W. Walsh Trust	162	55,000	340	1,375
Woodbourne Farm	220	127,500	580	2,775
Total	2900	1,345,425	464	26,279

Twenty-five years later, Seaview, overlooking the mouth of the Awatere River, became Montana's single largest Sauvignon Blanc vineyard.

The area of the nine properties bought by John Marris was 2900 acres (1174 hectares) (Figure 7.4). Montana paid $1.4 million for them – less than 20 per cent of what viticultural land would have cost in Hawke's Bay. In ten days Montana had secured options on an area of land equal to 80 per cent of the New Zealand vineyard at that time. And they bought more Marlborough property later the same year, including the site for their planned Riverlands winery. In the far right column of his table John Marris listed his 'commission' as real estate agent. 'Unfortunately,' he chuckled, 'Pyne Gould Guinness were not paying their agents a commission then.' Had these 2900 acres all been plantable in Sauvignon Blanc the vineyards alone would have been worth about NZ$235 million by 2005. At the end of this ten-day shopping spree the vineyard transactions were not quite complete. Frank Yukich had secured the deals by paying a 10 per cent non-refundable deposit from his own pocket. The board of directors of Montana, who knew nothing about these Marlborough purchases, by now included the Seagram representatives who had recently taken a 40 per cent stake in the company and were to lead the distribution of Montana's wines in North America and

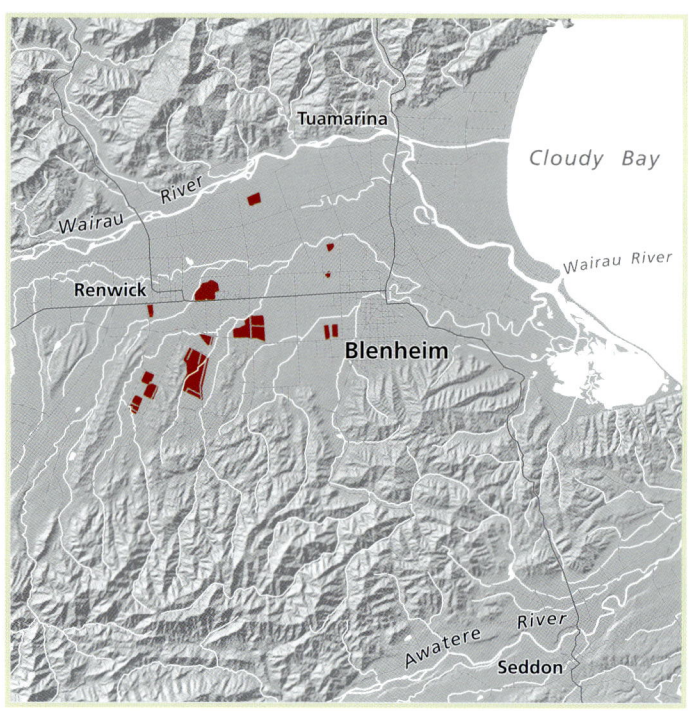

Figure 7.4 Properties bought by John Marris for Montana Wines, July 1973

internationally. At its July 1973 meeting the board refused to endorse the managing director's purchases.

Frank Yukich called Wayne Thomas for help. Thomas was at the University of California, Davis, learning modern propagation techniques for vines so that Montana's aggressive planting programme could be achieved. He convinced four scientists of the Department of Viticulture and Oenology at the university to sign a letter attesting to the suitability of Marlborough to 'successfully grow grapes of the early maturing varieties'. At its next meeting the Montana board approved the purchase, its Seagram representatives apparently convinced by Thomas and the United States scientists. But the relationship between the board and its managing director would never be the same. In 1977, Frank Yukich resigned as deputy chair – the position the Montana directors had squeezed him into.

Prior to this parting of the ways, Frank Yukich and Montana missed no opportunities for publicity. His Marlborough venture was launched on 24 August 1973. Dignitaries invited to the planting of the symbolic first vine on the biggest vineyard ever planted in

Montana's first Marlborough vine planting, 1973. From left, Alex Corban (president of the Wine Council), Frank Yukich (managing director of Montana), David Beattie (former Montana chairman and later Governor-General), Ronald Davison QC (the new chairman of Montana), and the local priest conducting the blessing. Alex Corban seems more interested in the vine cutting than the ceremony. *Dick Scott Collection, Auckland War Memorial Museum – Tāmaki Paenga Hira, PH-2008-4*

Marlborough

New Zealand included the Labour Prime Minister Norman Kirk. Kirk was not available, but David Beattie (Chief Justice and former chair of the Montana board, later to be Governor-General) took his place. Yukich turned on the full Dalmatian ceremony of the time – the blessing of the vineyard by the local priest, the taste of wine for the new vine, lambs barbecued on the spit. Other dignitaries from the adolescent wine industry were there including R. K. Davison QC, the chair of directors of Montana at the time, as well as Alex Corban, who in 1975 became the first chair of the newly formed Wine Institute of New Zealand.

By the end of 1973, Montana had planted 1200 acres (486 hectares) of vines in the Brancott, Fairhall and Woodbourne vineyards. During the dry summer of 1973/74, 80 per cent of the cuttings of some varieties died – not an auspicious beginning for the region that by 2000 would grow over 40 per cent of New Zealand's vineyard and provide 80 per cent of its major export wine – Sauvignon Blanc. Those growing grapes in Marlborough had much to learn. They learned quickly.

Sauvignon Blanc was not the preferred variety in 1973. The special qualities of the aromas it achieves in Marlborough were yet to be discovered. Instead, Riesling-Sylvaner, the cult white variety and wine of the moment (now called Müller Thurgau), and Cabernet Sauvignon (certainly not an 'early maturing' variety) dominated the vineyards planted by Montana in the twelve weeks from late August 1973. The decision to plant Cabernet was influenced by its international standing as one of the primary varieties of Bordeaux and by the quality of the wines recently produced out of Hawke's Bay.

Learning the Marlborough environment

Montana and the first grape growers

Just as Canterbury has its first four ships, Marlborough has its first nine properties and first ten growers. The nine properties were those bought by Montana in July 1973 (Table 7.1). The ten growers were those who planted grapes on their own land in 1978, initially to supply Montana. By concentrating its purchases in the Southern Valleys, Montana avoided the stoniest soils further north towards the Wairau in the Rapaura area. Their choice was not surprising. Until now, all of the experience of the Montana vineyard team had been on the heavier clay or clay-loam soils of the Waitakeres and Mangatangi and the alluvial soils of Gisborne and of the Heretaunga Plains, Hawke's Bay. To provide a matrix for the gravels, the Montana viticulturists wanted some finer materials in the soils to make cultivation easier and to be confident that vines would thrive. Nevertheless, this was the first time that a large area of vineyards had been planted on such gravelly soils in New Zealand.

Planting Montana's Brancott vineyard.
Pernod Ricard Winemakers New Zealand Ltd

Montana's purchases established its own beachhead and influenced the choice of many subsequent buyers and competitors. By the end of 1973, when it had bought further land in the Omaka Valley to the west, and the Riverlands site for their winery to the east, it seemed as though Montana's properties commanded the east–west axis of the Wairau Valley with the Southern Valleys as the core. Their Woodbourne vineyard confidently straddles the Middle Renwick Road less than a kilometre west of the airport. The Fairhall vineyard on New Renwick Road leads into Brancott Road where the view of the Brancott vineyard from 'Rob's Knob' is expansive, especially by the early twenty-first century when vines fill the valley and sweep on to the hills. Rob Muldoon, Prime Minister between 1975 and 1984, became a strong advocate of the New Zealand wine industry. Rural Marlborough responded by informally naming the commanding viewpoint overlooking the Brancott Valley after him.

As its knowledge of the soil and atmospheric environments of the different locations accumulated, Montana sold some land. This included parts of the J. M. Walsh and

Marlborough

Giles properties between Hawkesbury and Brookby Roads because they were too wet. The Omaka land on the Waihopai Valley Road was sold because of concerns about possible frost damage. The Gardiner property on New Renwick Road was also sold.

Local reactions

Montana's entry into this traditional pastoral farming and cropping region was not universally applauded. Within a week of the announcement, Marlborough Provincial Federated Farmers had met and staked out its position. Its president, Mr F. J. Murray, raised two main concerns with the *Marlborough Express* – hormone sprays and corporate farming:

> . . . he drew attention to the restrictions on the use of chemicals near vineyards and their disturbing economic and farm management effects on the lucerne, pea, fruit and grain growing industries in the district near the vineyard. . . . Once this company is established, the second bad feature of this land venture is that corporate farming is going to completely oust the family farm unit from this worthwhile economic venture.

Neal Ibbotson of Saint Clair Family Estate and Allan Scott of Allan Scott Family Winemakers, two of the first ten grape growers, confirm the vehement response of the existing landowners when the scale of the Montana purchases became evident. Ibbotson recalls the chairman of the county council telling him at a subdivision hearing that 'the land in Marlborough had been used for sheep and wheat ever since his grandfather had been a boy and as long as he was chairman it would continue to be used for that purpose'. Long-term Marlborough resident and experienced crop farmer Allan Scott, one of the first of the Marlborough grape growers to export wine to the United Kingdom, captures the concern of the mixed crop and livestock farmers who saw the possibility of their land being bought and planted in vines:

> All of a sudden you had a huge company coming in, pulling fences down, running roughshod over the locals and putting these sticks in the ground. Everybody was laughing and saying frost will wipe everything out, too cold for grapes, and all these funny things. All in all, the wise people were saying it's not the frost that's going to get you, it's the dry weather – the nor'westerly.

A late convert to grape growing, Ian Gifford, maintains his view concerning the original debates and makes a cogent argument from his own perspective. When the Gifford family finally planted grapes on their property in the late 1990s, the father and son chose the least suitable parts of their property for growing crops for seed. The vineyards of the Southern Valleys 'were in a water-short area and we and everyone else were saying that is where the grapes should grow. Anyway, they don't want to be encroaching on this good, arable land.'

Such concerns gained little immediate traction. The mayor of Blenheim came out strongly in support of Montana's initiative and the *Marlborough Express* was full of praise. The boldness, size and likely economic impact of the project received most attention. Montana had foreseen and partly finessed these local concerns by having discussions with central government – notably the Minister of Lands, Matiu Rata – before they took options over the properties they acquired. Nevertheless, the views of Federated Farmers continued to influence the Marlborough County Council.

In 1973, the same year that Montana planted its first vines, John Forrest was leaving his hometown of Blenheim to attend Otago University:

> I flew out of here in mid-February '73 – my first plane flight. We turned right over this property and I looked down and it was one sheep per hectare and brown and stony and dusty. I said, 'I'm never coming back to this bloody backwater!'

In 1988, disenchanted with his career as a research molecular biologist in the restructured DSIR, he returned, and with his wife Brigid, a general practitioner, started Forrest Estate Wines, one of the most successful medium-sized vineyards and wineries in Rapaura. This family enterprise is also multi-regional, becoming a partner in the Cornerstone vineyard on Gimblett Gravels, where John could realise his passion for growing and vinifying Cabernet Sauvignon in addition to his attraction to Riesling, Sauvignon Blanc and Pinot Noir.

The right to plant vines

Between 1973 and 1977, Montana was the only enterprise planting vines in Marlborough. By the time other landowners applied to plant vines, they were considered a 'conditional use' in Marlborough County's District Scheme largely because of the restrictions on spraying chemicals within 5 miles (8 km) of horticultural crops.

It fell to one of Federated Farmers' 'family farm units', owned by Phil and Chris Rose, trading under the name of Kesteven Farm Ltd, finally to open the way to a new cluster of enterprises and innovation in the Rapaura locality by establishing their right to grow grapes distant from the Montana plantings in the Southern Valleys. In early August 1978 the application of the Roses to establish a vineyard on Giffords Road attracted 46 objections including from the Marlborough Catchment Board. After the Marlborough

County Council Planning Committee recommended that their application be declined, the recently formed Wine Institute of New Zealand entered the debate, arguing strongly for freedom of choice for landowners. Montana made a cogent case against the limitations of allowing regulations over spraying herbicides to restrict land-use change and even threatened to send the cuttings it was about to plant in Marlborough to Gisborne. At its September meeting, the Marlborough County Council overturned the recommendation of its Planning Committee and made grape growing a 'predominant use' everywhere south of the Wairau River.

The way was clear for the Roses and all landowners in the region to participate in the Marlborough wine industry. The applications of J. E. and A. Marris (later Wither Hills), N. R. and J. M. Ibbotson (later Saint Clair) and A. H. and J. A. Dodson, plus two applications from Montana, were approved without further discussion. The large companies could now begin sourcing some of their grapes from specialist growers almost anywhere on the Wairau Plain and more widely. The shape of the New Zealand *filière* established by growers from Gisborne and Hawke's Bay was strengthened. In some years, grape growers have since provided up to 70 per cent of the New Zealand harvest, although the figure is now down to about 50 per cent.

This decision of the Marlborough County Council to make grape growing a predominant use had immediate effects on the geography of the industry, especially in Rapaura. By 1982 the area in grapes on Foxes Island, the area north of the Opawa River, was substantial. As in Auckland, Gisborne and Hawke's Bay, competition between Montana and Corbans was enlivened in Marlborough when, in late 1979, Corbans (by then controlled by Rothmans) bought three properties to assemble its first large parcel of land fronting Rapaura and Jacksons Roads. This corner was to be the site of its Marlborough winery built in 1989.

On the Stoneleigh farm purchased by Corbans from A. L. Ferguson in 1981, Sauvignon Blanc was one of the six varieties planted. An alternative node to the Southern Valleys was born. The cluster of cellars on or near Rapaura Road, and from its junction with State Highway 6 towards Renwick, is now denser than on any other part of the Wairau Plain (Figure 7.5). The Southern Valleys saw fewer vineyards and wineries established in the late 1970s and early 1980s, although some were to prove pivotal. In 1979, Ivan Sutherland planted his first vineyard on Dog Point Road less than a kilometre from the Brancott vineyard, as did P. and W. Walsh nearby and the Hogans (Te Whare Ra) and the Roughans.

In 1983, by the end of its first decade, Marlborough's area in vines had increased steadily to reach just over 1000 hectares – about half that of Gisborne or Hawke's Bay at the time. Only four Marlborough enterprises crushed any grapes in the South Island during this first decade: Montana, Te Whare Ra, Hunter's and Le Brun. By 1983 the two important vine-growing areas – Montana's plantings in the Southern Valleys dating

Table 7.2: Varietal evolution (% of Marlborough vineyard in five main varieties)

1980		1990		2000		2010	
Müller Thurgau	42	Müller Thurgau	29	Sauvignon Blanc	47	Sauvignon Blanc	76
Cabernet Sauvignon	12	Chardonnay	19	Chardonnay	22	Pinot Noir	10
Gewürztraminer	11	Sauvignon Blanc	15	Pinot Noir	13	Chardonnay	6
Chardonnay	7	Riesling	10	Riesling	7	Pinot Gris	4
Riesling	6	Cabernet Sauvignon	8	Semillon	3	Riesling	2
5 main varieties	78	5 main varieties	81	5 main varieties	92	5 main varieties	98

from 1973 and the group of grape growers in the Rapaura area from 1978 – formed a belt of vines between the Wairau River and the Southern Valleys and between Blenheim in the east and Renwick in the west (Figure 7.5).

Further vineyard and winery expansion

The expansion of the wine industry in Marlborough to the present occurs in three further stages: the remainder of the 1980s, the 1990s, and the 2000s. In each stage a different geography of the vine emerges, strongly influenced by the expansion of existing enterprises and by new grape growers and wineries entering the industry. In the early 1980s, with neo-liberal reform looming, it would have been difficult, perhaps impossible, to predict Marlborough's future sequence over these next three decades.

Stage one: 1984–1990

Marlborough probably fared better than any other wine region during the difficult economic times of the mid- to late 1980s. Certainly, no other region had a renowned Sauvignon Blanc cellar built in the same year that central government announced a vine-pull scheme to save the New Zealand wine industry. Cloudy Bay, although started by an Australian, found friends in New Zealand because Corbans (Brierley) and the Australian firm Wolf Blass jointly owned the Marlborough Cellars winery. These associations certainly influenced the Rapaura area and Marlborough internationally.

'Mate, do you want to try a real Sauvignon Blanc?' asked Ross Spence of David Hohnen at the Cape Mentelle winery, Margaret River, Western Australia in 1984. When Joe Babich got a bottle from the boot of their car, many lives were changed. Hohnen

Table 7.3: Marlborough grape varieties, 1975–2010 (hectares)

Grape variety	1975	1980	1990	1995	2000	2005	2010
Palomino	-	8	16	-	-	-	-
Muscats	-	20	20	19	<1	<1	<1
Chenin Blanc	-	21	20	16	1	2	1
Pinotage		32	31	25	17	16	14
Müller Thurgau	129	324	405	250	59	10	3
Gewürztraminer		87	35	34	39	66	84
Chardonnay	-	55	270	697	887	1120	1089
Sauvignon Blanc	-	33	211	845	1900	6212	14,611
Pinot Gris	-	-	-	2	37	185	780
Riesling		49	140	217	266	369	446
Pinot Noir		25	44	206	528	1676	1986
Cabernet Sauvignon	45	94	117	250	85	54	28
Cabernet Franc	-	-	3	19	11	3	3
Malbec	-	-	1	4	7	9	6
Merlot	-	-	15	109	94	108	89
Syrah			3	5	3	7	7
Total Marlborough listed (ha)	174	748	1259	2693	3932	9831	19,141
Other varieties (ha)		26	164	367	122	113	154
Total (ha)		774	1423	3060	4054	9944	19,295

was on a plane to New Zealand by the end of the year, had hired Australian Kevin Judd as winemaker, and bought some land opposite Corbans on Marlborough's Jacksons Road. By the end of 1985, the Cloudy Bay winery was built. In the meantime, Hohnen had made his 1985 vintage of Cloudy Bay Sauvignon Blanc in Corbans' Gisborne winery under telephone instructions from Kevin Judd who was making the 1985 vintage for Selaks in Auckland with grapes from Marlborough. Hohnen's grapes had been supplied by Corbans who had agreed to relinquish some of their Marlborough crop provided that in the 1986 vintage their Stoneleigh brand could be made in the Cloudy Bay winery.

By 1989, when the Corbans winery was built, half of Cloudy Bay's grapes came from their own vineyards under the direction of their new viticulturist, Ivan Sutherland, who with Allan Scott and Colin Muir was among the first grape growers for Cloudy Bay. Until 1989, when he started his own brand, Scott was national viticultural manager for Corbans and encouraged Rapaura locals to grow for the Stoneleigh brand.

A third prong to this node of Rapaura *terroir* pioneered by Phil and Chris Rose was the Nobilo/Selaks/Webber triumvirate whose vineyards on Hammerichs Road backed onto the Cloudy Bay operation. The largest part of these vineyards was not developed

Marlborough's Southern Valleys, reaching in toward the Wither Hill ranges from the Wairau Plain.
Jim Tannock Photography

until 1987 when, together with Corbans and Cloudy Bay, they reinforced an alternative concentration of vineyards and wineries to those in the Southern Valleys. By the early twenty-first century, John Webber had almost 300 hectares in vines and was one of the largest grape growers on the Wairau Plain.

Despite such developments, instability and uncertainty characterised much of the 1980s. Corporate battles for control of Corbans, Cooks, Penfolds, Montana and McWilliam's, combined with a perceived oversupply of grapes that triggered the vine-pull scheme of 1986, resulted in no net increase in the area in vines in Marlborough until 1989. In reality, 210 hectares were pulled out in the South Island, almost all of it in Marlborough, and replanted the same season in different varieties. The statistical illusion of no growth reflects the inadequate information from central government agencies in a perpetual state of reform after 1984, until the Wine Institute of New Zealand (later New Zealand Winegrowers) took responsibility for collecting its own data on the area planted in vines from 1989.

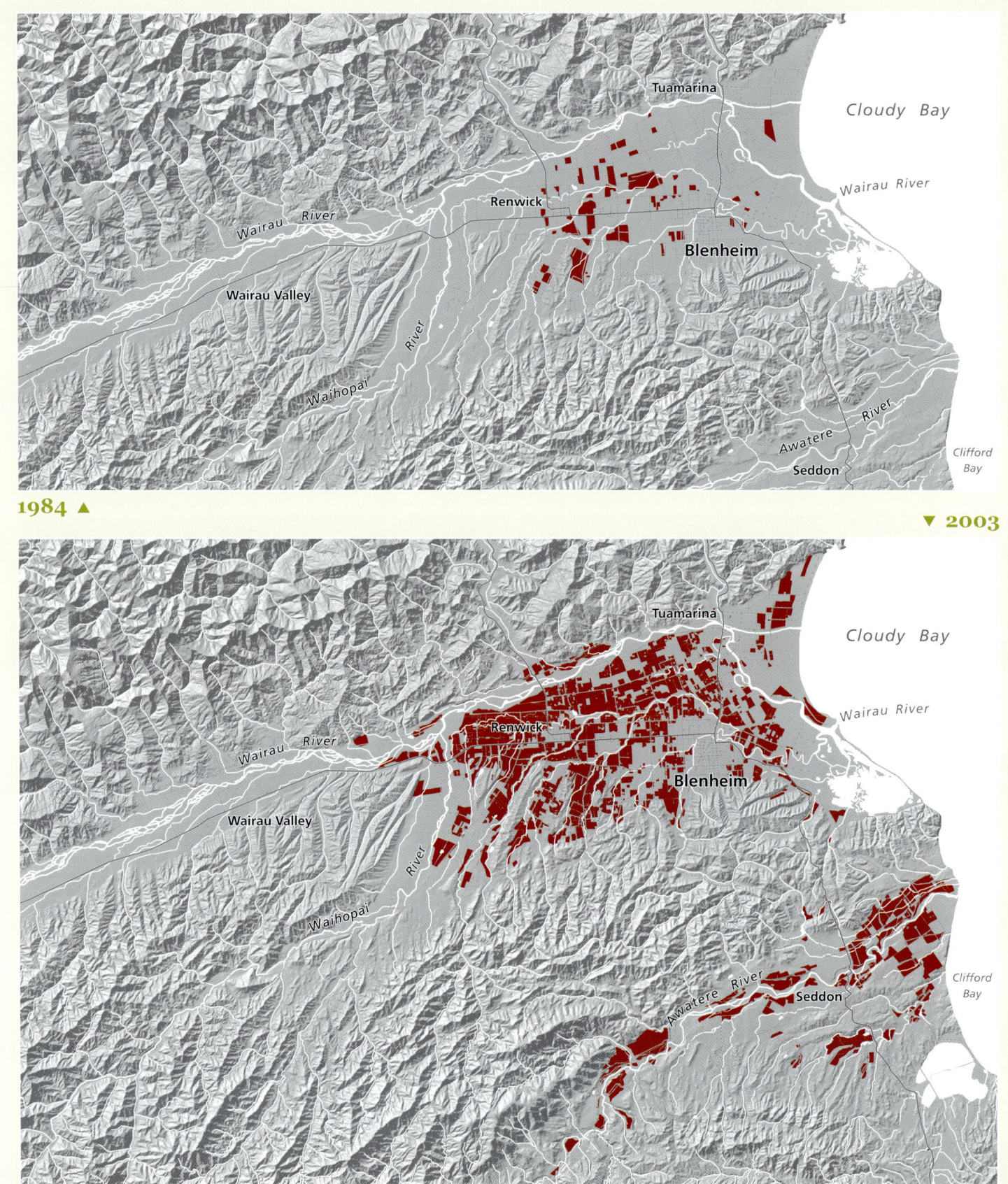

Figure 7.5 The evolution of the Marlborough vineyard, 1984, 1989, 2003, 2008

Tuamarina
Cloudy Bay
Wairau River
Renwick
Wairau River
Blenheim
Wairau Valley
River
Waihopai
River
Awatere
Seddon
Clifford
Bay

1989 ▲

▼ 2008

Tuamarina
Cloudy Bay
Wairau River
Renwick
Wairau River
Blenheim
Wairau Valley
River
Waihopai
Awatere River
Seddon
Clifford
Bay

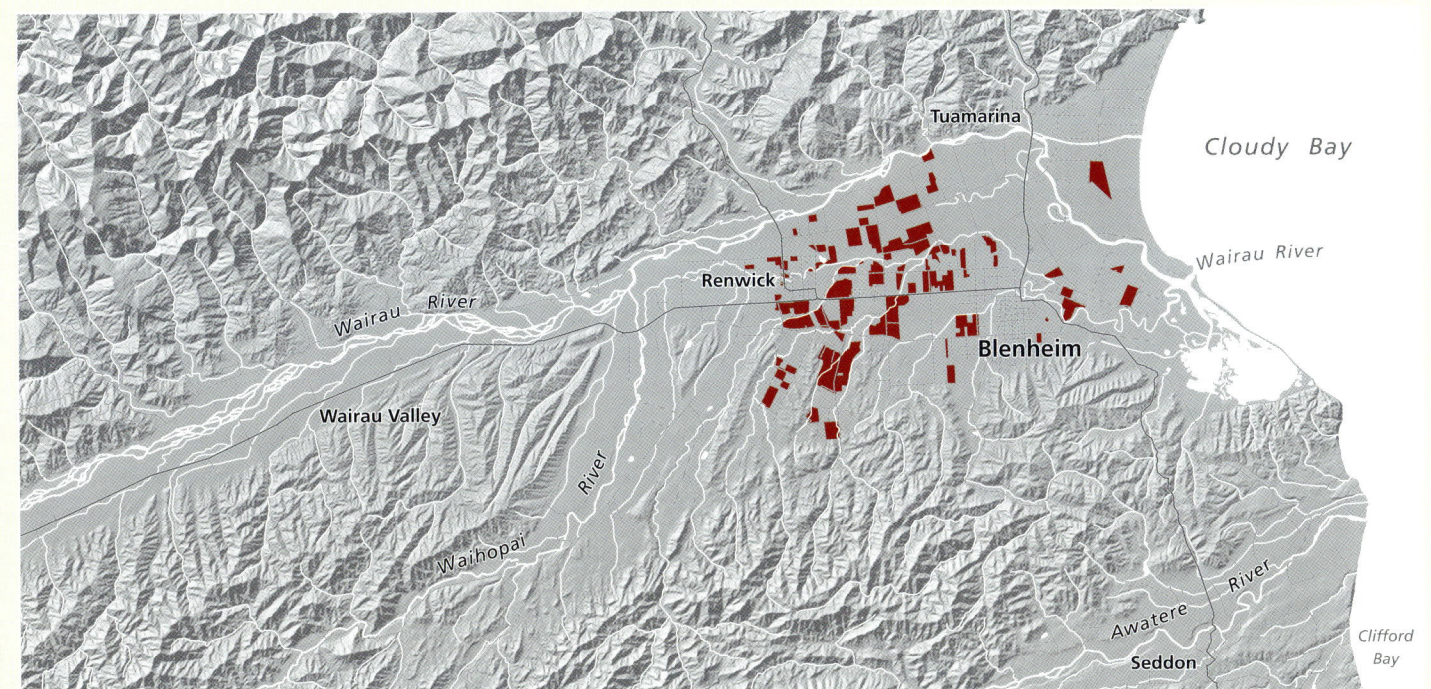

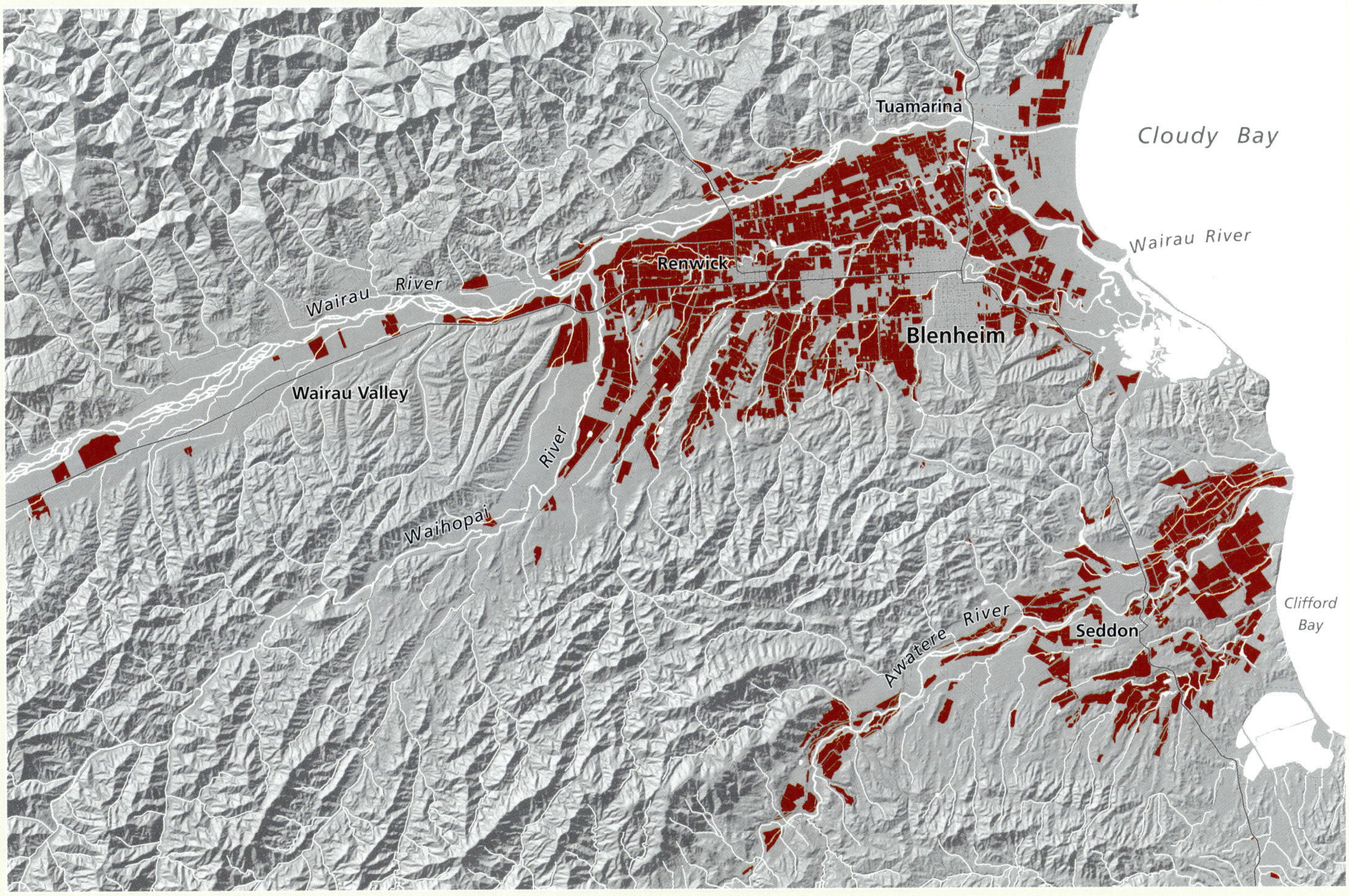

The varieties pulled out in Marlborough under the Lange government's Wine Industry Assistance Package of 1985–86 demonstrate the scattergun approach that most growers had taken to their original plantings. Out came 57 hectares of Müller Thurgau leaving 383 in the ground – still more than three times the area of any other variety in Marlborough at that time. More than 10 hectares each were also removed of Gewürztraminer (40 ha), Riesling (30 ha), Pinotage (16 ha) Chenin Blanc (15 ha), Chardonnay (11 ha) and Semillon (11 ha). Even by 1985, the year the Cloudy Bay winery was registered, people were reading their taste buds. Of the 53 hectares of Sauvignon Blanc planted, only 0.5 were removed in 1986. By 1990 the area in Sauvignon Blanc in Marlborough had reached 211 hectares; and by 1995 with 845 hectares planted, it was the dominant variety.

In this newest of the major winegrowing regions, grape growers and wine companies used the $6,175 per hectare provided by government to improve their mix of varieties. By now, they had learned which ones performed well on some of Marlborough's different sites and what the market was demanding. Many enterprises also replanted varieties on resistant rootstocks to overcome the phylloxera that was identified in the Wairau Valley in 1982. In the first rush to plant, most vines had been cuttings on their own roots. The pool of knowledge and practical experience that had accumulated in Marlborough in its first seventeen years of growing vines and making wine was to prove invaluable in the next period of growth.

Enterprises that were beginning to expand were adversely affected by the high interest rates of the late 1980s. Jane Hunter, for instance, was forced to sell her vineyards and later to buy them back when the economy stabilised. John Marris ran into similar difficulties with the large apple orchards that he had recently established. To recover his financial position, he had to call on his experience in property sales and development by buying a hilly block of land and subdividing it for rural residential blocks, some parts of which were later planted in vines to supply Wither Hills. Champagne corks certainly stopped popping after New Zealand's 1987 stock market crash.

Overall, apart from a small area of vines in Conders Bend – an indicator for the next decade – and larger areas in the upper Brancott and on the fan of the Taylor River, west of Blenheim, the pattern of vines in 1989 shows little change since 1982. Some growers had increased the size of their vineyards, but few vineyards had been established beyond the boundaries of the 1982 plantings.

Stage two: the 1990s

By the early 1990s the area in vines began to increase steadily again. So too did the investment in wineries, with more than 30 beginning during the decade (Figure 7.5).

This was a period of consolidation and new investment. Well-funded grape-growing enterprises appeared, some with capital accumulated from other industries, some with an affiliation and written agreements to supply particular wineries. Local landowners who had been waiting more cautiously on the sidelines began planting. Even more migrants from the North Island purchased land and planted grapes.

From 1990 the total area in vines was very much influenced by plantings of Sauvignon Blanc as its distinctive qualities and acceptance on the local and international markets became widely recognised. In 1989, Marlborough had 144 hectares of Sauvignon Blanc in production. At the millennium the total Marlborough vineyard reached 4000 hectares with about half of it in Sauvignon Blanc.

Unfortunately, no maps of vineyards exist for 2000, but the 2003 Marlborough District Council map of vineyards shows a transformed Wairau Valley (Figure 7.5). The western end of the valley has been occupied by vines at a speed and to an extent unprecedented in the region. The higher flood plain and undissected terraces bounded by the Wairau and Waihopai rivers and State Highways 6 and 63 has become the largest area of continuously planted vines in Marlborough and New Zealand. The wide entrance to the Omaka Valley is almost as solidly planted as the Brancott. Availability of water has strongly influenced this rush to the west. The strong aquifer there, together with the availability of land in large parcels, attracted the big companies such as Delegat's and Montana, while smaller companies such as Seresin could also find suitable parcels of land in this western rectangle.

The geography of local entrepreneurial association has gradually become less marked in Marlborough, but still lingers. Montana's original plantings in the Southern Valleys were supplemented in 1994 by the acquisition of land in the Rapaura area where a large block was leased on the southern side of Rapaura Road less than a kilometre from the original Roses' block. In the late 1990s it became even more committed to the higher flood plain when it purchased the radiata pine forest at Conders Bend, felled the trees and planted mainly Sauvignon Blanc. Montana initially branded this Sauvignon Blanc as Conders Forest. Infilling occurred everywhere that vines were already planted at the beginning of the 1990s and new areas were pioneered. Nobilo planted a large vineyard on the pea gravels of the Rarangi coastal area, while from the mid-1990s vines were established on the more accessible eastern bank of the Waihopai by both Spy Valley and later Nobilo.

In the early 1990s the vine leapfrogged to the Awatere Valley. Two main stimuli were important – local initiative, from landowners in the Awatere of which Vavasour Wines was the earliest with its first crush in 1989, together with the possibility of buying less expensive land, of similar potential for viticulture, as in the Wairau Valley. Both small and large enterprises were important in the Awatere's development as a viticultural region.

Villa Maria Estate Ltd saw the possibility of increasing their vineyards by securing land in the Awatere and getting investors involved in a viticultural enterprise to supply them with grapes. Seddon Vineyards and later Terra Vitae Vineyards were born. Other investment groups such as Brackenfield followed. Saint Clair Family Estate also committed to the Awatere in the early stages of the valley's development – a vision influenced by Neal Ibbotson's knowledge of the Awatere from his previous career as a land valuer and viticultural consultant.

Just before the millennium, with the terraces upstream of State Highway 1 in the Awatere catchment rapidly being acquired for vines, Montana made the bold move of planting their large Seaview vineyard on the gentle slopes overlooking the Pacific on the right bank of the Awatere. While these maritime-influenced slopes make early spring and late autumn frost most unlikely, sea breezes reduce daytime temperatures during the summer months providing cooler growing conditions than most of the Awatere. The Montana initiative was paralleled by Peter Yealands beginning an aggressive planting programme on rolling land further away from the sea than Montana's property.

Villa Maria's Awatere Valley vineyards. *Villa Maria*

Looking up the Awatere Valley from the coast. *Bruce Jenkins/PhotoNewZealand*

As in the Wairau Valley, the diversity of growing conditions throughout Marlborough enhances the diversity of fruit flavours from different soils and in different atmospheric environments. Jane Hunter, one of the most experienced wine entrepreneurs of the region, emphasises the value of the region's diverse soil and atmospheric conditions:

> I mean we've got this block here that is a very low-cropping, low-vigour vineyard. And 2 kilometres back down the road we've got two of our major Sauvignon Blanc vineyards and you'd think that they were in a different country the soil is so heavy. There's not one stone in it. And so you get rain coming in over the hills. The vineyard just doesn't even blink at it. The positive thing for a winery of our size is it gives us such wonderful fruit flavours because there is such a diversity of fruit coming in.

When different sites in the Awatere Valley are added to the overall Marlborough mix, the potential to use the different qualities in the grapes from different parts of the region to blend them into distinctive, or even consistently similar, wines from vintage to vintage becomes apparent. Marlborough, like Champagne, is primarily a

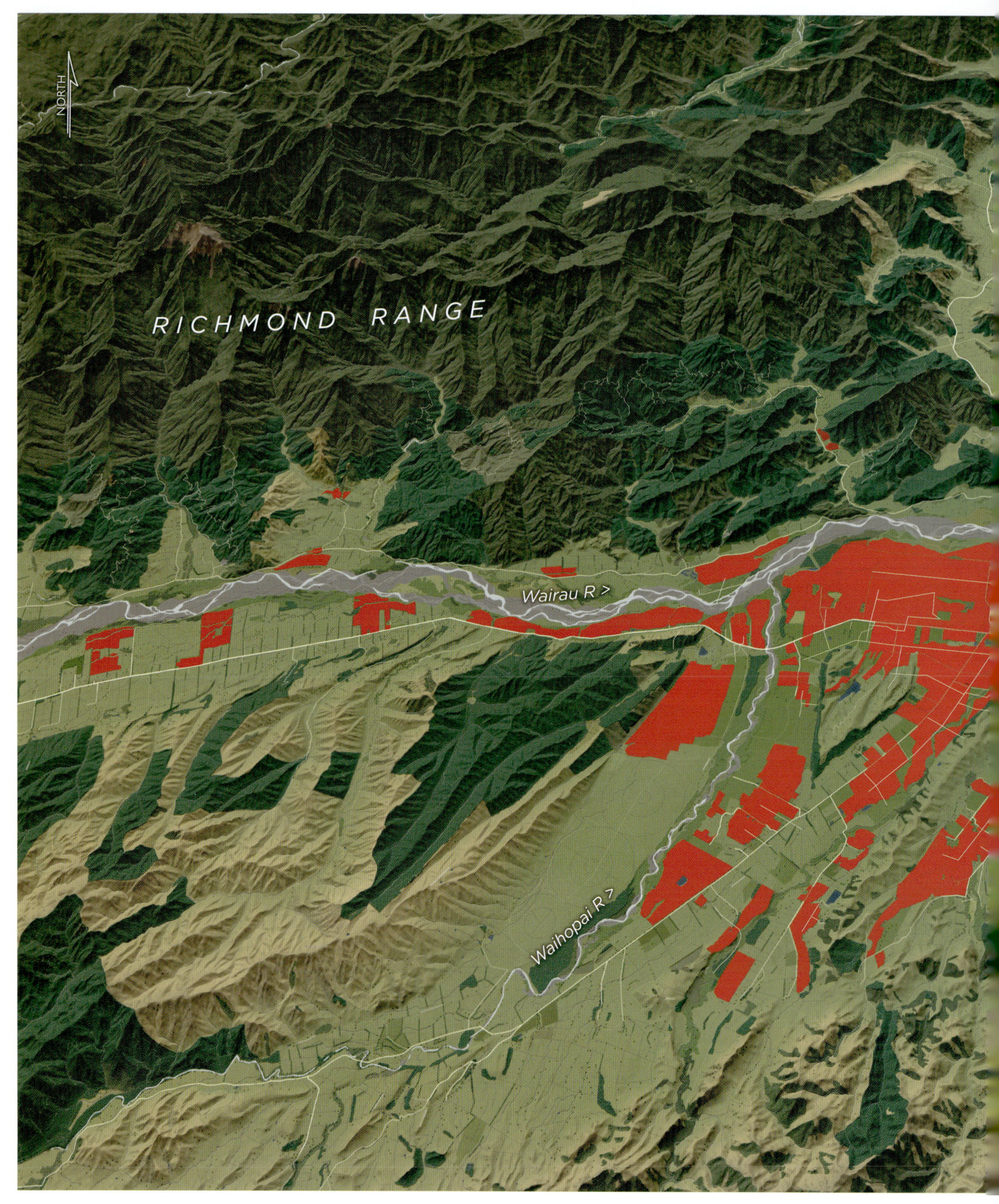

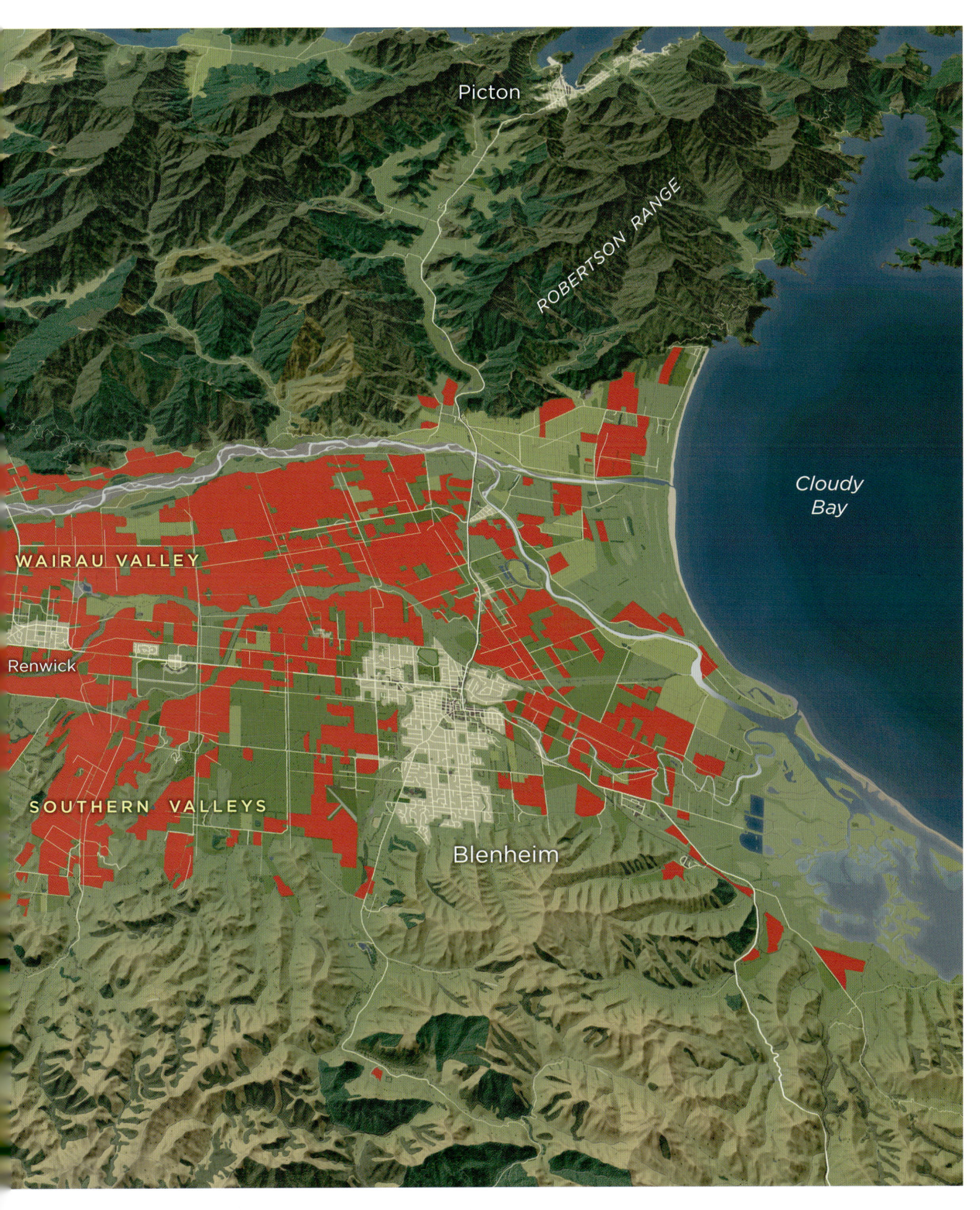

regional brand. These two regions also have similarities in the way their industries are organised which enhances the possibilities. Grape growers who sell to wineries, who also grow their own grapes, are common to both regions. Companies – or in the case of Champagne, co-operatives – have a variety of different fruit that can be blended to attain the styles and qualities they are seeking. Enterprises in both regions also have the capacity to maintain or modify their style of wine by changing their sources of grapes from year to year.

When vintages are variable from region to region and from year to year, New Zealand wine producers have the added advantage of being permitted by legislation to include up to 15 per cent of wine from outside their region, or indeed 15 per cent of grapes other than those varieties named on the front label. Champagne producers have an analogous flexibility as far as variety is concerned because they can choose the proportions of Chardonnay, Pinot Meunier and Pinot Noir that they include and not be required to name them. French producers may not blend any grapes from other regions, although in the past – notably in periods of difficulty such as after the ravages of phylloxera in the late nineteenth century – fraud, artificial wine and false labelling were endemic.

Both regions have a mix of soil types over small areas with subtle differences, as well as more marked trends in atmospheric environments. Some climatic differences, such as the influences of distance from the sea on temperature in Marlborough, are reasonably predictable. In both regions grape growers who supply different wine companies therefore produce grapes with different qualities, not only because the soils and microclimates are different but also because the people growing them have different viticultural styles and aspirations. Large companies, in particular, are able to source their grapes from the same or different growers from year to year. Co-operatives in Champagne have a similar diversity of supply although without the flexibility of being able so readily to change suppliers.

Stage three: post-2000

The rapidity of plantings in Marlborough in the twenty-first century surprised many observers and prompted the renewed interest of the Marlborough District Council to record and map their growth. Even the relatively conservative figures of New Zealand Winegrowers show the area in vines increasing by almost one and a half times between 2000 and 2005 – from just over 4000 to almost 10,000 hectares (Table 7.3). Marlborough District Council's monitoring of vineyards for irrigation and other infrastructure suggests that growth has been even faster.

This rapid growth is associated with strong international demand for Sauvignon Blanc, reinvestment of profits by existing wine enterprises, more enterprises being established in Marlborough and, especially, the acquisition of some large and medium-sized New Zealand companies by international conglomerates. These infusions of capital have stimulated bolder acquisitions of land to plant more vines, especially Sauvignon Blanc and Pinot Noir.

Vineyard plantings since 2003 show two revealing spatial patterns. First, plantings peripheral to the core of the Wairau Valley have been substantial. Vines have jumped the Wairau to its north bank, filled in most of the available flatter land at the heads of the Southern Valleys, and added substantial areas to the east and north of Blenheim on soils that were formerly considered to be less suitable for vines. By the end of 2005 the density of vineyards eastwards towards the coast on the low-lying land between Blenheim and the Wairau was greater than it was in 1990 in the combined Southern Valleys and Rapaura. These more coastal vines are often on what were originally poorly drained soils as the alluvium here is generally finer than further upstream and contains more clay. They include some sandy areas from former dunes that drain more freely. Large parcels of vines have also been established on both banks of the Waihopai and in the Omaka Valley.

Second, and perhaps even more significantly, wine companies and grape growers have planted on the ridges separating the Southern Valleys. These include Pernod Ricard NZ with its Terraces vineyard, Dog Point, and Clos Henri – the southern hemisphere Sauvignon Blanc outpost of the Bourgeois family of the village of Chavignol in Sancerre.

Shortage of easier land partly necessitates this move to the hills, but experienced growers like Ivan Sutherland argue convincingly that the hills may grow better, or at the least different, grapes and wine – especially, in his opinion, Pinot Noir. The clay and clay-loams have a much higher capacity for retaining moisture than the gravels of the plain. Some of these hillier parts have more exposure to solar radiation and some slopes have better natural protection from frost through cool-air drainage. Close monitoring of the soil moisture, using neutron probes or direct measurement of the vines' uptake of water, makes it possible to reduce irrigation to a minimum or even eliminate it as the vine ages and its roots are established at deeper levels. Cost savings on irrigation water can be significant.

The Awatere valley and hills

With the river roughly in the centre of its valley, the Awatere has a more classical form than the Wairau. At its widest point the Awatere's land available for planting is less than 5 kilometres across with the active riverbed occupying about a kilometre of that. The river also reveals the origins and variability of the valley sediments for all to see. Crossing the rail and road bridge just before Seddon, you see the terraces of various ages perched tens of metres above the active riverbed. As the river has sliced through these terraces it has exposed the strata that underlie them. Vineyards now define the outline of the surfaces of the terraces for 20 kilometres up the river.

While the Awatere has its own special attraction, it remains something of an adjunct of the Wairau, almost a grape-growing outpost. It seems highly unlikely that the large companies, already with cellars on the Wairau Plain, will establish processing facilities in the Awatere. Nevertheless, the vineyards that are snaking into the hills southwards from Riverlands along State Highway 1 and from the south towards the Dashwood Pass seem to be making an effort to link the two.

As in the Wairau, the acceleration of growth in the last decade has seen parts of the Awatere, such as east along Redwood Road from State Highway 1, packed with vines. The easy slopes away from the river on the south bank have been planted and vineyards in large parcels are appearing on the road to Ward and further south.

The imperative of a Marlborough brand

In the late 1990s, when the scrabble to buy the remaining land in Marlborough intensified as the corporates, now with deeper financial backing, became more aggressive, another smaller, Yukich-like raid was made on Marlborough. This time Sauvignon Blanc vineyards in production were the target (Figure 7.6). During 2000, Giesen Holdings Ltd, in association with the South Island iwi Ngai Tahu, bought 14 parcels of Sauvignon Blanc vineyards ranging in size from 12 to 45 acres, and a winery site – a total of 350 acres or 142 hectares of vineyards. It was suggested at the time that they were paying about

One part of Giesen's extensive Marlborough vineyard. *Giesen Wines Ltd*

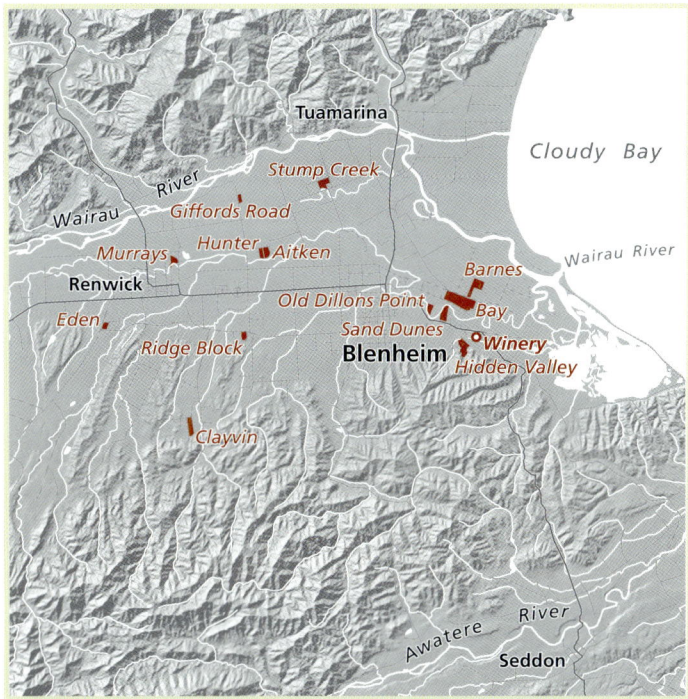

Figure 7.6 Beginning in 1993, Giesen Holdings bought pockets of land across the Wairau Valley, enabling them to discover the unique properties of different environments over time.

$135,000 per hectare for Sauvignon Blanc vines, which would make a total investment of over $19.2 million. In a period of months, Giesen transformed from a Canterbury company known for their Rieslings to a Marlborough label growing predominantly Sauvignon Blanc.

Other companies have used different approaches to associate themselves with Marlborough and to diversify their brand. In the early 1990s, Ross and Bill Spence established that Matua Valley was no longer merely a West Auckland company by introducing the Shingle Peak label – a much less expensive alternative strategy made possible because they had already secured their Marlborough grape growers and vineyards.

One conclusion about vine environments in relation to the sequence of vineyard development is inescapable. While it is generally accepted that Sauvignon Blanc from Marlborough has distinctive aromas and flavours compared to other parts of the world, it is being produced from soils that are extremely variable – from coarse gravels to deep alluviums to former sand dunes or marine gravels. It would seem that the atmospheric environment of the vine in Marlborough, which varies on a much coarser scale than the soils, is the integrating environmental influence. Kevin Judd, former chief winemaker and managing director of Cloudy Bay, is unequivocal on the reason for the distinctiveness of Marlborough's Sauvignon Blanc: 'It's primarily climatic – there's no doubt about that.' Yet even this explanation is not conclusive, because many other viticulturists and winemakers argue that Sauvignon Blanc grapes, or wine from the Wairau compared with the Awatere, and certainly from localities within the Wairau, all have distinctive characteristics.

In an oblique aerial view across the Southern Valleys, as recently as 2005 a single large area of flat land stood out as not yet being colonised by the vine. On the western bank of the Waihopai River is the former Bankhouse Station backed by its distinctive, arrow-like ridge. This enterprise has since been branded as Winegrowers of ARA. It is on the high and undissected terraces of the Waihopai. Its two main soil types are Renwick – the same as much of the Southern Valleys; and Waimakariri – the same as Conders Bend. Many potential buyers looked at this site as having potential for growing vines but were cautious because of its reputation for being colder in the cusp seasons than much of the Wairau Valley and vulnerable to late-spring and early autumn frosts. All but a small part of it is over 100 metres above sea level. Being well inland from the sea breezes originating from Cloudy Bay, its summers are hot. The circles from centre-point irrigation systems, growing pasture for fattening cattle, are clearly evident when viewing Bankhouse Station from Google Earth. These have provided some cash flow while the vineyards have been developed.

The viticultural plan for ARA is to limit or even eliminate frost damage while providing water for an ambitious irrigation system using large storage reservoirs. As in Chablis, the part of Burgundy most vulnerable to spring frosts, the watering system is overhead sprinklers, not drip irrigation. By coating vulnerable buds and young leaves in mist and thin layers of ice, they can be protected from several degrees of frost. Overhead irrigation systems also mimic rain. They can be used to charge the soil moisture until the appropriate time when fruit begins to change colour (veraison) and the soil moisture gradually decreases. The roots of vines are in this way encouraged to penetrate more deeply and find their own equilibrium with their environment until irrigation can be reduced.

By choosing this path, ARA are pushing beyond the climatic limits that others have so far been prepared to accept in the Marlborough region. It would be surprising if, given their frost precautions – at relatively low cost compared with alternative systems – their risks are any greater than for other localities of the Wairau Plain such as parts of the Southern Valleys where the ponding of cold air is common. It is also unlikely that the risk is any greater than for Central Otago growers who are now planting at elevations higher than 400 metres, or the large number in Hawke's Bay who have not yet invested in frost protection.

Delimiting Marlborough?

When the first European surveyors arrived on the Wairau Plain they lived on rafts of logs in the swamp near Blenheim, colourfully called Beavertown. By the time vines were planted in 1973, the Wairau Plain had already been transformed by artificial drainage, especially the lower eastern half. Controlling flooding using stopbanks had been practised for over a century and a comprehensive flood-control scheme was developed after 1960. These conservation efforts had extended into the hills. For much of the twentieth century the name Wither Hills was associated more with such efforts in soil conservation in the catchment of the Wairau than with wines.

With the wine industry now so important to the local economy, it might be assumed that differences between the citizens of the Marlborough district and those growing grapes would have dissipated. Yet, since the head-on court battles in the 1970s to establish the rights of landowners to grow grapes, other issues to do with the vine have taken their place. Two stand out – the voracious demands of the wine industry for water, and the effect of the vine monoculture on the landscape and ecology of the Marlborough region.

Aquifers, and water rights to access them through bores or direct pumping from surface streams and rivers, have been the traditional means of providing irrigation water. As demand for water rights has grown, the supply has dwindled, until in some areas no more water can be allocated. The Southern Valleys, with their large vineyards, intermittent streams and less abundant aquifers, are the main area of water deficit. The solution of the Marlborough District Council, after pressure from vineyard landowners in the area, was the Southern Valleys Irrigation Scheme funded by a combination of capital contributions and targeted property taxes (rates) from the users. Designed to provide water to 4000 hectares of land south of Renwick, it is now in operation.

In 2002 the Marlborough District Council commissioned the Wairau Plain Landscape Concept Guidelines in response to

> considerable public concern . . . at large vineyard expansion causing rapid landscape change on the rural Wairau Plain. A key concern is the loss of trees. Looking after the landscape and ecology of the Wairau Plain is considered of local and international importance.

The aim was to encourage, not coerce, landowners to plant native grasses, shrubs and trees on private land and that set aside for flood control, and to recapture something of the original ecology of the plain.

The guidelines identify four types of country – the Dry Plain, Spring Country, Old Dune Country, and Coastal Lands. While these categories are useful to represent the indigenous vegetation suitable for planting, they also identify the diversity of

Harvest at Yealands Estate.
Yealands Estate Wines Ltd

habitats that the grapevine has colonised and modified. As far as the vine is concerned, the Dry Plain is no longer dry. This was the preferred site of planting up to the late 1990s. Since then, grapes have successively extended their domain into the Spring Country, the Old Dune Country and the Coastal Lands. The Wairau Plain, Awatere Valley and Marlborough region are nearly full of vines.

The irrepressible Peter Yealands thinks differently. An early advocate of the Awatere Valley as an alternative growing area to the Wairau, he announced in late 2006 his intention to continue planting large areas in vines there and further south. In the early 2000s he had established an average of 125 hectares of vines annually and later increased this to over 150 hectares. By 2008 he owned over 1000 hectares in vines, over 90 per cent of which were Sauvignon Blanc. His Awatere winery has a final capacity to process 20,000 tonnes of grapes – or 2500 hectares of grapes, assuming an average of 8 tonnes to the hectare. Given that the Awatere Valley has an area in grapes approaching that of Hawke's Bay, and Yealands was only its third winery after Vavasour and The Crossings, the need is obvious. Some grape growers in the Awatere and further south will undoubtedly use the Yealands facility to have their own wines made under contract as they attempt to capture a higher proportion of the profits from their vineyards.

Peter Yealands' vision is not confined to the Awatere Valley. His Marlborough region extends further south. Purchase of the Flaxbourne Station south of Seddon allows him to continue to increase his vineyard land, although at a slower rate because much of it is too hilly. But his vision extends still further. Well aware of the importance of irrigation water in almost all South Island viticultural regions, Yealands has plans for an irrigation scheme to service the Ward area. The Marlborough District Council and the Environment Court turned down his initial application for water rights from the Awatere. He responded with a new scheme. His plans include extending his development of vineyards in the Ward area and further south to Kekerengu and perhaps later into the catchment of the Clarence.

The Yealands' and other initiatives south of the Awatere bring Marlborough's regional boundary into contention. In revising the regional and district boundaries of Marlborough in its 1989 determination, the Local Government Commission placed considerable emphasis on catchment boundaries and less on communities of interest, accessibility to urban centres and the economic geography of regions. The decision to transfer Kaikoura County to the Canterbury region was contentious at the time. There is little doubt from an economic perspective that the former Kaikoura County would benefit itself and New Zealand by being tied, as it was historically, to the Marlborough brand.

Enterprises in the Marlborough story

Chris and Judy Simmonds, grape growers

Marlborough grape growers came from many different backgrounds but most have one characteristic in common: they are enthusiastic about their *métier*. Chris and Judy Simmonds are no exception. Their opportunity arose when a Blenheim real estate agent and friend visited them in 1985 to let them know that 'some crazy Australian who was buying land from Corbans had to get rid of 60 acres because the government of the day would only let a foreign company own so much land'. The Australian was David Hohnen buying land to plant grapes for his new enterprise, Cloudy Bay. He was selling 60 acres in three 20-acre parcels. Their real estate friend suggested that they might 'perhaps get someone else in partnership to run it for them to grow grapes. So we bought 20 acres.' Contemporaneously, Ivan Sutherland was setting up his own, much larger, grape-growing enterprise. He also bought 20 acres of land from Hohnen as did Kevin Judd, Cloudy Bay's first winemaker. Ivan was keen to establish 50/50 partnerships with relations, friends and acquaintances. Chris and Judy Simmonds also took up this opportunity.

Chris, who had worked in banking for most of his life, had many people asking him 'what do you know that I don't? Four thousand dollars an acre is an awful lot of money to pay for poor land in Matthews Lane, which runs off Jacksons Road.' When they met with Hohnen, who was going to buy their grapes, Chris and Judy almost had second thoughts. He told them he had found a good name for his company: Cloudy Bay. Chris remembers replying: 'You're crazy – no one would put the word "cloudy" on a bottle of wine!' Hohnen, owner of the highly successful West Australian company Cape Mentelle, replied: 'Well, we put "mental" on a bottle of wine and it's done pretty well!'

Chris and Judy Simmonds served their grape-growing apprenticeship on this 20-acre property they bought from Hohnen and were fortunate to have Ivan Sutherland as their 50/50 partner. He managed the vineyard and was committed to producing Pinot Noir and Sauvignon Blanc – indeed all grape varieties – to the highest possible standard. In 1987, Hohnen offered him the opportunity to run the viticulture at Cloudy Bay. Ivan had begun planting the Sutherlands' own vineyard, Dog Point, in 1979 and it had become one of the largest family-owned vineyards in Marlborough. For their part, Chris and Judy were also prepared to experiment with the latest ideas on managing the vines' canopy on the variable soils of the Wairau Valley. They were sufficiently confident that they were 'always looking to buy something bigger, because the numbers just looked so good'.

They found the larger property they were seeking in 1992. It was 60 acres (24 ha). Chris 'was able to bail out of banking completely and became a full-time grape grower at that point'. Over the next eight years they gradually replanted or top-grafted the half of the new property that was growing vines and developed the rest. By the millennium, the 60 acres were in vines. Half of the new vineyard was in Sauvignon Blanc with the remainder in Chardonnay, Pinot Noir, Riesling and 3 acres of Gewürztraminer. Developing such a vineyard was a considerable accomplishment, especially when the family were living in Christchurch until 1997, where their youngest child was in fifth form (year 11) and their twin daughters beginning university. They built a cottage on the property, and as Chris says, 'I was coming up here every second week and spending the other week recovering!' During this period, a nearby grape grower, Philip Walsh, was managing the property for them. Chris admires Philip's knowledge and considers that

> we keep each other going quite well, because he's been in this game for a long time and has different skills and we work well together. One of the things I set out to do right from the beginning was to be able to do every job – and I've done everything it's possible to do on a vineyard, I think.

With the new vineyard, Chris was keen to experiment with a variety of ground covers and irrigation techniques to even out the vigour of their vines. On this southern side of the Wairau Valley the soils are heavier and more clayey. Because the Wairau River drains to the east, and Chris wanted his rows to be north to south so that berries on both sides of the row get their share of sun, the rows are at right angles to the alluvial deposits that change with distance from the river: 'We're trying to do different things down the same rows to try and balance the performance of the vines.' He familiarised himself with the work of Dr Peter Dry at the University of Adelaide and was lucky enough to have him visit and assess the 3 acres of vines that Chris was trialling.

The irrigation technique involves watering each side of the vine alternately. In the new Simmonds vineyard the roots appear to have responded by going deeper rather than spreading, as the research by Dry suggested. Chris is particularly impressed by the results he has achieved with Pinot Noir where the vines are producing fewer short shoots. With his Sauvignon Blanc, he has managed to keep yields at a level of about 5 tonnes to the acre (12 tonnes per hectare), and for the best-quality Pinot Noir about 3 tonnes to the acre (just over 7 tonnes per hectare). With their Marlborough Riesling, they produce two qualities of grapes – one as close as possible to 4 tonnes per acre (8.5 tonnes per hectare) for the best quality, and the other at about 6 tonnes to the acre (about 14.5 tonnes per hectare). As with all vineyards, the vagaries of the weather, when combined with the difficulty of pruning to a particular yield, means that the number of bunches per plant must be reduced closer to vintage when the level of the yield can be assessed more accurately.

Chris Simmonds prefers the simpler and less expensive vertical shoot positioning (VSP) method of trellising, although he did inherit 3 acres on the Scott-Henry system on the first vineyard he purchased:

> I think that with VSP and good canopy management to expose the fruit at the right level, and get a nice high canopy going, we can grow as good, if not better, fruit.

In his first fifteen years as a grower he sold his grapes to a variety of wine companies, with most of it initially going to Corbans, 'but we terminated that arrangement'. He cites his Gewürztraminer vineyard as an example of the way he has since associated with different wineries as his vines matured and he became more experienced. For five vintages he sold most of his Gewürztraminer to Cloudy Bay, before in 1999 selling to John Forrest who won a gold medal with it. This wine was also the best in its class at the 2000 Romeo Bragato Wine Awards.

By the 2000 vintage Chris had settled on supplying three companies of small to medium size – Forrest and Highfield Estate in Marlborough, and the Auckland firm De Redcliffe. These smaller wine enterprises, and particularly Forrest Estate, keep Chris in touch with their progress in producing wines from his grapes:

> John Forrest rings me up and says, 'Look, come over, we'll do a tank tasting of the Sauvignon.' That's just a heck of a lot of fun and he is just an amazing fellow. I've learned a lot about wine from him.

The ideas Chris bounces off John sometimes have their repercussions in Forrest's own business when, after one of these discussions, 'he goes back to his viticulturist and says "I want you to try such and such". The viticulturist commonly replies, "Oh, you've been talking to that bloody Simmonds again!"'

Chris agrees with John Forrest's approach to deciding when grapes should be picked. As vintage approaches, John monitors the state of maturity of the berries by their sugar and pH but picks each variety when he thinks the flavour of their fruit is right. Highfield has an even more flexible system: 'If fruit are ready prior to reaching their top figure, they come in and say, "We'll take it now and pay the top figure."' Chris is adamant that he never wants to grow for a very large company again. When supplying Corbans in the 1990s the price that growers received was related primarily to the sugar level (brix) of the grapes which, to be fair to both parties, requires careful measurement in the vineyard. Chris was unhappy with the differences between his and the company's measurement of these sugar levels.

The banker in Chris emerges when he discusses his pride and joy – the spreadsheet he developed to monitor the performance of his vineyard: 'I put all the variables into it, including row spacing, plants per hectare, and so on and so forth – and it works really, really well.' He began assembling the information when they bought their first vineyard and the spreadsheet's utility has increased year by year as more information accumulates, until it has become his main recording and management device. Its value derives from the variety of scales he can analyse. These range from the whole vineyard to a single parcel of land, to the performance of a particular variety or even clone: 'I now have a spreadsheet that I can run any vineyard through in the space of 20 minutes and give you a four-year projection on its performance.' He even uses it to convince his grape-growing friends to modify their viticultural practices:

> I've got a friend whose property we put into the spreadsheet and as a result of which he is top-grafting his Müller Thurgau – it was this that convinced him. He sort of knew that he needed to do that, but when you really looked at what he's making off that variety he actually made the change.

Cloudy Bay, Dog Point and Greywacke

Cloudy Bay, together with Dog Point and Greywacke, have been extremely influential in establishing New Zealand's local and international reputation for producing fine wines from several varieties, but especially Sauvignon Blanc and Pinot Noir. From the mid-1980s, members of the Healy, Judd and Sutherland families held responsible positions at Cloudy Bay. After the French firm Louis Vuitton Moët Hennessey (LVMH) bought Cloudy Bay in 2003, members of these three families established their own enterprises. The Sutherland and Healy families built a winery to complement the Sutherland vineyards, and in 2008 Kevin Judd launched the label that he had first registered in 1993: Greywacke. Kevin's last year as CEO of Cloudy Bay was 2008. By 2010 his name was back in the Annual Report of New Zealand Winegrowers, this time as proprietor of Greywacke. The trio's seamless transition was smoothed by their deep knowledge of growing fully flavoured grapes in the Marlborough environment and capturing the nuances of their qualities in the wines they produced.

Almost all the sites from which Judd sources the grapes for his new label – which 'is primarily based on two varieties, Sauvignon Blanc and Pinot Noir'– are part of the portfolio of vineyards owned by the Sutherland family. However, Greywacke's Sauvignon Blanc wines are nothing like the standard Marlborough model. Judd is striving for fuller flavours, greater mouth weight, and a more integrated wine. Moreover, with his 'wild' Sauvignon, as with his more conventionally fermented wines, the strong asparagus and capsicum flavours characteristic of many New Zealand Sauvignon Blancs are undetectable.

Kevin Judd is a strong believer in fermenting a proportion of the grapes he crushes with indigenous yeasts from the locality where the grapes are growing. These 'wild' ferments give distinctive flavour, mouth weight and aromas to the resulting wine. He still inoculates some ferments with commercial yeasts. These two approaches give him flexibility in blending the final wines. By fermenting in small and medium-sized tanks and in barrels he is able to vary the proportions of the rustic flavours from the wild ferments of Sauvignon Blanc or even Pinot Noir with the less distinctive wines from the more conventional ferments.

Fortunately, Judd is comfortable with harvesting his grapes at night and by machine, whereas Ivan Sutherland and James Healy of Dog Point favour hand-picking in the daytime. By harvesting at night, Judd is able to mesh with Dog Point's vineyard and winery scheduling. During vintage these practices see the three key figures of Dog Point and Greywacke on quite different working and sleeping schedules. Kevin is able to organise the mechanical harvesters, receive the grapes, and see to their pressing and allocation to barrels or stainless-steel tanks in the deep of the night. The bunches of Pinot Noir are already cool when they begin their cold soak in temperature-controlled stainless-steel tanks immediately after they reach the winery.

Dog Point winery had a long gestation. When, in 2003, David Hohnen sold Cloudy Bay to LVMH neither James Healy nor Ivan Sutherland was surprised. They had been working together for more than eighteen years, James as production manager and a winemaker while Ivan was running Cloudy Bay's viticulture as well as being a director of the company. Moreover, their two families had been closely associated with the Cloudy Bay enterprise. Wendy Healy worked in administration there, as did Margaret

Hand-sorting Pinot grapes at Dog Point. On the job are the four partners in the business, the accountant, the gardener, and Ivan Sutherland's sister.
Dog Point Vineyard

Sutherland who also kept a watchful eye on the books of the Dog Point enterprise. When the sale of Cloudy Bay was announced the two families launched their plan to build their own winery to operate in conjunction with Dog Point Vineyard.

The Sutherlands brought to the partnership access to their 240 hectares of mature vineyards. The Healys brought James' rich experience of vinifying Cloudy Bay's Sauvignon Blanc, Chardonnay and Pinot Noir over eighteen vintages and Wendy's understanding of the administration and finances of a wine business. All four individuals were well aware of the need to keep cash flow ahead of expenditure.

Dog Point's buildings are attractive, well-insulated, functional sheds each built when the enterprise needed and could afford them. Their main distinction is their height. Inside, barrels of Pinot Noir are stacked to the roof. At the entrance of the single-storey administration building, a wall of gabion baskets – the rectangular wire cages that South Island road makers use to keep slips at bay – echoes the Marlborough landscape. Regrettably, few wine buyers have the opportunity to observe this enterprise at work. Dog Point has become one of a handful of New Zealand wine producers with strong international recognition of its brand and sells 89 per cent of its wine offshore. This result has not come without intense commitment from its principals, Ivan Sutherland and James Healy. The wines that emerge from this cool cellar are anything but simple. Like all wine enterprises, its success rests on having close control of the vineyard as well as the winery.

The Forrests in Marlborough

A presence in two regions – a minority partnership in the Cornerstone vineyard in Hawke's Bay at the junction of Gimblett Road and State Highway 50 in conjunction with the development of their own Marlborough enterprise – has provided deep insights for John and Brigid Forrest. Both are doctors – Brigid in medicine and John with a PhD in molecular biology – which is why they call one of their Rieslings 'The Doctors'. Cash flow from Brigid's medical practice was essential in enabling them to buy land, service their debt, and develop a successful wine enterprise.

The land they initially purchased in Marlborough was 28 acres. Over the 1988 vintage, John worked with, and learned from, the talented winemaker Alan McCorkindale before setting up his own vineyard that winter, planting 8 acres of vines in this first year. Within three years, 16 acres of the Forrests' Marlborough land was planted and the vines trellised. The previous owner had planted 10 acres of the property in apples and these were one year old when the Forrests bought the land: 'Brigid made me keep the apples, and lucky we did because we cashed in on the great years of apple income of '92, '93 and '94 before they sort of crashed in '97, '98.' Several other aspiring grape growers in Marlborough, such as John Marris who purchased more land for grapes in the late 1980s, recount similar experiences of benefiting from high apple prices over the three years while they waited for their grapes to bear fruit.

The grape varieties the Forrests planted in their first years included some surprises. John admitted to 'one real mistake – because I could never afford to buy good Pinot Noir as a student and right through my post-doc life, I had a very low opinion of Pinot Noir!' (There speaks a Bordeaux lover with experience in California and the Barossa.) From the classical red varieties, he chose instead

> some Cabernet, some Merlot, some Franc, a bit of Malbec, and from the whites, Sauvignon in a higher proportion (thank goodness), and a bit of Pinot Blanc too – God knows why – which I have now ripped out. And a little bit of Semillon.

When the 10 acres of young apple trees had served their purpose, they were pulled out and replaced by more Sauvignon Blanc and some Riesling.

In 1993 the Forrests managed to buy 25 acres of land right next door. This parcel was invaluable because it provided better access to their cellar door, which was becoming an increasingly important part of their business. John also devised an ingenious way of funding the purchase. The Auckland company buying some of his grapes helped finance the purchase of the land in return for a guaranteed ten-year supply of a proportion of the Sauvignon Blanc and Riesling from the new vineyard. However, development of the Forrest enterprise did not come without compromises. For ten more years the Forrests continued to live in a converted Skyline shed, investing in their vineyard and winery rather than building a house.

John has definite ideas on the intricate interactions between the profitability of wines made from different varieties of grapes and the soil types where they are grown. He draws on his experience growing Cabernet and Merlot on the Gimblett Gravels of Hawke's Bay compared with Sauvignon Blanc grown in Marlborough. As he points out: 'Gimblett Road took two and a half times as long to reach positive cash flow as Marlborough.' The Forrests' red varieties grown in Hawke's Bay are cropped at lower yields per hectare than Marlborough Sauvignon Blanc and irrigation must be sensitively handled to avoid diluting their flavours. Most important of all, these wines need some time in the bottle before they are sold. These factors cumulatively make the Cabernet Merlot wines noticeably more expensive. The comparison with Sauvignon Blanc is stark:

> Sauvignon Blanc is a fantastic grape in Marlborough because come August of each year you can put it in a bottle, and come 20th of October someone's paying you for it. Wonderful!

The importance of yield of grapes per vine or per hectare is an essential element of the Forrest winemaking philosophy and practice:

> At about four and a half tonne per acre, the textural quality of Sauvignon Blanc begins to diminish, but not the flavour. You've got to get beyond six, six and a half tonne before you see significant losses in flavour in the good years. If it's a poor year, then at six and a half tonne you'll never get it past the green and grassy. But in an average year you can push it into a flavour spectrum of currants and gooseberries that the world wants, particularly the English. I believe the US market wants something slightly riper and more complex.

Four and a half tonnes per acre is over 10.5 tonnes per hectare. These are very high yields compared to those for the Premier Cru and Grand Cru vineyards of a region such as Burgundy, or even Sancerre, where yields are restricted under the appellation laws. It does appear that even when produced at higher yields in the natural environment of the Marlborough region (and some other parts of New Zealand), Sauvignon Blanc grapes do reach an intensity of flavour that is more difficult to achieve in other parts of the world.

After the establishment phase, which lasted until the mid-1990s, the Forrest winery was often larger than necessary for the tonnage of grapes their company harvested – an 'overcapacity' which rests on the variability of Marlborough's weather in the early autumn and the effects it can have on different varieties:

> If you get a frost, you've got ten days to get the fruit off and avoid that leafy character. You can get rain – you've got ten days to sort of grab things. If it's really hot, rather than having three or three and a half weeks to do your Sauvignon Blanc vintage, you've got to do it in 10 days.

In the years of temperature extremes, such as 1998, this strategy paid off handsomely:

> Up until then '90 was our previous hottest year. I knew how quickly flavours change here for Sauvignon. So I was awake to that and we started vintage on the 14th of March. I didn't plan to, but when I saw how quickly things were changing in the vineyard – completely unripe on one side of the row, to overripe on the other – I said, 'God, we've got to move here!' But I had the capacity built in to do it. We were finished by the 1st of April for Sauvignon.

Such flexibility from staged investment in the winery, coupled with astute observation of the vineyards' responses to different weather and climate events in each season and across the years, can make substantial differences to the profitability of winegrowing enterprises.

John and Brigid Forrest have improved the probabilities of success for their wine enterprise in other ways. Although partly fortuitous, establishing and maintaining a substantial presence in two regions has enabled them to present a much stronger portfolio of wines to their distributors. On marketing trips within New Zealand, but especially overseas, John Forrest captures some extra kudos by bringing out some of his well-made Bordeaux blends from Hawke's Bay, often at the end of a trade tasting. These wines can be compared and contrasted with his Pinot Noirs from their firm's diverse sites in Marlborough. Few companies of their moderate size are able to do this as effectively.

The flexibility of the Forrest enterprise runs even deeper. At various stages in its evolution John has emphasised the grape-growing arm of the enterprise and at others the winemaking. For more than a decade, John has supplied Merlot and Cabernet grapes from their Cornerstone vineyard to Villa Maria's Esk Valley winery for their reserve wines. Conversely, from their first vintage, John has always been prepared to 'send bulk wine off to Australia quickly, all up-front money, pre-paid'. Such strategies smooth the seasonality of the Forrest income:

> Those wines for Cardmember go into a mixed case – you've only got to make the best wine in a carton, not the best wine in the world. And 80 per cent of Cardmember is paid by the 20th of May when I have to pay for fruit, for winemaking, and all sorts of other things.

Such efficient and enduring links bring the Forrest enterprise much closer to the Australian wine market.

Wairau River Wines

The Lincoln College (now University) diplomas and degrees in valuation and farm management were attractive qualifications for the next generation of South Island farming families in the 1960s and 1970s. Lincoln graduate Phil Rose admits to being 'another one of those':

> I was born and bred in Marlborough. In fact just down the road. I had property which basically was a mixed cropping and dairy farm. So I came from very much different circumstances to what we're in at the present time.

Diversifying into viticulture changed the life of Phil and his wife, Chris.

Following a three-year OE, he and Chris married in October 1972 and returned to New Zealand in December. With his two older brothers, Phil was running several family properties in the Spring Creek area, which as he points out, 'is of course much heavier ground than out this way. It's really good dairying and cropping country, although grapes are going in there now.' The Rose brothers also ran 'a contracting firm that included a maize harvesting and drying business – we were into all sorts of things'. With all three brothers married and with young families, they agreed to go their own ways.

One of the properties bought by the Rose boys in 1973 was 257 acres on Giffords Road. When they distributed the family land among the three of them this stony property was growing lucerne (alfalfa) to be dehydrated, pelletised and sent to Japan as stock feed. His two older brothers were not interested in it. Phil contrasts this land with the soils at their Spring Creek property: 'We didn't have a stone on our property at Spring Creek. I'd never had anything to do with stones!' In contrast, he describes the Giffords Road piece of land as 'quite a light, gravelly property'. In the allocation of the different parcels of land among the three sons, Phil and Chris Rose 'took this property on. We had seen grapes growing in similar soils in Europe and our buying it almost coincided with Montana's first planting in the Brancott area.'

Their entry into grapes was hastened when the price of diesel more than doubled in the early 1970s. They were irrigating their lucerne crops using diesel-powered pumps

'I'd never had anything to do with stones,' recalls Phil Rose from Wairau River Wines. *Jim Tannock Photography*

that they moved from well to well and the cost of pumping large quantities of water in this way severely reduced their profitability. When John Marris suggested that they might consider growing grapes for Montana, Phil and Chris grasped the opportunity and planted the single acre of grapes that they were permitted as of right before the Marlborough County Council made grape growing a restricted activity outside the Southern Valleys. Further plantings were delayed while the Roses and their legal team, with Montana's support, argued their case before the Planning Tribunal. They were finally successful.

Their original application had been to plant 60 acres in three lots of 20 acres. Phil Rose was not one to convert their farm to grape growing without further investigation. He knew the Ministry of Agriculture and Fisheries scientist Paul Pollack who was now stationed at Gisborne and specialising in vineyard management so they went to see him. Whereas Pollack was very supportive of their winegrowing plans, the Gisborne growers they visited were saying:

> 'What are you going to grow grapes in Marlborough for? It's too cold down there. What are you putting in?' And I said, 'Well, I don't know yet. We've applied to establish a 60-acre vineyard.' I remember the looks we got. And then they said if we'd been from Canterbury we probably would have said we were planting 500 acres!

Phil and Chris Rose first planted 20 acres of Müller Thurgau followed the next year by 20 of Palomino, and in the third year another 20 acres of Müller Thurgau. Their cuttings, only some of them rooted, came from Montana and they were planted in rows 3 metres apart with 1.6 metres between the vines. Their choice of Palomino, the variety from which sherry is made, was surprising given that the grape varieties for table wines were by now asserting their superiority, but some of the major companies originating in Auckland, including Montana, were still making quantities of fortified wine. From the beginning, they irrigated their vineyard, but the only extruded pipe they could buy locally varied in diameter from 15 to 17 or even 18 millimetres:

> Even fittings were non-existent. There was very little knowledge about what to do and how to do it. We'd meet at Henk Ruesink's, at Merrill Hadfield's or at Neal Ibbotson's place and you'd have a look and see what was going on, and you know, who'd made a cock-up doing this or whatever. That was the way we learned.

Negotiations over the price the wine companies were prepared to pay for grapes in Marlborough were initially reasonably amicable but inevitably became contentious:

> We used to like negotiating with Mate Yukich, because he was such a gentleman. And he would sit down and you'd have a few drinks with him and you could guarantee by the end of the day everyone was happy. We got into difficult circumstances with some of the CEOs of Montana and of course in later years with Peter Hubscher of quite protracted and sometimes not very nice negotiations.

The price for Marlborough Müller Thurgau during the late 1970s and early 1980s was usually 'between $350 and $450 a tonne'. With yields over 10 tonnes per hectare, growing grapes compared favourably with the income from other crops cultivated on the Wairau Plain, although trellising and other setting-up costs were high. Phil and Chris Rose continued to grow for Montana for fifteen years.

They also kept buying and planting more land and supplying these grapes to other wineries, including Hunter's, Nobilo, Matua Valley and Penfolds. In the vine-pull scheme of 1986 they decided to pull out their Palomino vines but these wineries convinced them to pull out their Chardonnay instead. With their higher yields and low production costs, the hybrids, and other varieties from the previous era, persisted longer than expected. Over the same winter, the Roses replaced these Chardonnay vines with cuttings of Sauvignon Blanc on their own roots. Despite the presence of phylloxera in Marlborough, in 2001 these same Sauvignon vines continued to produce their best fruit.

To keep their enterprise viable they also sold 37 of the 257 acres they started with. Selling this land, including the house on it, recouped half of the cost of the original property. While their grapes came into bearing, they continued to use their orcharding skills to grow several other crops. These included 10 acres of apricots, 15 acres of nectarines, and until the winter of 2001, 50 acres of apples.

In 1992 the Roses bought 150 acres on Rapaura Road and a further 10 acres nearby as a possible site for their winery, because by now they fully appreciated the advantages of these more meagre soils for growing grapes, provided they could irrigate them, especially in their early years. Phil Rose evocatively refers to the Rapaura area as a 'sort of strugglers' flat'. He remembers this land from his childhood and how the sun burnt it off in summer and it was really just wasteland apart from 'some quite old established orchards, many of them quite small'. Without irrigation these would have been difficult sites on which to grow grapes but Phil Rose knew much about irrigation from his experience irrigating and processing their lucerne crops. With these additional land purchases they planned to have a total of 300 acres of grapes planted by the spring of 2002 with 200 acres of it in Sauvignon Blanc.

John Belsham made the first wine for the Roses under their Wairau Valley label in 1990 in the Rapaura winery. Not surprisingly, it was Sauvignon Blanc. After the difficult vintage of 1995, in a four-way partnership with Matua Valley (Ross and Bill Spence), Nautilus (owned by wine distribution company Negociants) and John Belsham (Foxes Island Wines), the Roses bought the Rapaura winery. Their wine was made there for a further five years before they decided they needed their own winery:

> This Rapaura winery has really served us very, very well in the last ten years. But circumstances are changing. Matua has been taken over by Beringer Blass and they have already signalled that they are going to grow. I think the demand on the Rapaura facility will grow enormously in the next few years and it's probably going to be something that's twice the size. Instead of a 5000-tonne winery it'll be a 10,000-tonne winery in another three or four years that is going to require considerable investment from us as a 25 per cent shareholder. And we've just decided that we think we'd be better putting that money into something that we own ourselves and control one hundred per cent. Moreover, the harvest window is not getting any bigger. And virtually all the increase in production is for Sauvignon Blanc, which all falls within about a two- to three-week window.

The similarity with John and Brigid Forrest's arguments for having adequate capacity to harvest Sauvignon Blanc quickly, when it is ripe and ready, is striking. No wonder the mechanical harvesters are often working at night during the Marlborough vintage.

The Roses' decision to build a winery also fitted with the life course of their family and their enterprise:

> Our youngest son is almost a winemaker. He's got this semester at Lincoln to finish. Rapaura is a contract facility and we have permanent staff on hand who do everything for everyone

under our instructions. It's not the sort of place that really lends itself to fostering more family involvement, which we can see coming up in the next generation. Hence our decision to step out.

The Roses decided to build a boutique winery with a capacity to vinify 1000 tonnes of grapes but with the possibility of expanding later.

Phil and Chris attended their first London Wine Fair in 1990 where they worked on the stand of their friends from Hunter's Wines. The small Marlborough winegrowing community of the early 1990s was close-knit and co-operative. While in London, the Roses established contacts with distributors and settled on an agent to represent their wine in the United Kingdom. They exported their first two containers of Sauvignon Blanc to England in late 1990 and the wine sold extremely well. In 1991 they took out the trophy for best Sauvignon Blanc at the Air New Zealand Wine Awards. 'We had to have a minimum of 50 cases to enter. And we had about 56, I think!' The rest of the wine – which had been bottled at Matua Valley in West Auckland because at that time the Rapaura contract winery had no bottling line – was already on its way to the UK.

With their 300 acres of vines on a diverse set of sites the Roses have no intention of having contract growers. They pick all of their blocks separately, because even though almost all their vineyards are 'on these Rapaura lighter soil types, there is a lot of variation within it. We keep them in separate batches and ferment them through.' Although they have each batch analysed comprehensively they also rely heavily on tasting and discussion to decide their final blends: 'We get those results every week. We do keep that in the back of our minds. But it's very, very much on flavour and balance.'

Asked whether his education at Lincoln and experience on his parents' property helped him move into viticulture, Phil Rose replies:

> Yeah, very much so. I mean we've been growing things all our lives really. It was just something different. Vines are relatively easy things to grow once you understand the sort of philosophy of a vineyard.

Marlborough's Sauvignon Blanc is New Zealand's Sauvignon Blanc

The Wairau Valley's distinctive shape, its fine-grained variability in soils, and subtle differences in temperature with distance from the sea and changes in elevation made it the ideal territory to experiment with planting varieties of *Vitis vinifera* native to the cooler climates of Europe, including Sancerre in the Loire Valley. The Wairau River was less co-operative when it came to laying out vineyards. Its course, and those of most of its tributaries, is roughly west to east, meaning that the sedimentary deposits of gravels, sands and silts (deposited from floods before the river and its tributaries were contained by stopbanks) also roughly parallel the river. With rows of grapes preferably aligned north to south for maximum exposure to the sun, each row tends to cross the bands of sediments, with the result that the vigour of vines often varies along the row. There is no simple solution to this dilemma other than to be aware of it and fertilise the vines to even out their vigour and yields.

Two varieties of white grapes have been especially important in Marlborough's evolution as the dominant winegrowing region of New Zealand. Müller Thurgau was the first, Sauvignon Blanc the second. For the fifteen years between 1975 and 1990, Müller Thurgau made up 27 per cent of all grapes grown in New Zealand. In quantity of grapes harvested each year, its dominance was even stronger, because its yields were higher than for most other *vinifera* varieties. From its inception, wine made from Müller Thurgau flaunted its accessible and fruity flavours that attracted a new generation of New Zealand and international wine drinkers, regardless of whether it was packaged in bottles or cardboard casks. Wine companies worked very hard to tweak their style of Müller Thurgau and increase their share of the market. For instance, Nobilo's White Cloud, a version of Müller Thurgau with a small proportion of Muscat added late in the vinification, gathered an almost cult following. But Müller Thurgau's prominence did not last and by 2000 it had fallen to 4 per cent of the national vineyard.

For grape growers, wine enterprises and consumers, Sauvignon Blanc's affinity with Marlborough's natural environment has proved a much more lasting legacy. Marlborough Sauvignon Blanc was initially a wine made in the vineyard. Its distinctive aromas and flavours baffled the wine community when it first appeared on the New Zealand and Marlborough grape-growing graphs of 1980 (Table 7.3). By then Sauvignon Blanc made up less than 2 per cent of the New Zealand vineyard. It reached 18 per cent by 1995 to eclipse the rapidly declining Müller Thurgau. By 2005, Sauvignon Blanc was 35 per cent of the national vineyard and by 2010 it was 53 per cent. Its rise to be the dominant New Zealand white wine was startling but not surprising. Its particular contribution was to introduce many New Zealand and international wine consumers to a new, palatable, crisp white table wine, with strong aromas and flavours that most of them could recognise instantly.

Pinot Noir entered Marlborough's mix of varieties in a very deliberate way. Montana, with Peter Hubscher as CEO and Tony Hoksbergen running the viticulture, instigated a planned Pinot Noir programme in 2000. This initiative, together with other Marlborough enterprises increasing their plantings of Pinot, saw its area grow from 528 hectares in the year 2000 to 1986 hectares in 2010 – an average growth rate of 146 hectares per year over the decade (Table 7.4). But this increase was dwarfed by the expansion in the area of Sauvignon Blanc over the same decade. Its Marlborough vineyard increased from 1900 hectares to 14,611 – an average rate of 1271 hectares per

Overleaf: Hand-harvesting Pinot Noir in Fairhall, Marlborough.
Jim Tannock Photography

Marlborough

year despite the annual plea from Philip Gregan, CEO of New Zealand Winegrowers, for enterprises to manage the supply of Sauvignon Blanc being cultivated in the regions.

Despite the babble of the 'Anything But Chardonnay' set in the United States, New Zealand Chardonnay between 1980 and 2000 showed a very similar sequence of growth to Sauvignon Blanc. Indeed, for these two decades, Chardonnay was a slightly higher proportion of the national vineyard, reaching almost 28 per cent by 2000 before falling to 18 per cent in 2005 as more Sauvignon Blanc was planted. Between 2000 and 2010, the slight increase in the area of Chardonnay planted in the Marlborough vineyard was much more similar to Pinot Noir's sequence than to Sauvignon Blanc's (Table 7.4). From 887 hectares at the millennium, Chardonnay reached 1089 hectares by 2010 – an increase of just 202 hectares or an average of 20 hectares per year. Marlborough, like most of New Zealand's winegrowing regions, also has Chardonnay among its top five varieties, but only in Gisborne is Chardonnay the most planted variety. Without the unique characteristics of Sauvignon Blanc, Marlborough's vineyard would probably be much closer to Hawke's Bay's in size.

This transformation of the Wairau and Awatere valleys into Sauvignon Blanc vineyards largely happened in the first decade of the new millennium. In the year 2000 these two valleys were growing 1900 hectares of Sauvignon Blanc. Five years later their Sauvignon vineyards were 3.3 times bigger with 6212 hectares planted. By 2010, New Zealand was growing 16,910 hectares of Sauvignon Blanc, of which Marlborough grew 14,611 hectares. All other viticultural regions of New Zealand (Auckland, Gisborne, Hawke's Bay, Wairarapa, Nelson, Canterbury, Waipara and Central Otago) made up the remaining 2299 hectares.

From the first commercial plantings of Sauvignon Blanc in Marlborough in 1980 through to the present, grape growers, winemakers and scientists have considered, contemplated and analysed the strong aromas, flavours and textures that give Sauvignon Blanc grown in Marlborough its unique qualities. As early as 1974 when John Marris was project manager for Montana Properties Ltd, he boldly proclaimed in a seminar presented at Lincoln College that 'the Marlborough region is a proven wine grape-growing area'. He emphasised in particular the suitability of the soils of the Wairau Plain, pointing out that he had already investigated soil profiles on a variety of different sites:

> I have carried out extensive surveys on our own and surrounding properties using a backhoe. The variability is quite incredible, and almost without exception, the southern side of the Wairau Plain will require deep ripping to some extent. I believe the majority of the soils in both regions will support grapes, and as mentioned earlier, feel that climate is a greater limiting factor.

Table 7.4: Sauvignon Blanc, Pinot Noir and Chardonnay in the Marlborough vineyard

Grape variety	1975	1980	1990	1995	2000	2005	2010
Sauvignon Blanc (ha)	–	33	211	845	1900	6212	14,611
Sauvignon Blanc (% of total)		4	15	28	47	62	76
Pinot Noir (ha)		25	44	206	528	1676	1986
Pinot Noir (% of total)		3	3	7	13	17	10
Chardonnay (ha)	–	55	270	697	887	1120	1089
Chardonnay (% of total)		7	19	23	22	11	6
SB + PN + Ch (% of total)		14	37	58	82	90	92

Winemaker Kevin Judd is just as unequivocal on the reason for the distinctiveness of Marlborough's Sauvignon Blanc when he insists that 'it's primarily climatic'. The two points of view are not necessarily contradictory. Few grapes were planted when John Marris thoroughly explored the region's variability in soils.

The general skills and knowledge about growing crops that its farmers brought to viticulture were fundamental to Marlborough's success. Grape trellises are little more than slightly sophisticated fences. Landowners and contractors in the region were quick to realise this and bring their ingenuity to bear to adjust their designs and speed the planting. No individual captured the spirit of contract grape growing more adroitly than the late Henk Ruesink. When payment for Sauvignon Blanc was by the tonne and grapes were in short supply, he configured his trellising and adjusted his pruning to maximise the vineyard's yield of the variety. As John Forrest considers his own learning curve in establishing their vineyard he reflects on the skills of the Wairau and Awatere farmers who adopted grape growing:

> That's an unsung strength of our Marlborough industry, and why we've been so successful so quickly – you've got this intellectual pool of farmers who had all the skills to be grape growers, just weren't growing grapes. They were growing sheep, or maize or barley.

Marlborough's Sauvignon Blanc is truly New Zealand's Sauvignon Blanc.

8

Central Otago

In certain parts of this district, where a good aspect and well-sheltered spots are available, the cultivation of the vine may be undertaken, but judgment must be exercised in the selection of varieties to be planted, and cultivation and pruning methods must be adopted that meet the requirements of the colder vine-growing regions.
– ROMEO BRAGATO (1895)

After a Lincoln College seminar in 1976, Tom McDonald, the managing director of McWilliam's Wines in Hawke's Bay, asked Ann Pinckney her plans when she graduated with her Master's degree in horticultural science. She replied: 'Grow grapes in Central Otago.' The sceptical Scot's reply was unequivocal: 'You'll never grow grapes down there, lassie!' McDonald's response captures a common attitude among members of the established industry of the time who were almost all growing their grapes in the North Island. They made their judgements on the basis of their experience in regions like Auckland, the Waikato, Gisborne and Hawke's Bay where variability in temperatures is less than in regions with a more continental climate such as Central Otago.

Bob Knappstein, the highly respected McWilliam's viticulturist, responded similarly when he visited Central Otago in 1972:

Chard Farm in the Kawarau Gorge. *Rob Suisted/ www.naturespic.com*

> On the day of the visit, 16 December, Riesling-Sylvaner were still partly in flower and on the customary optimum period to harvest, this will make for a late harvest in mid-April.... Two fellow grape growers endorsed that this variety would have been flowering at this stage in mid-November in Auckland.

Viticulturists frequently relate events in the phenology of the vine – such as bud burst, flowering or veraison – to local climatic conditions. Knappstein was arguing that vines growing in Central Otago would not have sufficient time to ripen their crop. But Central Otago is more than eight degrees further from the equator than Auckland. During Central's growing season, days are noticeably longer and climatic regimes are quite different. The later flowering of all grape varieties in Central Otago is itself a response to lower spring temperatures. Such late flowering helps protect the vines from late-spring frosts. Providing that sufficient solar energy is available later in the season to ripen the grapes, the late flowering need not be a problem. Moreover, low precipitation in Central Otago means that picking is less likely to be hurried by rain, although an early autumn frost may result in senescence of the leaves. Viticulturists now argue that Central's long autumn with warm days and cool nights stimulates the transfer of flavour and colour compounds into the berries of Pinot Noir.

In the late 1960s and early 1970s, therefore, Central Otago – not Marlborough or Wairarapa or Nelson or Hawke's Bay – became the focus of the climate/vine debate in New Zealand. Between 1967 and 1972 the journal *Wine Review* (edited by Dick Scott) ran a series of articles on the Ministry of Agriculture's grape trials on R. V. (Larry) Kinnaird's orchard at Earnscleugh, Central Otago. Scott visited the trial and wrote four short pieces. S. J. Franklin (Horticultural Advisory Officer, Alexandra) published two articles, one in *Wine Review* and one in the *Journal of Agriculture*. Scott's characteristically provocative piece titled 'Otago (2) High hopes meet official caution' exposes the tensions he perceived between the official views of the Department of Agriculture and those of the local residents and politicians. Under the heading 'Lukewarm Officialdom' Scott's angle was that:

> Given an ounce of encouragement there will be no shortage of individuals ready to pioneer a Central Otago viticultural industry. Sharp frosts and searing summers, isolation and irrigation – these are no deterrent to the enthusiasts *Wine Review* spoke to on a recent visit.

The difference between the advice of the North Island scientists at the Te Kauwhata Viticultural Research Station and the Central Otago advisory officer, Steve Franklin, is revealing. In May 1967, in answer to a written enquiry from an Otago resident interested in planting grapes, the representative of the research station replied:

> Penfolds, I am told, looked at the South Island for wine production but settled on the North Island. My advice to you is to do likewise; or at least go into your venture with the knowledge that you may come across insuperable problems.

The local view was more informed and less extreme. For a start, Franklin showed more intimate knowledge of Central Otago's sites:

> Heat trap areas... are known to ripen stone fruit somewhat earlier than the average for the district. Such heat trap areas could be ideal for production of early to early-mid-season grape varieties. One has to live in Central Otago for several years, and spend time poking round the district, to get to know these spots or to realise their extent.

He added the following:

> As vines do not normally come into growth before October only the last half of the frost fighting season would be a worry. In many seasons there would be no damaging frosts within this period, and in fact there were none in the season just past. Apples are at their most frost tender over the same period and it is not often necessary to light frost pots in an apple block.

Central Otago residents who knew the history of the region could also point to successful cultivation of the vine in the past. Even during the growing seasons of these debates, fruit from small parcels of vines in the region were being successfully ripened. As Scott implied, local winegrowers were likely to treat the debate as a challenge to prove the North Islanders wrong. Rolfe and Lois Mills of Rippon Vineyard certainly adopted this stance by planting a kaleidoscope of varieties before recognising that in their environment, a few kilometres from Wanaka, Pinot Noir performed best.

The mix of varieties in Central Otago has changed dramatically in the two decades from 1989 when the New Zealand Wine Institute collected the first reliable information on the varietal mix of regions. Pinot Noir has always been the dominant variety in this region. Its dominance has increased decade by decade and most noticeably in the twenty-first century. In 1990, Pinot Noir made up 22 per cent of the Central Otago vineyard; by 2000 it was 49 per cent; and by 2010 it was 78 per cent (Table 8.1). Marlborough, with 76 per cent of its vineyard planted in Sauvignon Blanc, is the only other region where a single variety is almost as dominant.

Two other varieties, Riesling and Sauvignon Blanc, have always been among the top five varieties in Central Otago during the last 20 years. Pinot Gris appeared as one of the five main varieties in the late 1990s and has since become the second most important variety, although, at just 9 per cent of the regional vineyard, well behind

Pinot Noir. It looks destined to remain the second most-planted variety and the most important white variety for some time. Riesling is a possible challenger as several of the Central winemakers, including Blair Walters of Felton Road, are intensely interested in vinifying Riesling to achieve a wine of intense aromas and flavours but with low alcohol. In 2000, Chardonnay made up 22 per cent of the Central Otago vineyard but by 2010 it was just 4 per cent. It seems fated to remain a lesser variety except for those enterprises making sparkling wine.

Central Otago's aspiring winegrowers stared down the scepticism of the ill-informed North Islanders by encouraging scientists to study the weather and climate of the region more thoroughly. Gordon Cossens, a scientist at MAFTech's Invermay research station in Mosgiel, investigated the temperature regimes of this climatically complicated region and provided winegrowers with reliable information to supplement their empirical experiments. The outcome of these efforts was the creation of one of New Zealand's most vibrant and exciting wine regions.

Horticulture, viticulture and Romeo Bragato

Horticulture and market gardening developed in Central Otago from the 1860s. Like similar mid-nineteenth-century gold-mining regions in California and Australia, small agricultural and horticultural enterprises sprang up to service the miners and their communities. In Otago the predominantly Anglo-Celtic population later used the abandoned water races, constructed for sluicing gold, to develop irrigated pip- and stone-fruit orchards growing predominantly apricots and cherries as the lowland foundations of the local rural economy.

Among the kaleidoscope of cultures attracted to Central Otago by gold was Jean Désiré Ferraud from France. On the west bank of the Clutha, just south of Alexandra, the name Frenchman's Point records the spot where in 1863 he and a group of others struck it lucky. In 1864 he used the proceeds to purchase a property of 100 acres (41 hectares) near the mouth of the Waikerikeri Valley. Ferraud was elected the first mayor of the municipality of Dunstan (now Clyde) in 1866. By 1870 he and his family were growing over 1200 vines as well as a variety of fruits on 'Monte Christo'. He sold this land in 1882 and moved to Dunedin where he became a partner in a firm that made wines and cordials.

Ferraud probably planted Pinot Noir. One of his wines, a 'Burgundy', won a merit award at Sydney in 1881. At that time the name Burgundy was more likely to mean the Pinot Noir grape, whereas in the resurgent wine industries of Australia and the United States of the 1960s the word Burgundy was used for wine from almost any red grapes. In the second half of the twentieth century, for instance, Gallo's Hearty Burgundy was

Table 8.1: Varietal evolution (% of Central Otago's vineyard in five main varieties)

1990		2000		2010	
Pinot Noir	22	Pinot Noir	49	Pinot Noir	78
Riesling	21	Chardonnay	22	Pinot Gris	9
Sauvignon Blanc	15	Pinot Gris	9	Chardonnay	4
Gewürztraminer	14	Riesling	8	Riesling	4
Cabernet Sauvignon	9	Sauvignon Blanc	6	Sauvignon Blanc	2
Total of 5 main varieties	81%	Total of 5 main varieties	94%	Total of 5 main varieties	97%

Table 8.2: Area in Pinot Noir by region (hectares)

	1990	2000	2010		1990	2000	2010
Auckland	30	17	24	Marlborough	44	528	1987
Waikato	2	5	8	Nelson	4	34	196
Gisborne	17	39	76	Canterbury	21	120	438
Hawke's Bay	36	118	379	Central Otago	4	136	1202
Wairarapa	20	101	465	New Zealand	178	1098	4777

Note By 2010, 220 hectares of Hawke's Bay Pinot Noir and 167 hectares of Marlborough's were used for sparkling wine. In 2000, Waipara grew 54 hectares of the total Canterbury Pinot Noir and by 2010, 313 hectares.

one of California's most popular jug wines, but very little, if any, of it saw Pinot Noir grapes. Bragato almost certainly visited the former Ferraud property. In an 1893 photograph (two years before Bragato's visit) vines were still growing against its stone winery. If the twentieth-century DSIR trial in Central Otago is taken as an example of survival without irrigation, other vines may also have survived on the Ferraud property. The trial was abandoned and the irrigation turned off in 1978 but its vines were still bearing fruit in 2002.

Early attempts at viticulture received approval when Croatian-born, Italian-trained scientist Romeo Bragato visited New Zealand. Bragato, Viticultural Expert to the Government of Victoria, Australia, arrived in New Zealand on 19 February 1895 under instructions from the Premier of Victoria, and at the invitation of the New Zealand government, to assess the prospects for viticulture in the colony. Central Otago was the first region he visited, commenting:

> . . . the grapes, notwithstanding that the vines had been high trained, were perfectly ripe. This was on the 25th February, a convincing fact to me that the summer climatic conditions here are conducive to the early ripening of the fruit.

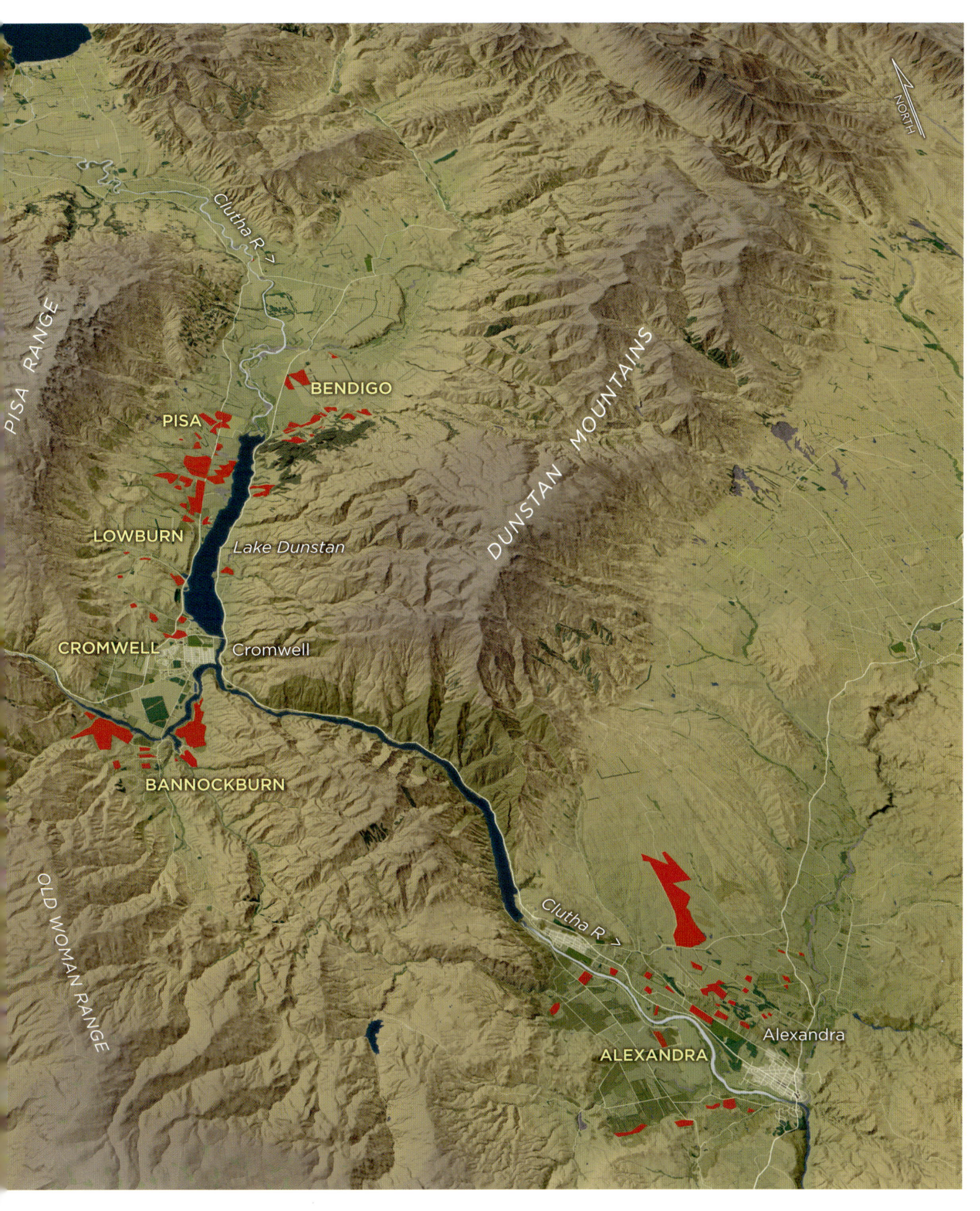

He did not identify the variety, but today's grape growers would not be picking anywhere near this early in the season. Writing of the Queenstown area, he said:

> In certain parts of this district, where a good aspect and well-sheltered spots are available, the cultivation of the vine may be undertaken, but judgment must be exercised in the selection of varieties to be planted, and cultivation and pruning methods must be adopted that meet the requirements of the colder vine-growing regions.

Other scientists were later to echo his caution.

By the end of the nineteenth century, therefore, Central Otago had shown its potential to ripen varieties of *Vitis vinifera* and make wine from them, but it took over 80 years before a prestige wine industry emerged. The successful cultivation of classical varieties of grapes and the making of wine in Central Otago during the 1860s and 1870s influenced this revival of viticulture a century later. Franklin mentions Jean Désiré Ferraud by name, while newspaper articles about the DSIR trial of the early 1970s quote an Italian viticulturist (undoubtedly Bragato) having said that the area was 'pre-eminently suitable for the growing of wine grapes' without mentioning his caveats.

Central Otago's terrain and sub-regions

With its vines and wineries spread over an area four times larger than the Hawke's Bay wine region and about twice as large as that of Marlborough, Central Otago is the most dispersed of New Zealand's wine regions. Yet Central's area in vines is about one third that of Hawke's Bay and about 7 per cent that of Marlborough. Vines in Central Otago are clustered in what the local winegrowers call sub-regions, some of which are over 100 kilometres apart. Each sub-region has its own distinctive history, style, character and contribution to the story of the evolution of winegrowing here. As the wineries gradually acquire land in several sub-regions, their local distinctiveness erodes, although the quality of their wine may improve as they discover better sites for growing Pinot Noir. The six sub-regions commonly identified are: Wanaka; Gibbston and the Kawarau Valley; Luggate to Cromwell (Clutha and Lake Dunstan right bank); Tarras to Cromwell, including Bendigo (Clutha and Lake Dunstan left bank); Bannockburn; and Alexandra.

The terrain of Central Otago is aptly described as 'basin and range'; valleys of varied widths are separated by substantial mountain ranges. The Clutha and Kawarau rivers and their tributaries provide the network to relate this terrain to the distribution of the region's vineyards and wineries. The Clutha sets the north–south trend. From its source at Lake Wanaka it flows southeast for 20 kilometres before being joined by the

Lindis River just before the first arm of the triangular Loop Road leading to the former mining town of Bendigo. The Clutha then carves south, the Pisa Range to its west and the Dunstan Mountains to its east. After the Kawarau River joins it at Cromwell the Clutha continues slightly east of south to Alexandra, the northern ridge of the Garvie Mountains to its west.

The Kawarau River has its source in Lake Wakatipu from where it sweeps eastwards around the northern fringe of the Remarkables, skirting the triangular tip of the Carrick Range before continuing eastwards to join the Clutha at Cromwell. This complex terrain, sculpted by these two rivers and their tributaries, results in slopes with many different aspects, parts of valleys that are shaded even during summer, and steeper slopes that in other countries are planted in vines (such as along the Rhine in Germany) but in Central Otago still grow tussock.

One way of revealing the relationships between vines and their terrain is to predict location of vineyards (and land with potential for planting them) by using measurements of the terrain that also strongly influence the weather and climate of the region. Three criteria are used in the digital terrain model that follows: elevation, slope, and aspect. Elevation has a direct effect on temperature. The decline in temperature with height (lapse rate) is about 1°C per 100 metres of elevation. The difference in elevation along the valley of the Clutha is small and the differences in temperature subdued. Between Lake Wanaka and Alexandra the change in elevation is only 100 metres. As a result the difference in temperature between the two locations directly attributable to elevation is about 1°C, although many other influences, notably aspect, affect the climates of individual sites.

In contrast, changes in temperature as a result of elevation are spectacular over short distances between valleys of the Clutha and Kawarau and the adjacent hills and mountains. Differences in elevation of 500 to 1000 metres between the floor of a valley and the nearest major ridge are common. As a result, daytime temperature differences of between 5°C and 10°C over a few kilometres are also common. Elevation has a major influence on precipitation and wind. Being in the rain shadow of the Southern Alps, most of Central Otago receives under 600 millimetres of precipitation annually. Irrigation is essential here. Gordon Cossens' work also established that in terrain such as that of Central Otago the lapse rate varies from between 0.3°C to the widely quoted 1°C.

Slope also influences the potential for winegrowing. Slopes of over 15 degrees make mechanical cultivation difficult. Central Otago's western hills and mountains are much steeper than those further east. The Remarkables, and further north the Crown Range and mountains west of the Cardrona River, have very few slopes less than 15 degrees. To the east, the Pisa and Dunstan ranges have been smoothed by glacial action, and a much higher proportion of their slopes are less than 15 degrees, especially their north- and west-facing ones. Nevertheless, the majority of gently sloping land suitable for

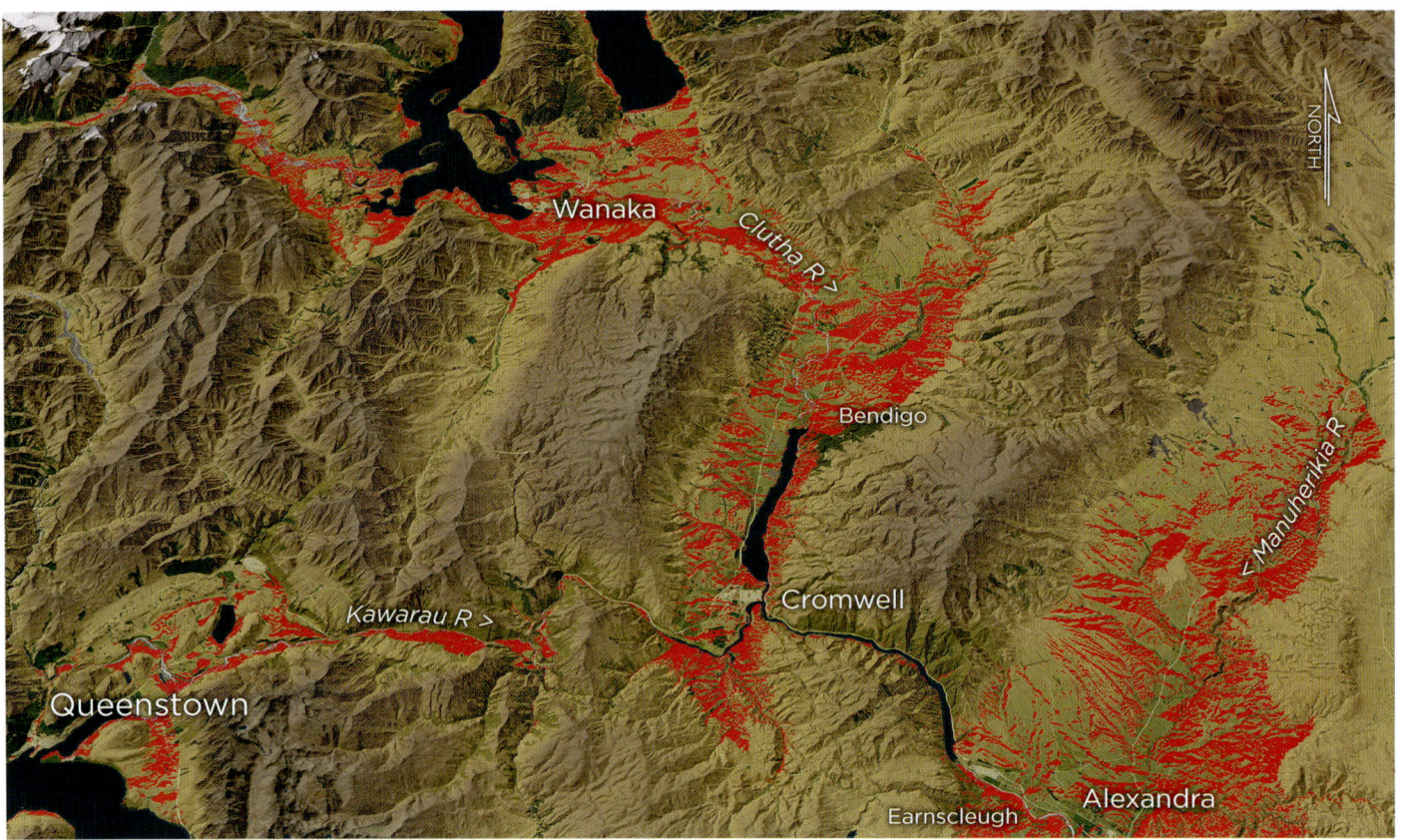

Figure 8.1 Altitude, slope, and aspect as environmental constraints on viticulture in Central Otago. The map identifies land with elevation of less than 400 metres, a slope of less than 15 degrees, and a northwest through northeast aspect.

vines under present climate conditions is in the river valleys, or very close to them. The main hazard along these valleys is spring frosts from cool-air drainage onto flat land. Winegrowers have often chosen adjacent slopes to avoid this hazard.

When it comes to aspect, a distinction again exists between the western and eastern parts of the Central Otago wine region. Those localities where vineyards are dense – the Gibbston locality along the Kawarau, the Clutha–Lake Dunstan valley (including Bendigo), Bannockburn and Alexandra – all have a high proportion of northerly facing slopes. Again, the valleys of the Cardrona and Nevis rivers establish a clear boundary between the northwestern, triangular third of Central Otago where northerly facing slopes are scattered and scarce, and the remaining two thirds of the region. East of the Cardrona–Nevis line, vines are much more dominant in the landscape.

When elevation, slope and aspect are combined on one map, the potential land for vineyards in Central Otago is defined (Figure 8.1). This map identifies almost all the

Table 8.3: Terrain (and associated climate) influences on vine sites in Central Otago

Elevation (m)	<330	<350	<400
Land area suitable for vines (ha)	19,540	25,560	40,260

Note The calculations are based on three criteria: elevation; slopes of <15 degrees; and an aspect of northwest through northeast. For this table, only the elevation is allowed to vary.

places where some vines are already planted; it also indicates the parts of the region that are likely to attract attention for future plantings. Even when a strict limit is put on elevation by considering land only under 330 metres, almost 20,000 hectares is classified as being suitable for vines (Table 8.1). Easing this elevation restraint to less than 400 metres doubles this figure to 40,000 hectares. In 2010, New Zealand's total area in vines was 33,428 hectares and Central Otago's about 1500 hectares. It thus seems highly unlikely that Central Otago will run out of vineyard land in the immediate future.

On the north- and west-facing slopes of the higher terraces at Bendigo, Pinot Noir has been planted as high as 400 metres. It ripens here because the favourable aspect of these slopes increases annual solar energy by up to 120 degree-days annually and offsets their higher altitude. Chinamans Terrace, as it is known locally, is a kilometre from Rudi Bauer's original Bendigo plantings on the southern arm of the Loop Road and the same distance from the Perriam homestead of Bendigo Station. South towards Cromwell along State Highway 8, the aspect of the Lakeside Vineyards is more westerly. Here, a variety of owners have intensively planted from almost on the lakeshore to about 400 metres. They include Misha's vineyard and Devil's Creek. Many other favourable sites at similar altitude exist in the region.

The most surprising results from this digital terrain model are the large areas of land suitable for viticulture in the Manuherikia catchment. When combined with the well-established orchards and other smallholdings along the Earnscleugh and Alexandra–Fruitlands Road, this southeastern corner of Central Otago contributes well over half the 20,000 hectares of land below 330 metres identified as being suitable for vines. The Earnscleugh and Fruitlands roads have a long history of successful intensive horticulture by orcharding enterprises, and viticulture has made only small inroads there. Farms practising pastoral agriculture in the Manuherikia and adjacent smaller catchments are more likely to be subdivided for vines than those holdings already successfully growing other horticultural crops.

Central Otago also has the advantage of much cultivable land at higher elevations not planted in vines. These higher slopes are likely to become more important in the future. At present many of them are not warm enough to ripen the available clones of

The north- and west-facing slopes of the Bendigo Terraces provide a sun trap that enables winegrowers to plant as high as 400 metres above the Loop Road.
Alan Kwok Lun Cheung

Pinot Noir. Two things are likely to change this: new clones of Pinot Noir and global warming. Scientists in the research establishments of several countries are attempting to breed cultivars of Pinot Noir that will mature in a shorter growing season. When these are available, sites now viewed as marginal will be re-evaluated. Global warming will further enhance the attraction of these higher sites because Central Otago viticulturists will be able to use planting at higher altitude to ameliorate its effects. Both factors will increase Central Otago's area in land suited to viticulture.

Even without such environmental and technical changes, the land suitable for planting vines, notably Pinot Noir, is considerable. Constraints of climate and terrain are not the main restriction to increasing the area in vines in Central Otago. Access to suitable sites is likely to be more limiting. Many of them are at higher elevations and part of viable, although extensive, livestock farming operations. It will require landowners to make these sites available or plant them in vines.

In the round of planting on greenfield sites from the mid-1990s into the new millennium the economic rent (return on investment) to be gained from winegrowing was sufficient to encourage runholders to free up land. Windfall gains of $15,000 per hectare from land sold for viticulture in localities such as Bendigo were difficult to resist when the market for fine wools from merino sheep was faltering. Whether demand for Central Otago wine will continue to grow at a similar rate is difficult to predict hard on the heels of a set of economic uncertainties in the first decade of the twenty-first century. But the international market for wines of high quality and reputation from exotic, beautiful places will continue to increase. Central Otago's vines and wine landscapes enhance its attractiveness to tourists and to the international market for its wine.

Viticultural trials

Central Otago, like other regions of New Zealand praised by Bragato, saw few grapes planted until the late 1970s. The stirrings of the table wine industry in Hawke's Bay, Auckland, and its extension into Gisborne during the 1960s aroused local and scientific interest in many parts of New Zealand including Central Otago. The region's reputation for orcharding led two departments of central government – the Department of Agriculture and the Department of Scientific and Industrial Research – to establish grapevine trials starting in 1962. The interest in grape growing was stimulated by government's rural policy, which offered generous tax breaks and low-interest loans for intensifying rural production, and the horticultural euphoria sparked by kiwifruit that swept the rural economy.

The objectives of the two trials were different. The Department of Agriculture one was to test the 'hardiness' of varieties in a region such as Central Otago, and the DSIR one to test varieties known to be suitable for unfortified table wines. A summary of the varieties of vines grown in the Department of Agriculture trial run from 1962 to 1973 and the DSIR trial that ran from 1972 to 1978 illustrates the sea change that was beginning to emerge in New Zealand viticulture. The hybrids (especially the Seibels), bulk producers such as the Muscats and Müller Thurgau, and the sherry grape Palomino dominated the Department of Agriculture trial. These were the foundation of New Zealand's fortified wines and continued to be important in the 'bag-in-box' wines of the 1970s and 1980s because by then the vines of these varieties were mature and bearing heavy crops in Auckland, Gisborne and Hawke's Bay. However, it does show that the South Island and Central Otago were on the Department of Agriculture's viticultural radar a decade before Montana's move into Marlborough in 1973.

The DSIR trial of the 1970s had a quite different suite of varieties. It concentrated on the *vinifera* wine varieties and clones that dominate the cooler regions of France and Germany. Some of these, especially Chardonnay and Riesling, had begun to show their potential in twentieth-century New Zealand during the 1960s. Others were yet to perform. The plantings (with their main French regions of origin in brackets) included Pinot Noir and Chardonnay (Burgundy), these two plus Pinot Meunier (Champagne), Gewürztraminer and Riesling (Alsace), as well as Gamay (Beaujolais), Cabernet Sauvignon (Bordeaux) and Syrah (Rhone Valley). Also included were a few of the hybrids and recently bred German varieties such as Stein. Pinot Gris had been planted in the earlier Department of Agriculture trial.

Results from these trials encouraged both the pioneering growers, some of whom took cuttings from the vines, and those who organised the experiments. But the fuller incorporation of their stories into the folklore of the region had to await the development of the late twentieth-century wine industry in Central. Once commercial production was established, producers, consumers, publicists and journalists reinvoked and re-established these histories and extended the association of the region with the vine back to Ferraud and Bragato.

Pioneers of the modern industry

By the early 1980s, five growers had established vineyards in Central Otago. They were Alan Brady, founder of Gibbston Valley Wines; Verdun Burgess and Sue Edwards of Black Ridge; the Grant family of William Hill Vineyards; Rolfe and Lois Mills of Rippon Vineyard west of Wanaka; and Ann Pinckney of Taramea Wines. Pinckney was the first to establish a winery, on the Speargrass Flat east of Queenstown, and several of the other enterprises made their first wines there. This group's motto was to 'plant and to hell with it'.

Rippon Vineyard became something of a viticultural trial in its own right and Rolfe Mills a willing source of knowledge to potential growers. 'If MAF or anybody else said it wouldn't grow here, I'd plant a few vines,' he declared. Rolfe and Lois Mills first planted the hybrid Seibels in 1974, to which they added Albany Surprise in 1975, with the bulk of the vineyard being planted in 30 varieties in 1981. New clones of Pinot Noir were added in 1985.

The Grants of Alexandra experimented with a few vines a decade before Rippon. Bill (William Hill) Grant, a schoolteacher at the time, planted about a hundred cuttings of the table grapes Gros Colman and Black Hamburg shortly after buying property near Alexandra in 1962. They were killed by a heavy copper spray. His 1974 cuttings and nursery of Chasselas and Palomino came from the Department of Agriculture trial on the Kinnaird property. Pinot Noir, Chardonnay, Gewürztraminer and Müller Thurgau vines from Blenheim were added in 1979. The William Hill vineyard remained smaller than Rippon until the Grants, with son David now in the business, purchased a mobile bottling plant. This attempt to diversify their enterprise became difficult to sustain in

The bereted bon vivant Rolfe Mills of Rippon Vineyard was one of a small group of Central Otago enthusiasts who built a wine industry out of nothing. *Rippon*

the economic conditions of the early twenty-first century and the family firm filed for bankruptcy in 2009.

Both the Grant and the Mills enterprises were initially relatively indiscriminate about the varieties they planted, taking a decade or more to establish their preferred varieties. In one sense, this hesitation was surprising, because by the early 1970s the classical varieties of *Vitis vinifera* were beginning to show their superiority in the North Island regions. Moreover, Central's DSIR trial of 1972–78 included all of the *vinifera* varieties that were to prove successful in the region, including both Pinot Noir and Riesling. On the other hand, both William Hill and Rippon were initially hobby vineyards, remote from other commercial vineyards and wineries and the year-to-year accumulation of knowledge that was more characteristic of West Auckland, Gisborne, Hawke's Bay and even Marlborough at the time.

Ann Pinckney, who had met Professor Helmut Becker of the Geisenheim Grape Breeding Institute when he visited New Zealand in 1978, also favoured the Germanic varieties in her first plantings (she 'met Gewürztraminer' during a six-week stint in

Central Otago

Alsace), and with Dr Rainer Eschenbruch of the Te Kauwhata Viticultural Research Station undoubtedly influenced her Speargrass Flat neighbour Alan Brady. Brady initially tried a small number of varieties without knowing how they might perform on his Gibbston property. In 1981 he planted 100 cuttings each of Pinot Gris, Gewürztraminer, Müller Thurgau and Chasselas. When he had mixed success, partly because of inexperience, he took the advice of Eschenbruch and planted the Germanic variety of the moment, Müller Thurgau. Within a year, after increasing contact with Rolfe Mills and Ann Pinckney, he had replaced the Müller Thurgau with 3000 Riesling plants and 4000 Pinot Noir. In these 1984 plantings he also experimented with Pinotage and Cabernet Sauvignon. Empirical experience soon showed him that neither was suited to Central Otago: 'The Pinotage never ripened. But it looked wonderful – big, healthy-looking bunches. It was as green as anything with very high acid. It wasn't any good.'

Three observations stand out from the Brady chronology: he was willing to experiment; he was temporarily attracted to (or advised to plant) the popular varieties of the moment; and he rapidly adjusted to plant varieties that were proving successful in Central Otago. Within four years of his first planting he had settled on Pinot Noir and Riesling as the two main varieties at Gibbston Valley Wines, supplemented by Pinot Gris and Gewürztraminer from his original plantings. It is unlikely that the transition would have been as quick if similar learning had not already occurred among several of the other pioneering growers. These four varieties are among the principal varieties of the elite wine regions of northern France and southern Germany – Burgundy, Champagne and Alsace.

The serendipity of dispersed plantings

The efforts of these first five enterprises to plant a significant area in grapes illustrated key features that were important to learning about the suitability of natural environments of the Central Otago region for different varieties of *Vitis vinifera*: they made production rather than location decisions; they were dispersed but interacted closely; they were liberal in passing on their knowledge; and they possessed a mixture of talents.

All the first five growers owned their land and decided to plant grapes on it rather than searching more widely for suitable sites. From the point of view of adding to the store of knowledge of Central Otago's viticultural environments, their dispersal proved enlightening. The five were sufficiently spread (Wanaka; Alexandra and the Earnscleugh Road; Gibbston in the Kawarau Gorge; and Speargrass Flat) that the north–south extent of the localities suitable for vines, and a large part of the east–west extent, were clarified by their success or failure with different grape varieties. This dispersal, together with the interaction among the owners, built the initial spatial knowledge of Central Otago's natural environments. Rolfe Mills, Ann Pinckney and Alan Brady met regularly. They made wine in the Taramea winery on Pinckney's property on Speargrass Road and were the forerunners of the Central Otago Winegrowers Association.

Three of the currently important clusters of vineyards and wineries – the Gibbston locality in the Kawarau Gorge (often now loosely referred to as Gibbston Valley after its first winery), Alexandra (William Hill Vineyards), and the schists along Earnscleugh Road (Black Ridge) – have all become successful localities for vines. By the mid-1990s some of the local grape growers, now with considerable experience of different parts of the region, such as Michael and James Moffitt (the sons of Bill and Sybilla Moffitt of Dry Gully Vineyard) and actor Sam Neill, had bought land and planted on the northeast-facing ridge of schists.

Despite the Wanaka area having its well-known Rippon Vineyard and winery, this locality has so far seen only small areas planted in grapes. Much of the land surrounding Rippon is steep and difficult to cultivate. Moreover, Rolfe and Lois Mills had first choice of land in the vicinity. Subsequently, owners of high-country runs were reluctant to sell small parcels of land, especially when the price of land was rapidly increasing. The area of Speargrass Flat (Taramea Wines) has also seen few vines planted. Growing grapes over several seasons helped Ann Pinckney to establish empirically the patterns of one of the main hazards to viticulture in this part of the region. Her experience in fighting frost on her own property and in establishing vines on her mother's nearby land helped establish the low probabilities of success there (Ann was initially reluctant to use smudge pots for frost control anyway because in her other life as a Karitane nurse she did not want to have soot fall on the nappies drying on the clotheslines of the Speargrass Flat).

Four aspects of the Central Otago experience inform the general story of the importance of learning in the regional specialisation of New Zealand winegrowing. First, empirical experimentation by growers on specific sites was the initial means of establishing the suitability of parts of the region for particular varieties of vines and the quality of wine that could be made from them. Second, winemakers working for the first few wineries extended this spatial knowledge by processing grapes from other sites. Taramea was the first of these wineries. Once Gibbston Valley Wines had established their own fermentation facilities in the Kawarau Gorge they began processing grapes on contract or buying them from vineyards in other localities. Their knowledge of the other localities in Central Otago soon widened, placing them in a much stronger position to choose where they would source their grapes from, to obtain qualities of flavour and aroma to enhance the wines made from their existing sites. By 2010, Gibbston Valley Wines owned about 10 hectares in the Gibbston locality but

sourced grapes from over 60 hectares elsewhere in Central Otago, some on land they had purchased and some bought from grape growers.

Third, this *filière* structure – grape growers (often aspiring winegrowers) with small areas in vines selling to the few wineries or having wine made by them under contract – was secured through local capital establishing the Central Otago Wine Company. This is a contract winemaking company in Cromwell partly funded by actor Sam Neill that makes wine for different labels from vineyards scattered throughout the region. From harvest to bottling and beyond, its principal winemakers (Mike Wolter followed by Dean Shaw) became repositories of knowledge of the qualities of the region's wines, especially of the dominant variety Pinot Noir and its variations from many vintages and across a wide range of sites. This knowledge filtered through to other participants in the industry.

Fourth, the distinctive *filière* of this region was reinforced by the organisation of particular enterprises. Until the early twenty-first century, Peregrine Wines sourced

The Gibbston Valley looking west towards Lake Hayes and Queenstown. *Alan Kwok Lun Cheung*

almost all of its grapes from its own contract growers. These are not contract growers in the sense in which the term is used in other regions – that is, farmers who already own land and plant grapes on part of their property. Many of the Central Otago growers are New Zealand or international professionals who either purchased their land and house site from Wentworth Estates, the associated company that subdivided and marketed the Gibbston lowland portion of Wentworth Station, or took advice on purchasing other land from Greg Hay of Peregrine or other informed locals. Purchase of the 4-hectare sites from Wentworth initially included the contracting of the planted grape crop back to Peregrine who also tended such vineyards. The distinctive blue Peregrine vineyard sign designating their contract growers has dotted the landscape of Central Otago from Gibbston to the side roads of Lowburn, and from Bendigo to Northburn Station. Peregrine was marking out its territory just as Cloudy Bay signposted its Marlborough vineyards when it was first established.

Central Otago's vine climates

The decision in the 1970s to dam the Clutha River and build a hydroelectric power station near Clyde was highly controversial. Sluicing for alluvial gold from the 1860s, followed by dredging for gold in the twentieth century, had already degraded the lowland landscape of much of Central Otago. Locals were polarised by the prospect of their unique landscape and close communities being split and divided by a 50-kilometre lake from the dam at Clyde to the Loop Road, Bendigo. Construction finally commenced in 1982, the dam was commissioned in 1992, and Lake Dunstan filled in 1993. At the junction of the Clutha and Kawarau rivers the lake flooded the lowest and oldest part of the historic mining town of Cromwell. It also affected the narrow Kawarau Gorge that links Cromwell with Arrowtown and Queenstown.

The National government of the 1970s and early 1980s and the Labour government from 1984 placated Central Otago's rural population by providing funds for a joint study by the Ministries of Agriculture and of Works to investigate the possibilities of intensifying the rural production of Central Otago. Scientists in the regional offices of these two central government agencies focused on establishing the temperature and wind patterns along the upper Clutha and Kawarau rivers. Grapes were included as one of the main crops to be considered, although the weather and climate information which was compiled could be applied to a variety of annual and perennial crops. MAFTech's Gordon Cossens organised much of the data collection and analysis and was lead author on most of the reports.

This detailed scientific work was disseminated in a series of publications that were printed sub-region by sub-region as the research was completed. Those contemplating winegrowing in Central Otago, including local landowners, devoured the information. The strength of the research derives from the close network ('swarm' in the climatological jargon) of temporary climate stations the researchers established in each sub-region. The fine resolution of the network, when integrated with the longer climatic record of the meteorological stations of Central Otago, established the seasonal temperature regimes and wind patterns of the localities where grapes might be grown. The topoclimatological studies identified potential vineyard sites in new localities – notably in the Lowburn area, on both sides of Lake Dunstan, near Bendigo, as well as at Bannockburn and the higher terraces along Lake Dunstan. No other wine region in New Zealand had such a comprehensive analysis of its weather and climate.

By the early to mid-1980s, empirical knowledge of the performance of different grape varieties was accumulating rapidly among the first group of wine enterprises and could be generalised and verified against the detailed information from the data collected by Cossens and others. By the early 1990s, the second wave of aspiring winegrowers such as Stewart Elms, the Dicey family and Steve Green of Carrick were able to differentiate

Table 8.4: Favoured locations for possible Central Otago vineyards

Locality	Growing degree-days >10°C Oct–April	Average Daily °C January			Annual mm precipitation	Air frosts Sept/Oct
		Max	Min	Mean		
>1100 Degree-days						
Bannockburn	1290	25.2	11.2	18.2	400	7
>1000 Degree-days						
Cromwell to Pisa	1100	24.4	11.0	17.7	400	10
Cromwell Gorge	1100	24.1	11.9	18.0	400	6
Alexandra to Clyde	1030	23.2	10.7	17.0	350	8
Bendigo	1040	23.8	9.8	16.8	400	8
>900 Degree-days						
Wanaka	940	24.1	10.4	17.3	660	9
Gibbston	910	24.1	9.3	16.7	600	6
>800 Degree-days						
Roxburgh–Dunbarton	890	23.1	9.8	16.8	500	6
Arrow Basin	890	23.8	8.8	16.3	650	6

the climates of different parts of Central Otago and be more confident in their choices of where to buy land and plant.

Cossens' research demonstrated that the accumulation of energy over the growing season varies considerably from one locality of Central Otago to another (Table 8.4). Two of the three places where grapes were already planted (Gibbston and Wanaka) both accumulate fewer than 950 degree-days over the growing season, whereas Alexandra (1030) and Bendigo (1040) receive appreciably more solar energy. The results from Bannockburn are even more persuasive. Its degree-days during the growing season are at least 350 higher than Wanaka and Gibbston and more than 150 higher than all other districts. The conclusion is clear: the first plantings in Central Otago were not in the most favourable places for coaxing grapes to reach physiological maturity.

One caveat needs noting. The low night temperatures of Gibbston and Wanaka are the main influence on reducing their average temperatures. Daily highs are much more similar across all of these sites. The same is true of Bendigo. Such high diurnal ranges of temperature encourage the development of flavour compounds as the berries of Pinot Noir ripen. Nevertheless, the differences in day/night temperatures of these first vineyards is not sufficient to change the general conclusion that other parts of Central Otago had climatic advantages over Gibbston and Wanaka for growing grapes. However, any environmental disadvantages became less significant as the Central Otago wine region matured. Wineries in the Kawarau Gorge could diversify their sources of grapes by buying or growing them in sub-regions such as Bendigo or Bannockburn where the probabilities of ripening grapes every year are higher. Moreover, Gibbston and Wanaka had other advantages that compensated for their climatic limitations. In both summer and winter, vehicle traffic counts are much higher through these localities than other rural parts of Central Otago. Wineries in the Kawarau Gorge benefit hugely in both their tasting rooms and restaurants from direct sales to this passing traffic.

The Cossens publications became available between 1985 and 1990 when the interest in planting vines was about to take off. From about 1995, when fewer than 50 hectares were planted, the area in vines in Central Otago increased sharply (Table 8.5). By 2000 it had reached 280 hectares and by 2005 this had more than tripled to 978 hectares. By 2010 it was 1540 hectares with Pinot Noir making up 78 per cent of the total area in vines. During this rapid expansion, Pinot Noir vineyards appeared on a much wider range of sites. Cossens' work had alerted many of the new and established grape growers to the environmental advantages of these alternative sites. They were able to make more informed choices on where to plant Pinot Noir. New vineyards appeared on the western side of Lake Dunstan in localities from Queensbury to the outskirts of Cromwell. On the eastern side of the lake, Ardgour, Bendigo Station (the Loop Road and the Terraces) as well as Cairnmuir and Bannockburn have all become important concentrations of vines.

The following extracts typify the clear and realistic advice Cossens provided for existing and aspiring grape growers:

Table 8.5: Grape varieties in the Central Otago region, 1990–2010

	1990		1995		2000		2005		2010	
Variety	ha	%	ha	%	ha	%	ha	%	ha	%
Pinot Noir	4	21	50	33	136	49	755	77	1196	78
Pinot Gris	1	5	8	1	24	9	70	7	143	9
Chardonnay	2	11	43	28	61	22	60	6	67	4
Riesling	4	21	14	9	21	8	47	5	66	4
Sauvignon Blanc	3	16	15	10	15	5	24	3	31	2
Gewürztraminer	3	16	8	5	9	3	11	1	17	1
Cabernet Sauvignon	2	11	1	1	1	1	1	<1	–	–
Other	–	–	13	13	13	3	10	1	20	1
Total	19	100	152	100	280	100	978	100	1540	100

… the development of a wine industry south of the Waitaki will be confined to those localities which are within a few kilometres of the 45th parallel and below 400m altitude.

The most favoured localities, very suitable for cool climate wine production, are the semi arid brown-grey earth soils at Bannockburn, those from Cromwell to Pisa and about Alexandra to Clyde. All have mean January temperatures of 17°C or higher and 1000 to 1250 GDD [growing degree-days] in degrees Celsius October to April.

The thermal conditions at any of the above locations can be enhanced by shelter, slope, and aspect. Shelter adds some 100 GDD. On the other hand, each additional metre in height loses about one GDD but increasing altitude can make sites less frost prone in the critical September to November period.

The risk of frost is always present so site selection is of prime importance in reducing this. Sites should preferably be sloping … slightly elevated above the intermediary terrace and away from the areas of severe cold-air ponding.

The daily mean maximum humidity is about 88% (roughly 9.00am), the minimum 53% (roughly 3.00pm). Absolute minimum humidities can be as low as 10%, but less than 30% is not uncommon for September through March.

Within all localities are high terraces which, on the data available, would appear to be suitable for vineyards having particularly the necessary vineyard soil characteristics. The thermal regime, indicated by the mapping, was warmer than anticipated. However … the terraces are exposed to the wind and lack shelter.

To mature grapes satisfactorily vineyards should be no more than 80m above the lower terrace of the Clutha or Kawarau Rivers and not more than 400m altitude above sea level. All sites above 400m should be viewed with great caution.

In spring frost kill depends on whether buds are wet or dry. Critical temperatures for dry sprouts in spring are -1.5 to -2.0°C (air temperatures), for wet sprouts it is as warm as -0.5°C.

Accumulation and sharing of knowledge

Nigel Greening's search for a suitable site in the late 1990s demonstrates how he conducted his own investigation before plucking up courage to approach the high priests of Central Otago winemaking:

Then as I learned my wines I started talking to people. I found the soil maps and started studying those. And then I got the topographic maps and started marking every slope that went the right way on the maps. I got a four-wheel drive and started driving. And I did that for about four or five months.... So I plucked up courage and knocked on Rudi Bauer's [Quartz Reef] door. He was very supportive, He said, 'Well, all your homework is good.' He said I ought to go and knock on Alan Brady's door [Gibbston Valley], which I did.... So I then went into phase two where I steadily narrowed it down to 30 sites then got it down to about twenty. Alan looked at about ten of them with me.

Nigel Greening bought the apricot orchard on Cornish Point before later buying Felton Road.

Numerous other new enterprises have emerged through experienced personnel leaving established ones and starting their own. Rob Hay who launched Chard Farm in the late 1980s was winemaker for Gibbston Valley while Chard Farm was being established. Greg Hay, Rob's brother, was running the viticulture for Chard Farm before he became involved in the Wentworth development and Peregrine. His influence there built on his previous experience, including knowledge of the quality of grapes from Gibbston sites compared with others in the region. The list of winemakers for Rippon Vineyard (Table 8.6) includes Rudi Bauer and Clotilde Chauvet, both of whom later returned to Central Otago and for twelve years were in partnership making *Méthode Traditionnelle* at Quartz Reef.

Alan Brady began his small Mount Edward winery in 1998 after he sold most of his shareholding in Gibbston Valley to Mike Stone, the American casino owner based in Wanaka. Steve Davies returned to New Zealand in 1999 after experience in California, initially to be winemaker for the recently formed Akarua in Bannockburn shortly after Sir Clifford Skeggs established it as one of the largest continuous areas in vines in the region. Davies then became winemaker for the Carrick winery, almost directly opposite on the Bannockburn Road and owned by Steve Green, the former chief executive of the Otago Regional Council and collaborator with Robin Dicey before Mt Difficulty was established.

The Annual Report of New Zealand Winegrowers lists all the country's wineries in three categories: those producing over 4 million litres of wine annually (large wineries); those producing between 200,000 litres and 4 million litres (medium); and those producing less than 200,000 litres annually (small). These lists of wineries and grape growers make it possible to establish the scale of production in the Central Otago region. In 2010, just four wineries – Amisfield Wine Company, Chard Farm, Mt Difficulty and Peregrine Wines – were in the medium category of wineries. Central Otago's remaining 98 wineries each produced fewer than 200,000 litres of wine annually, many much less than this. With 1540 hectares of vines in production in 2010, the average area of grapes per winery in Central was 15.1 hectares. On average, therefore, they had about the same area in vines as family operations in the prestigious appellations of the Côte d'Or, Burgundy. For those wine enthusiasts wishing to visit a region where most wineries are small, and owned and operated by families, Central Otago is the ideal choice.

Moreover, very few enterprises in Central Otago declare themselves as grape growers. In the 2010 New Zealand Winegrowers Annual Report only eleven Central Otago enterprises are listed as grape growers. This figure gives the region the lowest proportion of grape growers to wineries of any major winegrowing region in New Zealand. It also suggests that almost 90 per cent of the enterprises involved in winegrowing consider themselves as wineries because they make wine commercially, even though they may not yet have their own winery. This situation is likely to change. Localities within Central Otago such as the Kawarau Gorge and Bannockburn already have sufficiently dense clusters of wineries to attract substantial numbers of New Zealand and international tourists. As the number of successful wineries increases, the demand for grapes grown locally will follow. Verbal or written contracts with the small number of local growers are already zealously guarded.

Fine wines and fine wools

Fine wines are woven into the story of fine wools. The homesteads of high-country runs (stations) nestle into sheltered spots along the basins of Central Otago (Figure 8.2). These pockets of easier-sloping, sometimes irrigated land are the most productive on these properties and were often planted in lucerne or other crops. Parts of many are now in vines. Owners or traders of the traditional, large, family-owned pastoral farms of the South Island have entered grape growing or the development and selling of their land for vines. The owners of Northburn Station, one branch of the Pinckney family, first grew grapes for Peregrine. After developing their own successful vineyard in consultation with Greg Hay they then subdivided land along their road frontage on the eastern shores of Lake Dunstan and sold these parcels as vineyard land. They have also successfully diversified the sources of income from their own high-country run. Ten kilometres further north, owners of the numerous vineyard sites formerly part of Bendigo Station – of 'Shrek' the unshorn merino wether fame, owned by John and Heather Perriam – include Gibbston Valley and Quartz Reef as well as the Perriams and many other growers.

In 2008 the Central Otago Winegrowers Association published a map showing 42 wineries in their region. Just like the homesteads of the high-country runs, the wineries have clustered mainly in the accessible valleys and lowlands of the region. The settlement of Gibbston and the valley of the Kawarau River offer the best example.

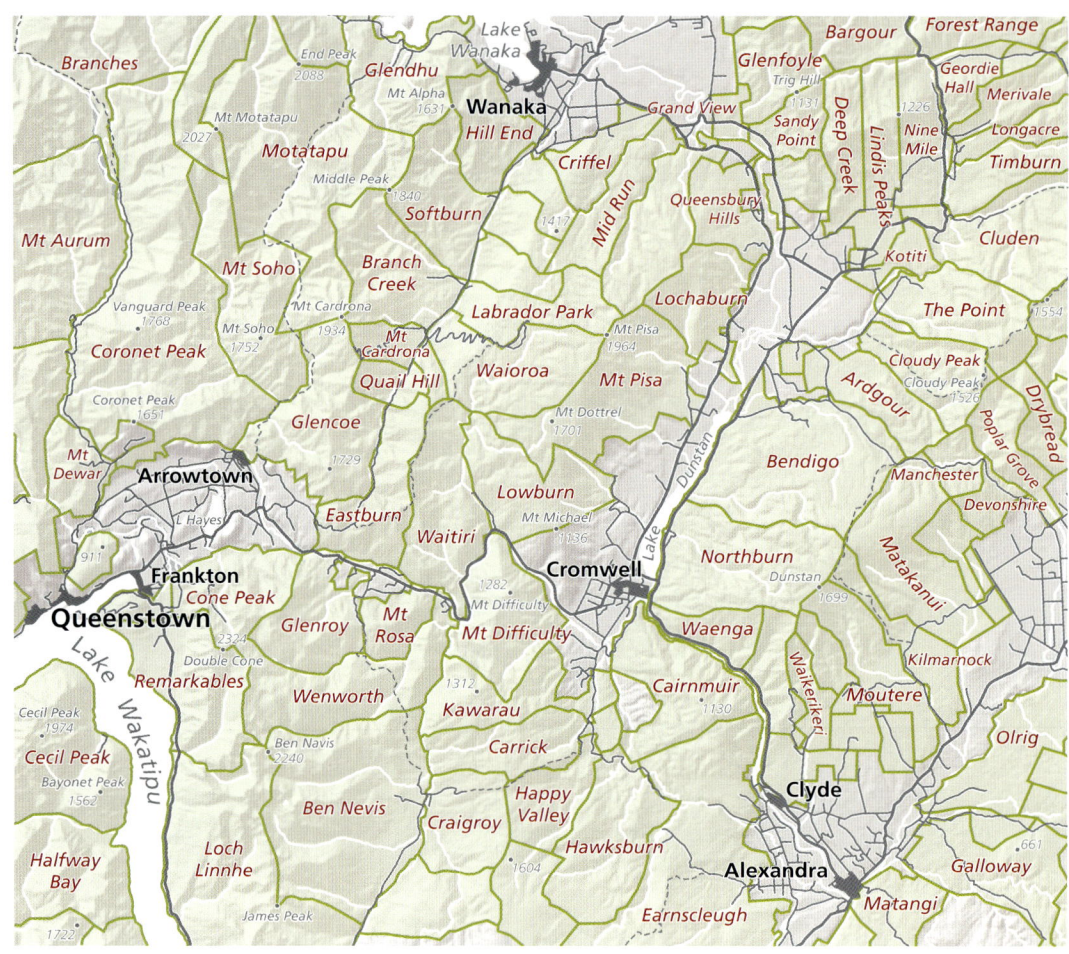

Figure 8.2 High-country runs of Central Otago

From the imposing Nevis Bluff in the east almost to Lake Hayes in the west, five high-country runs had their boundaries along the Kawarau River. From the south, three runs – Wentworth, Mount Rosa and Glenroy – fronted the Kawarau River and the parcels of freehold land along it. From the north, the two runs of Waitiri and Eastburn do the same. These former gold-mining localities have a rich history. Wine enterprises have mined this history by appropriating the names of sheep runs, settlements and features of the natural landscape. Mt Difficulty, Gibbston Valley Wines, Waitiri Creek, Mt Rosa and Coal Pit are all examples.

Maps of the vineyards and wineries of Central Otago, alone or combined, cannot yet capture the spatial organisation of the winegrowing enterprises of this region. Some wineries are still located in the industrial area of Cromwell, the settlement that housed most of the workers when the Clyde dam was being built. When the workforce left in the early 1990s, surplus industrial buildings in Cromwell were a windfall for many wine and other enterprises. They could rent or buy them at reasonable cost and concentrate on developing their vineyards while gradually purchasing winery tanks and equipment. Some new wineries, such as Rockburn, have since been built on sites in Cromwell. Resource consents for drainage and other essential requirements are often easier to obtain in such well-serviced industrial estates than for greenfield sites in the countryside.

Enterprises in the Central Otago story

Rippon Vineyard

Rolfe Mills was a scion of the Sargood family of clothiers. From 1912 to 1940, Percy Sargood ran the firm's South Island operation out of Dunedin. He also owned over 46,000 acres of high country that included the Wanaka Station. This land was sold when Sir Percy died, although one of his daughters managed to buy back about 3000 acres of it. It was here, on the shores of Lake Wanaka, that Rolfe Mills spent many of his childhood summer holidays.

The Sargoods' primary business was textiles, clothing and footwear. Rolfe was managing their South Island operations from Christchurch when in 1973 the company merged with a similar firm, Bing Harris. He took this opportunity to leave the trade and build a house clad with mud bricks on 85 hectares of the family land west of Wanaka. With his wife Lois, and two young children Sarah and Nick (soon to be three when a second daughter Charlie was born), the family settled in rural Central Otago. They started Rippon Farm in 1973, the same year that Frank Yukich of Montana planted vines in Marlborough.

Living on the spectacular Rippon site was Lois and Rolfe's primary attraction to the land but they were also committed to using it productively. They were torn between breeding and grazing goats and planting vines. Rolfe initially knew more about wines than he did about vines. He had visited some of the renowned wine regions of Europe, notably Portugal, where he was intrigued by the similarities between the schist soils of the Oporto region and those of Central Otago. He was also intent on finding out which varieties of grapes would grow on their Wanaka land. Their first vines were planted in 1974. By 1981 they had about 2 hectares planted in a kaleidoscope of hybrid and *vinifera* varieties from Baco 22A to Pinot Noir, some of them quite unsuited to making table wines of distinction in Central Otago.

Their goat enterprise was successful but both Rolfe and Lois were more interested in their vines. To help them decide if they would commit to producing wine commercially,

Summer evening at Rippon, Lake Wanaka. *Rippon*

they spent 1981 living and working on a vineyard in France and took their children with them. They chose the village of Sigoulès about 7 kilometres from Montbazillac and 15 kilometres from Bergerac, east of the elite appellations of Bordeaux. The two oldest children were enrolled in the local school and became fluent in French, an experience that was later to benefit Nick professionally.

This sojourn convinced Rolfe and Lois to keep developing Rippon although it also alerted them to the depth of the commitment required to carve out a successful life in wine. Rolfe, by then 57, was later to declare in a discussion with journalist Ric Oram:

> Time beat me. When I came back from France I realised that winemaking is not a hobby but a skilled profession. Difficulties there were, but not really in the growing of the grapes nor the ripening of them. The only problem was you cannot change overnight, throw your collar and tie away and become a viticulturist.

But time did not beat the Mills family. Rolfe and Lois continued to develop Rippon and its reputation. Their children extended it.

Rolfe and Lois were slow to make wines in commercial quantities, but after their experience in France, they recognised the need to take technical advice. In 1985 they arranged to send 200 kilograms of grapes north to the Te Kauwhata Viticultural

Table 8.6: Winemakers employed at Rippon Vineyard

Winemaker	Nationality	Years
Tony Bish	New Zealander	1986–89
Rudi Bauer	Austrian	1989–92
Clotilde Chauvet	French	1993–95
Axel Rothermel	German	1996
Ben Kagi	Australian	1997
Russell Lake	New Zealander	1998–2002
Nick Mills	New Zealander	2003–

Research Station to be made into wine and assessed professionally. They left their Müller Thurgau on the vines as long as possible to reach optimal ripeness but lost much of the crop to birds. Not to be thwarted, the following year they netted the vines and their first crop of Müller Thurgau was successfully fermented and bottled at Te Kauwhata where Rainer Eschenbruch endorsed the quality of the grapes and the resulting wine. This confirmation convinced them to employ Tony Bish from Hawke's Bay as their first winemaker in 1986. They went on to employ a series of professional winemakers many of whom were also knowledgeable viticulturists (Table 8.6), building an enviable reputation for their wines in the process.

Nick Mills, who took over the viticulture and winemaking at Rippon from 2002 (his father died in 2000), attributes his own commitment to the vine and wine to Rudi Bauer. Between 1989 and 1992, when Nick was in his late teens and Rudi was working at Rippon, they spent time together – pruning, planting and talking. 'Rudi sort of instilled in me the feeling that viticulture and winegrowing was something that I could potentially fall in love with,' says Nick. 'I got inspired at that time.' But Nick had another talent to explore. He was a freestyle skier in the New Zealand team preparing for the Nagoya Winter Olympics when at the end of 1997 he hit a control gate in a high-speed turn and 'lost my leg out behind me and blew it completely to bits. So that dream was out the window!' His next four years were spent at the Beaune Polytechnic studying viticulture and oenology and working in the vineyards of Burgundy.

During the 1980s and 1990s, winegrowers in Burgundy became more and more concerned with reducing, or eliminating, many of the chemicals that had crept into their vineyard management. Centuries of growing vines on the same sites, and the increasing reliance on herbicides in the twentieth century, had resulted in the accumulation of undesirable chemicals in these vineyard soils. Tertiary institutions were embracing organic and biodynamic practices in the vineyard and cellar, teaching them and integrating Burgundy's vine and wine history into their courses – notably the strong manual work ethic and respect for the vine held by the Cistercian order. Nick Mills was exposed to these ideas both in his studies and on the enterprises where he worked during his *stages*, or periods of practical experience. This experience deepened his commitment to organic and biodynamic practices and also to the people who were exploring and introducing them.

At enterprises like Domaine Jean-Jacques Confuron in the commune of Prémeaux-Prissey in the Côte d'Or, where organic and biodynamic practices were embraced, Nick Mills began accumulating a sophisticated knowledge of the biology of the vineyard and cellar. During his four years on the Côte from 1999 through 2002, Nick did *stages* at a number of diverse enterprises. With the 1999 Confuron experience under his belt, in 2000 he grasped the opportunity to work with Nicola Potel who is from a Volnay family but at the time was setting up a *négociant* business in Nuits-Saint-Georges. Here was a unique opportunity to experience the different nuances of the aromas, texture and flavours of Pinot Noir grown in the different communes of Burgundy by participating in their vinification. For the 2001 vintage, he arranged a job with Pascal Marchand at the Domaine de la Bougère, pruning and working in the cellar until the spring of 2002. Lastly, he worked in the prestigious Domaine de la Romanée Conti vineyard and cellar from April 2002 before heading home. Experience garnered at all these enterprises prepared Nick for his return to Rippon Vineyard.

He came back to a 15-hectare vineyard with 12 hectares of vines in production, about nine of them in Pinot Noir. By Burgundian standards the vineyard was a suitable size for a family holding. His experience in France had made him certain of one thing: 'I was already convinced about biodynamics.' His was a practical rather than an ideological attraction to the approach. Minimal intervention in the growing of the grapes and in converting them to quality wine is his philosophy and Central Otago is the ideal place to practise it. Its dry atmosphere reduces the incidence of many diseases that are a problem in other grape-growing regions of New Zealand. Consequently, Nick did not even consider using herbicides to control unwanted plants. He disced the whole vineyard and 'created the mound underneath the vines so I could work the under-vine cultivator properly'.

From the beginning, Rippon Vineyard was organic. Achieving this certification required them to vinify grapes from their own vineyard only. When Rolfe and Lois began planting vines at Rippon no vineyards existed within tens of kilometres of them. They limited their applications of sprays until their practices were certainly organic, and verging on the biodynamic. As the operation became more commercial and Rolfe became less involved in the day-to-day and seasonal management of the vineyard Rippon drifted from its earlier ideals of limited intervention in the life of the vines. By the late 1990s, when nearby Wanaka growers pressed them to buy small quantities of Pinot Noir, they obliged and their organic status was compromised.

Nick Mills' biodynamic beliefs in the benefits of manual labour and observation in growing grapes of quality have had consequences for everyone who is working at Rippon in the twenty-first century. Practices embedded in the Burgundian tradition are incorporated into daily organic and biodynamic routines. Parcels of mature Pinot Noir vines have been named after ancestors – Emma's Block for the great-great-great-grandmother of the current generation of the Mills family and Tinker's Field for the late Rolfe.

Twenty years earlier Nick had bought a hand hoe for Rolfe in Switzerland. They had fitted it with a kanuka handle. Hand cultivation of the vineyard had been part of their regime when Nick was growing up: 'We were buying hand hoes from Mitre 10 and we went through dozens and dozens of them.' But the rugged Swiss hoe had outlasted all others. So Nick used it as a template and had 20 more of them made up:

> And we do an hour hand-hoeing every morning, across the board, everyone on the property. We arrive in the mornings, we shake everyone's hands, we look each other in the eye and we go out and do an hour's hard yakka every morning. It really galvanises a team. We're in this together. That's the shop people, that's the winery people, that's the office people, it's everyone.

Rolfe Mills would undoubtedly have admired the depth of Nick's tribute to this lineage and this place.

Quartz Reef

When Rudi Bauer arrived in New Zealand in 1985 he was probably the best-qualified *vigneron* in the country. He had already spent nine years studying the theory and practice of viticulture and winemaking, punctuated by regular examinations, and had worked in vineyards and cellars with international varieties such as Riesling, Pinot Noir, Pinot Gris and Müller Thurgau as well as grapes native to Austria or Germany such as Zweigelt, St Laurent and Grüner Veltliner.

In March 1985 Rudi began working at Mission Vineyards in Hawke's Bay where he stayed until June 1989. During those years he took three winter breaks – the first to cycle around the South Island, the two others to extend his international experience with vintages at Simi in the Sonoma Valley, California and at Sokol Blosser in Oregon. In the winter of 1989 he planted the second block of the Rippon Vineyard with Robin Dicey who was advising Rolfe and Lois Mills on their viticulture. Rudi had already established a reputation as a winemaker based on notable wines he was involved with at Mission, including their 1985 Gewürztraminer, 1987 Pinot Noir and 1989 Reserve

Semillon. Winning Rippon's first gold medal for Pinot Noir in 1990 enhanced his reputation as well as confirming his skills in the Central Otago environment.

Rudi left Rippon at the end of 1992 to work at the Giesen Wine Estate where he was one of their principal winemakers until November 1997. In accepting this position Rudi was not spurning Central Otago. By 1991 he had discovered the land he coveted on Bendigo Station and remained intent on exploring the possibility of establishing his own vineyards and cellar in Central: 'I always wanted to come down here. That was a very clear call.' His wife, professional photographer Suellen Boag, grew up in Dunedin and is equally as enthusiastic about Central Otago and especially Arrowtown where she spent holidays as a child.

Giesen's brief for Rudi, undoubtedly influenced by his success at Rippon, was 'to improve their red wine portfolio'. He was responsible for grapes from their Canterbury property, from land the Giesens owned in Marlborough, and for grapes bought from Marlborough growers. The experience included working with white grapes – notably botrytised Riesling, Müller Thurgau, Sauvignon Blanc and Pinot Gris – but what confirmed the direction that Rudi wished to take was clear: 'What for me was the best was dealing with Pinot Noir from two more regions.' He added the distinctive Canterbury (Burnham) and Marlborough Pinots to his Otago experience.

In 1996, Rudi Bauer visited John and Heather Perriam to discuss the possibility of planting grapes on their Bendigo Station. 'He asked whether we'd be interested in forming a partnership,' recounts John Perriam. 'He was looking at the Loop Road. I told him to bugger off because I was running around the world at that stage setting up Merino New Zealand.' The Loop Road is a triangular side road with two entrances off State Highway 8 east of Lake Dunstan, about 30 kilometres north of Cromwell. At its eastern apex is the site of the former gold-mining settlement of Bendigo. Loop Road is on a flat terrace between 210 and 220 metres above sea level. On the southern arm of its triangle a relatively gentle concave slope rises above this terrace until at about 280 metres it becomes too difficult to cultivate with a tractor.

Rudi Bauer had long admired the slope as a site for a vineyard. He had observed it often from across the Clutha when driving between Wanaka and Cromwell: 'And you look at it, and you say, "That's not good enough, it's west facing", you know. And of course I made a mistake!' They visited the site where Suellen used her watch in relation to the position of the sun to convince Rudi that the slope was within 10 degrees of due north. He became more enthusiastic, even harbouring thoughts of establishing a monopoly over a large chunk of these slopes.

Rudi and Suellen were keen to use the name 'Bendigo' for the nascent enterprise, but firms in the winegrowing area of Bendigo, Victoria in Australia had already captured that intellectual property. Within a 10-kilometre radius of Loop Road are numerous colourful names from Central Otago's gold-mining era, especially of the creeks draining

Winter 2011 at Rudi Bauer's Quartz Reef. *Suellen Boag*

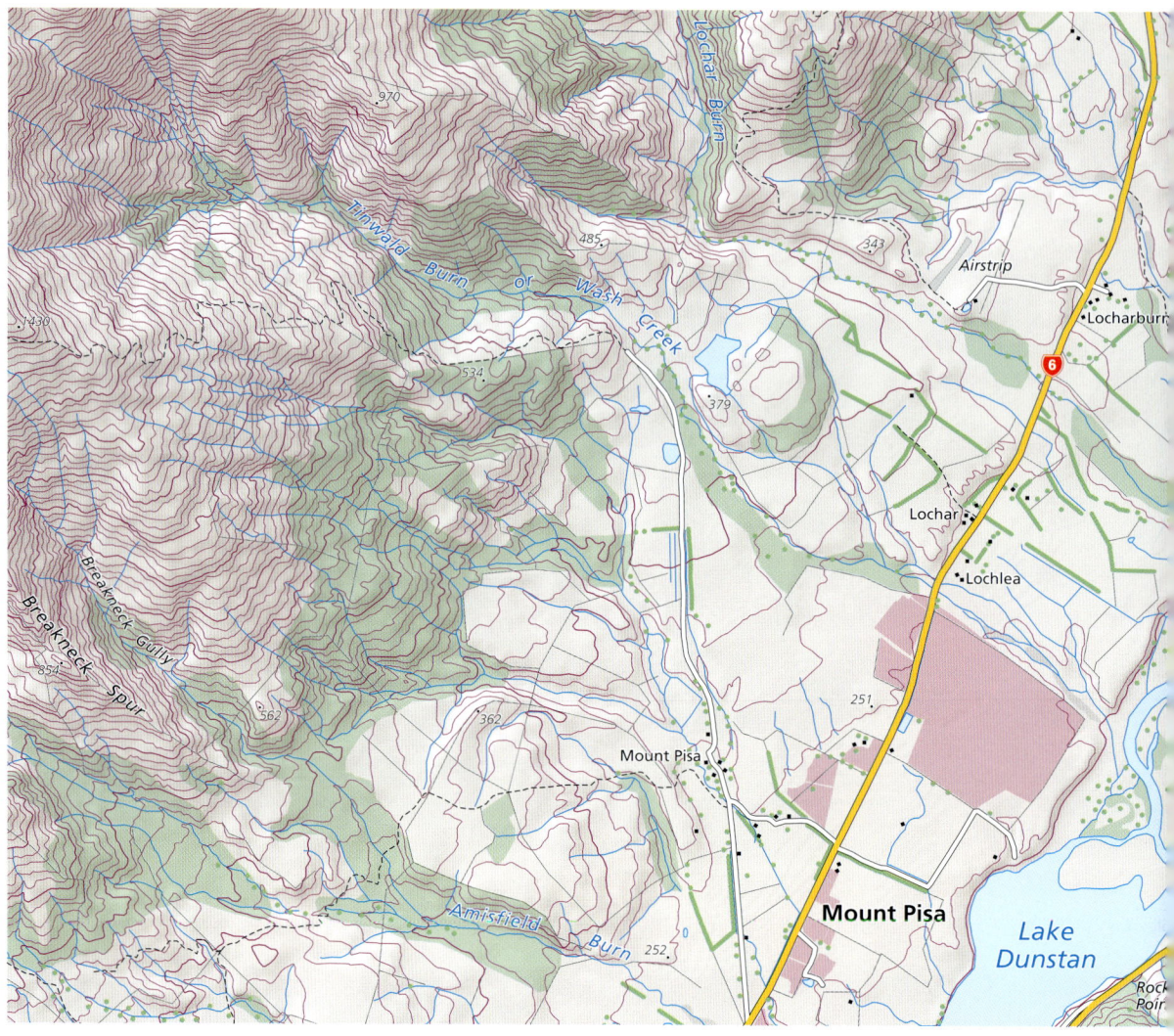

Figure 8.3 Loop Road, Lake Dunstan, and the Bendigo Terraces

the hills south and east of Bendigo – Shepherds, Rise and Shine, Aurora, Chinamans, Pigeon, Raupo, Green Valley, Devils, John Bull, and even Firewood and Brewery. Rudi and Suellen chose the evocative name Quartz Reef even though Quartz Reef Creek and Quartz Reef Point are on the adjoining Northburn Station to the south of Bendigo Station.

John Perriam was more interested in Rudi Bauer's proposal than he initially let on, but had told him to 'go away and if you can find us another partner in the old world that had a marketing infrastructure in place before we planted a grape then I'd think about it'. Three months later Rudi was back with the name of Clotilde Chauvet of Champagne.

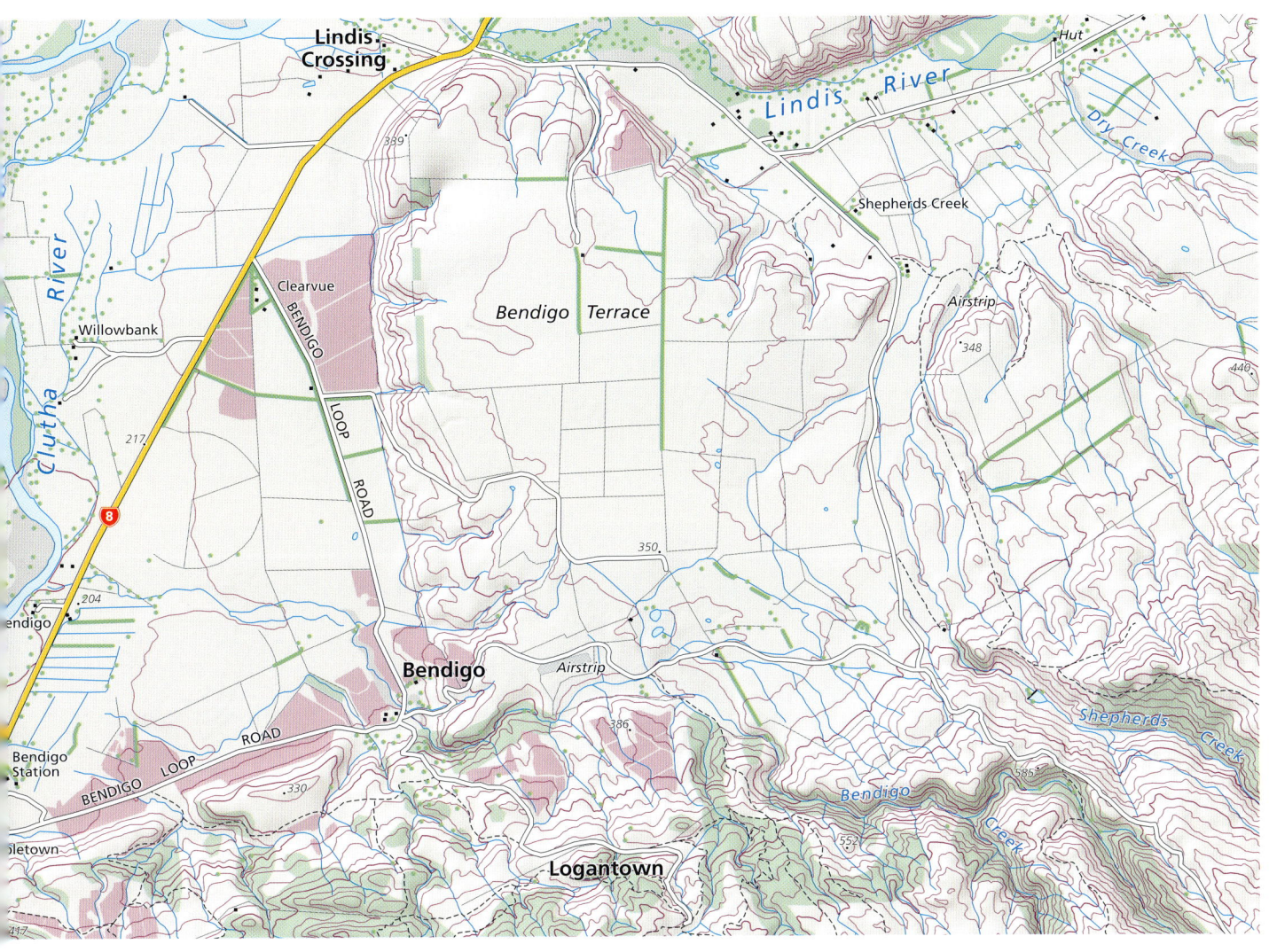

Her family owned a small, successful Champagne house in Épernay. Perriam's response was to fly to France and spend time getting to understand the Chauvet enterprise as the family's guest. That experience, together with his respect for Rudi's knowledge and winemaking skills, convinced him to go ahead.

In 1996, Rudi Bauer, Clotilde Chauvet and John Perriam formed the Bendigo Estate Partnership. Bendigo Station had been the first high-country run to go through tenure review in 1986. This allowed owners to freehold some land while ceding vulnerable natural environments to the Department of Conservation, in some cases with closely controlled grazing rights. Perriam tried to convince the Department of Conservation to include the Bendigo slopes in the land reverting to the state because it was costly to keep the rabbits under control and was growing little tussock or other grasses: 'I had tried to talk DOC into taking all the land right down to the road because it was full of rabbits. Now it's some of the most valuable land!' Until Rudi's approach, Perriam had been unaware of the potential of the Bendigo slopes and higher terraces for growing grapes. But he did know the micro-environments of Bendigo station well.

Rudi had taken temperature readings on the proposed Bendigo land that confirmed its suitability for Pinot Noir. Its temperatures during veraison were very similar to the commune of Aloxe-Corton in the Côte de Beaune. Clotilde Chauvet's experience at Rippon and skills in vinifying sparkling wine complemented his and were essential in producing the non-vintage Quartz Reef *Méthode Traditionnelle*. His plans for the future possibilities for the organisation of the enterprise were already clear:

> Trevor Scott, one of our partners, bought another 15 hectares just beside ours. So the plan is that it runs with us, under one label, which makes a lot of sense. That's a total of about 30 hectares. Let's say on average that's 250 tonnes, that's 20,000 cases-plus. I do believe in time, most of the sparkling wine would be sourced from contract vineyards. I think that's possibly a good call. Have the foundation and then we are not put under pressure. Basically we'll do what Montana does now. We realise that we cannot rely fully on grape growers. We really have to do it ourselves. Maybe we could aim for 50 per cent.

Rudi recognises the advantage of having two strings to his Central Otago bow – Pinot Noir backed by a *Méthode Traditionnelle*. Clotilde Chauvet's involvement at Quartz Reef for the first 12 years of its life removed some of the mystique surrounding Champagne, and Rudi is himself now skilled in its vinification. His quick calculation of the yield necessary to achieve 250 tonnes of Chardonnay and Pinot Noir works out at just over 8 tonnes of grapes per hectare. In the communes of the Champagne region proper, yields are often much higher than this, even for wines originating from elite houses.

Mondillo Vineyards

Domenic Mondillo, who trained in restaurant management and culinary arts in the United States, owned two restaurants in Queenstown and, in his words, 'had the pleasure of employing Mike Wolter', who worked as a kitchen hand for him in the late 1980s while looking after Ann Pinckney's vineyard and winery:

> I ended up going out to the vineyard with Mike during the day, because we were only open for dinner, and also started helping Mike in the winery at Taramea. It was a privilege to know him as an individual – and he was a huge inspiration to me.

Wolter went on to establish the Central Otago Wine Company with Sam Neill and his death in a winery accident in 1997 was tragic both for his family and for the close-knit community of Central Otago winegrowers.

Domenic was friendly with other influential members of the small Central Otago wine community of the mid-1980s including Rob Hay (Chard Farm) and Greg Hay (Peregrine) as well as Alan Brady of Gibbston Valley. By the time he sold the first of his restaurants in 1990 and the second in 1992 he had already begun a comprehensive private apprenticeship in viticulture and winemaking. Domenic had participated in vintages for more than a decade and pruned at Gibbston and other vineyards in most years.

By 1996, having completed the Eastern Institute of Technology's viticulture and winemaking qualification, Domenic was running the viticulture for Gibbston Valley. His appointment there coincided with more Central Otago vineyards coming into production. The Bannockburn vineyards of Mt Difficulty and Felton Road, for example, were beginning to bear fruit in the mid-1990s but their wineries were not yet built. For the vintages of 1995, 1996 and 1997, Gibbston Valley bought substantial quantities of Pinot Noir fruit from them. Being one of the first functional wineries in Central Otago made it possible for Gibbston Valley to begin increasing its production with grapes bought from growers who were intending to make their own wine later. At the same time, it needed to start planting more of its own vineyards against the day when this contract fruit was no longer available.

The first vineyard developed was in Alexandra, just beside the racecourse on Dunstan Road, in 1999, and under Domenic's stewardship Gibbston Valley also convinced John Perriam of Bendigo Station to sell them some land. It first purchased and planted two blocks on the gentle slopes west of the Quartz Reef vineyard. As the qualities of Bendigo's north-facing, higher terraces were recognised, many other enterprises, including Gibbston Valley, continued acquiring land there. It has two parcels on the Chinamans Terrace, named after the creek draining the lower slopes of the Dunstan Range, as well as a large parcel east of School Creek on what has been christened Schoolhouse Terrace. By the end of the first decade of the twenty-first century, Gibbston Valley had accumulated a total of 75 hectares in six parcels as well as leasing several other vineyards, including two from John Perriam.

Domenic and Ally Mondillo planted two of their own vineyard sites in the Bendigo locality. One is above the apex of the Loop Road with its highest point at 305 metres and the other further east on the Schoolhouse Terrace that is 388 metres at its highest

Mondillo's four vineyards on terraces above the Loop Road, Bendigo.
Alan Kwok Lun Cheung

point. They bought these sites from Bendigo Station for $15,000 per hectare when land suitable for viticulture in Marlborough was selling at over ten times this price. Their four interconnected vineyards above the Loop Road are on three levels all facing slightly west of north with steeper land separating them but linked by carefully sculpted tracks. They are all exposed to the afternoon sun. Pommard vines (clone 5) make up 40 per cent of the total and the more recently selected Dijon clones (114, 115, 667 and 777) make up the remaining 60 per cent of the vineyard's Pinot Noir clones. At this stage of the evolution of their enterprise the Mondillos are making only two wines – Pinot Noir and Riesling. Their winery equipment consists of just three 6-tonne stainless-steel fermenters and Rudi Bauer vinifies the grapes for them in Cromwell. They vinify only about 25 or 30 per cent of the grapes they grow and Pernod Ricard buys the rest.

Right from the first vintage in 2004 the Mondillo Central Otago Pinot Noir impressed judges in blind tastings and won a haul of medals. With the vines now older, and Domenic and Rudi understanding the Bendigo environment more deeply, recent vintages have eclipsed earlier results. The Mondillo 2008 Pinot Noir was awarded a gold medal and judged champion wine at the 2010 Royal Easter Show. By 2009 their Pinot Noir came from vines being grown sustainably and received a 'Pure Gold' in the Air New Zealand Wine Awards of 2010. These local results have been endorsed by commercial success in the United States.

The vineyards along the Loop Road are an excellent example of the need to be wary of spring frosts in Central Otago. In the spring of 2003, for example, frost significantly reduced the crop on some of the vineyards on the Bendigo flats. Aurora's crop was severely affected. Even the lowest rows of Quartz Reef's Loop Road vineyard had some frost damage because the cool air ponded near its poplar shelterbelt and flowed back to the vineyard. Gibbston Valley responded by installing fans for frost protection on its two more gently sloping vineyards west of Quartz Reef. Frost-protecting fans are also installed on two of the Mondillos', almost flat, Loop Road vineyards.

To avoid 'green' flavours in his wine, Domenic Mondillo does his best to keep his yields down, but not too low, somewhere over 5 tonnes but less than 8 tonnes per hectare. He believes that if yields are any lower there's a danger of prematurely getting high sugars in Pinot Noir before getting ripeness. The objective should be to maximise the flavour development without the sugars being 'ridiculously high', as too many shrivelled berries give a port-like character to Pinot Noir that is 'equally undesirable as green flavours'. Like other viticulturists in Central Otago, during the late spring and summer he measures and keeps a close eye on the evapotranspiration numbers each week. In many vineyard regions of New Zealand viticulturists expect the canes to reach about the top of the post at flowering. Domenic's experience of numerous sites in Central Otago suggests that the canes seldom reach this level by flowering. He sees his overriding role in the vineyard as achieving a balance between helping the vines to grow while limiting their vigour. This involves being careful with applications of water, in particular, and also fertiliser.

In future, the Mondillos intend to sell fewer grapes and produce more wine under their own label, and to this end have set aside a portion of land for a winery site. But Domenic's long experience of winegrowing makes him cautious: 'You know, you've got to walk, and then you've got to walk quickly, before you can run. But I suppose long-term, I'd like to be processing all of the fruit into wine.' The downturn of the New Zealand economy and those of its international wine markets temporarily slowed these developments, but Domenic and Ally Mondillo's experience, enthusiasm and initiative are likely to see their plans implemented sooner rather than later.

Felton Road

It is an international wine brand that also happens to be the name of a road in Bannockburn, Central Otago. Together with winemaker Blair Walters, Stewart Elms put Felton Road on the world wine map.

His family had been New Zealand hoteliers for four generations in Dunedin and, without planning it, working in the family business provided Stewart Elms with the ideal mix of knowledge and experience to start a small, elite vineyard and winery. He and his wife managed the City Hotel for sixteen years, a tenure which coincided with the period of import licensing for wines and spirits. They obtained a wholesale licence and for the decade between 1966 and 1976 imported wine from a variety of countries, France being the most important. Buying and selling wine became a significant part of their business and their life included trips to Europe. In 1976 they leased the hotel and wine and spirits part of the family enterprise and began looking for land.

Eventually they bought a farm at Palmerston, about 60 kilometres north of Dunedin, on which a farm manager looked after the stock and Stewart the crops. These included 60 acres of blackcurrants – 'which was really my first introduction to horticulture'. They soon had a contract to supply Beecham, the marketers of Ribena, and farmed their land for 17 years before again changing direction when Stewart noticed that Lincoln University had started a wine science programme. In 1990 he enrolled in this one-year postgraduate programme in horticultural science:

> I thought I'd better find out about this grape-growing business before I attempted it – you really want to know what you want to grow before you decide where you're going to buy the bit of land.

The DSIR had just published a soil map of the Bannockburn locality and Cossens' maps of temperatures expressed as degree-days were also available:

> Blackcurrants were a pure coincidence – whereas growing grapes was something I wanted to do. So I learned about it and then chose the land where I thought I could grow Pinot. I really just overlaid the heat accumulation data over the soil map and put a mark with a pin where it looked to be. And essentially we thought it was almost identical to what the climatic situation was in Beaune. Not as wet, but climatically very much the same sort of temperature curve.

His comparison with Burgundy is accurate, although average monthly temperatures in the growing season are about 1.5°C higher in much of the Côte d'Or. Cossens' work had established the similarity between the temperature regimes in Central Otago and those of the Côte de Nuits and Côte de Beaune. Within Central, Cossens had also demonstrated that Bannockburn was the locality with the warmest growing season, even though his data spanned only a short period (Table 8.4).

In the summer of 1991, Stewart decided to have his first look at the Bannockburn land on Felton Road. When he arrived, the owner was cutting hay. By chance, Stewart knew him from Dunedin, and he agreed to sell him a total of 49.5 hectares, even being prepared to modify the subdivision boundaries to include part of a shingle fan of Lochar soils that looked suitable for vines. 'So it was the only bit of land I looked at, you know. We had no hesitation in proceeding with it.'

The site of the Elms vineyard is especially favourable. Its shallow valley faces due north and is protected from wind by low hills on either side. About 5 kilometres to its west, the main ridge of the Carrick Range runs north–south. Its highest peak is Mt Difficulty (1285 m) and most of the ridge is over 1000 metres. This ridge protects the Elms and Calvert vineyards, indeed most of the Bannockburn vineyards, from the worst of the nor'westers.

The Calvert vineyard is across the road from the Elms vineyard. Calvert's slopes are gentler and its Bannockburn silt-loams from lake sediments are deeper. It slopes slightly east of north towards Cromwell. These vineyards along the northeast side of Felton Road are about 500 metres from the Kawarau River. Its banks here are 200

Table 8.7: Vineyards of the Felton Road enterprise, 2010

Name	Varieties and area (ha)	Year planted	Vines per hectare	Clones	Soils
Elms	Pinot Noir 8.1 Chardonnay 4.1 Riesling 2.2 Total 14.4	Blocks 1–9 1992–94 Blocks 10–13 2001	2667 4000	A variety of clones planted on their own roots and on various rootstock. Replanting has increased diversity.	**Waenga** 40-cm loess over schist. Preferred for Pinot Noir. **Lochar** Thin loess over schist gravels (up to 3 m) with bands of sandy clay loam. Preferred for Chardonnay and Riesling.
Calvert	Pinot Noir 8.5 Riesling 0.8 Chardonnay 0.8 Total 10.1	Lodge Block 1999 Arum, Willows, Springs Blocks 2001 House Block 2003	2500 3500 3500	**Pinot Noir** UCD5, 6, AM10/5, B115 **Pinot Noir** B667, B777, B115 **Riesling** GM198.19, 110 **Chardonnay** D55	**Bannockburn** Deep silt-loams. From lakebed sediments (tertiary clays) and quartz sands along with quartz and schist gravels.
Cornish Point	Pinot Noir 7.3 Chardonnay 0.3 Total 7.6	25 blocks 2000 Clones are on one of three rootstocks: 101.14, Riparia Gloire or 3309. Eight blocks are on their own roots.	4040	**Pinot Noir** B114, B115, B667, DRC Abel, AM10/5, UCD 5, UCD 6 **Chardonnay** D95	**Manuherikia** Moderately deep, fine, sandy loams. Loess (windblown) soils developed on river gravel and from schist parent material.

Note The Cornish Point vineyard became part of the enterprise when Nigel Greening bought Felton Road in 2000. Felton Road has also leased a vineyard in Gibbston.

Central Otago

metres above sea level. To their northeast these vineyards face the long corridor of the bed of the former Clutha River, now Lake Dunstan. On this side of Felton Road and a little lower are the vineyards of the Olssens (owned by Mark Weldon) and Robin Dicey, the spur-pruning enthusiast who has been a major influence on viticultural practices in Central Otago.

When Stewart began preparing the Felton Road land for vines he avoided reshaping the terrain of the property, apart from smoothing one small knob, but the prospective vineyard area was ripped and the subsoil broken up. He also wanted to get a more definite idea of the soil profiles so 'just got a fellow with a digger to make half a dozen coffin-like holes' and was pleased that they 'seemed to conform with the soil map'. To establish the air flows and cool-air drainage of the property he 'came up from Palmerston at ten o'clock at night and let off a few borer bombs just to see what was there, to see how the frost situation would be, and the air movement situation was satisfactory'.

Picking (far left) and punch down (left) at Felton Road. *Felton Road*

He used the recent DSIR soil maps as a guide to matching varieties to soils and made bold decisions. The gravelly soils of the Lochar series, with their thin layers of loess, were planted in Chardonnay and Riesling. On the Waenga series – 'which the fruit growers around the area seem to prefer' – he planted Pinot Noir. 'But all I could see in it was there was a bit more clay, obviously. So I used those areas with more clay for Pinot.' In these initial plantings he did not so much choose the number of hectares of each variety he planted, as choose where on his almost 50-hectare property he planted each variety. This decision, coupled with the availability of suitable rootstocks and cuttings, decided the varietal mix.

After three years of planting, only 10 per cent of Felton Road's 11 hectares of vines were on rootstock. Grafted vines were in short supply during the mid- to late 1990s as grape growers and wine companies in all viticulture regions were aggressively planting. Stewart obtained many of his original cuttings from Chard Farm and some of his grafted plants from Montana's Marlborough nursery as well as a range of other sources.

Cuttings he bought one year disappointed him: 'So I really said to myself, unless I can get exactly what I want and good plant material, forget it.'

When his vines started bearing in 1995, Stewart sold all these grapes (and those from 1996) to Gibbston Valley Wines. The excellent quality of these wines, and their success in winning medals, were the primary stimulus to his building the Felton Road winery. His friendship with his laboratory partner at Lincoln College, winemaker Blair Walters, was the other. Blair, who was extending his practical experience in California, agreed to design a gravity-fed winery for the Felton Road enterprise. Stewart built it. The vinification facilities were state of the art for the time and have been little modified since, although the capacity of the winery has more than tripled. Blair accepted the position as winemaker for Felton Road in time for its first vintage of 1997. The winemaking tine of the Felton Road tuning fork was in place. Felton Road's Pinot Noir has been under allocation to distributors from then until the present and Blair continues to run the winemaking arm of the enterprise following its sale in 2000 to Nigel Greening.

Summarising his approach to viticulture, Stewart Elms remarks:

> I felt that essentially what we wanted to do was grow Pinot, so we selected what we thought was the best area to do it. Site selection is 90 per cent of growing grapes. If you've got a bigger problem, if you've got a lot of canopy management, if you've got a lot of thinning, [it] only tends to indicate that things are not well balanced and the site is not that appropriate. . . . It's hard work and as you get older you just can't handle the physical stuff. Well, if you do, you're pretty stiff for days after!

Cornish Point

Nigel Greening already owned Cornish Point vineyard when he purchased Felton Road from the Elms family. The high success rate of wine enterprises in Central Otago, despite the widespread belief that Pinot Noir was a difficult grape to grow and the limited experience of winemakers and investors there, had first stimulated his interest in the region and he became intimately acquainted with its terrain, soils and viticulture. Following some intensive fieldwork as he searched for suitable parcels of land, Nigel found a number of sites where the slope, terrain and aspect met his criteria. They ranged from Lowburn to Bendigo to the Felton Road locality. 'Another one we short-listed was the back paddocks beyond Felton Road that has now just been developed.'

Buying his preferred sites proved much more difficult because most were part of large sheep stations. When Cornish Point came on the market, he finally found what he was looking for. This triangular parcel of land at the confluence of the Kawarau and Clutha rivers has excellent cool-air drainage. Damaging frosts are rare on this site, as Cossens' work had shown for the whole of the Cromwell Gorge. Nigel was especially impressed by the enthusiasm of the locals for the quality of the apricots grown on this site: 'I'd spoken to a lot of locals and they'd all said, "Oh, the Cornish Point apricots, they're the first to ripen – best tasting apricots in the region."' Such direct physiological evidence was weightier than the limited climatic data available.

The owner was planning to subdivide a few sections on the site and sell the rest as a parcel but Nigel convinced him to sell it all. It is now in vines – 7.6 hectares. When he purchased the land he already had clear ideas for the configuration of the vineyard:

> My idea from the start was I wanted this to be a laboratory. I want to try every which way possible and see which way works. So the idea with this was to break it into blocks. And we sized the blocks to a convenient small fermenter size. So it's 25 blocks here, each the size of a 3-tonne fermenter.

The large number of small blocks was designed to allow as many combinations of rootstocks as possible with the clones of Pinot Noir available at the time (Table 8.7): 'Obviously with rootstocks we're trying to match the soils – we've got sixteen different combinations of clone and rootstock.'

To ensure production while the experiment proceeded and to keep costs down, half of the Cornish Point vineyard was planted in the popular clones proven in New Zealand (10/5, 5 and 6), all directly on their own roots. Nigel's ultimate aim for the clonal mix is much more ambitious. The most successful combinations of rootstocks and clones will replace these vines on their own roots: 'In ten years' time we'll have the entire thing on grafted plants with our dream team of clones!'

Nigel's vineyard experimentation was not restricted to clones and rootstocks. He seriously considered planting some of Cornish Point at the traditional Burgundian spacing of about 1 metre in the row and 1 metre between rows giving 10,000 vines per hectare. He finally decided not to complicate the Cornish Point experiment by increasing the density, as it would have required hand-cultivation of the vines, or a tractor and equipment suited to the narrow rows. But he couldn't resist planting a small area at this higher density on part of the Felton Road property: 'Just over an acre planted in Dijon clone 777. It's going to be our Grand Cru experiment!'

Nigel Greening also has some pretty futuristic ideas for marketing their wines online. A virtual, but real, winery would allow the consumer to, for example, order wines aged in different oaks, to know the physical characteristics of the sites that influence the tannin structure, sugar content and flavours of wines in different seasons, and order mixed cases of Pinot Noir that have been fermented and aged separately in different barrels. This approach is analogous to an appellation system, with the enterprise and its practices ensuring the integrity and distinctiveness of the wine, rather than a geographic parcelling of space based on assumed relationships between the natural environment and the wine's quality. Such an approach to marketing also makes commercial sense because retail sales would be made direct to the consumer.

Mt Difficulty

The arrival of Robin Dicey in 1992 was a technical fillip for Central Otago. Robin has grapes in his blood. His family owned land in the Western Cape, South Africa, and he went to school in Cape Town before completing qualifications in viticulture and oenology at Stellenbosch University. His OE included working in Modesto, California and in the Barossa Valley, Australia before he returned to Cape Town to take over the family farm in the mid-1960s: 'We did about 1400 tonnes of wine grapes, another 200 tonnes of table grapes, and about 120 tonnes of canning and drying grapes.'

The Diceys left South Africa in 1977 when Corbans offered him the job of setting up their Tolaga Bay vineyard on the East Coast. Three years later the family settled in the Bay of Plenty where he was involved with Horticultural Resources, an enterprise managing kiwifruit operations for absentee owners. While living in Katikati he was responsible for setting up the Morton Estate winery for Morton Brown. With its Cape Dutch-style building, Robin helped give it a South African flavour that was echoed in some of Morton Estate's wine labels. By this time he had added a comprehensive understanding of New Zealand horticulture and winegrowing to his South African training and international experience.

During a skiing trip to Wanaka in 1988 the Dicey family fell in love with the area and eventually bought land on Felton Road in 1990 and moved there in 1992, bringing sufficient of their own grafted vines from Katikati to plant a 13-hectare vineyard. By the millennium they had 3.5 hectares of Pinot Noir, 3.5 hectares of Chardonnay, 2 hectares of Riesling and 1 hectare of Pinot Gris in production. A further 3 hectares of young Pinot Noir were in the ground.

An unexpected bonus came with the purchase of the Felton Road site. The former owner, a bulldozer driver on the Clyde Dam, had considered planting vines on the property and employed a consultant to write an extensive report on its soils which came with the property. 'It was just bloody marvellous,' says Robin, 'a huge help!' When asked about other potential sites for new plantings in Central Otago, Robin enthuses:

> I don't think we have begun to be intelligent about it yet. There's any number of sites if you've got the imagination to go and work with them. I'd look for something that probably had more

Robin Dicey's high wire trellising at Mt Difficulty.
Matt Dicey

slope on it than this. It would be north facing, I would look for more protection. I wouldn't worry too much about the soils. I haven't come across a soil here yet that I feel uncomfortable to plant.

Robin quickly became an advisor and mentor to other Central Otago grape growers, many of whom had little formal training in viticulture. By 2000 he was managing fourteen vineyards of various sizes and advising on five others as well as consulting when the opportunities arose. In his spare time he started teaching a viticulture course at the polytechnic in Cromwell from 1992 and continued doing this into the twenty-first century. Members of the Central Otago winegrowing community, such as Steve Green of Carrick, who took the polytechnic course attest to its influence on both their own practices and maintaining the close personal relationships that are a feature of the community of Central Otago winegrowers.

Central Otago

When Robin Dicey came to Central Otago he rethought his whole approach to trellising vines. Identifying frost as the primary environmental problem on their flattish Felton Road site, his solution was to get the canopy and fruit higher off the ground because at screen height air temperature is up to 2.5°C higher than at ground level. To take advantage of this temperature gradient he configured his trellises with a single high wire (later increased to two) with the foliage sprawling downwards from this wire. Pinot Noir has this recumbent tendency naturally. Robin admits that his thinking was influenced by his distaste for cane pruning: 'I'll do anything to avoid cane pruning. I hate it, it's so damned expensive.' So he settled for a 'high wire system, unsupported foliage, just flopping foliage, spur pruned'.

After assessing the performance of different varieties on their Felton Road property he also reduced the area planted in Chardonnay on the basis of his North Island experience:

> Gisborne does it as well or better than we do. They can crop at a higher level than we can. With our lower tonnage and ripening ability, we shouldn't be stuffing around with it. And there's no great difficulty in making a good Chardonnay – you can do it in any grape-growing region in New Zealand.

Other growers had a similar view. As a proportion of the Central Otago vineyard, Chardonnay dropped from 22 per cent in 2000 to 4 per cent in 2010. Pinot Gris at 9 per cent and Riesling at 4 per cent have replaced it as the premium white varieties in the region.

Robin favours a low density of vines per hectare with 3 metres between rows and 2 metres between vines within each row. This spacing reduces the number of passes with the tractor when spraying or cultivating. Such reasoning makes sense when he explains that they have adopted Geneva Double Curtain (GDC) trellising. In this system the canopy is split to both sides of the vertical trellis. Such a configuration fits with the spur pruning and flopping canopy that he advocates:

> And the second thing was I'm of the opinion that we have enough power and enough guts in these soils to actually split the canopy on a Geneva Double Curtain and that's why they're so wide.... With a 3-metre-wide row and GDC, you effectively end up with a 1.5-metre-wide row.

While each vine has more space to extend its roots to support the more expansive canopy, some viticulturists would counter that with fewer vines per hectare and a large canopy each vine may not be able to ripen its fruit as effectively.

With experience working or consulting in most viticultural regions of New Zealand, Robin Dicey has a clear idea of the variability in the phenology (sequence of annual growth) of vines in different parts of the country. He uses Central Otago and Pinot Noir as his example. Bud break is usually in the first week of October, four or five weeks after Auckland, but there is local variability within Central: 'Gibbston will be ten days later.' He describes the Central Otago bud break as 'absolutely instantaneous and it's generally 100 per cent. Blind buds, sleepy buds, long-drawn buds, crescent buds, are almost unknown here.' He attributes this uniformity to the depth of winter chill, even though 'the experts will tell us that vines actually require very little winter chilling'. He concedes that the experts are probably right but that the vines still benefit from Central's cold winter. On the north side of Felton Road where the Diceys' Full Circle vineyard is located, flowering is mid-December and veraison in the second half of February into the first week of March. The Diceys are usually picking by mid-April. Since their first vintage in Central Otago, their picking date for Pinot Noir has varied by no more than ten days.

The Diceys started their own contract winery called Longburn Wines which began in a makeshift leased building in Cromwell and was the forerunner of the Mt Difficulty winery on Felton Road:

> Five of us, now four, started out getting together under one label called Mt Difficulty to enlarge our blending base and for security of supply. So [that] when they ring up from America and say 'We'd like 5000 cases', we don't have to say 'We've got our last 14, would you be interested in that?'

By 2010 their total area under production was 46 hectares and they had clearly established themselves as one of the four largest enterprises in Central Otago.

Mt Difficulty is a refined form of co-operative; the four participating growers describe it as a joint venture. With co-operatives being common in French, Italian and Spanish winegrowing and having served the New Zealand dairy industry well, why are they rare in this country's wine production? The answer lies partly in the nature of the primary material being produced. Compared with milk, grapes for wine are highly differentiable. Moreover, the quality of the grapes supplied to co-operatives tends to drift towards the lowest common denominator. In some seasons, producing a crop with the balance of sugar, acid and flavours to make wines of quality is very difficult despite the best efforts of those growing the grapes. Robin Dicey had managed a large co-operative in South Africa and was fully aware of such problems. To overcome the problem of variability in quality of grapes from different sources the four participants in Mt Difficulty agreed to restrict yields. With Pinot Noir, for instance, they aim for 7 tonnes per hectare.

Robin Dicey expresses a similar view to many local and international grape growers and winemakers when he calls Pinot Noir 'a finicky sort of thing'. In Central Otago:

it comes to physiological ripeness very nicely, sugar ripeness with a decent degree of residual acidity. One of those elements is always likely to drop off somewhere further north.

Central Otago has another natural advantage over many other regions growing Pinot Noir, including Burgundy. Low rainfall in autumn means that botrytis has never been a severe problem. In almost all regions where Pinot Noir is grown, humid conditions and the onset of fungoid diseases compromises the decision on when to pick. In too many places where this variety is grown the *vigneron*'s hand is forced before the grapes have reached physiological maturity and the flavours have fully developed. In the distinctive atmospheric conditions of Central Otago, growers are often able to leave grapes on the vine in the autumn without them being spoiled. Recounting his own experience of picking Pinot Noir at 27 brix, Robin marvels: 'It's unheard of because no one can hang Pinot to 27 brix without it rotting!'

Akarua

In the early 1990s, Sir Clifford Skeggs considered buying 10 hectares in the Bannockburn area and planting a vineyard. When he explored the economics of winegrowing his commercial experience soon revealed that 'you can't make money off 10 hectares'. By 2000 he had accumulated sufficient land to have most of 52 hectares of predominantly Pinot Noir grapes planted on the higher slopes of Bannockburn. His unpretentious brick winery 'Akarua' was nestled alongside the road to Cornish Point and the restaurant attached to the winery was operating. He had even established a small brewery in the same complex – something many winemakers avoid because of the yeasts active in one fermentation adding undesirable species to the other – ensuring that the brewing and winemaking were isolated.

Clifford Skeggs has Southland and Otago in his DNA. He was born and raised in Bluff, Invercargill and before venturing into winegrowing had already had a successful career in a variety of primary industries ranging from inshore and offshore commercial fisheries to mussel farming in the Marlborough Sounds, to deer recovery by helicopter and deer farming. While confident that his deep experience of marketing these products and the systems his firms had developed could be applied to wine, he also recognised that he needed expert advice. Robin Dicey suggested that he contact John Hancock, the experienced initiator and part-owner of Trinity Hill in Hawke's Bay, to advise him about his vineyard and its development. Hancock assessed the north-facing slopes of Bannockburn that Skeggs was considering and pronounced them suitable for Pinot Noir.

Keen to establish his winery as quickly as possible, Clifford Skeggs visited Marlborough to evaluate a number of its small and medium-sized wineries. He was not impressed

Looking northeast across Felton Road and the Kawarau River towards Lowburn. Akarua's recently acquired Felton Road vineyards sit in a long band below the hillside. *Akarua Winery*

by some of the outdoor 'tank farms' that he encountered and the general crowded appearance of some small wineries. This experience convinced him to build a winery capable of handling 600 tonnes of grapes – a yield of about 12 tonnes per hectare from the 50 hectares he had accumulated. He was aware that he was unlikely to achieve a yield this high in the Central Otago environment but also considered the possibility of buying in grapes locally, albeit an expensive option in Central Otago during the 1990s when many vineyards were being planted but few were yet bearing. The vineyard ended up about 80 per cent Pinot Noir with the remainder split evenly between Chardonnay and Pinot Gris. 'I don't sincerely believe it's the right land for Chardonnay,' Skeggs graciously concedes. 'However, I'll continue to drink it!' Many experienced vinifiers have expressed similar doubts about producing Chardonnay of consistent and distinctive style from grapes grown in Central Otago.

In mid-1999, Clifford Skeggs again used John Hancock to assess the winemakers who had applied for the position at Akarua. They appointed Steve Davies, a New Zealander with experience in Bordeaux and California (the Napa Valley and Caneros). Steve uses his Californian experience to interpret the Central Otago debate over the difficulty of producing Chardonnay of top quality in this region. He attributes this limitation to the paucity of different Chardonnay clones available in the 1990s when Central Otago was developing rapidly. When he returned to New Zealand in late 1998 most of the Chardonnay being grown in Central was Clone 6 that he considers

> analogous to Clone 4 which is widespread in California. And I don't know anybody who makes better than good Chardonnay out of Clone 4. There's Mendoza down here and that seems, at least in Gibbston, to set poorly and has high acid problems.

He also has some interesting observations about the influence of yield of grapes per hectare on the economics of winegrowing in Central Otago compared with parts of California:

> The figure that people will quote you around here – the people whose wine you respect, might be talking 6 or 7 tonnes per hectare depending on the site, and in the Napa I've worked with vineyards that will make wine of reserve quality at 5 or 6 tonnes per acre [12 to over 14 tonnes per hectare]. If you can get all of your grapes doing well, if you can get consistency through the yield, take good care of them, you can get a reasonably high crop and get good-quality wine out of it as well.

Given that most enterprises in Central Otago are cropping Pinot Noir at less than two thirds of what is common in Californian, it is not surprising that Central Otago Pinot Noirs are not cheap.

Although Clifford Skeggs recognised the commercial opportunities for growing grapes and selling wine within an easy drive of his home on the outskirts of Wanaka, he was also motivated altruistically. His aim was to produce wine of high quality at a reasonable price and market as much as possible from the restaurant adjacent to the winery:

> I've got a wee cafeteria in the front of the building and I want to build it up into a family environment for particularly the summer months. And I want to be able to provide wine and beer and reasonably good food at competitive prices for the younger people and their families.

The camping ground opposite his winery provides a small captive market, especially during the summer school holidays and the skiing season.

Son David Skeggs is now leading a revitalised Akarua with winemaker Andrew Keenleyside, who came to Akarua with seven years' experience working in the wine regions of California, Germany and Oregon. This team is likely to allay Clifford Skeggs' earlier concerns when his investment was looking precarious:

> I have developed it now to 52 hectares of planting and it's really grown like Topsy. I've got a very substantial investment in it now that I want to see through to maturity. But in the meantime it's just like pouring money down the drain. It's not the type of business I'd been acquainted with in the rest of my working life, I can assure you.

We are likely to see both grapes of excellent quality and more fine wines emerging from Akarua's low-yielding vineyards.

Grape growing 'on the edge'

We can learn more about natural environments and the way people assess them from Central Otago's experience in growing grapes and making wine than from any other New Zealand wine region. Central is often portrayed as being 'on the edge'. Beyond the edge is the way that the established wine industry of the North Island judged it when grapes and wine were being considered as a possible growth industry for Central Otago in the late 1960s and 1970s. Many industry figures who visited the region expressed doubts about Central's ability to ripen *vinifera* varieties and to establish an economically viable industry. Deceived by the limitations of the method used to assess it at the time – the degree-day – they read Central's climate wrongly.

The sinuous valleys, terraces and hillsides where vines are grown in Central Otago extend over large distances and present many variations in exposure, microclimates and soils. Local knowledge, local experimentation and entrepreneurship, local capital, local enthusiasm and local methods of developing vineyards that created capital saw winegrowing restarted here. Talented winemakers and viticulturists from outside the region were attracted. While the total area in vines is about one tenth the size of an average high-country run, they have a disproportionate impact on the landscape, people's perception of the region, and the local economy. During the growing season their green patchwork stands out from the dun-coloured tussock. From March onwards the shimmering white, brown or green of bird netting gradually gives way to the reds, oranges and browns of Central's autumn palette.

The geography of the region's development has been especially important. The wide distribution of the first five producers resulted in comparative knowledge of the diversity of the sub-regional natural environments, and the qualities of the fruit they produced. When combined with studies related to the Clyde Dam to gather the best microclimatic information of any region in the country, the mix was potent. Central Otago is a region making wine and one where winegrowing helps to make this region. It is now also New Zealand's most specialised wine region. A single grape variety – Pinot Noir – made up 78 per cent of its vineyard in 2010. As recently as 1990 the region was growing just 1 per cent of New Zealand's Pinot Noir. Ten years later it had increased its share to over 10 per cent, and by 2010 to over 25 per cent. Only Marlborough has a larger area in Pinot Noir. In the 25 years of Pinot Noir's primacy in Central it has not been seriously challenged by other varieties. Instead, growers have made sure that their replanting has included promising new clones of Pinot Noir while experimenting with white varieties to support it.

For a short time in the late 1990s it seemed as though Chardonnay might become the second most important variety but, as the growers themselves have discovered, it is surprisingly difficult to grow successfully here. Its area has remained static, although it seems certain to remain a lesser variety, including for blending in sparkling wine. By the millennium, Pinot Gris (145 hectares) had emerged as the second most important variety with more than twice the area of Chardonnay. Riesling has increased to be about the same area as Chardonnay. Expect more complex Rieslings with low alcohol levels to emerge from Central Otago as grape growers and winemakers refine their skills in vinifying it.

The sub-region of Bannockburn (Felton and Cairnmuir Roads) is a model of the likely future spatial organisation of winegrowing in Central Otago. These enterprises have their wineries built on the site of their main vineyards. The same is largely true of Gibbston and the Kawarau Gorge where all the wineries also have some vineyards. But increasingly most of these enterprises have either planted vineyards or buy grapes from localities where Pinot Noir has higher probabilities of reaching physiological ripeness every year. They are searching for greater complexities in the flavour profiles of their wines and more reliable yields of their varieties. Other parts of Central Otago still have an unfinished look to their wine landscapes. Buildings are scarce, roads unsealed and dusty in summer, and in winter the parcels of pruned vines lend a starkness to the landscape. But the stunning views of the encompassing hills and mountains almost always compensate for such limitations.

Clifford Skeggs' idealistic model to provide inexpensive wines to the proletariat, while admirable, is unlikely to eventuate in Central Otago. The low yields, rich flavour profiles and approachable tannins of Pinot Noir grapes grown in this region and matured in oak are expensive to produce. It is inevitable that they are too expensive to be quaffing wines. In other regions growing Pinot Noir, notably Burgundy, other varieties, such as Aligoté, are grown at much higher yields and become the everday apéritif, often enhanced by flavours from fruits such as cassis (blackcurrant liqueur).

In Mediterranean climates such as the Caneros and Napa Valley of California, varieties such as Chardonnay can be grown at much higher yields than in Central Otago while still producing rich flavours.

It is tempting to attribute Central's success with Pinot Noir to aspects of its natural environment. Its continental climate certainly distinguishes the region from most of the North Island and suits the Pinot Noir variety admirably. Small areas with analogous climates are found in interior Hawke's Bay and parts of the Wairarapa. Pockets of land in the interstices of the Southern Alps have similar climatic regimes to Central Otago but few have its accessibility and potential for selling wine on site at retail prices.

The affinity between clones of Pinot Noir and the continental climate of Central Otago would not have been realised as quickly without the experimental spirit and camaraderie of the first five growers. They shared knowledge with one another and, as Nigel Greening of Felton Road attests, were a willing source of advice to the wine enterprises that followed them. Robin Dicey's technical role in this second phase from the early 1990s was decisive. He brought a deep practical experience of setting up and managing vineyards and the viticultural practices of several countries. While many did not agree with his advocacy of spur pruning, his commitment to it stimulated debate and encouraged grape growers to understand the architecture of the canopy and the particularities of Central Otago's climatic regime and soils. Most of all, Central Otago winegrowers have managed to maintain their sense of close community despite the rapid growth of their region during the last decade of the twentieth century and the first of the twenty-first.

9

Metropolitan Vineyards and Cellars

In medieval France, every major settlement where grapes would grow had its vineyards nestled against the protective walls of the town. Vineyards adjoining some towns proved to make especially good wine. Bordeaux was one of them. Before the Bordeaux region specialised in the vine and wine it was a trading town, packed with merchants trading with England and the North Sea ports and transporting wines from the hinterland of Bordeaux as well as from regions to the south. The merchants and politicians of Bordeaux saw the opportunity to produce and trade wine, especially to Britain, and their entrepreneurship stimulated and built the local wine industry. Over centuries, *vignerons* learned and refined their skills until the wines were of superior quality to most other regions of France, and Bordeaux became one of the most successful and specialised wine regions in the world.

Proximity to a city continues to be an advantage for wine enterprises in any country. In three of the four metropolitan wine regions discussed in this chapter – Auckland and its region, Wellington and the Wairarapa, Christchurch and Waipara – association with a large city has had a marked influence on the location and character of the wine industry that emerged. As well as having the market and loyalty of its provincial city, Nelson's winegrowing is also influenced by the region's long history of growing a variety of fruit and vegetables, from quality apples to asparagus, to which grapes have been added as another successful crop.

Palliser Estate, Martinborough.
Palliser Estate

Table 9.1 The five dominant grape varieties for four regions, 2010 (% of regional totals)

Auckland		Wairarapa (Wellington)		Nelson		Waipara (Canterbury)	
Chardonnay	22	Pinot Noir	53	Sauvignon Blanc	39	Sauvignon Blanc	46
Merlot	16	Sauvignon Blanc	23	Pinot Noir	23	Pinot Noir	22
Cabernet Sauvignon	11	Chardonnay	8	Chardonnay	14	Riesling	20
Pinot Gris	7	Pinot Gris	5	Pinot Gris	10	Pinot Gris	6
Cabernet Franc	7	Riesling	4	Riesling	7	Chardonnay	5

Collectively, these smaller wine regions of New Zealand have the third largest area in vines after Marlborough and Hawke's Bay. With a total of 4042 hectares of grapes planted in 2010, they slot into the hierarchy of regions after Hawke's Bay (4947 hectares) and before Gisborne (2083 hectares). Waipara has the largest metropolitan vineyard of these smaller regions with a total of 1456 hectares of grapes in production. Waipara growers are highly protective of the identity of their locality and have been reluctant to be included in the larger entity of Canterbury. Given that the rest of Canterbury had just 323 hectares in vines in 2010, their reluctance is understandable. Nevertheless, with a total of 1779 hectares of vines in the combined Canterbury region, its total is fast approaching the area of vines recorded for Gisborne.

In each of the regional examples, the intersection of vines and wines with a particular city and its countryside has been different. Migration of Croatians from the Dalmatian coast to New Zealand, especially Northland and Auckland, was the initial stimulus to winegrowing in the Auckland region. Local landowners with strong political connections to Wellington were important in Martinborough and the wider Wairarapa. Nelson has the longest and most successful horticultural history of all these metropolitan regions. The French vineyards of Akaroa of the nineteenth century demonstrated that vines would grow in the Canterbury region, while in the twentieth century it took pioneering locals to demonstrate the potential of the Waipara area to make fine wines.

Auckland and its region

In the mid-twentieth century, vineyards and orchards dominated Lincoln Road, Henderson, which was lined with hoardings advertising fruit and wine for sale. While a few names from that period still survive – notably that of the Mazuran family – the sale in 2008 of the vineyard land of Collards Wines, and that of the quaintly named Mother's Cellar of the Farac family, marked the final stage of the urbanisation of that landscape.

Like some of the vineyards in the Graves area adjoining Bordeaux, the landowners have been unable to resist the imperatives of escalating property taxes, the problems associated with growing grapes in a built-up area, and the attraction of the capital gains associated with selling land now zoned commercial or industrial. Such decisions do not come lightly for the people who nurtured these vines and their enterprises in the sometimes difficult natural environment of West Auckland. Bruce Collard was driving past the family's beloved Shanty Block, renowned for its Malbec, when the digger was uprooting their vines. He burst into tears.

Yet, despite its small area in grapes, compared with Marlborough or Hawke's Bay, by some criteria Auckland remains the most important wine region in the country. Over 70 per cent of New Zealand wine is bottled or packaged in Auckland and most exports of wine leave through its port. At head offices in the city, executives and boards make major decisions concerning their companies that have vineyards, wineries and other assets distributed throughout New Zealand. From its Symonds Street headquarters,

Josip Babich began growing grapes in 1916. His descendants have developed a major family-owned enterprise with twelve vineyards around the country as well as wineries in Auckland and Marlborough. *Nigel Gardiner*

Metropolitan Vineyards and Cellars

299

New Zealand Winegrowers also plays its role, as it represents grape growers and wine companies within the country and internationally.

Transforming and revitalising the Auckland vineyard

The sequence of dispersal and growth of new localities growing grapes and making wine in the Auckland region has many nuances. From the beginning of the twentieth century, the Henderson-Oratia area had a number of vineyards and cellars, with Pleasant Valley Wines owned by the Yelas family and Corbans in Henderson being the first to emerge there. The second West Auckland concentration in Kumeu-Huapai originated in the 1930s and 1940s, with two families – the Brajkoviches and Nobilos – being among the first to grow vines there.

At mid-century, Croatians owned over 90 per cent of the enterprises holding winemaking licences in West Auckland. Many of them were part-time growers and winemakers, having often started their enterprise by making wine for family consumption. A number of these Croatian settlers had initially worked in Northland digging kauri gum or farming before migrating to the periphery of the country's largest city.

While these two main nodes of viticulture still exist, the Lincoln Road part of the Henderson-Oratia locality has largely been converted to urban uses, whereas inclusion in the special zoning for the Waitakere Ranges – which restricts further subdivision into small lots – means that Oratia's vineyards and orchards will now most likely survive.

The mixed fortunes of the Auckland region over the last 40 years are closely related to the actions of the enterprises involved in this region's wine industry. Many of them focused their attention on other parts of the country with higher potential to grow grapes for making unfortified table wine. In Poverty Bay (Gisborne), Marlborough, Hawke's Bay, and later in Waipara (Canterbury), Auckland companies let contracts to grow grapes, some of them purchased land, and they established and extended their presence in these regions. Metropolitan Auckland itself received its share of the capital invested because companies enlarged their existing finishing, bottling and administrative arms there. Improving the regional organisation of their systems of production, processing and distribution was one objective of these companies: Auckland has always been their main New Zealand market, and main point of departure for wine exports.

Quite separately from these multi-regional companies, a group of smaller enterprises have been launched in Auckland. People with knowledge and experience of winegrowing started most of them. They chose interesting and attractive places to live, permanently or at weekends, and to plant vines. Waiheke Island in the Hauraki

Gulf, a 35-minute ferry ride from downtown Auckland, was one such destination. The Matakana area, less than an hour's drive northeast of Auckland and also overlooking the Hauraki Gulf, was another. Both destinations proved to have the natural environments where varieties of *Vitis vinifera* grew well on mainly clay soils. Moreover, in both places these vineyards and wineries have associated winegrowing with fine food and high culture. Sculpture, art, and crafts flourish alongside neatly trimmed vines on north-facing slopes.

Serendipitously, some of the varieties native to Burgundy and Bordeaux grew as well here as in any other region of New Zealand, apart perhaps from Hawke's Bay. On Waiheke Island, Stephen White of Stonyridge Vineyard established an enviable reputation for the Larose label, while in Matakana, Jim Vuletic captured an international following for Providence – both of which are Bordeaux blends although the mix of varieties going into them is different. Wines from each of these enterprises have demonstrated that with the right sites, older vines and appropriate viticulture, grapes can be grown and wine made that sits comfortably alongside some of the best wines in the world. Much of this wine is sold offshore.

Some of the smaller vineyards and wineries that previously dominated Henderson-Oratia leapfrogged to other locations on the northwestern urban periphery of Auckland. The Collards were among the first to do so when they established their Rothesay vineyard east of Waimauku and within reasonable access of their winery and Shanty Block vineyard in Lincoln Road. Soljans of Lincoln Road successfully relocated to the largely rural belt between Brighams Creek and Kumeu. Their winery on this site seems almost incidental to the large café and reception centre that also serves as an outlet for their wines.

West Brook Winery, operated by winemaker Anthony Ivicevich and family, was formerly located on the ridge facing the Babich winery on land that is now occupied by housing. It has re-established on the hills east of Kumeu close to Riverhead Forest. Like many Auckland wineries, it now sources grapes from other parts of New Zealand as well as locally and Anthony has established a stellar reputation as a contract winemaker for other enterprises in the district.

The Babich winery persists in Babich Road, Oratia, with a small area in vines adjoining the winery, although it sources almost all of its grapes from Marlborough and other regions. Its current CEO David Babich, son of Peter and Lisa, refers to their enterprise as an 'asset company', alluding to the astute way that the family has bought and sold land as demand for housing in the vicinity of the winery has escalated. At Artisan Wines, Rex Sunde and family have been particularly active in encouraging Auckland residents to visit them at Parrs Cross Road, Oratia, where their organic vineyard and boutique winery and restaurant have a regular weekend craft and produce market with musical entertainment.

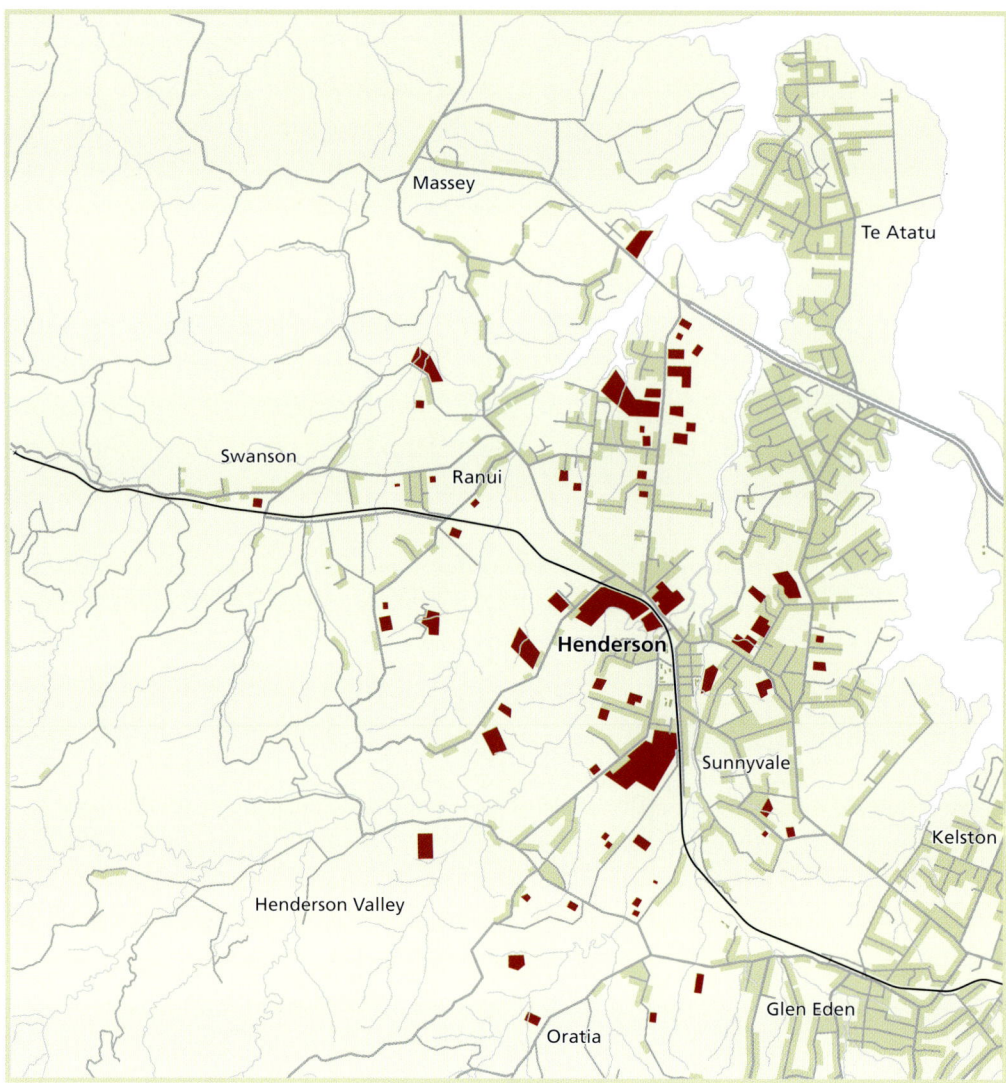

Figure 9.1 Vineyards of West Auckland, 1960

By 2010, the total area of vineyards on Waiheke Island and in the Matakana locality northeast of Warkworth was greater than the combined vineyard area of the two main Auckland viticultural nodes in the region during much of the twentieth century, Kumeu-Huapai and Henderson-Oratia. This group of more recent and emerging localities now has a similar area in vines to the Auckland vineyard in 1980 when the Ministry of Agriculture recorded 603 hectares.

Auckland's sequence of growth, then decline, followed by a noticeable period of growth in the last decade, has involved two interrelated changes. The first is a varietal revolution. The second is spatial. In 1980, 68 per cent of the Auckland region's 603

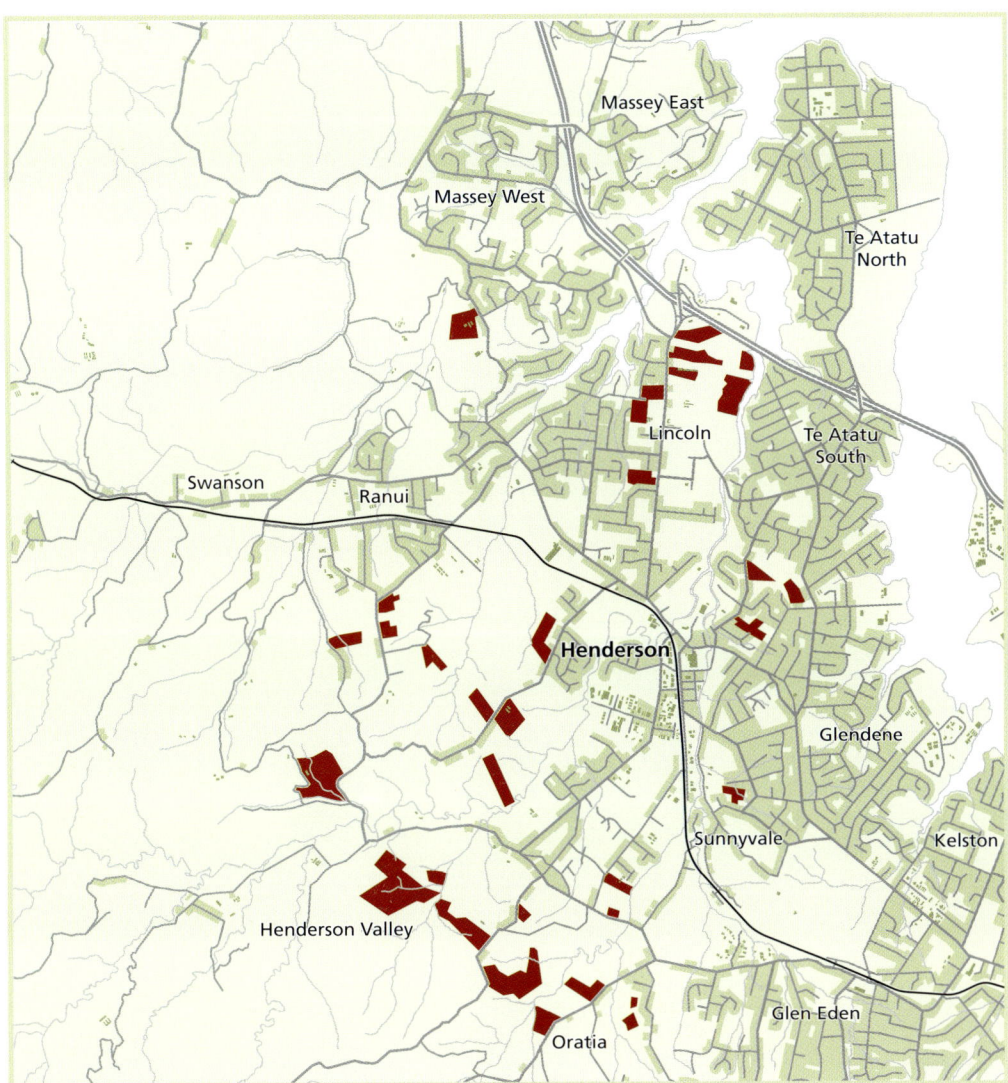

Figure 9.2 Vineyards of West Auckland, 1980

hectares in grapes were hybrids. By 1990 this proportion had fallen to under 20 per cent. These varietal changes also signal a spatial shift of winegrowing in the Auckland region towards the parts that receive lower rainfall and are less humid than the traditional area of West Auckland.

The owners of vineyards on Waiheke Island had already recognised that the classic varieties of Bordeaux would perform well there. Rainfall gradients from west to east are surprisingly steep across the narrow isthmus and peninsulas of the Auckland region, mainly because of the rain-shadow effect of the Waitakere Ranges which regularly receive over 2000 millimetres of annual rainfall and Henderson-Oratia about 1500

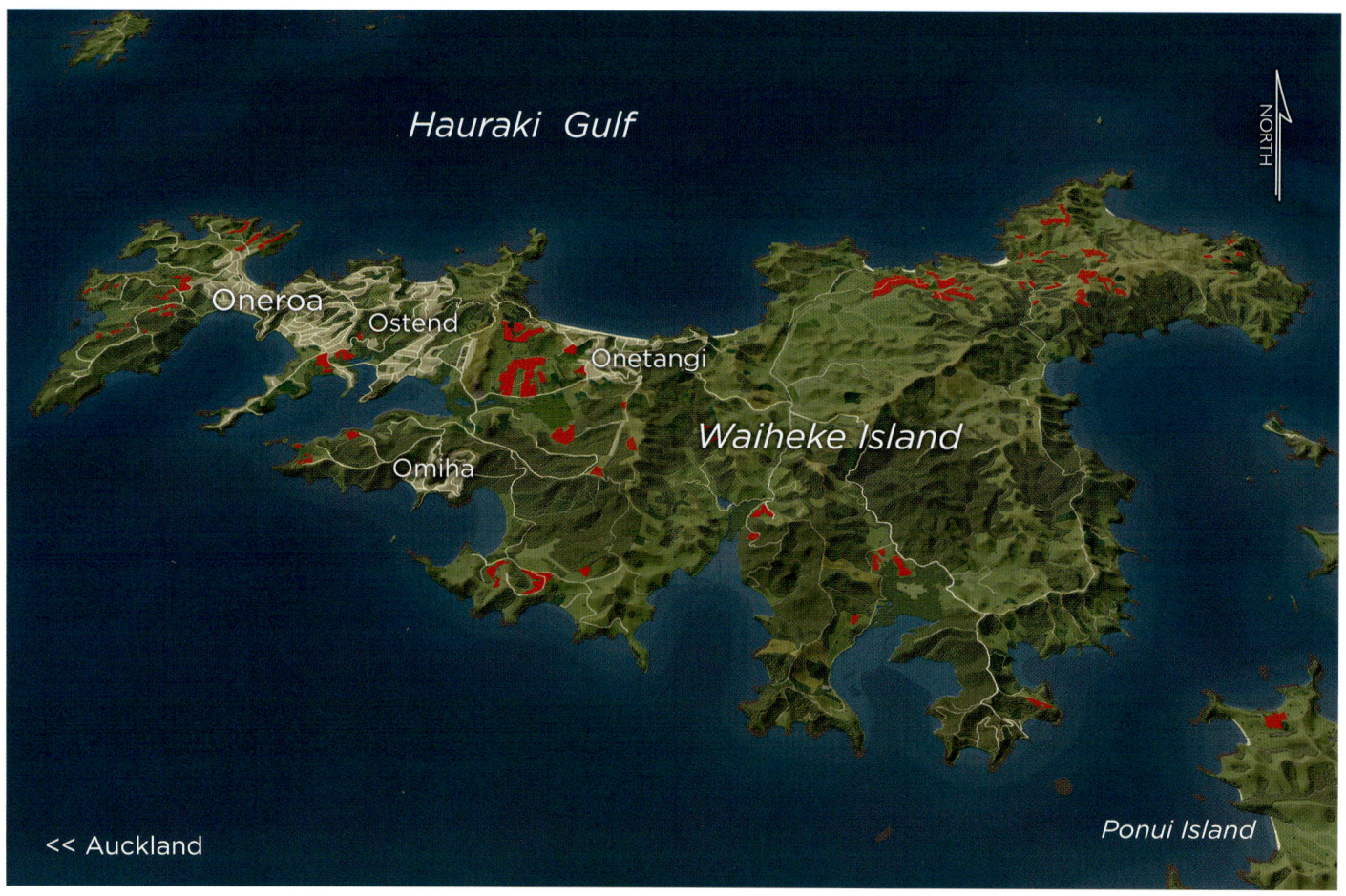

millimetres. In many years, parts of the east coast of the Auckland region and islands of its Hauraki Gulf have rainfall as low as 1000 millimetres.

The long axis of Waiheke Island is aligned east–west. A series of spine-like ridges roughly follow this alignment, with the result that the island has its share of north-facing slopes. Many of the successful vineyards have established on these slopes, especially those reasonably close to the north coast but seldom right on it where beach houses take first choice of the land. To ripen a variety such as Cabernet Sauvignon in the middle latitude, maritime climate of Auckland the vines need all of the accumulated energy that these sites can capture. Despite its small area, some pockets of land in the interior of Waiheke Island are sheltered from sea breezes and are noticeably warmer than those on the coast. On some of these large holdings, such as that of the Spencer family, favoured sites have been identified and planted in vines.

In the statistics collected by New Zealand Winegrowers, Auckland is identified as a region. However, many of the wine enterprises clustered around its urban periphery no longer identify themselves by their region. Instead, as with Waiheke and Matakana – each of which is an excellent example of the advantage of being a metropolitan vineyard – they prefer to build their reputation using the name of their immediate locality.

Auckland's varietal mix

Auckland now grows the most eclectic range of grape varieties of any region in New Zealand. In 2010 it had twelve varieties, each with more than 10 hectares planted (Table 9.2). The top ten of these are all classical winemaking varieties, but the eleventh wine on the list, Palomino, reminds us of West Auckland's chequered past when it was making mainly fortified wines and this sherry grape was one of the stalwarts. Buried

Table 9.2 Grape varieties in the Auckland region, 1990-2010

	1990		2000		2010	
Variety	ha	%	ha	%	ha	%
Chardonnay	33	11	86	22	121	22
Merlot*	21	7	67	17	86	16
Cabernet Sauvignon*	60	19	77	20	62	11
Syrah	-	-	11	3	45	8
Pinot Gris	7	6	11	3	40	7
Cabernet Franc*	7	2	30	8	37	7
Sauvignon Blanc	12	4	12	3	35	7
Pinot Noir	21	7	17	4	23	4
Malbec*	<1	<1	10	2	20	4
Viognier	-	-	-	-	11	2
Palomino	57	18	13	3	11	2
Pinotage	11	4	19	5	10	2
Gewürztraminer	5	5	<1	<1	9	2
Riesling	5	2	2	<1	3	<1
Semillon	12	4	10	3	3	<1
Seibel 5455	14	5	-	-	1	-
Baco 22A	7	2	-	-	-	-
Other	37	12	28	7	33	6
Bordeaux blends total*	89	29	184	39	205	38
Total	310	100	393	100	550	100

deeper in the list are two hybrids from that time, Seibel 5455 and Baco 22A. These were last recorded in 1990, although Seibel 5455 was again listed as having a single hectare in production in 2010.

Chardonnay, with 121 hectares planted in 2010, is now the dominant variety, making up 22 per cent of the region's vineyard. The varieties grouped together as the 'Bordeaux blends' – Merlot, Cabernet Sauvignon, Cabernet Franc and Malbec (marked with an asterisk in Table 9.2) – total 205 hectares and are now 38 per cent of Auckland's vineyard. More than 20 hectares each of Syrah, Pinot Gris, Sauvignon Blanc and Pinot Noir were also listed in Auckland's total area in vines of 550 hectares. When viewed in this way, Auckland's vineyard exposes its interesting story. Chardonnay and the Bordeaux varieties comprise 60 per cent of the Auckland vineyard and 89 per cent of it is now planted in classical varieties.

In all other metropolitan wine regions of New Zealand just five varieties make up over 90 per cent of their vineyard, whereas Auckland requires twelve to reach this threshold. Part of the explanation is the prevalence of the Bordeaux varieties in Auckland. They have been taken seriously here for a long time and in parts of the region such as on Waiheke Island and in Oratia old vines of these varieties are treasured. Viticulture in the Auckland region now benefits from being organised in a much more artisanal fashion than in some of the recently developed, larger regions of New Zealand. Auckland wine enterprises are prepared to grow small areas of Pinot Noir or Sauvignon Blanc despite the natural environment of the region not being optimal for them. Even 3 hectares each of Riesling and Semillon are recorded in Auckland's diverse heritage vineyard.

While in the 1970s and 1980s members of the North Island wine industry were questioning whether grapes would ripen in the South Island and prosper on its gravelly soils, the boot is now on the other foot. Some South Island growers question whether the Auckland climate has sufficient winter chill and diurnal ranges of temperature in the late summer ripening period for varieties of *Vitis vinifera* to prosper. However, the climatic data shows that many Northland and Auckland sites get their share of cool night temperatures in autumn and frosts in winter (see Chapter 4). Even more powerful evidence comes from the quality of the wines produced from local grapes by local enterprises. No example is more convincing than that of Kumeu River Wines located on the southern edge of the small town of Kumeu in West Auckland. The success of the Brajkovich family business amply demonstrates the importance of learning the nuances of the local environments in creating successful wine enterprises through hands-on experience.

An Auckland Enterprise

Kumeu River Wines

Much to the surprise of his colleagues in Central Otago and Martinborough, in the late 1990s Michael Brajkovich, winemaker and manager of the Kumeu River vineyard and winery west of Auckland, pulled out all of his Cabernet Sauvignon vines and replaced them with Pinot Noir. Earlier he had pulled out his Sauvignon Blanc and replaced it with Pinot Gris. After fifteen years' experience with the discarded varieties, and some experimental work growing their replacements, he considered that he could make much more elegant wine on his Kumeu sites with these different varieties.

Paying little heed to the environmental hype suggesting that it is the winter chill, diurnal ranges of temperature, and long and dry ripening period that gives the special qualities to Pinot Noir grown in the Wairarapa and Central Otago, Michael Brajkovich's philosophy, influenced by his French experience (at Pétrus, the prestigious Pomerol

Lyre trellising at Michael Brajkovich's Kumeu River Wines. *Warren Moran*

Metropolitan Vineyards and Cellars

chateau east of Libourne in the Bordeaux region), is that great wines are made from understanding the land where you find yourself growing vines and matching the varieties to it. He had already done this with Chardonnay. Now it was the turn of the other Burgundian variety, Pinot Noir, and a white from Alsace, Pinot Gris.

Kumeu River Wines has been setting national standards for some varieties from the 1980s, but up until the last decade the Brajkovich family were reluctant to source grapes from outside their immediate locality. Pressure from their international distributors saw them finally succumb to having a Marlborough Sauvignon Blanc in their range. But the fundamental philosophy of their enterprise is to grow their own grapes and supplement these by having a small number of local grape growers. They liaise with them regularly, indeed manage some of their vineyards as well as buy their grapes. No contracts are written. Instead they discuss price per tonne in January each year and arrive at a consensus. The success of Kumeu River wines in the local and international market – notably their elegant Chardonnays but Pinot Gris and Pinot Noir as well – is clear evidence that northern New Zealand will continue to feature in the country's list of fine wines.

When asked if for some reason it were impossible for him to establish in Canterbury, in which part of New Zealand would he plant grapes, pioneering winemaker Danny Schuster rattled off a list: 'Martinborough, Marlborough, Hawke's Bay. They're all great, even Auckland.' Invited to elaborate, he added:

> Well, because most people are in a hurry to get away from Auckland. And I think it's a challenge, number one. And number two, there's some great wines being made from grapes grown there. So obviously something must be right. I don't know what it is, but why not? Who the hell wouldn't want to make Chardonnay like Michael Brajkovich?

Wellington and the Wairarapa

Martinborough was a town, and the Wairarapa a region, just waiting for the vine and wine. The substantial Tararua Range 30 kilometres to the northwest of Martinborough, and the Rimutaka Range to the southwest, shelter the gently sloping and flat land northeast of Lake Wairarapa that is drained by the Ruamahanga River. The sprawling band of hills to the east of the Ruamahanga's catchment stretches for 30 kilometres to the east coast and limits the precipitation from that direction. As a result, along the axis of the Ruamahanga River between Martinborough and Masterton the rainfall is under 1000 millimetres annually and some parts of it receive less than 800 millimetres. Such lower precipitation and drier conditions prior to harvest were one of the main attractions to winegrowing in this part of the Wellington region.

A close reading of the maps of key climatic criteria in Chapter 4 shows that the Wairarapa meets all the essential criteria for winegrowing under cool-climate conditions. A substantial area east of the Ruamahanga River accumulates over 1200 growing degree-days. In the very hot 1998 season, a strip of land reaching up to 40 kilometres inland along most of eastern New Zealand from the Ashburton River to the Marlborough Sounds in the South Island and from Palliser Bay almost to East Cape in the North accumulated an extra 200 degree-days. Nevertheless, physical constraints of both terrain and climate, as well as the availability of parcels of land of suitable size for viticulture, limit the area suitable for winegrowing in the wider Wairarapa.

The Wairarapa's varietal mix

In the two decades between 1990 and 2010, the Wairarapa has become the most specialised of New Zealand's metropolitan wine regions (Table 9.3). As recently as 1990, eleven years after Neil McCallum of Dry River planted his vineyard on the Martinborough Terrace, Chardonnay and Cabernet Sauvignon were the second and third most-planted varieties in the region. Together, they made up over 40 per cent of the Wairarapa's vineyard. Sauvignon Blanc, with just 11 hectares planted, was the fourth most important grape. Subsequently, as winegrowers learned the nuances of this region's natural environments, and consumers became more informed, most wine enterprises in the Wairarapa have favoured Pinot Noir as their main red variety and Sauvignon Blanc as their white.

Table 9.3 Grape varieties in the Wairarapa (Wellington) region, 1990–2010

	1990		2000		2010	
Variety	ha	%	ha	%	ha	%
Pinot Noir	20	27	101	31	465	53
Sauvignon Blanc	11	15	51	16	197	23
Chardonnay	18	24	69	21	70	8
Pinot Gris	–	–	14	4	47	5
Riesling	2	3	25	8	32	4
Cabernet Sauvignon	13	18	25	8	14	2
Merlot	1	>1	17	5	12	1
Gewürztraminer	6	8	5	1	3	<1
Other	4	5	12	3	25	3
Total	74	100	328	100	871	100

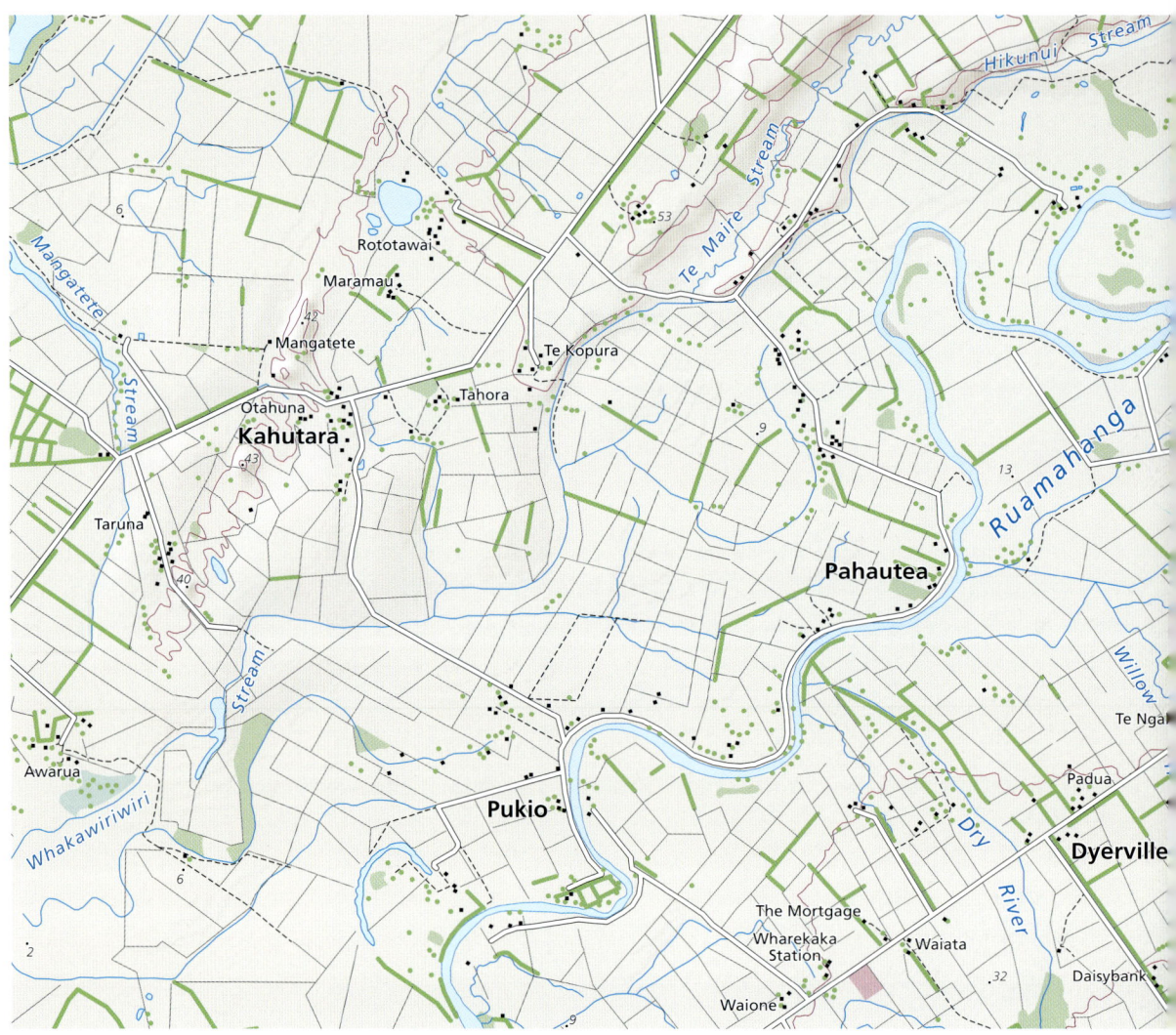

Figure 9.3 Martinborough vineyards in the Wairarapa

By 2010, Pinot Noir alone made up 53 per cent of the region's vines, and with Sauvignon Blanc at 23 per cent, accounted for over three quarters of the region's vineyard. Cabernet Sauvignon was just 2 per cent of the vineyard, while five varieties – Pinot Noir, Sauvignon Blanc, Chardonnay, Pinot Gris and Riesling – now make up 93 per cent. Riesling and Pinot Gris are relative newcomers to this region. Pinot Gris will probably continue to increase in importance, most likely at the expense of Chardonnay. The region's distinctiveness and reputation for making quality table wines from *vinifera* varieties is firmly established.

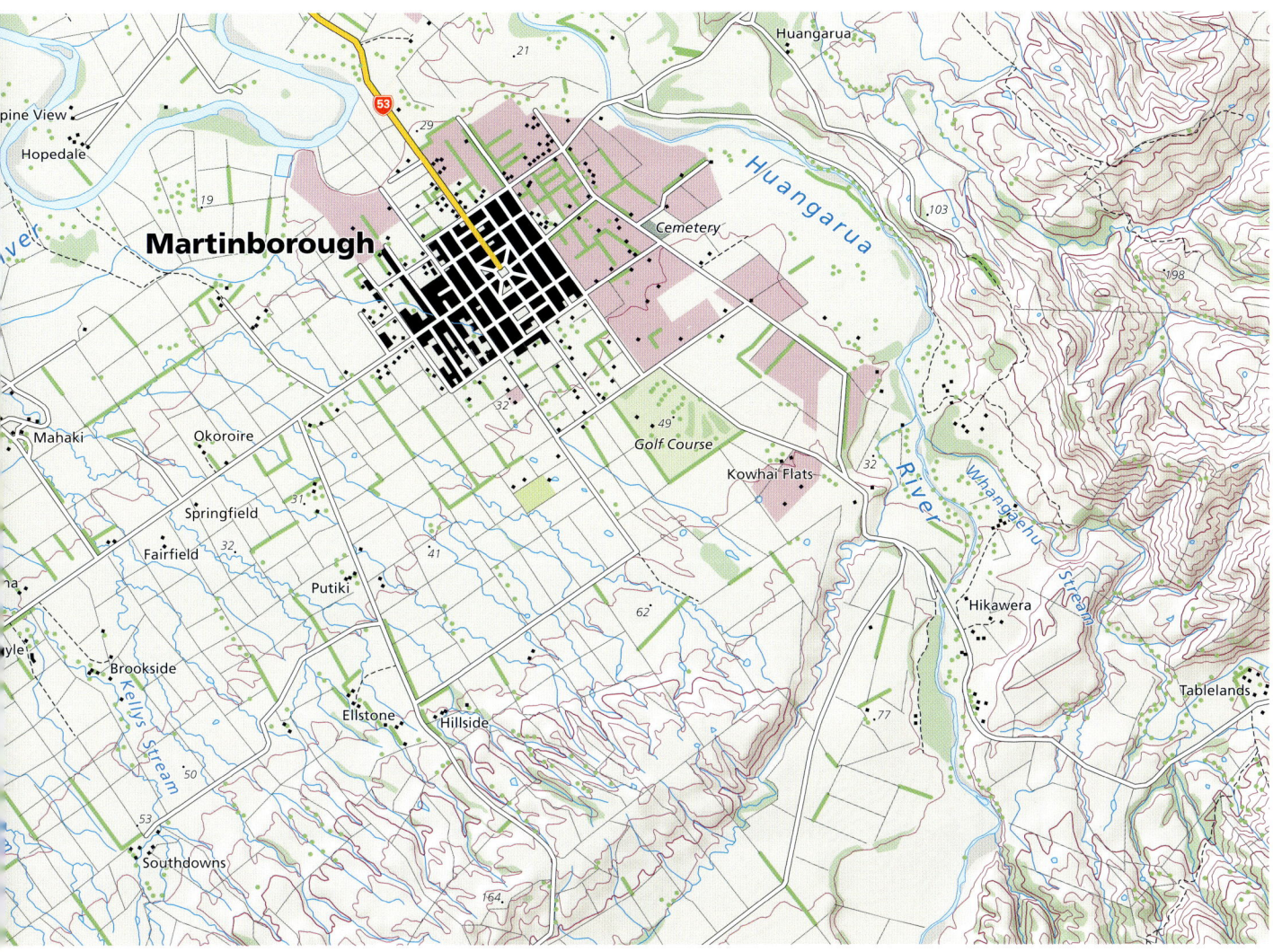

Low yields of grapes also differentiate the Wairarapa region. When calculated for the region as a whole, and for all varieties, enterprises in the region averaged 3.5 tonnes per hectare over the decade ending 2010. Only in Central Otago and Canterbury (Waipara) are yields at similarly low levels. That Sauvignon Blanc, the second most important variety in the Wairarapa, is always cropped at higher yields than Pinot Noir makes these results even more compelling. It is the owners' careful management of the 465 hectares of the region's Pinot Noir that is mainly responsible for the low yields. The predominance of Pinot Noir also ensures that the price of wine per bottle remains high. It is an expensive wine to produce, as its retail price reflects.

The Wairarapa yields are even more telling when compared with similar figures for some of New Zealand's larger winegrowing regions. On the average across all varieties,

Gisborne produces about 12 tonnes of grapes per hectare, Hawke's Bay 8 tonnes and Marlborough 8.5 tonnes. The varietal mix is distinctive in each of these regions, but the average figures strongly suggest that for enterprises in regions such as the Wairarapa to be successful they must ensure that their vineyards produce first-class fruit and their winemaking makes the most of its qualities. When their yields of grapes are lower they must also maintain the efficiency of all aspects of their business. Palliser Estate even monitors and controls the humidity in its winery to ensure that evaporation from its Pinot barrels is not excessive.

Enterprises in the Wairarapa story

Ata Rangi

In 1978 the local authorities of the Wairarapa, in collaboration with central government agencies, such as the Department of Scientific and Industrial Research and its Soil Bureau, organised a seminar in the small, sleepy town of Martinborough to discuss the suitability of this region for viticulture. Derek Milne, the scientist who had mapped and interpreted the soils of the region, was one of the presenters. Although intensely interested in the topic, Clive Paton was unable to attend, but he made sure he read the transcript of the presentations thoroughly. They helped to convince him of the region's suitability for viticulture, and by 1980 he had bought a 12-acre block of land on the Martinborough Terrace and was planting vines: 'Wish I'd bought 200 acres because it was only about $1,000 an acre then!'

Clive Paton is deeply interested in plants, in nurturing them, and in understanding their interaction with, and place within, their natural environments. He applied this sensitivity to the vines he planted, recognising that the dry summers and autumns that were a disadvantage for pastoral farming were ideal for some varieties of *Vitis vinifera*. Ata Rangi was one of the first four Martinborough enterprises to plant Pinot Noir by 1980. The others were Martinborough Vineyards, Dry River and Chifney Estate. His description of the land they bought identifies the key qualities that made the Martinborough, and later the Te Muna, terraces valuable viticultural land:

> This land is not that good for farming. It grows grass for about six months of the year. It's good for wintering stock and that's about it. I've done a little bit of cropping on some of our blocks just to get them broken up and quite often it's too dry in the pre-Christmas period to grow good crops. You really need the rain or irrigation.

Picking at Ata Rangi.
Pete Monk/Ata Rangi

Irrigating land for grazing livestock was uncommon in the late 1970s but irrigating vines on the free-draining Wairarapa gravels is essential. A much more intensive land use, such as viticulture, could earn the income that was necessary to be able to make a living off a much smaller piece of land, including the costs of irrigating when necessary. Clive was leaving a dairy farm of about 120 acres but initially only buying 12 acres to get his grape-growing enterprise under way.

Contemplating yields of Pinot Noir over the 20-year period since he had begun growing the variety at Ata Rangi, Clive thought it appropriate to reduce the period to 15 years because the vines from the Abel clone that he had planted in 1980 had taken at least five years to come into full bearing. He mused about vintages during the 1990s:

> It's been a gradual rise. In the early '90s, we were around 4000 to 5000 cases, and for a single family, at the prices we were getting, that was quite good. It gave us a little bit to put back into capital development. As we've gone on and the operation has expanded, we've had to increase. In '95 and '96 we had good crops, the best crops we'd had in our 20-year period, closer to 3 tonnes to the acre, and we were still able to make good wine. Any more than that and your wine starts going downhill. Most people prune and trim back to 3 tonnes to the acre and we thought

Metropolitan Vineyards and Cellars

we were on the pig's back. The last four seasons averaged one and a half tonnes for all sorts of reasons. The drought had an effect in '98 but we also had major trouble with flowering – it was in early December, we still get those southerlies coming through that pull temperatures down.

Fluctuations in the production of this small but innovative and internationally respected enterprise illustrate the way that variability in yield from vintage to vintage makes planning for a particular level of production difficult. One obvious solution for Ata Rangi would have been to buy in grapes to even out the variability in their production of wine. In the early days of winemaking in Martinborough, however, few surplus grapes were available in the district. Moreover, artisanal producers like Ata Rangi are reluctant to buy in grapes unless they originate from their own locality, preferably from their own or leased land where they can prune and nurture the grapes to suit the style of wine they wish to produce.

Winegrowers in the Wairarapa have long been convinced that low yields are necessary to make distinctive and fully flavoured wines, especially when vinifying Pinot Noir. The yield of Pinot Noir that Clive would be happy with is 2 tonnes per acre. In the French appellation system the levels of maximum production in Burgundy are prescribed under the appellation laws. At the top of their hierarchy, Grand Cru (loosely translated as first growth) wines are commonly set at 35 hectolitres (hundreds of litres) per hectare. Expressed as hectolitres, the yields achieved by Clive Paton at Ata Rangi (and other Wairarapa winegrowers such as Neil McCallum of Dry River) stack up alongside those prescribed in the French system very favourably. When expressed in tonnes per hectare the equation reads:

$$2 \text{ (tonnes)} \times 2.471 \text{ (acres per hectare)} = 4.942 \text{ (tonnes per hectare)}.$$

To convert these tonnes of grapes per hectare to quantity of juice for wine, a conservative multiplier is 0.7. In other words, seven tenths of the grapes are juice. So:

$$4.942 \text{ (tonnes per hectare)} \times 0.7 = 3.459 \text{ hectolitres of juice per hectare}.$$

This roughly rounds to 3500 litres of wine per hectare or, in the French vernacular, 35 hectolitres of wine.

In other words, Pinot Noir vines in the Wairarapa are being cropped at a similar level to the Grand Cru wines of Burgundy. No wonder the Wairarapa wines have the intensity of flavour and nuances on the palate that have seen them gather numerous awards. This comparison with Burgundy shows that their emphasis on low yields is paying off with improved quality, a lively demand for their wines, and the potential of higher prices per bottle.

Palliser Estate Wines of Martinborough

Richard Riddiford, whose great-grandfather was one of the first four settlers to farm sheep in the Wairarapa, is managing director of Palliser Estate Wines of Martinborough which was initiated by a group of investors in the early 1980s. Palliser's first vineyards were planted in 1982: 'But because we didn't really know what we were doing, we didn't produce much fruit until '89.' Australian-born winemaker Larry McKenna, long-term resident of the Martinborough Terrace, made Palliser's first Pinot Noir. When Richard Riddiford tasted it he was astounded:

> Nineteen eighty-nine was our first vintage. By some miracle it was not only drinkable, it was bloody good. And then we built this winery. We exported to the UK in '91 and it rolled out from there, really.

Marketing Palliser's wines in various countries takes up most of Richard's working hours. Switzerland has been a reliable and profitable export market, but he suspects that this success relies on the quality of the partner that they have there. He prefers the word 'partner' to the more common term 'agent', because he believes that the individual doing the selling for you should be taking as much interest in the qualities and price of the wine as the producer. Although it is a difficult market, partly because

Pinot Noir grapes, Palliser Estate. *Palliser Estate*

Metropolitan Vineyards and Cellars

many of its customers have only recently been introduced to wine, there have also been some bright spots for Palliser in parts of Asia. For instance, during the hiatus in Asian economic growth in the late 1990s, the Palliser brand was the only wine to increase in total sales.

From the beginning, Palliser decided to restrict their vineyard to five main varieties: Pinot Noir 40 per cent, Sauvignon Blanc 40 per cent, with Riesling, Chardonnay and Pinot Gris making up the remaining 20 per cent:

> And we do also make a *Méthode Champenoise* – a small amount though. We just make 700 cases simply because if we do good Pinot and Chardonnay, it's a natural progression. And there are occasions where the only thing people will drink is Champagne. But it's expensive and it's got a long lead-time, so we're not going to go into that big-time.

When asked if Palliser's broad intentions concerning the mix of grape varieties they planted had been realised, Richard replied:

> The only thing I've changed is Chardonnay, because we can't differentiate that on the world market. But with Pinot and Sauvignon, wherever I go in the world, it's easy to differentiate those. The Sauvignon is, by the mere nature of it, that New Zealand style, so exuberant really that it is not repeated anywhere else.

By the millennium Palliser had over 100 hectares in vines and were exporting about 55 per cent of their production. Richard believes that increasing exports of quality bottled wine is the primary imperative for New Zealand wine enterprises, and because most people in the international market look for reassurance he has 'always used other brands that are more famous than mine':

> Most people who taste your product don't know what they are tasting. So if they say, 'Where can I buy this?' and you say Harrods, then they think it's got to be all right. Which is a load of rubbish, but it's a mental process people go through. That's why the Wimbledon tennis tournament is also very important to us. It's another international brand name that's known the world over.

Similarly, the airline business provides wonderful exposure because when people get on the plane

> the rich ones turn left and the poor ones turn right. And if your wine is in the left-hand section, you don't need to worry about whether they've got any money or not – they wouldn't be travelling there if they didn't. And flying from New Zealand, it's a bloody long way to wherever

you're going, so they tend to remember what they drink. That's why I think Air New Zealand has been very important to the New Zealand wine industry.

Richard Riddiford has strong ideas on the influence of the youth of New Zealand winegrowing on the attitude of consumers to its wine and uses the example of Pinot Noir to illustrate his claim. When consumers are served several New Zealand Pinot Noirs and several Burgundian Pinot Noirs, and they taste them blind, some will prefer the local product and some the Burgundian. But when the consumers are shown the price, all of them will prefer the New World product. However, he is quick to point out that he does not see the Burgundian Pinots as competition but rather as the benchmark. He also suggests that New Zealand Pinot Noir 'hasn't got a regional style yet because even within Martinborough you will find quite distinct styles between Ata Rangi, Dry River, Martinborough and Palliser, and yet they are next door to each other'.

Richard also sees a bright future for Riesling grown in the Wairarapa and other localities in the South Island, although he points out that:

> For the last three decades, we've been told that Riesling is going to be the wine of the next decade, but despite what everybody says about it, unless you know and understand wine, people won't buy it. Knowledgeable people will, because it's still, I think, the world's greatest grape variety. It's as simple as that.

In 2010, Marlborough was growing 448 hectares of Riesling, Wairarapa 32 hectares, Waipara 286 hectares, the rest of Canterbury 52 hectares, and Central Otago 66 hectares. The total area of Riesling recorded for the whole of New Zealand was 986 hectares. Winemakers and wine enterprises in most regions of New Zealand, but especially Marlborough, Canterbury (particularly Waipara) and Central Otago, express similar views to Riddiford about the qualities of Riesling and have been supported by New Zealand Winegrowers. Yet, despite these communal efforts, and the quality of the wines being produced, Riesling remains obstinately reluctant to move off the shelves of supermarkets or out of the cellars of producers.

Martinborough Vineyard Estates and Escarpment Vineyard

Larry McKenna is one of the several colourful Australians who are stalwarts of New Zealand winegrowing and especially of Pinot Noir. In 1974 he enrolled full-time in the three-year Roseworthy Agricultural College degree, and from 1977 worked as an agricultural advisor for the South Australian Department of Agriculture including eighteen months at Port Lincoln. His OE consisted of another eighteen months in Europe during which he 'saw a lot of vines and drank a lot of wine'.

In 1980, when his close friend from high school, fellow Australian John Hancock, founding partner of Trinity Hill in Hawke's Bay, was winemaker at Delegat's in Auckland, he offered Larry a temporary job. Larry accepted with the intention of staying only for the vintage, but when he was offered a permanent position agreed to stay on. By 1983, Larry was a winemaker for the firm and remained there until late 1985 when he was offered the position of winemaker and general manager at Martinborough Vineyard including the offer to buy a 20 per cent shareholding in the company. His motivation for the move south was very definite:

> I was sick of receiving 25-tonne loads of grapes in the back of a truck that I'd never seen before. I wanted to be fully involved in all aspects of the business and particularly in the vineyards.
> To be a producer of very specialised, you know, uniquely qualified wine.

At this time, Martinborough Vineyard had 15 acres (about 6 hectares) in vines and was producing 40 tonnes of grapes annually.

Two families, the Milnes and the Shultzes, were the principal shareholders. Derek Milne, a soil scientist with the DSIR, had visited Germany in 1977 where he recognised the importance of free-draining soils, and low rainfall during the late summer and autumn, as two of the criteria for selecting suitable sites for vineyards. Perceiving the potential of some of the free-draining soils of the Wairarapa terraces for growing grapes, he bought land and encouraged other landowners to become involved. As Larry points out, Derek still insists that there is 'a very, very small area of this district that's suitable for growing grapes':

> But it's fair to say that the industry has moved much wider than he would ever have given it credit to be able to do. We're now in Gladstone, and Masterton, and south of here and east of here, but I think we are starting to identify those same soil types in lots of these areas – and Gladstone will be successful, and so will Masterton. I don't think south of here will be successful, but east of here will be.

The successful establishment of Craggy Range's vineyards under Steve Smith's guidance (see Chapter 6), but within a wider definition of the Wairarapa, adds weight to McKenna's argument.

When Larry told friends he was leaving Auckland to make wine in Martinborough, he was met with incredulity. At that time, fewer than 10 hectares of Pinot Noir was being grown in the Wellington region and fewer than 100 hectares in all of New Zealand. It was his first encounter with New Zealand Pinot Noir:

> When I came down here at the end of 1985 to look at this job I was shown a wine made from Pinot Noir out of barrels by amateurs that just blew me away. It was wine like I'd never tasted in New Zealand and it wasn't Cabernet! I thought if these guys can make wine on an amateur basis out of Pinot Noir that tastes and looks like this, whew, we're into it!

He spent the next fifteen years developing Martinborough Vineyard Estates into one of the Wairarapa's and New Zealand's most respected small vineyards and wineries. By 1999 it was producing 12,000 cases of wine. Pinot Noir was 40 per cent of the production, Chardonnay 30 per cent, Riesling 20 per cent, Sauvignon Blanc 10 per cent, along with a few hundred cases of Pinot Gris. Two thirds of the grapes for these wines came from their own vineyards. It continued to increase in size until in the 2010 Annual Report of New Zealand Winegrowers it was for the first time listed in the medium winery category of wineries as producing over 200,000 litres of wine (22,000 cases) annually.

After fourteen vintages at Martinborough Vineyard Estates, Larry was ready for a change. Although disappointed to be leaving the vines he had planted that were now coming into their best period of production, he was also excited to have an opportunity to set up a new vineyard and winery (alongside compatriots Robert and Mem Kirby of Australia's Village Roadshow) using the experience that he had accumulated in the Wairarapa environment.

His role as a consultant for winemakers growing Pinot Noir in the Wairarapa, and in other regions of New Zealand and internationally, had deepened his knowledge. The varieties they were going to grow were the easiest choice. Within each variety, the matching of rootstocks with clones, the type of trellising to use and the spacing of the vines were much more testing questions, especially because these decisions interacted intricately with the style of wine he wanted to produce. During a discussion in the early autumn of 1999 when he was planning the configuration of the new Escarpment Vineyard in Te Muna Road, Martinborough, he captured his dilemmas vividly:

> I have to look at the wine style I want and my vineyard management beliefs, and then say I'm going to be planting on this piece of flat land with this soil type – now what's the best rootstock/clone combinations and canopy management for that? I have some answers, but whether they're right or not, I don't know. What I can be dead sure of is they'll be more right now than they will be in ten years' time. In ten years they're going to be wrong. And I just have to accept that. Whatever I say in 1999 for my planting regime on my new block in 2000, I have to make that decision and not worry about it any more. Make those decisions, live with them, and then learn to manipulate the whole thing with irrigation, and bud numbers. The big decisions, the spacing, the rootstock, the clones and the variety have been made, and then you have to get the best out of those decisions by managing the block as effectively as you can.

Few *vignerons* get the opportunity to set up two successful wine enterprises in their lifetime. Larry McKenna is one of them.

Nelson and its region

If it were possible to rank those New Zealand regions with the climate, soils and terrain to make fine table wines, Nelson would be near the top of the list. Its mild climate with high sunshine hours, less extreme temperatures, and fewer frosts during the growing season than much of the South Island, gives it a distinctive natural environment. Its Moutere soils, with their gravels of various sizes in a matrix of clay, allow vines to be grown with limited, or even no, irrigation. The region also has the river-deposited gravel and silty soils of the Waimea flood plain where the Seifrieds and several other enterprises have planted some of their vineyards. Such varied terrain, with many north-facing slopes and adequate flat land, provides ample opportunities for aspiring winegrowers.

Between 2000 and 2010, Nelson increased its area in vines from 205 to 842 hectares – an increase of 637 hectares, or a quadrupling of its regional vineyard (Table 9.4). White-grape varieties made up 73 per cent of its vineyard in 2010. Sauvignon Blanc, with 327 hectares in vines, comprised almost 40 per cent, while Pinot Noir with 23 per cent was the only red variety with more than 10 hectares planted. However, a comparison between the varietal mix of the Nelson region with the varieties grown in the vineyards of

Table 9.4 Grape varieties in the Nelson region, 1990–2010

	1990		1995		2000		2005		2010	
Variety	ha	%	ha	%	ha	%	ha	%	ha	%
Sauvignon Blanc	6	13	43	31	54	26	245	38	327	39
Pinot Noir	4	9	15	11	32	16	143	22	196	23
Chardonnay	8	18	22	16	55	27	133	21	121	14
Pinot Gris	–	–	–	–	3	2	27	4	81	10
Riesling	7	16	23	17	34	17	50	8	56	7
Gewürztraminer	5	11	4	3	7	3	22	3	28	3
Cabernet Sauvignon	5	11	12	9	11	5	6	1	3	<1
Syrah	2	4	1	<1	–	–	3	<1	8	1
Müller Thurgau	3	7	2	2	–	–	–	–	–	–
Seibels	2	4	–	–	–	–	–	–	–	–
Other	3	7	15	10	20	10	17	3	33	4
Total	45	100	137	100	205	100	646	100	842	100

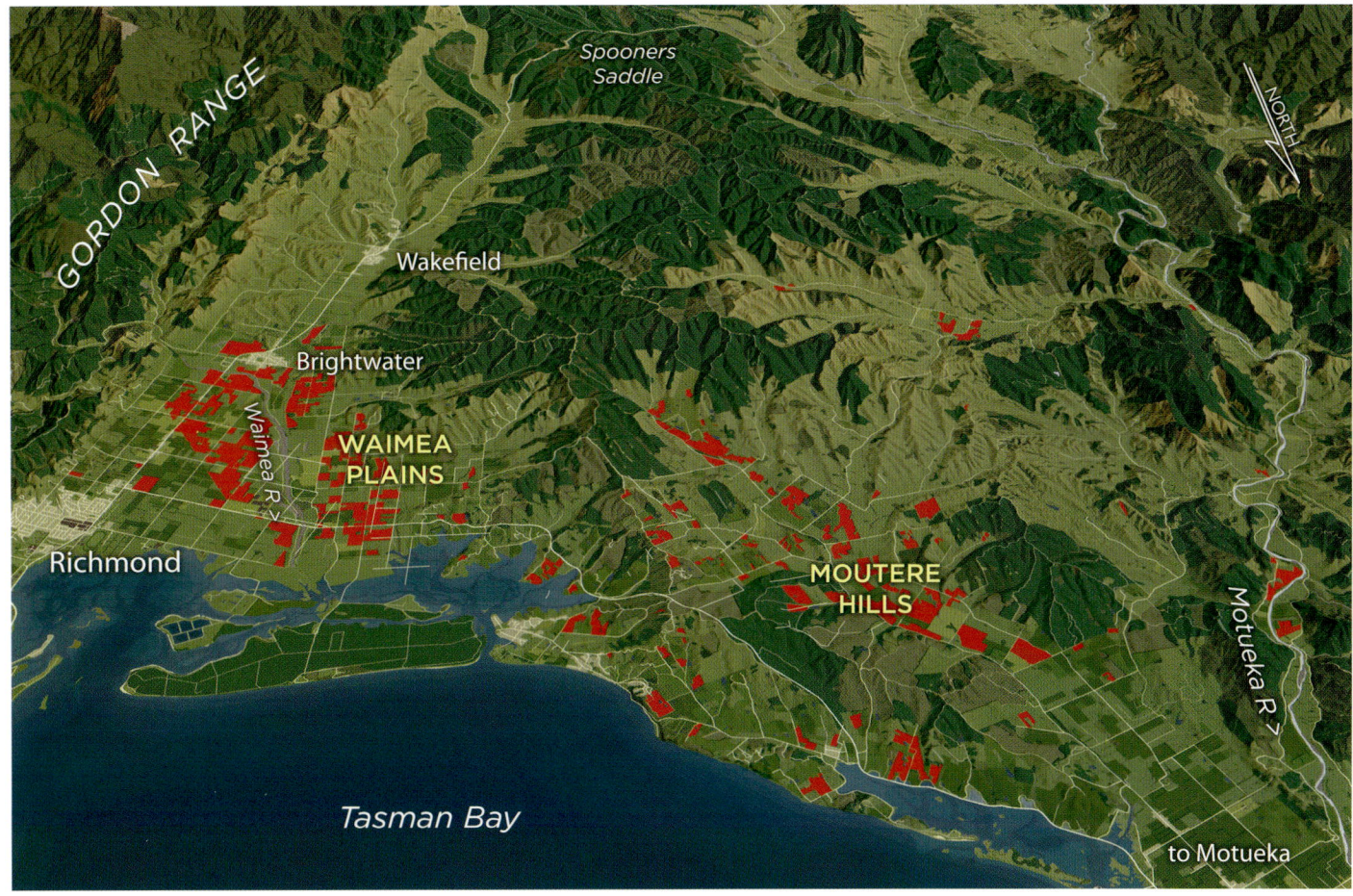

its largest enterprise, Seifried Estate, reveals some notable differences. Whereas for the region as a whole Sauvignon Blanc was 39 per cent of its vineyard, for the Seifrieds it was noticeably higher at 54 per cent. They have used their scale to compete aggressively with some of the large Marlborough companies on local and international markets, and being a well-established family company have the advantages of lower costs of production in Nelson and growing conditions that are just as favourable as in Marlborough.

Enterprises in the Nelson story

Seifried Estate

The seven vineyards of Seifried Estate vary in size from 19 hectares to 70 hectares and their total area is just over 250 hectares. Comprising 22 per cent of the Nelson region's vineyard, it is unlikely that any single enterprise is as dominant in any other viticultural region of New Zealand.

Hermann Seifried arrived in Nelson from his native Austria in 1971, recruited by the Apple and Pear Marketing Board to advise them on making cider, apple wine, or other products from the surplus apples that Nelson and New Zealand were producing at the time. He quickly recognised that the Nelson environment offered other opportunities. Both hops and tobacco were being successfully cultivated in the region, and from his horticultural training and experience in Austria, he knew that to ripen grapes fully they needed similar temperatures and length of growing season to hops. In 1973 he and his

Figure 9.4 Vineyards of the Waimea Plain

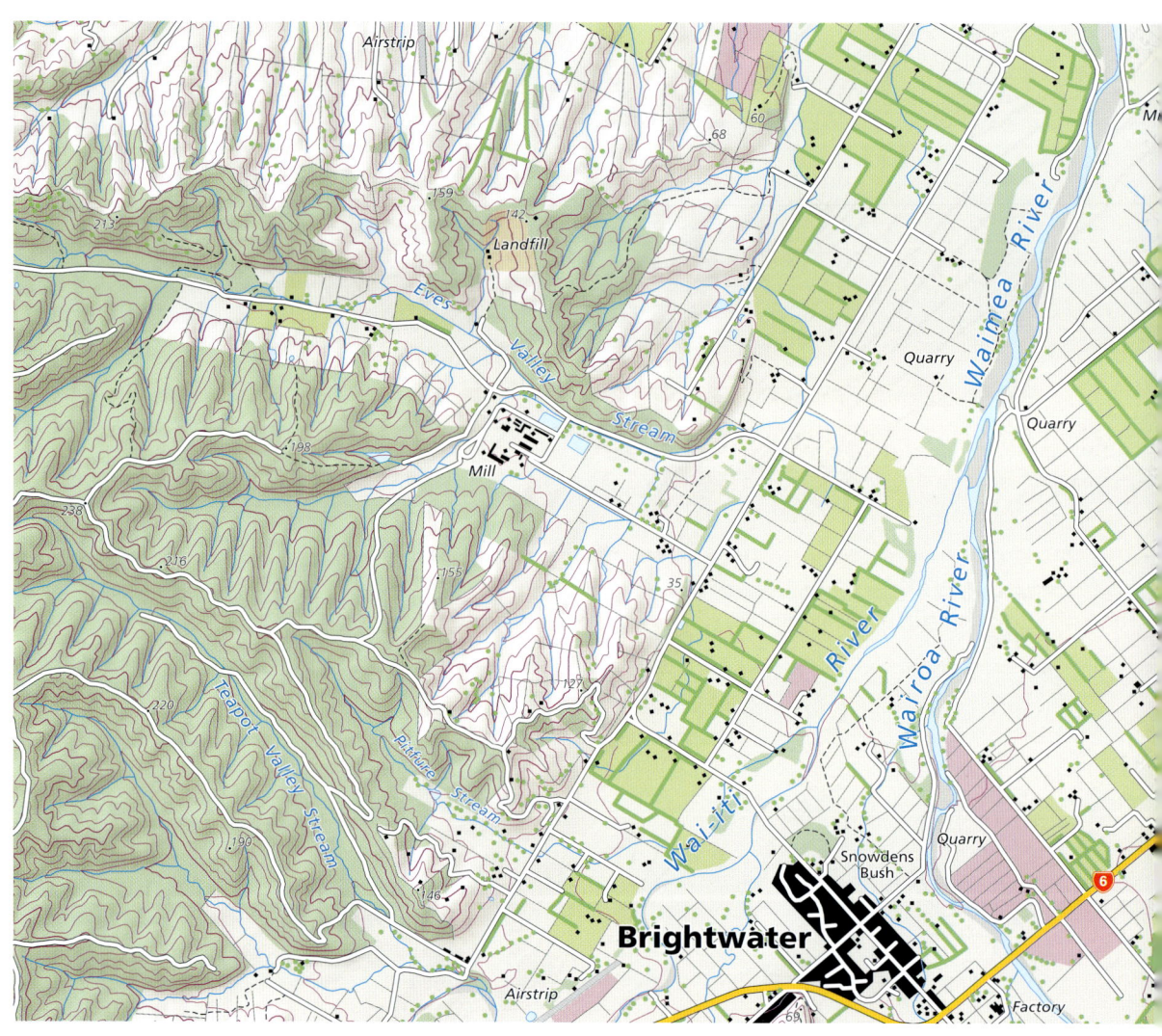

wife Agnes planted 2 hectares of Riesling and Gewürztraminer on the property they had purchased in the Upper Moutere Valley. Both varieties performed well. They built a winery on site and planted more grapes. With their vineyard producing excellent fruit, and their wines selling well, they began thinking more seriously about increasing production and launching a larger commercial operation. Their existing land in the hilly Upper Moutere area did not suit such plans because, on this site, drainage and waste disposal were difficult.

The Seifrieds made the bold decision to buy land and establish vineyards and a winery on Redwood Road, less than 2 kilometres west of the Waimea River but in the

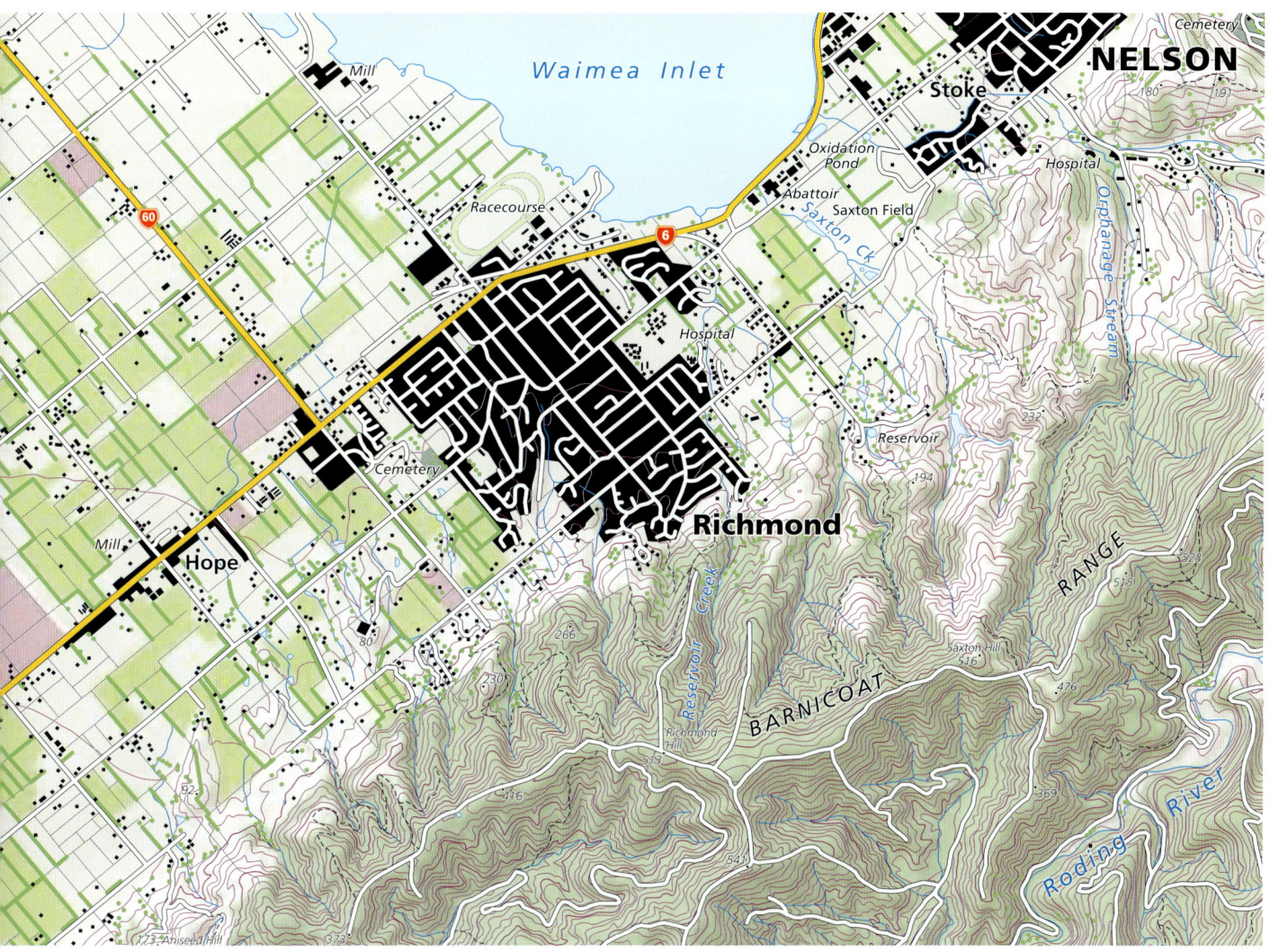

catchment of O'Connor Creek. The Seifrieds added value to these properties by building a dam, on a branch of the Eves Valley Stream, to provide water to their vineyards. These were acquired in 1980 (2004), 1990 (1998), 1993 (2004) and 1999 (1999) respectively – where the year in brackets is the date of their last plantings on each vineyard. Some of these sites, such as Redwood Valley, were planted over a long period as different parcels of the property were matched with particular varieties of grapes. In 2000 and 2007 the Seifrieds added two further vineyards: Brightwater, planted between 2000 and 2004, and Eden Road, in 2007 to 2008.

The tumbling terrain of its surrounding hills shelters the triangular lowlands of the Waimea and similar former flood plains. To the southeast the Richmond and Gorgon ranges rise to over 1000 metres, while northwest of the Waimea and Wai-iti rivers is a great wedge of forested hills that continues right to the valley of the Motueka River. The northward-flowing Moutere River, with the Moutere Highway in its valley, furnishes more gently sloping land suitable for horticulture. It was in this valley that several of the first Nelson vineyards were planted. Neudorf, the original Seifried vineyard and winery (now Kahurangi Estate) and Spenser Hill Estate are examples.

One limitation to increasing the area of vines planted in the Nelson region is the availability of land in suitably sized parcels, either on the Waimea Plain or further north towards Motueka. In Nelson, apple and stone-fruit orchards compete strongly for land on the Waimea and other former flood plains. In contrast, farms on the Wairau Plain in Marlborough had practised more extensive cropping before diversifying into viticulture, and as a result land parcels there were large. Wine companies wanting extensive vineyards could buy such properties or consolidate several adjoining parcels. As one of the Wakefield settlements of the 1840s, Nelson has had a longer history of more intensive farming, including orcharding. The average size of rural land parcels is smaller than in Marlborough and the density of rural population is higher. Consequently, large parcels of land for viticulture have been more difficult to find there.

Seifried Estate's seven main vineyards are dispersed over a 10-kilometre stretch of land on either side of the Waimea River from Redwood Road to just south of Brightwater (Figure 9.4). There are advantages to this spread of vineyards and grape varieties. Several of their vineyards have four or five different types of soil, and five have between three and twelve varieties of grapes planted on them. Where possible, the Seifrieds have matched the different varieties with specific soils, and in the process have gradually deepened their understanding of which varieties are performing best on the different sites. Where the soils are more uniform, they have been quite prepared to plant large blocks in a single variety.

Strong principles are driving the Seifrieds' planting policy. First, Sauvignon Blanc has always been their dominant variety. They achieved this by buying existing Sauvignon vineyards or planting up to half of each of the new sites they purchased in the variety. The Cornfield vineyard on Redwood Road was almost all planted in Sauvignon during the 1990s, the 20 hectares of Sauvignon planted in the Brightwater vineyard maintained their momentum into the new millennium, while the Eden Road vineyard is a 29-hectare monoculture of Sauvignon. By 2010, their 99 hectares of Sauvignon Blanc made up over 54 per cent of their total vineyard of 183 hectares – as mentioned above, a higher proportion than most other Nelson enterprises.

The second principle was to ensure that other aromatic varieties were a distinguishing feature in their portfolio of wines. Hermann's Austrian heritage and experience meant that New Zealanders would be introduced to wines made from Grüner Veltliner, Gewürztraminer, Riesling and Zweigelt. The third principle, to have Pinot Noir as their main red variety, was slower in being realised. After planting a small Pinot Noir vineyard of 1.9 hectares on Redwood Road East in 1998, a further 9.1 hectares of Pinot was planted on Redwood Road West the following year. The 16.3 hectares of Pinot on the versatile new Brightwater vineyard increased the total area in Pinot Noir to more than 27 hectares.

Other plantings in the Brightwater vineyard demonstrate that the Seifrieds are trying to achieve several new objectives. The characteristics of the different sites in this vineyard have encouraged them to experiment. They have planted between 1 and 2 hectares of each of the Bordeaux varieties and Syrah – a total of 6 hectares – an initiative which suggests that they think the favourable microclimates and soils in Nelson, and

For Austrian immigrant Hermann Seifried and his New Zealand-born wife Agnes, establishing the vineyard was a family effort.

Metropolitan Vineyards and Cellars

After establishing their first vineyards in the Upper Moutere Valley near Nelson, Seifried Estate expanded into the Waimea Plain. Here they grow Riesling in their Brightwater vineyard.

especially on their Brightwater vineyard, may be sufficient to ripen Cabernet Franc, Cabernet Sauvignon, Malbec and Merlot. In Nelson's sunny environment they may well be right. The twelve varieties planted on the Brightwater site also include more than 5 hectares each of Gewürztraminer and Riesling – a continuation of their commitment to the aromatic varieties. Any new vineyard belonging to the Seifrieds requires a compulsory planting of at least half a hectare of each of Grüner Veltliner and Zweigelt, so both of these are present too.

The Seifried family's vigorous colonising of the Waimea lowlands was not without controversy. Some of their purchases of land and applications for resource consent attracted lively opposition from local landowners but were energetically defended. At one stage, Hermann went as far as threatening to move their enterprise to Marlborough. But the Seifrieds were attracted to the coarse gravel soils of the Waimea Plain which were similar to those that were beginning to produce wines of quality in the Wairau Valley in Marlborough. Similar soils are found on the flood plain of the Waimea River northwest of Richmond and off Redwood Road facing Rabbit Island.

Viticulture had its first presence in the Nelson region on the Moutere gravels in the hills, but there has been a noticeable shift towards the gravels of the lower Waimea in the Brightwater area and further towards the mouth of the river. One consideration in such moves is that most of these gravelly soils are on flat or easily sloping land – conditions which make the laying out of the vineyard, including irrigation lines, simple as well as reducing the costs of weed control and harvesting, making larger-scale viticulture possible. Such attractions were a major consideration in an expanding enterprise such as Seifried Estate moving off the Moutere Hills, even though establishing the new site involved the major cost of building a large private dam to ensure sufficient water supply.

Neudorf Vineyards

The stylish weatherboard buildings, manicured forecourt, and mature vines with trunks as thick as a wrestler's forearms suggest that this enterprise takes wine seriously and has been around for the long haul. Tim and Judy Finn planted their first vines in 1979, six years after distant neighbour Montana had struggled to establish its first vineyard on the dry, gravelly soils of Marlborough's Wairau Plain. Getting Neudorf's Chardonnay and Pinot Noir vines to grow on the Nelson soils was much simpler. On the Moutere clays these varieties flourish without irrigation to the extent that excessive vigour needs to be carefully controlled.

Tim Finn trained as an agricultural scientist at Massey University, Palmerston North. In 1975 he was working at Ruakura Agricultural Research Centre on the outskirts of Hamilton, where, as part of his Master's degree, he was collecting data for his thesis on 'cows and stress'. The Te Kauwhata Viticultural Research Station was still operating and on Friday afternoons the scientists and graduate students from Ruakura would meet there to taste the house wines. Tim got to know the Te Kauwhata scientists, especially Tom van Dam and Rainer Eschenbruch who had recently arrived in New Zealand. Discussions at these tastings sparked his interest in wine.

With his thesis completed and bonded to the Ministry of Agriculture and Fisheries for two years, Tim was offered a choice of positions in several regions of New Zealand and chose Nelson where he was appointed as a dairy advisory officer. However, the choice had very little to do with the particular job and everything to do with the possibility of finding a suitable piece of land for viticulture. Accordingly, soon after their arrival the Finns 'looked around to see what was available in the area and to get a feeling for how viticulture would go', and met up with Hermann and Agnes Seifried who gave them a lot of good advice.

The Seifrieds had established their winery in the Moutere area in the mid-1970s and the Finns were also attracted to 'the hill country aspect' of this locality. It seemed like a nice area to live as well. Tim was looking for a north-facing block of affordable size and they found one that had been on the market for some time. Moutere is an old German settlement, and the last surviving member of one of the original settlers, the Bosselmans, owned this block. The Finns funded their purchase by arranging to subdivide the 50 acres that was for sale, buy the 23 acres with the house on it, and sell the rest to the neighbours. They bought the property in 1978.

Tim's background in agricultural science served him well in his new career. Despite the few vineyards in the area, he and Judy were able to keep in touch with winegrowing through colleagues in MAF. Their launch into grape growing also coincided with Lincoln College developing its viticultural and winemaking programme, which involved experimenting with different clones and varieties, and they would attend their

The original 1850 farm buildings and first plantings at Neudorf Vineyards. Tim and Judy Finn transformed the barn into an authentic New Zealand winery. *Tim Finn*

monthly tastings. They also kept in contact with Rainer Eschenbruch. Tim remembers very clearly the event that convinced him to give up his job visiting and advising dairy farmers in the northern part of the South Island and become a full-time winegrower. At a poetry reading he attended, Sam Hunt and the group he was performing with seemed

> so full of doing their own thing and were out there and saying to hell with it, that I handed in my notice the next day and gave up the safety of the steady job and came out here and worked full-time on the place.

With Tim working on the property and Judy continuing as a journalist for another three years while they established their vineyard and winery, the enterprise began to take shape, but not without sacrifices and hard work. Tim used his contacts at Te Kauwhata, and growing friendship with Hermann Seifried, to find sufficient cuttings on suitable rootstock to get the vineyard started. The varieties they planted were Cabernet Sauvignon, Chardonnay, Riesling, Gewürztraminer and what was being called Beaujolais, which as Tim points out, 'turned out to be an upright clone of Pinot Noir (clone 22) that had been wrongly named at Davis'. Neudorf's first vines were planted in 1979 and they picked their first small crop in 1981. By the year 2000, the only vines still in the Neudorf vineyard from these first plantings were the Mendoza Chardonnay and a small parcel of the clone 22 Pinot Noir.

In 1982, Tim sketched the plans for their winery, including a wine bar and restaurant, before passing them over to an architect for the final drawings. The Finns had decided to base the winery on the old barn that was one of the original buildings on the site – although 'it's hard to know what's remaining of it,' says Tim, 'the roof is still there!' – and construct it largely of timber milled from the property. They had several mature Douglas firs on their land and a good stand of macrocarpa. The Douglas fir timber was used mainly in the structure of the building and the winery was clad in macrocarpa.

However, the restaurant proved to involve more than either Judy or Tim had anticipated:

> We knew nothing about running a restaurant. It's terrible looking back on those days – it was just mayhem. We would run out of food and send someone off to Richmond, or Motueka, to try and find food. It was far more successful than we had ever imagined.

When they opened just before Christmas of 1982 they expected about 20 people a day, but in the New Year 'it jumped up to about 120 a day and there was no way we could handle that'. From 1988 they changed to become a 'Bring Your Own Food' restaurant.

Meanwhile, Tim continued to develop their vineyard and vinify their wine. In 1982 they picked about 10 tonnes of grapes from their property. In 1983 this increased to about 18 tonnes but in 1984 it dropped to about 12 tonnes:

> We were not controlling the vigour in the vineyard and we were getting poor sets. It's very easy to get a nice little crop off young vines with open canopies, but unless you know what you are doing in terms of your trellising systems, you suffer more disease and get less fruit. And I really wasn't up to it in terms of knowing what was going on there.

The pioneering work on canopy management of Richard Smart (see Chapter 4) was his salvation:

> We changed it all over to Scott-Henry [trellising] and started opening up the canopy and leaf plucking. All of a sudden we got the viticulture right from about '87 on, the fruit was so much better, and we really had some sort of control over the vineyard.

Neudorf's total production of grapes from their own vineyard during the late 1980s was between 25 to 30 tonnes but Tim was still not happy with the quality of the grapes they were producing. Sauvignon Blanc was returning more than twice as much as the other varieties such as Riesling or Gewürztraminer. So they began to make their varietal choices and the Gewürztraminer came out the next year. But 'it was really only through the '90s that we came to terms with crop reduction':

Neudorf's clay soils (left) shape the varieties they can grow – Chardonnay and Pinot Noir flourish, Sauvignon Blanc does not. Effective canopy management picked up from Richard Smart has been critical to improving the quality of the Neudorf grapes and wines. At right, Tim Finn, Richard Flatman, and Todd Steven survey the vineyard. *Tim Finn*

Through the mid-'90s we were starting to find out what grew best here, and you know, what we shouldn't do. In the end we realised that we shouldn't be growing Sauvignon Blanc up here – it's too vigorous on these clay soils. You are really fighting it right through summer because it's a very vigorous vine and Sauvignon Blanc doesn't like the overcrowding effect.

Their response was decisive: 'We just pulled it out!' Their revised strategy over the varieties they favour was that 'what we do best here is Chardonnay and Pinot Noir – and they suit us pretty well'. Questioned as to whether this was a site decision rather than a marketing decision, Tim explained their reasoning:

In the end we could see that Pinot was the only red we were going to do any good with, because it ripened here and it ripens well. We're aiming at the very top end of the market. And we had a taste of the top end with early success with the Chardonnay in '89, '90, '91 – we were right up there in international competitions.

Tim Finn rates Richard Smart's contribution to New Zealand winegrowing as 'huge to us, and huge to New Zealand at that stage in terms of understanding what needed to happen out there in the vineyard' – although 'I don't necessarily go along with all of what he says'. He sees Smart's particular strength as encouraging grape growers to

produce 'reasonable volumes of well-produced fruit for wines selling in the premium range'. Tim's objective is slightly different. He is aiming at the ultra-premium range and believes that Smart underestimated the importance of reducing yield to improve flavours. The philosophy at Neudorf is that 'even though you have got them all well displayed, you will actually get better fruit if there is less of it there'.

Rosie's Block at Neudorf carries the name of the owners' daughter. The high, north-facing block overlooking the Neudorf home vineyard was planted in 1999 in Chardonnay, with Riesling and Albariño added since. *Tim Finn*

Greenhough Vineyard

In 1990, Andrew Greenhough and Jenny Wheeler purchased a run-down 10-acre block at the southern end of Paton Road near the settlement of Hope with about 4 acres in vines. Around 2 acres were in Müller Thurgau, plus an acre each of Pinot Noir and Riesling, and two rows of Cabernet Sauvignon. As Andrew points out, 'it was all producing well, so it was good for total novices to have a bit of a play with'. The vines had been planted in 1979 so by then were eleven years old. Andrew and Jenny made no changes to the vineyard until 1993 when they ripped out the 2 acres of Müller and replaced it with Pinot Noir. Over the next three years to 1996 they developed an additional 4 acres of Chardonnay and began buying more land – 7 acres in 1993 and a further 10 adjoining acres in 2000, giving a total of 27 acres, half of it planted in vines. The unplanted land was earmarked entirely for Pinot Noir.

Additional fruit for the Greenhough enterprise, including Sauvignon Blanc, is sourced from contract blocks, as Andrew explains:

> Lifestylers are starting to add a vineyard to their list of requirements along with pony paddocks, so there's an opportunity now for people like us to go in and establish blocks the way we want them, set them up, plant them with what we want and manage them, and take fruit.

Andrew contributes his labour to the development of the block but the landowner pays for all of the posts, wire, vines and any other materials. This arrangement allows Andrew to have more control of the viticulture and to configure these vineyards to their own specifications without having to buy the land. The arrangement between the landowner and Greenhough Vineyard is a form of lease. Beyond the first four years, when the vines are coming into full production, they are guaranteed another ten years of access to the fruit, and beyond that, the right of renewal for a further period. In a region such as Nelson, where the population is increasing through migration, the potential demand for such land tenure arrangements in the rural areas is considerable. Andrew and Jenny increased the quantity of Sauvignon Blanc they were buying under contract to about 25 tonnes during their first ten years growing grapes.

Without this innovative method of increasing their access to grapes under their control they would not have been able to invest more in their own winery. They were trading off Andrew's skill in setting up vineyards for an assured supply of grapes in the future that they would be able to process with winery equipment they had paid for through their labour. Reflecting on the vulnerability of wineries that do not have access to grapes of the quality they would like, Andrew distinguishes two groups of enterprises in the Nelson wine *filière* that both complicate and open up opportunities:

> There are those landowners who want to make the investment and the improvements to their property as an asset but don't want to have anything to do with it. Then you get your growers who suddenly want their own label. So what was a secure grower relationship becomes insecure. I think that long-term leases, and being able to design the vineyard, gives me a lot more control – in terms of how I crop it, how I establish the vineyard, the plant density and all the rest – which is more and more significant I think.

Andrew keeps his canopy management 'as simple as I can get it really – and it is evolving'. As he explains, they inherited the original vineyard's planting densities with rows 3 metres apart and the vines from 1.8 to 2 metres in the rows. In his most recent plantings he has increased the density by spacing rows at 2.2 metres and the vines at 1.2 metres. He will plant some of his next vineyard at 2 metres by 1 metre. These vineyards have close to 4000 vines per hectare compared with the standard in most New Zealand vineyards of around 2000.

Andrew has several reasons for increasing the density of vines and having a single fruiting wire:

> The management is so simple. Pruning is simple. I see the pruning as the key, in the sense that you've got far fewer decisions to make on every vine. The options of what to lay down become reduced to a minimum – which is good in terms of employment because you don't have to have very experienced people working on your property. They can get to know what is required very easily and do a good job. And I think that's really important in terms of maintaining the standards that you want.

Close planting also results in more competition among the vines, which is especially valuable in a region such as Nelson where vines grow vigorously. But the competition is much less intense than is the case among the 10,000 vines per hectare that is standard practice in regions such as Burgundy.

Getting their enterprise operating to their satisfaction took considerable effort. Andrew emphasises that he had to 'serve his apprenticeship' in their own vineyard and winery for seven years before he was prepared to employ permanent labour. Through this period Andrew hired casual labour to assist him with particular jobs, and Jenny organised the pickers during vintage. By the millennium, Greenhough Vineyard was employing one full-time worker for the vineyard and winery.

Andrew describes the natural qualities of their home block:

> Up here we've got a foot to 18 inches of good topsoil, interspersed with river stone. And below that clay which is yellow and quite sticky and it's got rock scattered through it. These soils retain water well over the summer period.

Water allocations for irrigation were historically based on apple and kiwifruit requirements and they have proved more than adequate for the needs of Greenhough Vineyard: 'In a three-year period I used one third of one year's allocation.' Other areas on the plains are a little bit siltier and possibly more like parts of the Wairau Plain. Andrew believes that they can make much better Pinot from grapes grown on their site than those closer to Rabbit Island. He uses the evidence from the current pattern of land use southwest of Nelson, between Brightwater and Richmond, to make his point:

> You drive around here and you see a lot of market gardening and it's pretty easy soil. You can grow vegetables really well because there is a good topsoil, it's friable, and it's easy to work. It's versatile ground.

He takes issue with the argument that suggests these qualities make the area unsuitable for vines:

> But the myth that it was fertile, and if I planted vines at close spacing and had 15 buds or 16 buds per vine, then I'd have a massive vigour problem – that's proved totally unfounded.

More importantly, the behaviour of these vines gave Andrew the confidence to continue with planting at higher densities and using the vines to control the vigour of their adjoining plants:

> I think one of the advantages of taking these old vines that have been in the ground for quite a while and trained on 60 buds, and taking them right back to 25 buds and see what happened to them, gave me confidence to bring all my planting in closer, because I could see that they didn't go crazy. But at the same time it's got commercial advantages in that it's easy to work, it's easy to get onto in all conditions because it's free draining.

The quality of the wines that have emerged from this corner of the Nelson region suggests that he is right.

Waipara, Christchurch and Canterbury

In May 1973 the academic staff of Lincoln College, Christchurch organised a Saturday seminar titled 'Fruit wine making for the amateur'. At the modest fee of $1.50 per person it was sold out. In the same year, Montana, with Frank Yukich as managing director, planted its first vines in the Wairau Valley. The transformation of the land use and economy of the Marlborough region had begun. This event had a much greater immediate impact on the future of New Zealand winegrowing than the Lincoln College initiatives in Canterbury. By the beginning of the second decade of the twenty-first century, Marlborough's vineyard was almost 20,000 hectares while Canterbury's vineyard was approaching just 2000 hectares, or barely 10 per cent of Marlborough's area in vines, despite its much larger land area.

The difference in size of the two regions, their different local climates, different systems of established farming, and the ability of winegrowing to compete with these existing systems, suggest some of the reasons for the disparity. Only in the Waipara locality, 60 kilometres north of Christchurch, do vineyards and wineries dominate Canterbury's rural landscape. Here, soils are meagre, precipitation low, and the farms either originally quite small by Canterbury standards or willingly subdivided by their owners to sell to aspiring *vignerons*. Canterbury's sweeping coastline is over 300 kilometres long and exposed to easterly weather for most of its length. Waipara is one of the few localities protected from the east by substantial hills culminating in Mt Cass (525 m). In contrast, Marlborough's comparatively small Wairau and Awatere valleys have hills and even mountains partly protecting them from adverse weather from both the northwest and the southeast.

Canterbury's distance from established winemaking areas of the North Island such as Hawke's Bay, and especially West Auckland, also influenced its growth and style. Marlborough was an intervening opportunity for family and corporate enterprises from Auckland such as Babich, Corbans, Delegat's, Matua Valley, Montana, Nobilo, Selaks and Villa Maria. Auckland wine companies embraced the opportunity afforded by Marlborough to grow or buy grapes from a much more favourable natural environment than their own. In addition, land in Marlborough was initially reasonably priced.

As contract growers for Auckland enterprises, Marlborough landowners produced grapes of high quality. With land and grapes readily available in the Wairau Valley, it was unlikely that many of the Auckland wineries would source their fruit from Canterbury. During the 1990s, Corbans, which grew Riesling in Waipara and branded it as their Robard & Butler Amberley Rhine Riesling, was the exception. When Montana bought Corbans in 2000, and planted the 60-hectare Camshorn vineyard on State Highway 1 at its junction with Glasnevin Road, they finally announced their Canterbury presence.

New ways of farming

Lincoln College had an active and talented group of plant scientists in the early 1970s as well as strong connections with its alumni. Apple orchardist and cider maker Bill Turner was president of the Canterbury Fruitgrowers' Association when he approached the Lincoln microbiologist Dr Paul Mulcock over problems that he was having with his large-scale cider fermentations. Turner suggested that Mulcock apply to the association for a grant to fund this research. The application was successful and income from the grant was used to employ Danny Schuster. Schuster, whose hometown was Prague and who had trained at the Melnik Institute at Geisenheim, was something of a professional itinerant at the time as he deepened his already rich knowledge of viticulture and winemaking by working vintages in Australia, South Africa and New Zealand. Plant physiologist Dr David Jackson was also soon enfolded in the work of the group and in 1973 began a series of experiments to test the potential of a wide range of varieties of *Vitis vinifera* in the Canterbury environments.

The climate at Lincoln College, where the experimental vines were to be grown, fell well short of the weather and climate of sites in Central Otago or Marlborough. Between 1965 and 1975, before the Lincoln College plantings were bearing, the average number of

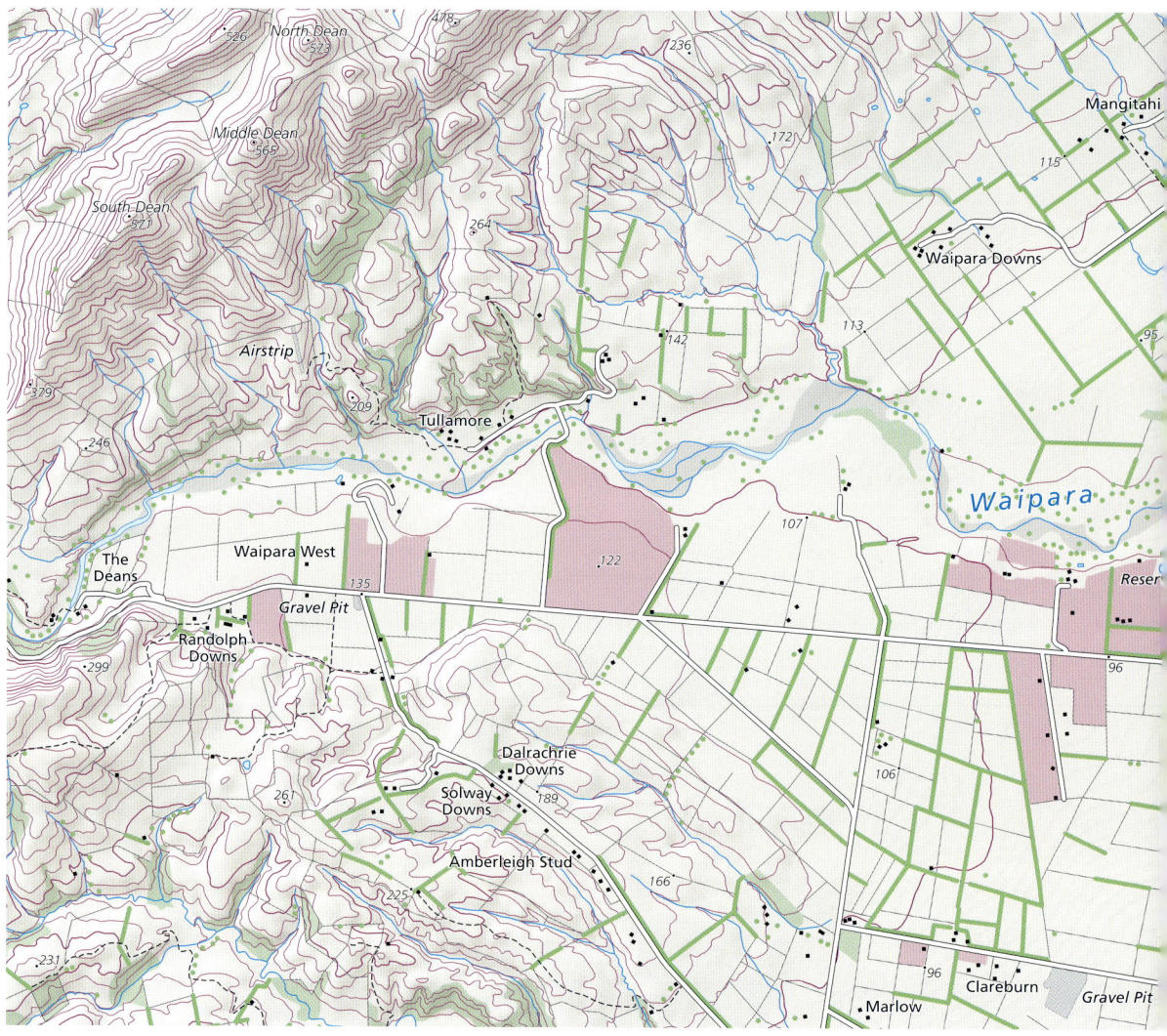

Figure 9.5 Waipara Valley vineyards and cellars

degree-days over the October to April growing season at Lincoln was 973. In subsequent years, the growing degree-days were as low as 630 (1975–76) and 880 (1978–79). Such low readings made little difference to the experimental work of the Lincoln scientists but did suggest that commercial winegrowers would need to search for the warmer parts of Canterbury where degree-days were above 1000 over the growing season.

In the early 1970s, rural landowners in the Canterbury region had two main influences encouraging them to learn about growing grapes. The traditional rural economy of the region was stuttering. Prices for grain, wool, sheep and cattle were volatile as New Zealand rural enterprises suffered from Britain joining the Common

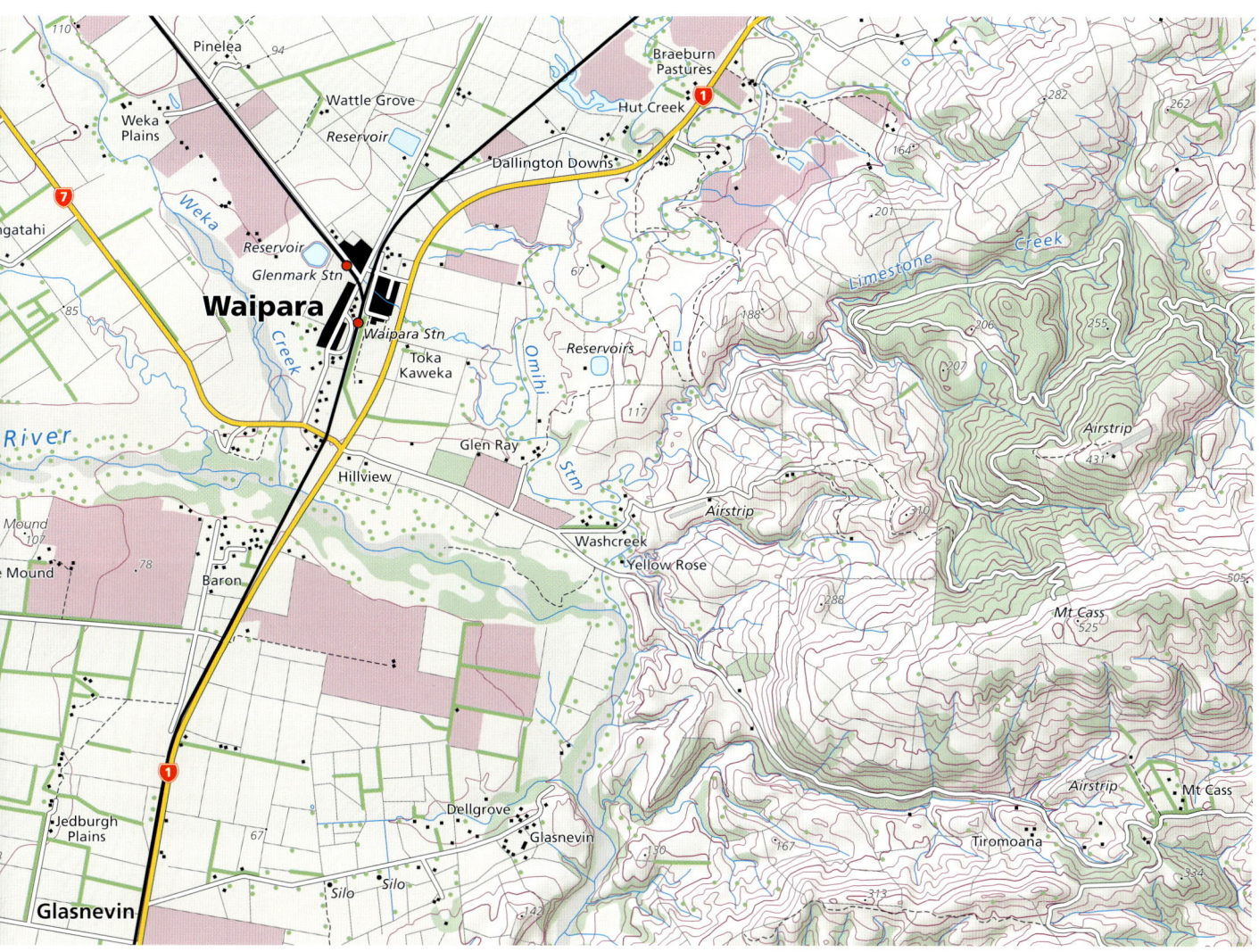

Market. Farmers in the Waipara Valley and vicinity were finding times especially difficult because many of them were running smaller pastoral farms that had always verged on being uneconomic. Most were farming free-draining, gravelly soils. Summer droughts and soil moisture deficits were common. The Ministry of Agriculture's farm advisory officers were encouraging those on smaller holdings to intensify their land use by diversifying into horticulture.

In 1972 a committee of Waipara farmers, after consultation with the Waipara County Council, asked the New Zealand Agricultural Engineering Institute at Lincoln College to conduct a feasibility study for a suitable irrigation scheme for their district. The Lincoln proposal was centred on a series of 'ring and gully dams' that were common in the arid parts of Australia. Such dams capture water from floods and other high flows

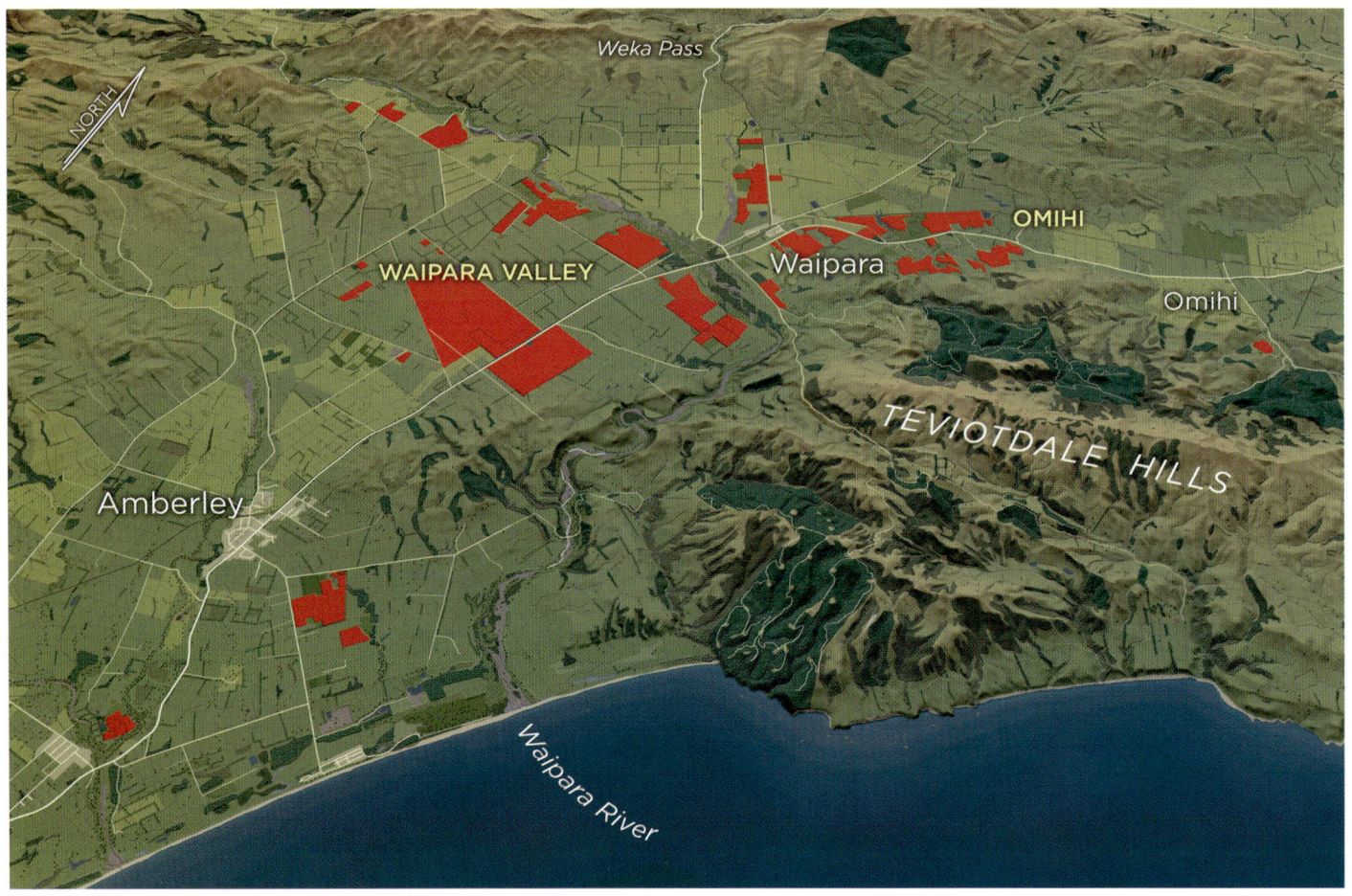

and store it in a local network of small catchments for mitigating summer droughts. When the final report was published in 1977 it recognised the potential for the scheme to promote the development of non-traditional farm enterprises at Waipara:

> The provision of irrigation . . . will allow the possibilities of new ways of farming to be explored. It is considered by the staff of the Department of Horticulture at Lincoln College that the area is well suited to the production of many horticultural crops including vineyard grapes.

Canterbury's terrain, climate and sub-regions

In terms of latitudinal stretch, Canterbury is the longest region in New Zealand, measuring over 300 kilometres from north to south. Between the foothills of the Southern Alps and the east coast are a variety of different terrains, mesoclimates and soils that contribute to an array of local environments suitable for growing vines. Most of the favoured sites are in north Canterbury where coastal hills, such as those adjoining Mt Cass, provide shelter from the cool easterly conditions and frost hazards in spring and to a lesser extent in autumn. Viticulture is not a strong competitor for land south of the urban periphery of Christchurch, where the Canterbury Plains are even more exposed to cool winds from the east and south.

The jigsaw piece that is Banks Peninsula separates the flood plain draining into Pegasus Bay north of Christchurch from the Canterbury Bight to its south. The braided, formerly glacial, rivers flowing from the Southern Alps to the east coast have deposited complex layers of coarse gravels, fine sands and clays. However, the desiccating 'nor'wester' – the Föhn wind that sweeps across the Canterbury Plains from the Southern Alps – brings high temperatures, often for short periods, to most parts of the region. While its drying qualities limit some fungus diseases, it is gusty enough to damage the delicate leaves of vines after bud burst, and will disturb the setting of fruit if it blows hard during flowering. Coupled with the low precipitation over most of the region, the nor'wester's drying effects mean that irrigation is necessary in almost all localities of Canterbury, especially when vines are being established.

Compensating for these adverse climatic characteristics, the crescent-like sweep of the foothills of the Southern Alps comes closer to the east coast about 40 kilometres north of Christchurch at Amberley. Ten kilometres further north, State Highway 1 and the railway line veer east of north at Waipara to parallel the coast. It is in this valley, and on the hills around it, that Canterbury winegrowing is concentrated. These low coastal hills continue in a northeasterly direction for a further 70 kilometres before the road and railway line are squeezed against the east coast 40 kilometres south of Kaikoura.

With vineyards scattered intermittently from its northern boundary with Marlborough, north of Kaikoura, to its southern boundary with Otago, the Waitaki River, the four localities with conspicuous concentrations of vineyards and wineries which have emerged in Canterbury are thus: north Canterbury, Waipara, the urban periphery of Christchurch including Banks Peninsula, and the rest of Canterbury.

From 1989, when New Zealand's regional administrative boundaries were changed, a chunk of what was previously Marlborough (most of the former Kaikoura County) became part of the Canterbury region. In terms of its physical characteristics, especially climate, this northern part of the region is more similar to Marlborough than to much of the Canterbury Plains. Such boundary adjustments were less important when few grapes were grown in the district, but with the establishment of the substantial Mt Beautiful vineyard by California-based New Zealander David Teece, north Canterbury is likely to receive more attention as a winegrowing area.

The urban periphery of Christchurch extends from Rangiora and the Ashley River to the Selwyn River. Wineries are densest here south of the Waimakariri in the West

Melton, Hornby and Lincoln area. Burnham was the original site of the Giesen winery before they purchased and leased land in Marlborough in 2000. Banks Peninsula, the first locality in Canterbury to have grapes planted in the mid-nineteenth century (by settlers sponsored by the French Nanto-Bordelaise Company), continues to grow grapes but its total area in vines is less than 50 hectares. Although vines have had a continuous presence there, often associated with restaurants, the vineyards of Banks Peninsula have never reached the potential that its many frost-free sites deserve.

Waipara, which begins at the catchment of the Ashley River north of Amberley and includes the small Kawhai catchment as well as the Waipara catchment, has by far the largest concentration of vines in the Canterbury region. Sheltered from the cold southeasterlies that are common in spring and autumn, the Waipara Valley regularly returns degree-day readings that are the highest in Canterbury and approach sites in the Wairau and Awatere valleys of Marlborough. Over the period from 1951 to 1980 (when it closed) the meteorological station at Waipara recorded an average of 1049 degree-days for the October to April growing season. Over the same period, Blenheim airport recorded an average of 1121 degree-days – just 72 more. Subsequent research has confirmed what Waipara winegrowers discovered empirically. On average, Waipara has the highest temperatures and the warmest grape-growing seasons in all of Canterbury north of Christchurch.

As Table 9.5 demonstrates, Waipara's vineyard has continued to grow more quickly than other parts of Canterbury until it now clearly dominates winegrowing in the region. Three varieties – Sauvignon Blanc, Pinot Noir, and Riesling – account for 87 per cent of the Waipara vineyard and 83 per cent of the Canterbury vineyard as a whole. By 2010, Sauvignon Blanc (662 ha) made up almost half of Waipara's vineyard, Pinot Noir (313 ha) 22 per cent, and Riesling (286 ha) 20 per cent (Table 9.6). Such statistics do not imply that more vines will not be planted in other parts of the wider Canterbury region, but with 1456 hectares of grapes planted as of 2010, Waipara is the first locality in Canterbury to have a concentration of vineyards and wineries that may be considered a distinct wine region.

John McCaskey of Glenmark Wines was very influential in stimulating winegrowing in Waipara by both actively experimenting with different varieties of grapes and later selling land, often in 10-acre blocks, to other aspiring winegrowers. The McCaskey family owned over 400 acres of land that had been the run-off for Glenmark Station. In the early 1960s, John planted cuttings of hybrid grapes in a nursery vineyard on sandy soils close to Weka Creek which were washed away by a flash flood – fortuitously saving Cantabrians from having to drink Baco 22A or Seibel 5455 instead of Sauvignon Blanc or Pinot Noir. Undeterred, John planted 10 acres of vines in 1981 with cuttings from Tim and Judy Finn's Neudorf vineyard in Nelson. These included Chardonnay, Cabernet Sauvignon, Gewürztraminer, Müller Thurgau and Pinot Noir. Glenmark

Table 9.5 Area in vines (hectares)

Year	2000	2005	2010
Waipara	210	573	1456
Rest of Canterbury	232	280	324
Total Canterbury	**442**	**853**	**1780**

Table 9.6 Grape varieties in the Waipara region, 1990–2010

	1990		2000		2010	
Variety	ha	%	ha	%	ha	%
Sauvignon Blanc	7	6	40	19	662	46
Pinot Noir	21	19	54	26	313	22
Riesling	26	23	32	15	286	20
Pinot Gris	7	6	7	3	83	6
Chardonnay	16	15	49	23	69	5
Cabernet Sauvignon	10	9	9	4	5	<1
Merlot	1	<1	10	5	6	<1
Other Bordeaux	0	0	4	2	4	<1
Gewürztraminer	5	5	1	<1	4	<1
Other	18	16	4	2	24	2
Total	111	100	210	100	1456	100

Note In 1990 the 'Other' category includes 13 hectares of Müller Thurgau.

Wines' first small vintage in 1985 was processed in their recently completed winery in the Glenmark Station barn. Its Waipara Red was well received and stimulated other smallholders to plant more vines.

Enterprises in the Waipara story

Rossendale Wines Ltd

Brent and Shirley Rawstron of Rossendale Wines were cropping farmers on the Canterbury Plains who were 'hit quite badly' by changes to government economic policy in the 1980s and 'quickly realised that if we wanted to survive we had to change'. With the demand for grain and vegetable crops rapidly falling, they decided to pursue opportunities to produce and export prime cuts of meat from their own beef-farming operation and have been doing so successfully since 1985–86. Once the beef enterprise was operating smoothly, the Rawstrons began to 'look around for something else we could do as a branded product'. Horticulture attracted them because they had been 'growing things for years', but they were concerned about the perishability of horticultural crops such as strawberries and raspberries, as well as the difficulty of differentiating them in the market:

> The wine industry gave us all the dimensions that we wanted in terms of a product that could be branded and differentiated, and also added very good value. If it didn't sell today, it was probably going to be a better product to sell tomorrow!

Robin Mundy from St Helena endorsed their choice of site, although he also advised them that 'grapes will grow anywhere', whereas plant physiologist David Jackson from Lincoln College made an even more positive assessment when he declared that 'grapes will grow well here'.

Before planting any grapes they considered possible markets for their wine, recognising from their experience with prime beef that the closest they could sell to final demand the better, and in 1983 bought a 'little cottage' over the river which had been the gatehouse for the original 15,000-acre pastoral station owned by a relative who had arrived on one of Canterbury's first four ships. The Rawstrons also considered the possibility of catering to the expanding population of this southwestern quarter of the city of Christchurch, deciding 'we have a building, we have an ambience, and we can really create something to bring them here, so we'll develop that as our restaurant to sell our wine'.

With this settled, 'we then went and got some grape cuttings from Robin Mundy and popped them in the ground'. In the first year they planted an acre of Pinot Noir and an acre of Chardonnay. By the millennium they had over 15 acres of grapes in their vineyard, all Chardonnay and Pinot Noir except for a small area of Gewürztraminer. The first grapes were planted in 1986 and 1987, the winery built in 1992, and the restaurant opened in 1994. Contemporaneously, they had both enrolled part-time in the postgraduate diploma in viticulture and winemaking at Lincoln College and completed it over three years. Even more impressive was the sales profile for Rossendale's wines by the year 2000. Over 50 per cent of their wine was sold through their own restaurant and cellar door. Of the remaining wine, 25 per cent was sold in Christchurch and its hinterland and the remaining 25 per cent was exported to the United Kingdom, Canada, Germany and the Pacific Islands.

In the Annual Report of New Zealand Winegrowers of 2010, Rossendale Wines is listed as one of the 74 New Zealand wineries producing over 200,000 litres (22,000 cases) of wine annually. By 2012, they had increased their production to 40,000 cases partly by extending their range of wines by annually purchasing and vinifying 14,000 tonnes of Merlot grapes from Hawke's Bay.

The Rawstrons had earlier recognised the need to own land on the Wairau Plain in Marlborough. Brent is convinced that this is the best locality to grow the aromatic varieties such as Sauvignon Blanc and Pinot Gris that the public have been demanding. The Rossendale enterprise now has access to several parcels of land growing these two varieties and Chardonnay on Hammerichs Road on the Wairau Plain. Brent believes that neither Canterbury nor the Awatere Valley can produce Sauvignon Blanc of similar quality.

Alan McCorkindale Ltd

Alan McCorkindale was born and bred in Hastings where his father was a refrigeration engineer who 'put the first refrigerated tank in for Tom McDonald'. After completing his studies at Victoria University of Wellington, he decided to work in a winery for six months before going overseas: 'So, in the summer of 1979 to 1980, Bob Knappstein gave me a job at McWilliam's in Hawke's Bay.' When the cellar foreman was injured he was offered that job:

> And then Bob came to me part way through the year and said, 'Well, how would you like to go up to Roseworthy and study winemaking and come back and be a winemaker for us?' And I said I had just had three years' study and didn't want to do that!

However, the more Alan thought about the offer, the more he warmed to the suggestion and decided to 'give it a crack'. While at Roseworthy, as part of his practical experience, he worked for McWilliam's in the Hunter Valley for two vintages as well as doing a vintage at Pipers Brook in Tasmania.

With his Roseworthy qualification in hand, Alan came back to New Zealand early in 1984 as assistant winemaker for McWilliam's. Cooks took over McWilliam's soon afterwards and he stayed at Cooks for 1985 but during the year applied for and won an exchange scholarship that Prime Minister Rob Muldoon had set up with the German wine scientist Helmut Becker when he had visited New Zealand. When Alan arrived in Germany in 1986 he spent a month immersing himself in the language before organising the details of his programme for the year, which included practical experience in Champagne and the Chablis district of Burgundy.

When winemaker Glen Thomas left Corbans in June 1988, Alan McCorkindale 'finished the '88 wines at Cloudy Bay', as at this stage Corbans' Marlborough winery had not been built but the company had arranged with Cloudy Bay to use theirs.

The McCorkindales moved permanently to Blenheim at the end of that year and stayed there until 1996. During that time as Marlborough winemaker Alan had responsibility for Corbans' Stoneleigh brand and as he explains:

> We took Stoneleigh from a fairly small production level – about 100,000 litres – right through to a million litres. We lifted it from sort of occasionally winning bronze medals to regularly winning gold medals.

He was also experimenting with making small batches of 'stickies', wines where the fermentation has stopped naturally as the alcohol increases and the wines still retain their residual sweetness:

> Fantastic wines, but they were like 450 litres, 500 litres and they were considered too small. If you can't buy it, there isn't much point in trying to win heaps of awards.

Since 1990 the McCorkindales had been looking for a small block of land in Waipara and Alan did 'a whole lot of scientific stuff, got a whole lot of maps because the first prerequisite was limestone soil'. He explains:

> If you want to produce wines that are nice and fresh and light and fruity and sell them quickly, you grow them on well-drained, gravelly, stony soil. If you want to produce a wine that is going to taste good in 30 or 40 years' time it grows on a limestone soil!

Alan focused on Waipara 'because of the quality of the Riesling we'd had from Joe Corban's Waipara block in '89 and '90'. The bite of the Riesling and its depth of flavour at a relatively low sugar level particularly impressed him.

When Alan left Corbans at the end of 1996 he did a vintage at Waipara West in Amberley in 1997 before shifting to Waipara and doing a vintage at St Helena in 1998. By 2001 he had planted 2 hectares of vines and a hectare of olives on their Waipara property but the McCorkindales were living in Christchurch for the children's schooling. He also built up his consulting business from that time, although being a highly respected consultant winemaker with experience in the main vineyard regions of New Zealand as well as Germany and France meant less time than he would like for their own Waipara vineyard:

> Because the thing I love the most is going up to Waipara and working in the vineyard. That's the best thing.

A tale of two vineyards

Through the Weka Pass on the road to Hanmer Springs is another new vine-growing area, rather difficult to name. Some people refer to it as Waikari after the small town 2 kilometres west of the Hanmer road, some as Waikari-Hawarden, and others as Pyramid Valley.

Pyramid Valley Vineyards

Mike and Claudia Weersing, of Pyramid Valley Vineyards, conducted what must be the most thorough and single-minded search for a particular *terroir* of anyone in New Zealand. American by origin, after a series of vintages in Burgundy and time in New Zealand, Mike decided that this country was where he wanted to grow grapes. While he was winemaker for Neudorf in Nelson he began hunting for the right piece of land.

He had a clear idea of his priorities. He believed that the Burgundian, rendzina soils of limestone origin were of primary importance in growing Pinot Noir without irrigation. Their chemical composition and capacity to retain moisture while allowing the root system to explore deeply are their essential attributes. The Weersings set about finding suitable sites in the South Island with similar soils.

Limestone deposits are quite common in both the North and South Islands, especially east of the axial ranges, as evident from the number of lime quarries scattered across many of the winegrowing regions of the country. But limestone suitable for lime and for quarrying does not necessarily indicate limestone soils. In many areas where lime is quarried, windblown deposits (loess) are the parent material of soils that sit on top of limestone. Such is the case for much of the limestone of Hawke's Bay and the Wairarapa. Fractured limestone with a high active lime component, and soils derived from this limestone, are less common in both islands.

After close exploration in the library and on the ground, the Weersings were reasonably sure that in Pyramid Valley, across the Weka Pass from Waipara and close to Waikari, they had found the closest equivalent to the limestone soils of the Côte d'Or. So they engaged soil scientist Emmanuel Bourguignon at Lincoln University to test their findings on the property they were considering buying. A series of soil pits dug to a depth of 2 metres on the most likely sites across the 50-hectare property established both the nature of the soils as similar to Burgundy and the variation of soils across the different sites – invaluable information for future plantings. These initial assessments were confirmed by analysis of samples sent to a soil laboratory in Burgundy.

The Weersings accordingly bought the property and proceeded to plant their vineyard on the best parcels of land using the soils and the orientation of the various

At Pyramid Valley, Mike Weersing has established a number of small, individual vineyards with their own soil properties. Vines are planted close, in the Burgundian fashion. *Pyramid Valley Vineyards*

slopes as their combined criteria. The Pyramid Valley has slopes facing north and east and they were able to choose small parcels of land with good air drainage and solar insolation. The area may not be as hot as parts of Waipara so they wanted to maximise the energy of their growing season as well as limiting the chance of damaging spring or autumn frosts.

Adopting the Burgundian configuration, rows are a metre wide and vines 800 millimetres apart in the row, giving 12,000 vines per hectare. Rootstocks were chosen to suit the alkaline soils and machinery imported from France to suit the spacing of the vineyards. The limestone story from Burgundy is so keenly co-opted by many wine drinkers that it now has another life in another place: North Canterbury, New Zealand.

Bell Hill Vineyard Ltd

The Weersings were not the first to plant grapes in the Waikari locality. Marcel Giesen and Sherwyn Veldhuizen boldly bought land on the site of a former lime quarry. Asked

Bell Hill: planted on limestone. *Warren Moran*

about their decision to be on limestone when the story told by the Burgundians often overemphasises their *agro-terroir* at the expense of the human effort and capital going into learning how to grow grapes and produce wine from particular sites, Marcel's answer was simple and memorable: 'We wanted to cover the possibility that they may be right!'

Their search for a suitable site may not have been as comprehensive as the Weersings' but their earlier start means they now have evidence from older grapes of the likely quality of their wines. The Pinot Noir from the Bell Hill vineyard has been widely acclaimed, in New Zealand and internationally. Meanwhile, Sherwyn and Marcel have affirmed the quality of their boutique site by continuing effort in the vineyard to overcome the difficulties with rootstocks growing in calcareous soils, and in the cellar by vinifications that express these soils.

As the Pyramid Valley and Bell Hill vineyard stories attest, Canterbury's potential for winegrowing on a grander scale should not be dismissed lightly. The size and intricate nature of the region's terrain conceals gems of sites that are just beginning to demonstrate their potential for growing grapes and making fine wines.

Varieties across the metropolitan regions

A direct comparison of the varietal mix of the four metropolitan vineyards traversed in this chapter highlights some intriguing correspondences (Table 9.1). All regions except Auckland have Pinot Noir and Sauvignon Blanc as their two main varieties, although their position in the hierarchy varies. With 76 per cent of its vineyard in these two varieties and the longest history of producing Pinot Noir, Wairarapa is the most specialised of the metropolitan vineyards.

It is not surprising that the South Island's two metropolitan regions, Nelson and Waipara, both have Sauvignon Blanc as their main variety. Grape growers and wineries in these regions plant it to help assure the success of their enterprises. Although their natural environments are different from Marlborough, and the resulting wines are different – especially when they come from some of the limestone soils near Waikari and on the hills of Waipara – if tasted blind, most consumers would find these wines difficult to distinguish from Marlborough's. With barrel fermentation, ageing on lees, and other practices that innovative winemakers are now adopting when vinifying Sauvignon, the resulting wines are becoming much more complex and interesting. Sophisticated winemaking has transformed some of the more overwhelming aromatic and capsicum flavours of New Zealand's traditional Sauvignon Blanc into wines that now improve with age.

Auckland is the maverick region in its varietal mix, but the explanation is simple. Although Chardonnay (22 per cent) is the single most planted variety, three of the Bordeaux varieties (Merlot, Cabernet Sauvignon and Cabernet Franc) together make up 34 per cent of Auckland's vineyard. In most years they ripen well there. Some Auckland enterprises also buy Sauvignon Blanc grapes, from Marlborough or other regions of the South Island, because it is difficult to grow locally. The former Goldwater Estate on Waiheke Island, now called Goldie Estate, is a good example.

Seven per cent of Auckland's vineyard is in Pinot Gris, although it is a demanding variety to grow in the region's humid environment. This suggests that local enterprises are keeping up with the current trends in consumer preferences. In fact, the area in Pinot Gris has been increasing in all of these metropolitan regions until it is the fourth most important grape variety in three of them and equal fourth with Cabernet Franc in Auckland. Its popularity and growth are largely at the expense of Chardonnay. Some

Overleaf: Looking across from Kennedy Point toward Te Whau Vineyard, Waiheke Island. *Nigel Gardiner*

vignerons are even prepared to grow Sauvignon Blanc in the Auckland region. Provided the viticulture is first class, why not?

The other sleeper variety beginning to awaken in these metropolitan regions is Riesling. In Waipara, Corbans and Montana (Pernod Ricard) have long shown that grapes from this *terroir* make excellent Rieslings. There is no reason why the versatile Nelson and Wairarapa should not follow this example. Nevertheless, the similarity of the varietal mix in all four metropolitan regions is rather surprising when the growing conditions in each of them are so demonstrably different. It will be interesting to observe their continued evolution.

10

A Natural Experiment

Forty years ago, I visited Les Boucherottes, a Premier Cru vineyard near Beaune in Burgundy. After a walk in the vines, I talked with the *vigneron*, and he offered to sell us a bottle of their 1947 vintage. I still remember the nuances inside that bottle – the waves of flavour coursing through. The land in Les Boucherottes is flat, the appellation not that prestigious, and many wine writers would not make much of it. But the people there had made the vine produce something special. The owners were out early in the morning working the vines, they had a deep understanding of their locality, they learnt from fathers and brothers, big companies and neighbouring vineyards.

It was not so different from the West Auckland that I remembered as a boy. In the 1950s, I worked in the vineyards and sprawling corrugated-iron Corbans buildings along Great North Road, Henderson. I plucked leaves and pruned alongside the extended Corban family – Najib, old and almost blind; Alex running the business and Joe the viticulturist; uncles and cousins. The Corban family had been growing grapes, making and selling wine for over 50 years. Their extended family, and the community growing grapes in West Auckland, had developed an understanding of how to make wine in the New Zealand environment for New Zealand consumers.

Corban's buildings, Great North Road, Henderson, March 1959. *John Thomas Diamond, Auckland Libraries, JTD-14A-00645*

The New Zealand wine industry was still in its infancy in the 1950s. Restrictive liquor legislation, a country that preferred beer or sherry, rootstock infected with phylloxera, a vineyard planted with varieties and clones very different from the classical varieties of France: all of these factors would not have made a knowledgeable French visitor particularly optimistic about the future of New Zealand wine.

But over the next 50 years the winemakers of West Auckland led the explosion of the New Zealand wine industry. The area in vines has increased from less than 1000 hectares in the early 1970s to over 35,000 hectares today. More than 2000 vineyards make up the New Zealand *filière* with developing regional and local specialities. And New Zealand wines are now recognised by wine writers and judges around the world for their distinctive qualities. The New Zealanders accomplished in 50 years what had taken the workers of Burgundy five hundred. What happened?

First came a geographical revolution. In 1960, the New Zealand wine industry was dominated by small, mostly Dalmatian, operations in West Auckland and a few large, mostly Australian, firms making wine in Hawke's Bay. Winegrowers continue to operate in both regions, and Hawke's Bay's wine industry has grown significantly, but over the following 50 years winegrowers expanded into Gisborne, Marlborough, Central Otago, Waipara, Martinborough, Nelson and Waiheke Island. And in those regions, the vine colonised frosty hillsides and gravelly soils, river terraces and limestone hill country that growers would not have taken a second glance at in 1960.

Second was a varietal revolution. During the 1960s and 1970s, New Zealand winegrowers moved away from fortified wines (ports, sherries and liquors) and the hybrids and varieties of the American grape *Vitis labrusca*, first to Germanic varieties like Müller-Thurgau, and then to the classical French varieties, Pinot Noir, Chardonnay and Sauvignon Blanc. By 2010, 70 per cent of New Zealand's vineyard bore white-skinned grapes. Three of these white *vinifera* varieties, Sauvignon Blanc with 52 per cent, Chardonnay with 13 per cent, and Pinot Gris with 5 per cent, together demonstrate the current specialisation of the national vineyard.

What drove the geographic and varietal revolution? With the 20/20 vision of hindsight, the most popular varieties of grapes in New Zealand and their geographic pattern could have been predicted from a close reading of the French wine regions and their climates. Our six most important varieties all originate in the coolest wine regions of France. From Champagne and Burgundy come Chardonnay and Pinot Noir. From Alsace comes Riesling and from the Loire Valley and Bordeaux, Sauvignon Blanc. Merlot and Cabernet are the two dominant red varieties in the prestigious appellations of Bordeaux. None of the traditional varieties of the warm climate viticultural area of France – the Midi – are important in New Zealand.

Within New Zealand the distribution of these varieties now follows an expected pattern. Merlot and Cabernet Sauvignon predominate in Hawke's Bay and on Waiheke

Island, two of the warmest viticultural regions in the country. Pinot Noir begins to become important in Martinborough and continues across Cook Strait being an important variety in Marlborough, Nelson, Canterbury and Central Otago for both still and sparkling wine. Sauvignon Blanc is overwhelmingly predominant in Marlborough and Riesling is an important variety in all of the Pinot Noir regions. Chardonnay, the unfaithful variety as Burgundians label it, is important in all of the New Zealand regions.

The natural environment – sunlight hours, temperature gradients, soil types, aspect and slope – has played a role in this geographical specialisation. We would expect nothing else. After all, the vine has its roots in the soil and leaves in the atmosphere. Frost kills buds. Nutrients are one foundation of aromas in the berries. *Terroir* has a biophysical foundation. But the problem with taking the direct explanatory path from the natural environment to wine is that it omits the viticultural and winemaking practices that intervene. Those practices all involve decisions by people, because the vine is a managed plant.

So to understand the wine, we need to understand the people. Successful wine enterprises, localities, regions and countries – in Henderson or Les Boucherottes – result from patient and persistent learning by people in the environment. These people are not passive observers of the soil or the atmospheric environment. They are part of it. They work in it and with it. They select the cultivars, shape the canopy, pluck and trim the leaves, decide what fertiliser and sprays to apply, and help to balance the crop carried in the particular environment of each year by each vine. It is through the experiences of people like Nick Nobilo and Nick Mills, Alwyn Corban and Ann Pinckney that we can begin to appreciate how environmental learning over time shaped vine and wine. In New Zealand, the expansion of viticulture has been so rapid that this learning has occurred at breakneck speed. How did the New Zealanders learn so fast?

First, New Zealand's distinctive *filière* has enabled learning to be shared. The wine *filière* in its simplest form is straightforward. The main sequences are the growing of the grapes, the making of wine, its bottling and packing, distribution and selling. But who owns and controls the various elements in the sequence makes a difference. In Burgundy, small family firms, run mostly by family labour, grow grapes and 70 per cent of those firms vinify their own wine. In New Zealand, family firms dominate numerically, but most of them grow grapes but do not produce wine. A few large firms dominate the production of wine, buying in grapes from different regions and growers. Alongside those firms, an array of smaller firms (though bigger than in Burgundy) make wine, often focusing on a high-end market.

The distinctive New Zealand *filière* enabled rapid learning. Individuals have moved frequently between levels – learning in a large, multinational winemaker; spending some time in a boutique firm; buying a piece of land to build their own business. Rudi Bauer and Kevin Judd epitomise this learning trajectory. Others, like the Thorpe family, have learned the business as grape growers for the large companies and then developed their own winemaking enterprise. Sometimes the relationships are remarkably intertwined. Kevin Judd, James Healy and Ivan Sutherland are all alumni of Cloudy Bay. When Healy and Sutherland began their new enterprise, Dog Point, it was not surprising that they found Judd was a skilled supplier of grapes to them while he also negotiated the use of their winery to make his Greywacke wines. The New Zealand *filière* is increasingly being shaped by a nascent family tradition of viticulture and winemaking – as the second and third generation of Croatian, Lebanese and other New Zealand families (Alwyn Corban, Nick Nobilo, or Nick Mills, for example) take learning from one firm to another, and one generation to the next.

The *filière* has shaped what has happened where and when in New Zealand winegrowing. It is unlikely that Alan McCorkindale would have established in Waipara if Corbans had not sourced grapes from there in the 1980s and if he had not made the award-winning Amberley Rieslings of that period. Nor would Montana have established its large Camshorn vineyard nearby in the twenty-first century and given a fillip to the Canterbury region and Waipara locality. Varietal and geographic learning was made possible by the distinctive New Zealand *filière*.

Second, science, particularly government science, has enabled a more rapid development of knowledge about soils, climate, varieties, clones and canopy management than would have been possible through empirical learning in the vineyard on its own. From the MAF farm advisory service, the Te Kauwhata Viticultural Research Station, the DSIR and other arms of government, prospective grape growers and winemakers gained reliable data about the physical environment and the available varieties and clones. Scratch many wine enterprises and a recycled government scientist will often emerge. Neudorf's Tim Finn is one: an agriculture degree from Massey, a thesis on cows and stress, a career as a dairy advisory officer for the Ministry of Agriculture, and then a winemaker. Scientific learning brought from overseas has also played a key role in the New Zealand industry. Increasingly, prospective winemakers graduate from international programmes like Roseworthy or the University of California, Davis. The contribution that the UC Davis Clone 15 Chardonnay has made to the high quality of Chardonnay in New Zealand is more evidence of the importance of international scientific work for the New Zealand industry.

New Zealand winegrowers were hungry for the science and used it to make decisions. Before buying the land that would become Matawhero Wines, Gisborne bookseller Bill Irwin drove around the river flats with Pullar's maps, studied the water table, and got into long discussions with the Department of Agriculture's horticultural advisory officer in Gisborne, Paul Cullen. To select the vines to plant, he wrote to Dr Helmut Becker at the Geisenheim Grape Breeding Institute in Germany, to Australia, to the DSIR, and eventually imported clones of Cabernet Sauvignon and Gewürztraminer from UC Davis in California. Irwin's deep engagement with scientific knowledge and his use of it to make decisions was not uncommon in New Zealand.

Finally, with the knowledge developed by their experience in the *filière* and from science, New Zealand winegrowers have been willing to experiment on the ground. When Frank Yukich bought 1174 hectares of land in Marlborough, the Montana board refused to endorse the purchase. Nobody then had the faintest idea that Sauvignon Blanc grapes grown in this environment would result in a wine with a distinctive array of aromas that is almost instantly recognisable and appealing to consumers in most wine-drinking countries. Just as large companies like Montana were willing to experiment at a national scale, small enterprises in the regions conducted, sometimes unknowingly, natural experiments of their own. In Central Otago, for example, Alan Brady, founder of Gibbston Valley Wines, Verdun Burgess and Sue Edwards of Black Ridge, the Grant family of William Hill Vineyards, Rolfe and Lois Mills of Rippon Vineyard and Ann Pinckney of Taramea Wines established vineyards across a full range of the region's climates and planted a whole range of varieties. It took a decade for the locals to discover by empirical learning the preferred varieties and locations. And even at the scale of the firm, experimentation is evident. On Te Mata Estate, for example, John Buck and family now run vineyards in three quite different Hawke's Bay environments and he has planted them in varieties used in the firm's current major wines (Cabernet, Chardonnay, Merlot) but also in varieties that may only substantiate their promise, or lack of it, a decade from now (Gamay Noir, Viognier, Petit Verdot). Experimentation and empirical learning has shaped and reshaped the industry's geography and varietal mix.

Rapid learning has produced a mature New Zealand wine industry in just 50 years. Each region now has its own distinctive localities and soils, its own environmental challenges, and increasingly its own set of varieties. The varietal composition of these regional vineyards has evolved as winegrowers have accumulated experience of how successfully different varieties grow in different localities and the quality of the wines that are produced there.

What are the current challenges facing the New Zealand industry? Some wine journalists, and even winemakers, are bemoaning the increasing varietal diversity of New Zealand's vineyards. Close analysis of the evolution of the national vineyard suggests they are barking up the wrong vine. In 2015, five varieties – Sauvignon Blanc, 20,266 hectares; Pinot Noir, 5564 hectares; Chardonnay, 3361 hectares; Pinot Gris, 2456 hectares; and Merlot, 1320 hectares – were growing a total of 32,967 hectares of vines or 92 per cent of the national vineyard. These figures suggest that the varietal mix of the New Zealand vineyard is in fact highly specialised.

In the last 50 years, most New Zealand winegrowers have sequentially relied heavily on two varieties of white grapes to establish their first *vinifera* vineyards and to profit from them – first Müller-Thurgau and then Sauvignon Blanc. In 1980, the planted area in Sauvignon Blanc was just 2 per cent of the national vineyard (73 hectares) but by 2015 its area had increased to 20,266 hectares, or 57 per cent of all New Zealand's grape plantings. I know of no other grape variety anywhere in the world that has become so dominant in a single generation.

Why the dominance of Sauvignon Blanc? Its unique position in international markets is obvious. Sauvignon Blanc from Marlborough, even when young, has a vibrancy, freshness and complex range of flavours that are unequalled in any other winegrowing region of the world. In short, it has a distinctiveness that is difficult, if not impossible, to replicate elsewhere. Jean-Marie Bourgeois, the Chavignol *vigneron* and Loire Valley *négociant*, is unequivocal: 'Sauvignon Blanc reaches its apogee in only two parts of the world – the Loire Valley, France and Marlborough, New Zealand.' He first tasted New Zealand Sauvignon Blanc on an internal European airline flight and was sufficiently impressed to explore New Zealand's wine industry exhaustively, buy land, and establish a large vineyard in Marlborough, Clos Henri.

But simple tonnage must also play a part. When the yields of the six main grape varieties grown in New Zealand are analysed, one strong conclusion emerges (Table 10.1). Despite the attempt of grape growers and wine companies to keep the yields of Sauvignon Blanc at a reasonable tonnage per hectare, the variety stands out because its average yields are noticeably higher than all other varieties. Over the decade from 2004 to 2013 Sauvignon Blanc has produced almost twice (1.96 times) the yield of the sixth variety, Pinot Noir.

Sauvignon Blanc is the mainstay of the New Zealand wine industry and has been important in all periods of its development. Such is the dominance of Sauvignon Blanc, and its importance to the cash flow of enterprises, that every region must have some. But such dependency on one variety makes the national wine industry vulnerable. It is important that New Zealand winegrowers continue to provide enterprises and regions

Table 10.1 The six main grape varieties in the New Zealand vineyard with their yields over the decade 2004 to 2013 (tonnes per hectare)

	2004	2005	2006	2007	2008	2009	2010	2011	2012	2013	Mean
Sauvignon Blanc	11.5	8.7	10.9	9.8	12.1	11.0	10.3	13.4	8.9	11.2	10.8
Chardonnay	9.8	7.8	7.1	9.9	8.6	8.8	6.8	6.7	7.1	8.4	8.1
Merlot	6.3	6.2	7.9	8.1	7.5	8.6	6.5	6.6	6.5	8.0	7.2
Riesling	8.5	5.9	7.9	6.9	9.3	6.5	5.5	6.2	6.5	7.5	7.1
Pinot Gris	5.0	3.4	4.8	5.3	9.0	7.6	7.3	10.3	6.2	8.9	6.5
Pinot Noir	6.2	3.9	5.4	4.7	7.1	5.8	5.0	6.5	4.3	5.9	5.5

growing Sauvignon Blanc with the resources necessary to explore this uniqueness. But there is also a need to look ahead to the day when other countries and enterprises are able to compete with the local Sauvignon Blanc and capture the complexity of this variety in all its forms.

What are the wines that could challenge Sauvignon Blanc? Knowledgeable New Zealand winegrowers have adopted serious experimentation in crafting sparkling wines. Within ten years after the first wines were produced in the Marlborough region, Montana set the trend with its Marlborough Cuvée in collaboration with its French advisors and financial partners, Deutz. In New Zealand's cool climate we can grow grapes with high yields and with the qualities required to make the base wines for *Méthode Traditionnelle*, primarily Pinot Noir and Chardonnay. Also important are the skills of talented and tenacious winemakers such as Alan McCorkindale who was one of the early vinifiers of *Méthode Traditionnelle* for Corbans in Marlborough. He has also demonstrated his skills in making dessert wines with high residual sugar and captivating flavours. Like several other winemakers, he is also producing Sauvignon Nouveau.

The ideal mix of varieties to succeed in producing *Méthode Traditionnelle* would be difficult to achieve using only those grapes currently cultivated in New Zealand's vineyards. While sufficient Chardonnay and Pinot Noir are being grown to ensure an expansion of *Méthode Traditionnelle*, New Zealand's present plantings of Pinot Meunier, the third variety commonly used in French Champagne, would restrict any immediate development of a substantial production of traditional sparkling wine as made in the Champagne region of northeastern France. In 2010, just 20 hectares of Pinot Meunier were being grown in New Zealand, 10 hectares of it in Hawke's Bay and 8 hectares in Marlborough. Although a rapidly increasing number of New Zealand wine enterprises are producing *Méthode Traditionnelle*, most of it sees no Pinot Meunier.

Would the absence of Pinot Meunier make much difference to the practices of producing New Zealand's *Méthode Traditionnelle*? The simple answer is probably not. In much of Champagne, both historically and today, the *syndicats* (unions of grape growers and winemakers) hold considerable power. In conjunction with the *négociants-manipulants* (merchants of Champagne), they strongly influence the structure of their organisations and their strength in the marketplace. In contrast, New Zealand winegrowing is much more lightly regulated with few restrictions limiting the practices of participants.

One characteristic of viticulture in Champagne is irrefutable. When it comes to managing the yield of grapes per hectare in France, the allowable maximum for vineyards in Champagne is very high. Yields of grapes of up to 15,500 kilograms per hectare (15.5 tonnes) are permitted, although this quantity varies from year to year according to both weather conditions during the growing season and to the state of the market. The *vignerons* of Champagne have managed to avoid the restrictions on

View across the Kawerau River to Mt Difficulty Wines, Central Otago. *Tim Hawkins.*

yield that apply to winegrowing in the elite appellations of Burgundy, Bordeaux and the vineyards of the Loire Valley. In these prestigious appellations yields as low as 30 hectolitres per hectare are required for Grand Cru wines and as high as 50 to 60 hectolitres per hectare for Premier Cru wines. New Zealand's natural environments for the vine are similar to those of Champagne during the growing season but the limitations on yields per hectare are much more liberal in France.

In 2012, for instance, the price of grapes in the Champagne appellation of France was €5.50 per kilogram. Similarly high yields (up to circa 100 hectolitres of wine per hectare) would be sufficient to provide the cash flow necessary to establish a serious *Méthode Traditionnelle* industry in southern New Zealand. Wine journalists have been touting Central Otago as a possible location while mid- and North Canterbury offer another strong possibility.

Alongside continual development of new wines and new varieties, we would expect to see the vine colonise new areas of the country. A number of factors have shaped the geographical spread of the vine in New Zealand over the last 50 years: sunlight hours, aspect and slope, soil profile, competition for land, and often also just the empirical success (or lack of it) of an existing winegrower. Some of New Zealand's historically strong winegrowing areas are now almost full: the Wairau Valley in Marlborough, the Ngaruroro River flats in Hawke's Bay. But the tentacles of vineyard expansion are evident in many regions – down into the hill country of Southern Hawke's Bay, up the Awatere Valley and further south, all over Waipara and Central Otago where slope and aspect allow.

Alongside physical geographical expansion, we will see increasing efforts to associate particular features of a landscape with New Zealand wines. The New Zealand trade mark Gimblett Gravels, for instance, is not primarily about gravels. Its origin is a group of producers owning, or about to own, land in a locality, finding a way of publicising their territory by defining it, and attempting to convince journalists and consumers that it has the eco-physiological qualities to make great wine. This sort of promotional *terroir* is becoming increasingly sophisticated.

Burgundians used to label New World wine regions like California *le royaume d'inox* (the kingdom of stainless steel). That was part of a wider outlook that saw the New World and Old World wine industries as having quite different cultures. But such a dichotomy hides more than it reveals. While many of the wine caves in Burgundy have heat-controlled tanks that are wired and computerised as carefully as a patient in intensive care, making a 'descente de cave' with, for example, Marcel Giesen at Bell Hill in Canterbury, is very similar to doing the same with friends such as the Cornu family in Ladoix and Maurice or Claude Chapuis in Aloxe-Corton. The topics of conversation are the same, the wines are more similar than one might imagine, the challenges of a variable climate and market hover in the air, and the discovery to be made opening each bottle fires them on.

Acknowledgements

This book represents a lifetime's work making sense of the New Zealand wine industry. To all of those who have helped me along the way and whom I cannot personally acknowledge here, my thanks.

The winemakers of New Zealand have been learning about the vine in the New Zealand environment for only 50 years – the winemakers of France have had 500. For that reason, we have much to learn from our friends on the continent. I thank in particular Jean-Baptiste Traversac, Philippe Perrier-Cornet, Phillippe Roudié and Jean-Claude Hinnewinkel. And over a number of years, we have been fortunate enough to live among the vines, particularly with the Cornu family at Ladoix-Serrigny in the heart of Burgundy.

In New Zealand, the study of the vine is even younger than the industry. Nonetheless, I have enjoyed the comradeship of a number of colleagues over the years, particularly Nick Lewis, Damian Martin and Eric Pawson.

Alongside scholars, I have learnt much of what is in this book from the winegrowers of New Zealand, and I am grateful to many individuals and enterprises for sharing their data, maps, time and knowledge. I have listed key interview subjects in the Sources, but they are a subset of a much bigger community. Those men and women have welcomed me into their wineries and homes, they have shared their wine and their ideas. This book is a product of that generosity.

Making this book has taken many years and many hands. I thank in particular cartographers Igor Drecki, Chris McDowall and the team at Geographx; the photographers, winegrowers and institutions who have supplied the photographs; publisher Sam Elworthy and his team Anna Hodge, Katrina Duncan, Louisa Kasza and Margaret Samuels at Auckland University Press; and editor Mike Wagg, proofreader Fiona Kirkcaldie and indexer Tim Vaughan-Sanders.

And finally, my gratitude to Pauline, for everything.

Sources

The world of wine

Asselin, C., Fanet, J. and Falcetti, M. (2011). Terroir et Internationalisation. *Revue Française d'Oenologie* 247: 24–29.
Bartoli, P. and Boulet, D. (1989). Dynamique et régulation de la sphere agro-alimentaire: l'exemple viticole. *Série Etude et Recherches – Station d'Economie et de Sociologie Rurales* 97. Montpellier: INRA.
Bartoli, P. and Boulet, D. (1990). Conditions d'une approche en termes de régulation sectorielle: le cas de la sphère viticole. *Cahiers d'Economie et de Sociologie Rurales* 17: 7–38.
Carbonneau, A. (1990). Influence de la conduite du vignoble sur la qualité des vins. In *Conditions du milieu et qualité du vin: environmental conditions and the quality of wine/animé par Pierre Huglin*, pp. 13–21. Académie d'Agriculture de France.
——. (1995). La notion complexe de terroir, chronique. *Le Progrès Agricole et Viticole* 112(2): 29–30.
Carbonneau, Alain, Deloire, Alain and Jaillard, Benoît. (2007). *La vigne: physiologie, terroir, culture*. Paris: Dunod.
Chapuis, L. (1980). *Vigneron en Bourgogne*. Paris: Robert Lafont.
Chidgey, C. (1984). *The century companion to the wines of Burgundy*. London: Century.
Combined working group of the Institut National des Appellations d'Origine (INAO) and Institut National de la Recherche Agronomique (INRA) into the two words *terroir* and *typicité*.
de Blij, H. J. (1983). *Wine: a geographic appreciation*. Totawa, New Jersey: Rowman and Littlefield.
Dion, R. (1949). *Grands traits d'une géographie viticole de la France*. Lille: Société de Géographie de Lille.
——. (1959). *Histoire de la vigne et du vin en France des origines au XIXe siècle*. Paris: Les Belles Lettres.
Dougherty P. H. (ed.). (2012). *The geography of wine: regions, terroir and techniques*. New York: Springer.
Fanet, J. (1991). Appellations d'origine et terroirs. In *La protection des terroirs viticoles*. Bordeaux: CERVIN.
——. (2001). *Les terroirs du vin*. Paris: Hachette.
Gadille, R. (1967). *Le vignoble de la côte bourguignonne, fondements physiques et humains d'une viticulture de haute qualité*. Paris: Les Belles Lettres.
Galtier, G. (1958). *Le vignoble du Languedoc méditerranéen et du Roussillon*. 3 vols. Paris: Université de Paris.
Halliday, J. (1994). *A history of the Australian wine industry 1949–1994*. Adelaide: Australian Wine and Brandy Corporation in association with Winetitles.
Hancock, J. M. (1998). What makes good wine? Climate versus terroir in determining wine-quality. *Science Spectra* 15: 74–79.
——. (1999). Terroir: the role of geology, climate and culture in the making of French wines by James E. Wilson, Feature review. *Journal of Wine Research* 10(1): 43–49.
Hinnewinkel, J.-C. (2004). *Les terroirs viticoles: origines et devenirs*. Bordeaux: Féret.
Jacquet, Olivier. (2002). Le statut viticole de la Bourgogne: un terrain de divergences syndicales entre la Saône-et-Loire et la Côte d'Or pour la délimitation de la Bourgogne. *Cahiers d'Histoire de la Vigne et du Vin* 3: 239–259.
Jacquet, O. and Laferté, G. (2005). Appropriation et identification des territoires du vin: la lutte entre grands et petits propriétaires du «Corton». *Cahiers d'Economie et de Sociologie Rurales* 76: 9–27.
——. (2013). La route des vins et l'émergence d'un tourisme viticole en Bourgogne dans l'entre-deux-guerres. *Cahiers de Géographie du Québec* 57(162): 425–444.
Johnson, H. (1971). *World atlas of wine*. London: Mitchell Beazley.
——. (1989). *The story of wine*. London: Mitchell Beazley.
——. (2006). *Wine: a life uncorked*. London: Phoenix.
Kliewer, W. M. (1968). Effect of temperature on the composition of grapes grown under field and controlled conditions. *Proceedings of the American Society for Horticultural Science* 93: 797–806.
——. (1977). Influence of temperature, solar radiation and nitrogen on coloration and composition of Emperor grapes. *American Journal of Enology and Viticulture* 28: 96–103.
Kliewer, W. M. and Lider, L. A. (1971). Effects of day temperature and light intensity on growth and composition of Vitis vinifera L. fruits. *Journal of the American Society of Horticultural Science* 95: 766–69.
Kliewer, W. M. and Torres, R. E. (1972). Effect of controlled day and night temperatures on grape coloration. *American Journal of Enology and Viticulture* 23: 71–77.
Laferté, G. (2002). La création d'une folklore vineux en Bourgogne dans l'entre-deux-guerres. *Cahiers d'Histoire de la Vigne et du Vin* 3: 261–277.
Landrieu-Lussigny, M.-H. (1983). *Le vignobles bourguignon: ses lieux-dits*. Marseille: Jeanne Laffitte.

Institut National des Appellations d'Origine. (1985). *A success story for France: l'appellation d'origine contrôlée.* Paris: INAO.
——. (1987). La protection internationale des appellations d'origine des vins et eaux-de-vie. Paris: INAO.
——. (1991). Composition, fonctionnement et competences de L'INAO. Paris: INAO.
Martin, D. (1999). The search for terroir – a question of management. *Proceedings of the 5th international symposium on cool climate viticulture and oenology, Melbourne,* pp. 1–4. Adelaide: Australian Society of Viticulture and Oenology.
Moran, W. (1988). The wine appellation: environmental description or economic device? In *Proceedings of the second international symposium for cool climate viticulture,* ed. R. E. Smart et al., pp. 356–60. Auckland: New Zealand Society for Viticulture and Oenology.
——. (1993). The wine appellation as territory in France and California. *Annals of the Association of American Geographers* 83(4): 694–717.
——. (2000). Culture et nature dans la géographie de l'industrie vinicole Néo-Zélandaise. *Annales de Géographie* 109(614–615): 525–551.
——. (2001). Terroir – the human factor. *Australian and New Zealand Wine Industry Journal* 16(2): 32–51.
Moran, W., Perrier-Cornet, P., Traversac, J.-B. and Rousset, S. (2000). Economic organisation and territoriality within the wine industry of quality: a comparison between France and New Zealand. *Actes et Communications – Institut National de la Recherche Agronomique, Economie et Sociologie Rurales* 17: 315–328.
Pitte, J.-R. (1997). Pour en finir avec le pseudo-terroir: les vrais facteurs de la qualité du vin. *Pratiques anciennes et genèse des paysage. Mélanges de géographie historique à la mémoire du Professeur Jean Peltre,* ed. André Humbert, pp. 195–212. Nancy: Université de Nancy.
——. (2005). *Bordeaux-Bourgogne: les passions rivales.* Paris: Hachette.
Ray, C. (1983). *Histoire d'un grand vin de Champagne: Bollinger.* Paris: Tallandier.
Richard, I. (1978). Aspects historiques de l'évolution du vignoble bourguignon. In *Géographie historique des vignobles,* ed. A. Huetz de Lemps, pp. 187–96. Paris: CNRS.
Robinson, J. (1999). *Oxford companion to wine.* Oxford: Oxford University Press.
Roudié, P. (1994). *Vignobles et vignerons du Bordelais (1850–1980).* 2nd edn. Bordeaux: Presses Universitaires de Bordeaux.
——. (2001). Vous avez dit 'terroir'? Essai sur l'évolution d'un concept ambigu. *Journal International des Sciences de la Vigne et du Vin,* numéro hors série, pp. 7–11.
Saint-Julien, H. (2004). *Bollinger: une certaine idée de Champagne.* Ay: Romaines Pages Editions.
Seguin, G. (1970). Les sols de vignobles du Haut-Médoc. Influence sur l'alimentation en eau de la vigne et sur la maturation du raisin. PhD thesis. Bordeaux: University of Bordeaux II.
——. (1983). Influence des terroirs viticoles sur la constitution et la qualité de la vendange. *Bull. OIV* 56(623): 3–18.
——. (1986). 'Terroirs' and pedology of wine growing. *Experientia* 42(8): 861–873.
Swinchatt, J. and Howell, D. G. (2004). *The winemaker's dance: exploring terroir in the Napa Valley.* Berkeley: University of California Press.
Unwin, T. (1991). *Wine and the vine: an historical geography of viticulture and the wine trade.* London: Routledge.
Vaudour, E. (2002). The quality of grapes and wine in relation to geography: notions of terroir at various scales. *Journal of Wine Research* 13(2): 117–141.
Vigreux, J. and Wolikow, S. (eds). (2001). *Vignes, vins et pouvoirs.* Dijon: Editions Universitaires de Dijon.
Vincent, E. (2005). Bilan et perspectives de l'édifice français des appellations d'origine. Paper presented at the Université européenne d'été sur le vin et la mondialisation. Perspectives historiques et enjeux contemporains (XIXe–XXIe siècles), 12–16 Septembre 2005.
Wilson, J. E. (1999). *Terroir: the role of geology, climate, and culture in the making of French wines.* Berkeley: University of California Press.

The development of New Zealand winegrowing

A. A. Corban & Sons. [1961?]. *Father to son tradition in wine making.* Henderson: A.A. Corban & Sons.
Berrysmith, F. (1968). Grape growing prospects throughout New Zealand. *New Zealand Journal of Agriculture* 117(1): 91–95.
Bradley-Streeter, D. (1994). New Zealand wines and vineyards: a bibliographic guide. Compiled as part of the requirements in LIBR 824, for the Diploma in Library and Information Studies.
Bragato, M. (1906). *Viticulture in New Zealand: with special reference to American vines.* Wellington: Government Printer.
Cooper, M. (1977). The wine lobby: pressure group politics and the New Zealand wine industry. MA thesis (Political Studies). Auckland: University of Auckland.
——. (1984, 1986, 1988, 1993, 1996). *The wines and vineyards of New Zealand.* Auckland: Hodder & Stoughton.
——. (2002, 2nd edn 2008). *Wine Atlas of New Zealand.* Auckland: Hodder Moa Beckett.
de Blij, H. J. (1985). New Zealand: Vinifera victorious. In *Wine regions of the southern hemisphere,* pp. 222–238. Totowa, NJ: Rowman & Littlefield.
Dunleavy, T. (2006). Wine Institute 30 years on. *New Zealand Winegrower* 10(2): 10–13.

Fairburn A. R. D. (1948). *Crisis in the wine industry*. Auckland: The Pelorus Press.
Forder, P. G. (1977). The Te Kauwhata Viticultural Research Station (1886–1977). MA research essay (History). Auckland: University of Auckland.
McMenamin, A. R. and Moran, W. (1989). *New Zealand vineyard survey, 1989*. Auckland: Department of Geography, University of Auckland.
McMenamin, A. R., Moran, W. and Hawke, D. (1989). *Vineyard regions of New Zealand, 1989*. Auckland: Department of Geography, University of Auckland.
Mabbett, J. (1997). Prehistory of the New Zealand wine industry. *Journal of Wine Research* 8(2): 103–114.
——. (1998). The Dalmatian influence on the New Zealand wine industry: 1895–1946. *Journal of Wine Research* 9(1): 15–25.
Moran, W. (1958). Viticulture and wine-making in New Zealand: its national and regional character. MA thesis (Geography). Auckland: University of Auckland.
——. (2000). Culture and nature in the geography of the New Zealand wine industry (Culture et nature dans la géographie de l'industrie vinicole Néo-Zélandaise). *Annales de Géographie* 109(614–615): 525–551.
——. (2007). Regions making wines, winemaking regions. *New Zealand Winegrower* 10(2): 32–38 and 10(3): 40–47. 2006 Romeo Bragato Address, published in two parts. Part 2 is titled: How wine was established in Marlborough, Central Otago.
Morris, J. (2006). *Wine makers and their labels, as printed by Falcon Press Ltd., printers to the wine industry*. Waitakere: J. Morris.
NZ Department of Industries and Commerce. (1961). *Wine in New Zealand*. Wellington: Department of Industries and Commerce.
NZ Industries Development Commission. (1980). *The wine industry development plan to 1986*. Wellington: The Commission.
Overton, J. (1996). The wine industry. In *Changing places: New Zealand in the nineties*, ed. R. Le Heron and E. Pawson, pp. 150–54. Auckland: Longman Paul.
Saunders, P. L. (1976). *Wine label language*. Auckland: Wineglass Publishing.
Scott, D. (1964). *Winemakers of New Zealand*. Auckland: Southern Cross Books.
——. (2002). *A stake in the country: Assid Abraham Corban and his family, 1892–2002*. Auckland: Reed.
——. (2002). *Pioneers of New Zealand wine*. Auckland: Reed/Southern Cross.
Stewart, K. (2010). *Chancers and visionaries: a history of New Zealand wine*. Auckland: Godwit.
Talmont, R. (1995). *New Zealand wineries & vineyards, 1996*. Auckland: Hodder Moa Beckett. [AA Leisure Guide.]
Thorpy, F. (1983). *Wine in New Zealand*. Auckland: Penguin Books.
Wall, K. N. (1999). Learning to make wine 'the Dallie way': exploring transformations and continuities in a New Zealand-Croatian winemaking community. MA thesis (Anthropology). Auckland: University of Auckland.
Wine Institute of New Zealand. (1979). *The New Zealand wine industry: a study and development plan*. Auckland: Wine Institute of New Zealand.
——. (1992). *New Zealand wine, 1993–2000: a working paper*. Auckland: Wine Institute of New Zealand.
Woodfin, J. C. (1928–29). Grape-vines for New Zealand conditions. *New Zealand Journal of Agriculture* 36(2): 106–110 and 39(4): 262–266.
——. (1938). Development of viticulture. *New Zealand Journal of Agriculture* 57(2): 124–126.
Workman, M. (1993). Geographic organisation of the wine industry in New Zealand. MA thesis (Geography). Auckland: University of Auckland.

Winegrowing in the New Zealand environment

Berrysmith, F. (1976). Viticulture in New Zealand, 1819–1975 – climate and varieties. *Annual Journal of the Royal New Zealand Institute of Horticulture* 4: 9–12.
Cossens, G. G. (1987). Agriculture and climate in Central Otago. In *Proceedings of the New Zealand Grassland Association* 48: 15–21.
Cossens, G. G. and P. D. Johnstone. (1987). *Climatology of the Alexandra District. Warm season growing degree-days*. Internal report. Invermay: Ministry of Agriculture and Fisheries.
——. (1988). *Climatology of the Upper Clutha Valley. Warm season growing degree days*. Internal report. Invermay: Ministry of Agriculture and Fisheries.
Ewart, A. (1974). Grape varieties in Poverty Bay. *New Zealand Journal of Agriculture* 129(4): 58–59.
Fitzharris, B. B. and Endlicher, W. (1996). Climatic conditions for wine grape growing: Central Europe and New Zealand. *New Zealand Geographer* 52(1): 1–11.
Imre, S. P. (2011). A multi-disciplinary study to quantify terroir in Central Otago and Waipara pinot noir vineyards. PhD thesis. Auckland: University of Auckland.
Imre, S. P. and Mauk, J. L. (2009). Geology and wine 12. New Zealand terroir. *Geoscience Canada* 36(4): 145–159.
Jackson, David and Schuster, Danny. (1987). The production of grapes & wine in cool climates. Wellington: Butterworths of New Zealand.
Jacometti, M. A., Wratten, S. D. and Walter, M. (2007). Management of understorey to reduce the primary inoculum of *Botrytis cinerea*: enhancing ecosystem services in vineyards. *Biological Control* 40(1): 57–64.

Jones, G. (2007). How climate change may affect viticulture in NZ; warming to advance harvest date? or CO2 to delay it?. *New Zealand Winegrower* 11(2): 47–51.
Limmer, A. (2006). Is global warming likely to affect our wine industry? and Global warming and our industry. *New Zealand Winegrower* 10(2): 87–88 and 10(3): 48–52.
Milne, D. (1978). South Island potential for viticulture. *Grapes and Wine Bulletin of Lincoln College* 22A.
Prescott, J. A. (1965). The climatology of vine (Vitis vinifera L.). The cool limits of cultivation. *Transactions of the Royal Society of South Australia* 89: 5–23.
Smart, R. E. (1985). Principles of grapevine canopy microclimate manipulation with implications for yield and quality: a review. *American Journal of Enology and Viticulture* 36: 230–239.
——. (1985). Some aspects of climate, canopy microclimate, vine physiology and wine quality. In *Proceedings of the international symposium on cool climate viticulture and enology*, ed. D. A. Heatherbell, P. B. Lombard, F. W. Bodyfelt and S. F. Price, pp. 1–19. Corvallis: Oregon State University Technical Publication, No. 7628.
——. (1988). Wind and water effects on wine quality. In *Proceedings of seminar 'Quality winegrowing – an industry perspective', held at the Marlborough Centre, Blenheim . . . 1987*, ed. A. P. Naylor, pp. 1–5. Auckland West: New Zealand Society for Viticulture and Oenology.
Trought, M. C. T. and Naylor, A. P. (1988). Irrigation responses in a cool climate. In *Proceedings of seminar 'Quality winegrowing – an industry perspective', held at the Marlborough Centre, Blenheim . . . 1987*, ed. A. P. Naylor, pp. 6–16. Auckland West: New Zealand Society for Viticulture and Oenology.
Woodfin, J. C. (1938). Development of viticulture: climate compares favourably with wine-producing countries. *New Zealand Journal of Agriculture* 57(2): 124–126.

The New Zealand context

Ballingall, J. and Schilling, C. (2009). *Economic impact of the New Zealand wine industry: an NZIER report to New Zealand winegrowers.* Wellington: New Zealand Institute of Economic Research.
Banks, G., Kelly, S., Lewis, N. and Sharpe, S. (2007). Place 'From One Glance': the use of place in the marketing of New Zealand and Australian wines. *Australian Geographer* 38(1): 15–35.
Barker, J., Lewis, N. and Moran, W. (2001). Re-regulation and the development of the New Zealand wine industry. *Journal of Wine Research* 12(3): 199–221.
Barker, J. P. H. (2004). Different worlds: law and the changing geographies of wine in France and New Zealand. PhD thesis (Law and Geography). Auckland: University of Auckland.
Bell Gully. (2006). *Winemaker's legal handbook*. [Auckland?]: Bell Gully.
Benson-Rea, M. (2005). Network strategy in the New Zealand wine industry: how firms in an industry understand and use their business relationships. PhD thesis (Marketing). Auckland: University of Auckland.
Beverland, M. B. and Bretherton, P. B. (1998). The strategic challenges facing the New Zealand wine industry. *Journal of Wine Research* 9(1): 55–64.
Beverland, M. and Lockshin, S. (2001). Organizational life cycles in small New Zealand wineries. *Journal of Small Business Management* 39(4): 354–362.
Dunleavy, T. (2007). NZ wine unveils new brand imagery. *New Zealand Winegrower* 11(1): 8–10.
Hamlin, R. P. and Watson, V. (1997). The role of the appellation in wine marketing – does the New Zealand wine industry know what it's getting?. *International Journal of Wine Marketing* 9(2): 52–69.
Howland, P. J. (ed.). (2014). *Social, cultural and economic impacts of wine in New Zealand.* Milton Park: Routledge.
Investment New Zealand. (2007). *New Zealand wine industry*. Wellington: Investment New Zealand.
Judd, K. and Campbell, B. (2009). *The landscape of New Zealand wine*. Nelson: Craig Potton.
Lewis, N. (2003). Associational governance and industry making: New Zealand winegrowers. *Proceedings of the 22nd New Zealand Geographical Society conference*: 319–323.
——. (2004). *The New Zealand wine industry: issues and status at vintage 2004, WIRI-NZTE Wine Industry Research Project*. Commissioned by New Zealand Trade and Enterprise. Auckland: Auckland Uniservices Ltd.
——. (2008). Constructing economic objects of governance: the New Zealand wine industry. In *Agri-food commodity chains and globalising networks*, ed. R. Le Heron and C. Stringer, pp. 319–323. Aldershot: Ashgate.
Lewis, N., Moran, W., Perrier-Cornet, P. and Barker, J. (2002). Territoriality, enterprise and réglementation in industry governance. *Progress in Human Geography* 26(4): 433–462.
Mabbett, J. (1998). Sociological aspects of the development and current structure of the New Zealand wine industry. PhD thesis (Sociology). Auckland: University of Auckland.
Moran, W., Perrier-Cornet, P. and Traversac, J. (2000). Economic organisation and territoriality within the wine industry of quality: a comparison between France and New Zealand. In *The socioeconomics of origin-labelled food products in agri-food supply chains: spatial, institutional and coordination aspects*, ed. B. Sylvander, D. Barjolle and F. Arfini, pp. 315–328. Versaille: INRA Editions, no. 17-1.
Murray, W. E. and Overton, J. (2011). Defining regions: the making of places in the New Zealand wine industry. *Australian Geographer* 42(4): 419–433.
Overton, J. (2010). The consumption of space: land, capital and place in the New Zealand wine industry. *Geoforum* 41: 752–762.
Overton, J. and Heitger, J. (2008). Maps, markets and merlot: the making of an antipodean regional wine appellation. *Journal of Rural Studies* 24(4): 440–449.

Parr, W. V. et al. (2007). The distinctive flavour of New Zealand sauvignon blanc: sensory characterisation by wine professionals. *Food Quality and Preference* 18(6): 849–861.
Pawson, E. (1997). Branding strategies and languages of consumption. *New Zealand Geographer* 53(2): 16–21.
Saker, J. (2010). *Pinot noir: a celebration of New Zealand's premium wine*. Auckland: Random House.
Schamel, G. and Anderson, K. (2003). Wine quality and varietal, regional and winery reputations: hedonic prices for Australia and New Zealand. *Economic Record* 79(246): 357–369.
Stewart, K. (2005). *The great wines of New Zealand*. Auckland: Viking.
Thomas, A. (2000). Elements influencing wine purchasing: a New Zealand view. *International Journal of Wine Marketing* 12(2): 47–62.
Thomas, A. and Pickering, G. (2003). Behavioural segmentation: a New Zealand wine market application. *Journal of Wine Research* 14(2–3): 127–138.
Wilson, M. M. J. and Goddard, R. (2004). Creating value in the New Zealand wine industry. *International Journal of Wine Marketing* 16(2): 62–73.

Data

The former DSIR's NZ Soil Bureau, LINZ (and its predecessors) and Metservice (and its predecessors) are the government bodies that have provided much of the data and science behind this book. Data about the New Zealand wine industry has been gathered through the years by a variety of organisations and individuals.

Berrysmith, F. (1961). 1960 survey of N.Z.'s vineyards. *New Zealand Journal of Agriculture* 103(4): 371–375.
——. (1966). Grape survey shows progress made in New Zealand. *New Zealand Journal of Agriculture* 113(2): 74–75.
——. (1971). 1970 survey shows rapid vineyard expansion. *New Zealand Journal of Agriculture* 23(1): 48–51.
——. (1976). Highlights of the 1975 vineyard survey. *New Zealand Journal of Agriculture* 132(6): 12–13.
Deloitte and New Zealand Winegrowers. (2008). *New Zealand wine industry benchmarking survey – vintage 2007*. Joint publication of Deloitte and New Zealand Winegrowers.
Jordan, D. and Veldhuizen, S. (1992). *New Zealand vineyard survey*. Unpublished report. Hamilton: The Horticulture and Food Research Institute of New Zealand.
McMenamin, Andrew and Moran, Warren. (1989). *New Zealand vineyard survey*. Auckland: Department of Geography, University of Auckland, for the Wine Institute of New Zealand.
Ministry of Agriculture and Fisheries. (1975). *New Zealand vineyard survey*. Wellington: Ministry of Agriculture and Fisheries.
——. (1980). *New Zealand vineyard survey*. Wellington: Ministry of Agriculture and Fisheries.
New Zealand Winegrowers and Bank of New Zealand. *New Zealand grape and wine industry statistical annual, 2000–2009*.
New Zealand Winegrowers. *Annual Report*, 2002–
New Zealand Winegrowers. *Vineyard register report*, 2012–
Wine Institute of New Zealand. *Annual report*, 1976–2001.

Gisborne/Poverty Bay

Interviews
Doug and Delwyn Bell, Bell Vineyard
Denis Irwin, Matawhero Wines
James and Annie Millton, Millton Vineyards & Winery
Roger McLernon, Montana
Warwick Bruce, Montana
Geoff Thorpe, Riversun Nursery
Bill Thorpe, Thorpe Horticulture, Longbush Wines
Nick Nobilo, Vinoptima Estate
Reid Fletcher, Waitaria Vineyard

Lewis, N. (2007). *Wines of Gisborne strategic plan*. Report prepared for Auckland Uniservices Ltd, Auckland.

Hawke's Bay

Interviews

Kim Salonius, Eskdale Winegrowers Ltd
Alwyn Corban, Ngatarawa Wines
Chris Pask, Pask
Kate Radburnd, Pask
Michael Collins, Pask
Grant Edmonds, Sileni Estates
Alan Limmer, Stonecroft
John Buck, Te Mata Estate
Rod McDonald, Vidal Estate/Villa Maria Estate

Johnston, P. and Arnold, N. (2007). Status of soil health in Hawkes Bay vineyards. *New Zealand Winegrower* 10(6): 76, 89.
McDonald, R. (1999). Pinot noir in Hawke's Bay, are we going to be surprised? In *Lincoln University Annual Grape & Wine School, Saturday 24 – Sunday 25 July 1999*, pp. 39–44. Lincoln: The School, Lincoln University.
Stewart, K. (1997). *Te Mata: the first 100 years*. Auckland: Godwit.
Taggart, P. (2004). *The quest: a search for Hawke's Bay's best Bordeaux-style wine*. Hastings: Hawke's Bay Today.
Tesic, D., Woolley, D. J., Hewett, E. W. and Martin, D. J. (2002). Environmental effects on cv. Cabernet Sauvignon (*Vitis vinifera* L.) grown in Hawke's Bay, New Zealand. 1. Phenology and characterisation of viticultural environments; 2. Development of an index site. *Australian Journal of Grape and Wine Research* 8(1): 15–26 and 27–35.
Yardin, (Rev. Father). (1890). On vine-growing in Hawke's Bay. *Transactions and Proceedings of the New Zealand Institute* 23: 528–531.

Marlborough

Interviews

Allan Scott, Allan Scott Family Winemakers
Chris and Judy Simmonds
Ivan Sutherland, Dog Point
John Forrest, Forrest
Kevin Judd, Greywacke
Jane Hunter, Hunter's Wines
Ian Gifford
John Marris, Montana/Pyne Gould Guinness agent
Neal Ibbotson, Saint Clair Family Estate
Phil Rose, Wairau River Wines
Chris Rose, Wairau River Wines
Damian Martin, Marlborough Research Centre
Gerry Gregg, Montana

Badger, R. P. (1994). Modelling grapevine physiology against climate: examples from Marlborough. MSc thesis (Geography). Auckland: University of Auckland.
Beer, C. and Lewis, N. (2006). Labouring in the vineyards of Marlborough: experiences, meanings and policy. *Journal of Wine Research* 17(2): 95–106.
Department of University Extension, Victoria University of Wellington and Marlborough Regional Development Council. (1978). *Development of Marlborough: a one-day seminar, Thursday 30 November, Chateau Commodore, Blenheim*. Wellington: Department of University Extension, Victoria University of Wellington, in conjunction with the Marlborough Regional Development Council.
Hayward, D. and Lewis, N. (2008). Regional dynamics in the globalising wine industry: the case of Marlborough, New Zealand. *Geographical Journal* 174(2): 124–137.
Greven, M. et al. (2003). The effect of reduced irrigation on yield and quality of sauvignon blanc grapes in Marlborough. *Australia & New Zealand Grapegrower & Winemaker* 474: 101–104.
Mills, T. S. (2006). Relations among geology, soil type and sauvignon blanc vineyard variation in Marlborough, New Zealand. MSc thesis (Wine Science). Auckland: University of Auckland.
Perry, P. J. and Norrie, B. P. (1991). The origins and development of a new world *vignoble*: Marlborough, New Zealand, 1970–1990. *Journal of Wine Research* 2(2): 97–114.
Riddell, P. (1988). Water requirements and irrigation design – Montana vineyards – Marlborough. In *Proceedings of seminar 'Quality winegrowing – an industry perspective', held at the Marlborough Centre, Blenheim . . . 1987*, ed. A. P. Naylor, pp. 17–25. Auckland West: New Zealand Society for Viticulture and Oenology.

Central Otago

Interviews
Sir Clifford Skeggs, Akarua Winery
Steve Davies, Akarua Winery
Verdun Burgess, Black Ridge
Nigel Greening, Felton Road
Stewart Elms, Felton Road
Blair Walter, Felton Road
Alan Brady, Gibbston Valley Wines
Domenic Mondillo, Mondillo Vineyards
Robin Dicey, Mt Difficulty Wines
Rudi Bauer, Quartz Reef
Rolfe Mills, Rippon
Nick Mills, Rippon
Ann Pinckney, Taramea Wines

Boardman, M. K. (1999). Central Otago wine: organisation and investment in a new regional industry. MSc thesis (Geography). Auckland: University of Auckland.
Bodkin, A. W. (1997). *Vines in the valley: the development of the wine growing industry in the Alexandra/Clyde district of Central Otago, 1864–1997 – a personal perspective.* Clyde: A. W. Bodkin.
Buchan, D. J. et al. (2000). *Going for gold: an analysis of the wine-growing industry in Central Otago.* Palmerston North: Horticulture and Food Research Institute of New Zealand.
Cull, D. (2001). *Vineyards on the edge: the story of Central Otago wine.* Dunedin: Longacre.
Oram, R. (2004). *Pinot pioneers: tales of determination and perseverance from Central Otago.* Auckland: New Holland.
Prater, J. (1988). Viticultural developments in Canterbury and Otago. In *Proceedings of seminar 'Quality winegrowing – an industry perspective', held at the Marlborough Centre, Blenheim . . . 1987*, ed. A. P. Naylor, , pp. 50–56. Auckland West: New Zealand Society for Viticulture and Oenology.

Metropolitan Vineyards and Others

Auckland
Interviews
Danny Schuster, Babich Wines
Peter Babich, Babich Wines
Alex Corban, Corbans Wines
Michael Brajkovich, Kumeu River Wines
Frank Yukich, Montana
Peter Hubscher, Montana
George Fistonich, Villa Maria

Baragwanath, L. (2010). *The Waiheke Project: overview of tourism, wine and development on Waiheke Island.* 2 vols. Auckland: School of Environment, University of Auckland.
Baragwanath, L. and Lewis, N. (2010). Lessons from a changing place. *University of Auckland news* 40(8): 5. [Summary of findings from the Waiheke Project.]
———. (2014). Waiheke Island. In *Social, cultural and economic impacts of wine in New Zealand*, ed. P. J. Howland. Milton Park: Routledge.
Benson-Rea, M. and Wilson, H. (1997). Coopers Creek and the New Zealand wine industry. *New Zealand Strategic Management* 3(1): 50–58.
Beverland, M. B. and Bretherton, P. B. (1998). The evolution of strategy in medium and large Auckland (New Zealand)-based wineries. *Journal of Wine Research* 9(1): 43–53.
Bretherton, P. and Simpson, K. (2003). Co-operating to compete in the wine industry: a case study of the Matakana region, New Zealand. *Proceedings of the 22nd New Zealand Geographical Society conference*: 309–313.
Marter, C. A. (2004). Development and contest on Auckland's urban fringe: a case study of the Matakana wine region. MA thesis (Geography). Auckland: University of Auckland.
Saintignan, A. (2009). The culturability, biodiversity and biogeography of a New Zealand vineyard yeast community. MSc thesis (Biological Sciences). Auckland: University of Auckland. [Kumeu River.]

Nelson
Interviews
Andrew Greenhough, Greenhough Vineyard
Tim Finn, Neudorf Vineyards
Hermann Seifried, Seifried Estate

Wairarapa
Interviews
Clive Paton, Atarangi
Larry McKenna, Escarpment
Richard Riddiford, Palliser Estate

McCallum, N. K. (1988). Developments in Martinborough. In *Proceedings of seminar 'Quality winegrowing – an industry perspective', held at the Marlborough Centre, Blenheim . . . 1987*, ed. A. P. Naylor, pp. 46–49. Auckland West: New Zealand Society for Viticulture and Oenology.
Howland, P. J. (2014). Martinborough: a tourist idyll. In *Social, cultural and economic impacts of wine in New Zealand*, ed. P. J. Howland. Milton Park: Routledge.

Waipara
Interviews
Alan McCorkindale, Alan McCorkindale Ltd
Marcel Giesen and Sherwyn Velduizen, Bell Hill Vineyard
Mike Weersing, Pyramid Valley Vineyards
Brent Rawstron, Rossendale Wines

Schuster, D. F., Jackson, D. and Tipples, R. (2002). *Canterbury grapes & wines 1840–2002*. Christchurch: Shoal Bay Press.
Tipples, R. (2007). Wines of the farthest promised land from Waipara, Canterbury, New Zealand. In *Wine, society, and globalization: multidisciplinary perspectives on the wine industry*, ed. G. Campbell and N. Guibert, pp. 241–254. New York: Palgrave Macmillan.

Index

Page references in **bold** refer to illustrations.

agro-terroir, 7, 9, 130, 347
Air New Zealand, 84, 102, 132, 234, 279, 317
Akaroa, 35
Akarua Winery, **80**, 290–93
Albany Surprise, 2, 10, 19, 25, 47, 89, 108, 254
Albariño, 116
Albonez, 1–3, 19
Alexandra, 248–50, 254, 256–57, 261, 263, 277
Alpha Domus, 177
Alsace, 59, 141, 256, 354
Amisfield Wine Company, 264
Amor-Bendall, 132
Anglo-Celts, 12, 34, 37, 244
appellations, 4, 54, 58–61, 73, 181, 228, 286, 360
Appellations d'Origine framework, 6, 54, 58, 73
ARA, 69, 75, 218
Arneis, 116
Arrow Basin, 261
Artisan Wines, 301
Ashwood Estate, **105**
Ashworth, Jo and John, 182
Ata Rangi, 312–14
Athens, **79**
Athfield, Ian, 167, **170–71**
atmospheric environment, *see* climate
Auckland, **14–15**
　climate, 63, 65, 303–4, 306
　as corporate centre, 45–46, 299–300
　early wine industry, 20–22, **24**, 298–300
　enterprises, 298–301, 307–8
　and Gisborne development, 84, 95, 107, 130
　production rates, 98–99
　regional vine distribution, 31, 38–42, 300–5
　soil, 306
　specialisation, 49–53
　varieties, 298, 305–6, 348–49
　West Auckland, *see* Auckland, West
Auckland, West, **viii**, **21**, **302–3**
　early wine industry, 9–10, 18, 20–22, 298–301, 353–54
　regional vine distribution, 31, 41, 43, **302–3**
Australia, 2, 54, 61, 113, 155, 229–30, 244–45
Averills, 20, 41
Avery, Graeme, 178
Awatea, 165, 167, 169
Awatere Valley, 45, 71, 154, 188–95, 209–11, 215–16, 218–21, 238–39

Babich, David, 301
Babich, Josip, 3, 17–18, 114, 203, 299
Babich, Peter, 3, 17, 71
Babich Wines, 17–18, 41, 84, 96, 140, 181, 301
Baco 22A, 19, 47–48, 52, 100, 103, 128, 142, 305–6
Bakano, 18, 48, 158
Ballins Industries, **19**
Banks Peninsula, 339–40

Bannockburn, 248, 250, 261–63, 265, 277, 280–81, 290, 294
Bauer, Rudi, 269, 271–76, 355
Bay of Islands, 34
Bay of Plenty, 39, 61, 90
Bay View, 22, 149
Beattie, David, 197–98
Bell, Delwyn and Doug, 114–20
Bell Hill Vineyard, 346–48
Belsham, John, 233
Bendigo, 32, 248–52, 261–62, 272, 274–78
Bendigo Estate, 275
Berrysmith, Frank, 99
biodynamics, 126–28, 269–71
Bish, Tony, 269
Black Pinot, 47
Black Ridge, 254
Blackberry Nip, **19**
Blanc de Blancs, 59
blends, 55, 59, 61, 131
Blenheim, 187–88, 194, 201, 203, 215
Boag, Suellen, 272, 274
Bond Road, 95, 110
Bonfiglioli, Rod, 124
Bordeaux, 19, 49, 53, 59, 68, 80, 139, 142–43, 148, 165, 177, 179–81, 185, 268, 297, 301, 305–6, 309, 341, 354, 360
botrytis cinerea, 76, 127
Bradley, Stephen, 178
Brady, Alan, 254, 256–57, 264, 277, 357
Bragato, Romeo, 25, 36, 47, 49, 135, 138, 144, 241, 244–48
Brajkovich, Mate and Melba, 20
Brajkovich, Michael, 307–8
Brancott vineyard, 199
Breidecker, 35, 106
Breweries, New Zealand, 22, 109
Bridge Pa, 146–47, **160**
Britain, 34–36
BRL Hardy, 129, 132
Brookefields Vineyards, 154
Bruce, Warwick, 97
Buck, John, 141, 156, 165–67, 181, 357
Buck, Wendy, 165–66
Bullnose vineyard, **56**, 154, 165–66, **168**
Burgess, Verdun, 254, 357
Burgundy, 4–6, 8, 18–19, 58–59, 77, 79–80, 103, 165, 184, 218, 228, 244, 256, 269–71, 301, 314, 317, 345–47, 353–55, 360–61
Busby, James, 34
Butler, Rosie, 182

Cabernet, 10–11
Cabernet Franc, 52, 55, 122, 142, 204, 298, 305–6, 348
Cabernet Sauvignon
　Auckland, 305–6, 348

Canterbury, 341
Central Otago, 245, 254, 262
Gisborne, 113–14
Hawke's Bay, 142, 145, 155, 159, 164, 167–68, 172, 354
Marlborough, 198, 203–4
metropolitan regions, 298
national varietal mix, 10, 19, 46–49, 51–52, 54–55, 59, 100–1
Nelson, 320
Wairarapa, 309–10
Cairnmuir Road, **80**
California, 70, 133, 245, 292
Campbell and Ehrenfried, 97, 109, 175
Canada, 2
Candia Road, **viii**, 1, 17–18, 26
canopy management, 8, 33, 41, 72, 74–77, 102, 116–17, 132, 173, 223, 288, 295, 329, 332–33
Canterbury
　climate, 61, 63–67, 81, 338–41
　early wine industry, 32, 334–38
　enterprises, 341–48
　regional vine distribution, 38–40, 45, 336–38
　soil, 339, 345–47
　specialisation, 49–54
　varieties, 245, 298, 341, 348–49
Capri Vineyards, **85**
Carignan, 58
Cemetery Road, 110
Central Otago, *see* Otago, Central
Central Otago Wine Company, 45, 258, 277
Chablis, 18–19, 59, 218
Champagne, 59, 211, 214, 256, 274–76, 354, 359
Chard Farm, 32, **240**, 264, 277
Chardonnay
　Auckland, 305–6, 348
　Canterbury, 341
　Central Otago, 244–45, 254, 262, 281, 286, 288, 291–92, 294
　France, 59
　Gisborne, 84, 88–89, 102–4, 106–7, **109**, 111, 113–16, 121, 131, 238
　Hawke's Bay, 142–43, 155, 157–59, 164–65, 167–69, 172, 174, 178, 183
　Marlborough, 203–4, 208, 238–39
　metropolitan regions, 298
　national varietal mix, 10, 19, 46–50, 52–54
　Nelson, 320, 330
　Wairarapa, 309–10, 316
Chasselas, 47, 52, 100–3, 111, 142
Chauvet, Clotilde, 269, 274–76
Chenin Blanc, 10, 47, 49, 52, 102–3, 106, 126–27, 142, 204, 208
Chile, 123
Christchurch, *see* Canterbury; Waipara
Church Road winery, 17, 150

371

Claret, 18–19
climate
    Auckland, 63, 65, 303–4, 306
    Canterbury, 61, 63–67, 81, 338–41
    Central Otago, 61, 63–67, 71, **74**, 80, 242–45, 249–51, 260–63, 276, 279, 288–90, 293–95
    cool climate imperatives, 71–75
    culture and, 77–80
    environmental limits, 10, 58, 61, 81, 293
    and French varieties, 4, 59–61
    Gisborne, 61, 63, 65–67, 69, 81, 89–90
    Hawke's Bay, 61, 63–64, 66–67, 80, 144–48, 183–84
    managing variability, 70–72
    Marlborough, 65, 67–68, 71, 188, 211, 214, 217–18, 234
    microclimate, 77, 102
    Nelson, 320–21
    and New Zealand vines, 61–70, 80–81, 355
    Wairarapa, 61, 64, 66, 80, 183–84, 308–9
Clive River, 146
Clone 6 Chardonnay, 115, 121, 292
Clone 15 Chardonnay, 104
clones
    in Central Otago, 251–54, 278, 285
    in Gisborne, 98, 112–13, 115–16
    improvements, 44, 76, 81
    knowledge of, 41
    production process, 8
Clos de St Anne vineyards, **118–19**
Clos Henri, 215
Cloudy Bay, 188, **191**, 194, **213**
Cloudy Bay winery, 83, 187, 203–5, 221–22, 224–27, 356
Clutha, 248–49
Clutha River, 248–49, 260, 263
Clyde, 260–61, 263, 266
Coleraine, 165, 167, 169–71
Collard, Bruce, 299, 301
collective bargaining, 115, 117
Collins, Michael, 172–74
Concord, 2, 19, 47
Conders Bend, 208–9
Constellation Brands, 12, 89, 116, 132–33, 143, 152, 154
Cook, James, 83
Cooks Wines, 26, 176, 205
Coopers Creek, 84, 116–17
Corban, Alex, 3, 18, 48, 110, 114, 197–98, 353
Corban, Alwyn, 17, 111, 141, 149, 156, 159–62, 172, 355
Corban, Brian, 160, 162
Corban, Joe, 110, 353
Corban, Najib, 110, 353
Corbans
    in Auckland, 20, 22, 41–43, 45, 84, 300, 352–53
    in Canterbury, 335, 349
    in Gisborne, 95–98, 108–10, 115, 117, 120
    in Hawke's Bay, 140
    in Marlborough, 202–5
    Montana competition, 38, 95, 97, 108–10, 116, 131, 175–76, 202
Cordier, 176–77, 185
Cornish Point, 284–86
corporate centre, Auckland as, 45–46, 299–300

corporate influence, 105–8, 116–17, 131, 299–300
Cossens, Gordon, 244, 260–62, 280
Cottage Block, **109**
Cowley, Peter, 166
Crab Farm Winery, **138**
Craggy Range, 152, 177–81, 318
Crawford, Kim, 132, 177
Cresta Doré, **158**
Croatians, *see* Dalmatians
Cromwell, 248–49, 258, 261, 263, 266–67, 285
Crownthorpe, 154
Cullen, Paul, 111, 356
Cuvée, 359
cyclones, 69, 81, 90–91

Dalmatians, 11–12, 20–22, 24, 35, 37, 84, 96, 128, 198, 298, 300, 354
Dartmore, 150
Davies, Steve, 264, 291–92
Davison, Ronald, 197–98
degree-days, 70–72, 144, 261, 263, 336, 340
Delegat, 75, 84, 140, 143, 152, 154, 181, 185
Delegat, Jim, 185
Delegat, Nick, **28**
Depression, 37
Destiny Bay, 83
Dicey, Robin, 286–90, 295
Dicey family, 260, 282, 286–90
Dijon clones, 278, 285
Dion, Roger, 4–7, 53
disease resistance, 2, 10, 24, 36, 47, 76, 81, 99, 102, 115, 155
dispersion
    environmental learning in, 80–81
    viticultural, 32, 38–46, 53
distribution, regional
    evolution of, 31–33, 38–46
    varietal specialisation, 49–54
Dog Point, 215, 222, 224–27, 356
Dominion Breweries, 22, 109, 176
drainage, 78–81, 148
Dry, Peter, 223
Dunbar, John, 162
d'Urville, Dumont, 34

Earnscleugh Road, 256–57
East Tamaki, 176
edaphic environment, *see* soil
Edmonds, Grant, 178
Edwards, Sue, 254, 357
Elephant Hill Wine Estate, **134**
Elms, Stewart, 260, 280–84
environment
    atmospheric, *see* climate
    culture and, 77–80
    edaphic, *see* soil
Escarpment Vineyard, 317–20
Eschenbruch, Rainer, 162, 256, 269, 328
Esk Valley, 22, 46, 138–39, 141, 146, 150, 158–59, 174–75, 181, 184, 229
Eskdale, 111, 149, 158
Eskdale Winegrowers, 156, 158–59
Europe
    climate, **60**
    introduction of *vinifera*, 34–37
    naming influence, 19, 54

overproduction, 2
Evans, George, 115
Ewart, Andrew, 100–1, 104, 113

Fairburn, A. R. D. (Rex), 26
Fairhall vineyard, 199
Family of Twelve, 128, 132
Felton Road, 244, 277, 280–84
Ferraud, Jean Désiré, 244–45, 248
fertiliser, production process, 8
filière, 46, 95–98, 105, 130, 148, 258, 354–57
Finn, Judy, 327–29, 340
Finn, Tim, 327–31, 340, 356
First World War, 37
Fistonich, George, 18, 139, 174–75, 178, 181
Flatman, Richard, **330**
Flaxmere, 149, 153, 184, 220
Fletcher, Reid, 105–6
Flora, 115
Forrest, Brigid, 227–30
Forrest, John, 201, 223–24, 227–30, 239
Forrest Estate Wines, 201, 223
fortified wines, 18, 53, 84, 135, 253
France
    climate, 59–61, 68–69
    environmental determinism, 78–79
    terroir, 4–6
    vinifera, 31, 35, 47, 53–55
Franklin, Steve, 242–43
Fraser Shingle, 152, 163, 175, 181–82
Fredatovich, Peter, 20
Frederickson, Aidan, 178
Fromm winery, 111, 113
frosts, 73–75, 80–81, 154, 218, 250, 261, 263, 279

Gadille, Rolande, 4–6, 53
Gamay, 59, **79**, 103, 254
Gamay Noir, 143, **168**
Garnham, Rachel, 178
Geisenheim, 115
Geographical Indications (Wines and Spirits) Registration Act 2006, 54
geography
    and production, 2, 18–19
    varietal specialisation, 54
    of *vinifera*, 33–37
Germany, 35, 54, **88**, 112
Gewürztraminer
    Auckland, 305
    Canterbury, 341
    Central Otago, 245, 254–56, 262
    Gisborne, **82**, **94**, 102–4, 106–7, 111–14, 121, 126, 128–29, **129**
    Hawke's Bay, 157, 164, 182
    Marlborough, 187, 203–4, 208, 223
    national varietal mix, 10, 47, 49, 54–55
    Nelson, **3**, 320
    Wairarapa, 309
Gibbston, 32, 248, 250, 256–59, 261–62, 265, 294
Gibbston Valley Wines, 254, 256–58, 266, 277
Giesen, Marcel, 346–47, 361
Giesen Holdings, **216**–17, 272, 340
Gifford, Ian, 200–1
Gimblett Gravels, 124, 146–47, 149, 152, 160–61, **173**, 175, 179–82, 185, 228, 361
Gimblett Road, 45, 78, 151–52, 172, 228

Gisborne, **86–87**, **118–19**, *see also* Poverty Bay
    awards, 132
    climate, 61, 63, 65–67, 69, 81, 89–90
    corporate influence, 105–8, 116–17, 131
    early wine industry, 10, 25–26, 34, 83–89, 354
    enterprises, 95–98, 107–31
    filière, 95–98, 130
    future of industry in, 131–33
    growers, 96–102, 114–20, 124–28, 130–31
    Montana-Corbans competition, 95, 107–10
    production rates, 100, 107
    regional vine distribution, 38–41, 44
    soil, 91–95, 117, 120, 129–30, 133
    specialisation, 49–53
    varieties, 49, 98–104, 106–7, 131, 245
    yields, 85, 88–89, 103–4, 117, 133
Gisborne Wine Company, 121, 123
Glazebrook, Gary, 159–62
Glenmark Wines, 340–41
Glenvale Wines, **19**, 22, 42, 135, **140**, 154, 164, 174–75
GM 312-53, 115
Golden Slope Ltd, The, 122
Goldwater Estate, 348
Gough, Peter, 161–62
goût de terroir, 4
government
    Select Committee recommendations, 26–29
    trials, 253–55
    vine-pull scheme, 34, 38, **40**, 44, **46**, 49, 85, 102, 121, 124, 130, 138–39, 151, 203, 205, 208
    Viticultural Research Station, 36, 47, **78**, 162, 242, 256, 268–69, 327, 356
grafting, 124
Grant family, 254, 357
Grape Growers Council, New Zealand, 159
Graves, 59, 299
Great North Road vineyard, 110
Green, Steve, 260, 287
Greenhough, Andrew, 331–34
Greenhough Vineyard, 331–34
Greening, Nigel, 263–64, 284–86, 295
Greenmeadows, 22, 34, 149–50
Gregan, Philip, 98, 238
Grenache, 58, **168**
Greywacke, 224–27
Groshek, Paul, **viii**, 1–2, 10, 18–19, 26–27
growers
    Central Otago, 254–59, 265
    corporate influence, 105–8, 174, 300
    Gisborne, 96–102, 105–8, 114–20, 124–28, 130–31
    Hawke's Bay, 138–41, 162, 174, 176
    Marlborough, 198–99, 201–3, 208–9, 214, 221–24
Grüner Veltliner, 325–26
Gunn Estate, 177

hail, 73, 161
Hamilton, Jim, 182
Hancock, John, 183, 290–91, 318
Hanmer Springs, 345
Hapara Road, **85**
Harrison, Richard, 182
Hastings, 22, 139, 144, 184
Hauraki Plains, 64
Havelock hills, **166–67**

Havelock North, 22, 35, **134**, 149, 184
Hawke's Bay, **11–12**, **56**, **76**, **136–37**
    Central, 182–84
    climate, 61, 63–64, 66–67, 80, 144–48, 183–84
    early wine industry, 9–11, 17–19, 22–26, 36, 84–85, 139–41, 154–58, 180, 354
    enterprises, 158–180, 184–85
    family operations, 141
    filière, 148
    future of industry in, 180, 184–85
    growers, 138–41, 162, 174, 176
    production rates, 98–100, 185
    regional vine distribution, 38–42, 44–45, 148–54
    soil, 139, 145–49, 152, 154, 160–61, 163, 173, 177, 179–82
    specialisation, 49–53
    varieties, 49, 141–43, 245
Hay, Greg, 264, 277
Hay, Rob, 264
Healy, James, 225–27, 356
Healy, Wendy, 225–26
Heinz, 152
Henderson, **14–15**, 41, 110, 298, 352–53
Henderson-Oratia, 20–21, 24, 300–2
Heretaunga Plains, 135, 139, 143, 145, 149–52, 181–82, 185
Highfield Estate, 223–24
Hinnewinkel, Jean-Claude, 7
hoar frost, **80**
Hock, 17–19
Hogan family, 126, 202
Hohnen, David, 187, 203–4, 221–22, 225
Hoksbergen, Tony, 235
Hoskins, Nick, 124
Huapai, 49, 114, 128
Hubscher, Peter, **23**, 90, 131, 155, 161, 169, 176, 185, 235
Hunter, Jane, 208, 211
Hunter's Wines, **186**, 202
hybrids, 46–48, 53, 84, 89, 99, 128, 131, 253–54, 303

Ibbotson, Neal, 200, 210
imports, 26–29, 36
Indevin Partners, 38
Institut National de la Recherche Agronomique, 6, 78
irrigation, 44, 64, 73–75, 173, 215, 218–19, 221, 223, 249, 313, 337–38
Irwin, Bill, 101, 111–13, 356
Irwin, Denis, 3, 96, 111–14, 132, 157, 164
Irwin family, 89
isotherm, 61, 64
Italy, 19, 54, 142

Jackson, David, 335, 342
Jacksons Road, 202, 204
Jerez de la Frontera, 18
Johansen, Gary and Malcolm, 182
John, Brother, 157
Johnson, Hugh, 57–58
Judd (growers), 96
Judd, Kevin, 204, 217, 221, 225, 239, 355–56

Kagi, Ben, 269
Kaikoura, 221, 339

Kaikoura Range, 188, **190**
Kaiti, 91
Kalberer, Hätsch, 111, 113
Kasza, Denis, 3, 18, **23**, 48, 114, 155, 177
Kawarau Gorge, **240**, 257, 260–62, 265, 294
Kawarau Valley, 248–50, 265–66
Kemblefield Estate Winery, 154, 177
Kendall-Jackson Vineyard Estate, 132–33
Kennedy Point, **350–51**
Kerr, Graham, 165
Kesteven Farm Ltd, 201
Keuka, **79**
Kim Crawford Wines, 177
Kirk, Norman, 198
Knappstein, Bob, 114, 155, 241–42, 343
Korokipo Road, 169
Koura Bay, 83
Kumeu, 20, 41, 110, 301, 307–8
Kumeu River Wines, 25, 307–8
Kumeu-Huapai, 24, 300, 302

labrusca, 2, 24, 47, 99, 354
Lake, Russell, 269
Lake Dunstan, 248, 260, 262, 274, 282
Lake Hayes, **259**
Landfall, 121
Lange, David, 208
Langlois, 35
Languedoc-Rousillon, 116, 142
Lazy Bay, 83
Le Brun, 202
Lebanese, 12, 356
Leonard, Warren, **28**
Les Maranges, 59
licences, **24**, 27–29, 36
Lime Rock, 182–83
Limmer, Alan, 111, 141, 156, 159, 162–65, 181–83
Limmer, Glennice, 163
Lincoln College, 334–38
Lincoln Road, 20, 298, 300–1
Lindauer, 89, 97, 104, 131
Linnaeus, 124
Lion Breweries, 97, 176
liqueurs, 10, 18, **85**, 89
Loire Valley, 59, 354, 358, 360
Lombardi Wines, 154
Longbush Wines, 121–23, 131
Loop Road, 272, 274, 277–79
Love, Matt, 150
Lucas, David, 26, 176
Luggate, 248
Lyttton Road, 130

Mabbett, Jason, 34–35
Mackenzie country, 66–67
Mâconnais, 59
Malbec, 19, 55, 142, 159, 204, 305–6
Mangatangi, 84, 99, 111, 198
Manuherikia, 251
Manutuke, 92–93, 100, 121, 127
Marist Brothers, 34
Marlborough
    awards, 223, 234
    branding, 216–18
    climate, 65, 67–68, 71, 188, 211, 214, 217–18, 234
    early wine industry, 10–11, 84, 187, 195–203, 354

Index   373

Marlborough *(cont.)*
   enterprises, 32, 176, 187–88, 195–215, 221–34
   growers, 198–99, 201–3, 208–9, 214, 221–24
   production rates, 98–100, 239
   regional vine distribution, 38–40, 42–44, **206–7**, 214–15
   Sauvignon Blanc association, 57–58, 69, 71, 198, 234–39, 357–58
   soil, 188–95, 198–99, 211, 214–15, 217–18, 222, 234
   specialisation, 49–53
   varieties, 202–4, 208, 245
   yields, 223, 228, 239
Marris, John, 31, 195–96, 208, 227, 238
Marsanne, 116
Marsden, Samuel, 34
Martin, Damian, 69
Martin, Neal, 129, 169
Martinborough, **296, 310–11**
   climate, 65, 71, 308–9
   early wine industry, 11, 32
   enterprises, 312–20
   specialisation, 53
Martinborough Vineyard Estates, 317–20
Mason, H. G. R., 28
Massey, W. F., 37
Matakana, 31, 45, 53, 301–2, 305
Matariki Wines, 177, 185
Matawhero, 91–93, 95, **105**
Matawhero Wines, 111–14, 132, 164
Matua Valley, 41, 84, 96, 140, 217, 233
maturation, 8
Mazuran, George, 20, **33**, 298
McCaskey, John, 340–41
McCorkindale, Alan, 126, 227, 343–44, 356
McDonald, Rod, 174
McDonald, Tom, 3, 18, 22–23, 48, 155, 175, 177, 241
McDonald's Wines, 22, 42, 135, 139, 154, 175, 177
McKenna, Larry, 315, 317–20
McLernon, Roger, 83, 97, 107–8, 130
McWilliam's Wines, 17–18, 22–23, 42, 48–49, 135, 140–41, 150, 154–56, **158**, 175–76, 205, 241, 343
Mendoza Chardonnay, 104, **109**, 115–16, 164
Mere Road, 151, 162–64
Merlot
   Auckland, 41, 305–6, 348
   Canterbury, 341
   Gisborne, 101, 103–4, 106–7
   Hawke's Bay, 142, 145, **168**, 172, 174, 178, 183, 185, 354
   Marlborough, 204
   metropolitan regions, 298
   national varietal mix, 10, 46–47, 49, 51–52, 55, 59
   Wairarapa, 309
Méthode Traditionnelle, 187, 264, 276, 359–60
metropolitan vineyards, 297–98, 305, 348–49
microclimate, 77, 102
Middle Renwick Road, 199
Midi, 73, 354
Milburn Cement, 152, 175, 181
Mills, Lois, 243, 254, 257, 267–71, 357
Mills, Nick, 269–271, 355
Mills, Rolfe, 243, 254–55, 257, 267–71, 357
Millton, Annie, 89, 124–28, 131

Millton, James, 89, 117, 124–28, 131, 161
Millton Vineyards, 124–28
Milne, Derek, 31, 318
Ministry of Agriculture, 32, 47, 97–100, 103
Mission Estate, 22, 34, **140**–41, 150, 154, 157, 271
missionaries, 34
Moffitt, James and Michael, 257
Mondavi, Robert, 133
Mondillo Vineyards, 276–79
Monkey Bay, 83
Montana
   in Auckland, 41, 45
   in Canterbury, 335, 349, 356
   Corbans competition, 38, 95, 97, 108–10, 116, 131, 175–76, 202
   in Gisborne, 83–84, 89, 91, 95–98, 107–8, 115, 130–31
   in Hawke's Bay, 140, 150, 154, 169, 175–77, 185
   in Marlborough, 32, 42–44, 52, 176, 187, 195–203, 205, 210
MontGras, 123
Mooney, Paul, 157
Morris, June and Michael, 165–66
Morton Estate, 154
Mouats family, 183
Mourvèdre, 58
Moutere, 320, 326–27
Mt Difficulty Wines, **30**, 264, 266, 277, 286–290
Muaga Vineyards, **viii**, 18, 26
Mud House, 89
Muir, Colin, 204
Muldoon, Rob, 199, 343
Müller Thurgau
   Central Otago, 253, 256, 269
   Gisborne, 84–85, 88, 100–3, 105–6, 111, 115, 120–21
   Hawke's Bay, 139, 141–42, 174, 180
   Marlborough, 198, 203–4, 208, 232, 235
   national varietal mix, 10, 19, 46–49, 52, 54
   Nelson, 320
Mundy, Robin, 342
Muscat, 47–49, 52, 102–4, 106–7, 204, 253
Myers, Douglas, 109, 165

Napa Valley, 70, 133, 292
Napier, 22, 144
Nautilus, 233
Neill, Sam, 257–58, 277
Nelson, **3, 5, 13**
   climate, 63–65, 67–68, 320–21
   early wine industry, 10
   enterprises, 321–34
   regional vine distribution, 31, 39, 321
   soil, 320, 324, 326, **330**, 333–34
   specialisation, 49–54
   varieties, 298, 320–21, 348–49
Neudorf Vineyards, 5, 13, 327–31, 340
New Plymouth, 35
New Renwick Road, 199–200
New World wines, 2, 34, 105, 317, 361
Ngakoroa Road, 129
Ngaruroro River, 45, 75, 139, 143, 146, 148–52, **156**, 160, **168**, 181, 184–85, 361
Ngaruroro Terraces, 146–48, 151–52, 154, **156**
Ngatapa block, 125
Ngatarawa, 154

Ngatarawa Wines, 17, 111, 149, 156, 159–62
Nobilo, 38, 41, 48, 83–84, 96, 143, 152, 154, 204, 209
Nobilo, Mark, 128
Nobilo, Nick, 3, 49, **82**, 84, **94**, 114, 126, 128–30, 132, 355
Nobilo, Steve, 128
Norman family, 182–83
North America, 24
Northland, 34–35, 38–39, 61, 65, 98–99

Opou Station, 125–26
Oratia, 108, 301, 306
organic wines, 1, 126–28, 269–71
Ormond, 95, 110
Ormond Road, 114–20
Otago, Central, **246–47**
   awards, 272, 279
   climate, 61, 63–67, 71, **74**, 80, 242–45, 249–251, 260–63, 276, 279, 288–90, 293–95
   early wine industry, 10, 32, 242–48, 254–59, 354
   enterprises, 254–59, 263–65, 267–93
   growers, 254–59, 265
   regional vine distribution, 38–40, 45, 248–53, 256–57
   soil, 281–83, 293–95
   specialisation, 49–54, 257, 294
   trials, 253–55
   varieties, 243–45, 251–54, 262
Otaki, 34
Othello, **79**
overproduction, 2, 27, 102
Oyster Bay, 83

Palliser Estate, **296**, 312, 315–17, **360**
Palomino, 18–19, 47–49, 52, **79**, 101–3, 142, 204, 232, 253, 305
Parker, Chris, 117
Pask, Chris, 141, 156, 162–63, 169–74
Pask Winery, CJ, 156, 169–74, 181
Paton, Clive, 145, 312–14
Patutahi, 91–93
Peabody, Terry, 178
Pegasus Bay, 83
Penfolds, 20, 41–42, 84, 96–97, 115, 140, 176, 205
Peregrine Wines, 258–59, 264, 277
Perle, Jack, **78**
Pernod Ricard, 12, 17, 38, 89, 131, 143, 150, 152, 154, 175–77, 185, 215, 349
Perriam, Heather, 265, 272
Perriam, John, 265, 272, 274–77
Perrier-Cornet, Philippe, 78–79
Petit Verdot, **168**
phylloxera vastatrix, 24, 36, 47, 53–54, 73, 99, 115, 155, 214, 354
physiological processes, 8
Piedmont, 116
Pinckney, Ann, 241, 254–57, 355, 357
Pinot Chardonnay, 19, 48
Pinot Grigio, 104
Pinot Gris
   Auckland, 305–6, 348
   Canterbury, 341
   Central Otago, 243, 245, 254, 256, 262, 286, 288, 294
   Gisborne, 88, 103–5, 107, 142–43

Hawke's Bay, 182
Marlborough, 203–4
metropolitan regions, 298
national varietal mix, 47, 52–54, 59
Nelson, 320
Wairarapa, 309–10, 316
Pinot Meunier, 59, 254, 359
Pinot Noir
Auckland, 245, 305–8
Canterbury, 245, 340–41, 355
Central Otago, 32, 243–45, 251–52, 254–56, 258, 261–62, 270, 272, 276, 278–81, 286, 289–92, 294–95, 355
France, 4, 58–59
Gisborne, 89, 101, 103–4, 107, 114, 120–21, 127, 245
Hawke's Bay, 142–43, 159, 174, 182–83, 245
Marlborough, 187, 203–4, 215, 223–25, 235–37, 239, 245, 355
metropolitan regions, 298, 348
national varietal mix, 10, 46–47, 49, 51–55, 81
Nelson, 245, 320, 325, 330, 355
Wairarapa, 245, 309–11, 314–19, 348, 355
Pinotage, 49, 52, **79**, 103, 204, 208, 305
Pleasant Valley Wines, 300
Pollack, Paul, 231
Pommard clones, 278
port, 10, 18, 24, 89
Porter, Rolph, 107
Pouilly, 59
Poverty Bay, **86–87**, *see also* Gisborne
Corbans in, 95
early wine industry, 26, 88–89
growers, 96–102
production rates, 98–99, 107
soil, 85, 92–95, 117, 120, 129–30, 133
usage of name, 83–84
varieties, 98–104, 106–7
precipitation, 61–64, 80–81, 144–45, 188, 261, 290, 303–4, 308
Prescott, James, 61, 64, 71
prices
collective bargaining, 115, 117
price fixing, 108
price wars, 106
yield influence on, 104
prohibition, 20
Providence, 301
Pullar, Alan, 91, 93–95, 111
Pyramid Valley Vineyards, 345–46

Quartz Reef, 271–76
Queenstown, 248, **259**

Radburnd, Kate, 172–74
Rapaura, 201–4, 209, 233–34
Rata, Matiu, 201
Rawstron, Brent and Shirley, 341–43
Read, Mark, 150
Read, Nigel, 150
Redwood Valley, 3
regional distribution
evolution of, 31–33, 38–46
varietal specialisation, 49–54
Reichensteiner, 52, 103, 115, 131
Revington, Ross, 121
Rhine Riesling, 103, 111

Rhine Valley, 112
Rhone Valley, 116, 142–43
Richmond Range, 188, **191**, **212**
Riddiford, Richard, 315–17
Riesling
Auckland, 305–6
Canterbury, 340–41, 344, 349
Central Otago, 243–45, 254–56, 262, 281, 286, 288
Gisborne, 111, 126
Hawke's Bay, 182
Marlborough, 187, 203–4, 208, 223
metropolitan regions, 298
national varietal mix, 10, 19, 46, 49–50, 52–55, 59
Nelson, 320
Wairarapa, 309–10, 316–17
Riesling-Seibel, 115
Riesling-Sylvaner, 19, 48, 84, 100–1, 198, 242
ripeness, 72–74, 77, 81, 102, 145, 242, 251–52, 261, 288
Rippon Vineyards, 32, 243, 254–55, 264, 267–72
Riverlands, 154, 196, 199
Riverlea vineyard, 110
Riverpoint Road, 95, 110–11
Riversun Nursery, 120, 123–25, 132
Roberts, Daniel, 132
rootstock, 8, 44, 47, 173, 285
Rose, Chris, 201–2, 204, 230–34
Rose, Phil, 32–33, 201–2, 204, 230–34
Rosie's Block, **331**
Rossendale Wines, 341–43
Rothermel, Axel, 269
Rothesay vineyard, 41, 301
Rothmans, 109, 176, 202
Roxburgh-Dunbarton, 261
Ruakumara Range, 92
Ruesink, Henk, 239
Russell, Dudley, **16**, 18

Sacred Hill, 154, **156**
Saint Clair Family Estate, 202, 210
Salonius, Kim, 111, 141, 155–56, 158–59, 163–64
Salonius, Trish, 156
Sancerre, 59, 228, 234
Sauternes, 18, 59, 129
Sauvignon Blanc
Auckland, 305–6
Canterbury, 340–41, 343, 348
Central Otago, 243, 245, 262
France, 59
Gisborne, 103, 107, 115, 122, 132
Hawke's Bay, 142–43, 164, **173**–74, 182–83
Marlborough, 11, 32, 57–58, 69, 71, 187, 198, 203–4, 208–9, 214–18, 224–25, 228, 233–39, 355, 357–58
metropolitan regions, 298, 348
national varietal mix, 10, 46–47, 49–50, 52–55
Nelson, 320, 324–25, 329–330, 348
Wairarapa, 309–11, 316
Schuster, Danny, 308, 335
Scott, Allan, 200, 204
Scott, Dick, 108–10, 242
Scottish Presbyterians, 12
Seagram, 41, 197
Searle family, 114, 132

Seaview, 195–96, 210
Second World War, 20, 26, 34, 37
Seddon Vineyards, 210
sediments, Quaternary, 61–64
Seguin, Gérard, 69
Seibel 5437, 48, 52
Seibel 5455, 19, 47–48, 52, 142, 305–6, 320
Seifried, Agnes, 325, 327
Seifried, Hermann, 321–22, 325–27
Seifried Estate, 3, 321–26
Selak, Mate, **28**
Selaks, 84, 96, 204
Select Committee recommendations, 27–29
Semillon, 52, 59, 103, 106–7, 115, 203, 208, 305–6
Seneca, 108
Shaw, Dean, 258
sheep runs, 265–67
sherry, 10, 18, 24, **85**, 89, 354
Sherry, Sweet, **19**
Shingle Peak, 217
Shiraz, 143
Sileni Estates, 177–78, 180
Simmonds, Chris, 221–24
Simmonds, Judy, 221–24
Skeggs, Clifford, 290–94
Smart, Richard, 3, 76–77, 102, 132, 154, 162, 178, 329–31
Smith, Geoff, 178
Smith, Ron, 151
Smith, Steve, 175, 178, 180–81, 318
soil
Auckland, 306
Canterbury, 339, 345–47
Central Otago, 281–83, 293–95
culture and, 77–80
Gisborne, 91–95, 117, 120, 129–30, 133
Hawke's Bay, 139, 145–49, 152, 154, 160–61, 163, 173, 177, 179–82
Marlborough, 188–95, 198–99, 211, 214–15, 217–18, 222, 234
Nelson, 320, 324, 326, **330**, 333–34
and New Zealand vines, 61, 80–81, 355, 357
in production process, **8**, 11
terroir, 4
Soler, Joseph, 35
Soljans, 301
Southern Alps, 64, 66, 80, 249, 338–39
Southern Valleys, 189, 194, 198–99, 201–3, 205, 209, 218–19
Southland, 64
Spain, 19, 35, 142
Sparkleburg, **19**
Speargrass Flat, 256–57
specialisation, varietal, 49–55, 257, 294
Spence, Bill, 217, 233
Spence, Ross, 203, 217, 233
Sperling, Spatz, 111
spraying, 126
St Arnaud Range, 188
St George Estate, 155
Station Road, 128
Steven, Todd, **330**
Stonecroft Wines, 111, 143, 156, 162–65, 181
Stoneleigh, 204, 344
Stonyridge Vineyard, 301
stopbanking, 90, 92, 145, 219
sunshine hours, 61, 67, 81, 90, 188

Index 375

supermarkets, 29
Sutherland, Ivan, 204, 215, 221–22, 225–27, 356
Sutherland, Margaret, 225–26
Swanson Road, **20**
Syrah, 52, **56**, 142–43, 162, 164, **173**, 185, 204, 254, 305–6, 320

table wines, 1–2, 18–19, 24–25, 27–29, 48, 53, 84, 98, 135
Taradale, 150–51
Taramea Wines, 254, 257
Tarndale slip, 92
Tarras, 248
Tasman Bay, 83
Taupaki, **43**, 110
Te Arai River, 126
Te Awa Farm, 177
Te Awanga, 22, **134**, 139, 149, 181
Te Kauwhata
   early wine industry, 25–26
   regional vine distribution, 31, 38
   Viticultural Research Station, 36, 47, **78**, 162, 242, 256, 268–69, 327, 356
Te Mata, 36, **56**, **134**, 149
Te Mata Estate, 22, **140**, 143, 154–57, 165–71
Te Whare Ra, 126, 202
Te Whau Vineyard, **350–51**
temperance movement, 34, 36–37, 53–54
temperature, 61, 64–75, 81, 144, 249, 261, 263, 276
Tempranillo, 143
Terra Vitae Vineyards, 210
terroir, 4, 6–8, 52, 55, 58, 132–33, 179, 204, 345, 355
Thomas, Dave, 128–29
Thomas, Wayne, 31, 43, 195, 197
Thorpe Brothers Wine, 121, 123, 131
Thorpe family, 89, 120–24, 131–32, 355–56
Tietjen (growers), 96, 122, 132–33
Titirangi, 176
Tolaga Bay, 66
Traminer, 164
Traversac, Jean-Baptiste, 78
trellising, 8, 44, 76–77, 102, 162, 173, 223, 232, 287–88, 295, **307**, 329, 332–33
Trinity Hill, 143, 177, 318
Tukipo River Estate, 183
Tukituki River, 146, 148, 150–51, **156**, **170–71**, **179**, 184
Turner, Bill, 335
Tutaekuri River, 139, 146, 148–50, 154, **156**, 165, **168**, 184
Tynan, Roger, 182
typicité, 6

UCD4 Gewürztraminer, 112
UCD4 Traminer, 164
UCD7 Cabernet Sauvignon, 112, 164
unfortified wines, 2, 17–18, 253, 300
United Kingdom, 2
United States, 2, 70, 197, 244–45
Upper Moutere, 5, 326

Valley Road vineyard, 110

van Dam, Tom, 162
varietal mix (national)
   corporate influence, 105–8
   evolution of, 10, 31–33, 46–49, 354
varietal mix (regional), *see under the names of specific regions*
varietal specialisation, 49–55, 58
Vavasour Wines, 209–10
Veldhuizen, Sherwyn, 346–47
vermouth, 18
Vicieli, Brian, 83
Vidal, 18, 22, 35, 46, 135, 139–41, 143, 154, 157, 174–75
Vidal, Anthony Joseph, **35**
Villa Maria, 12, 18, 38, 46, 139–41, 152, 157, 174–75, 181, 210, 229
Vincor, 132
vine-pull scheme, 34, 38, **40**, 44, **46**, 49, 85, 102, 121, 124, 130, 138–39, 151, 203, 205, 208
vinifera
   disease resistance, 24, 47, 76, 155
   distribution of, 10, 22, 38–40
   geographical history of, 33–37, 58
   regional production, 98–101
   varietal mix, 31, 46–49, 131
   varietal specialisation, 49–55
vini-terroir, 7, 9
Vinoptima Estate, **82**, **94**, 126, 128, **129**, 130
Viognier, 103, 116, **168**, 305
virus status
   improvements, 44, 76, 124
   knowledge of, 41, 124
   production process, 8
Virus Type 3, 124
Viticultural Association, **33**
viticulture
   dispersion, 32, 38–46, 53
   environmental factors, 62–67, 70–72, 77, 80–81
   imperatives, 71–75
   specialisation, varietal, 49–55
   studies, 31–32, 75–76, 98–99, 260
   technologies, 2, 7–9
   trials, 253–55

W. and R. Smallbone Ltd, 96–97, 109
Waiheke Island, 31, 45, 53, 63, 80, 300–306, 348, **350–51**, 354–55
Waiherere, 95
Waiherere Wines, **88**, 97, 107
Waihopai, 75, 218
Waikari, 345–46, 348
Waikato, 38–39, 64–65, 98–99, 245
Waimea Plain, 64, 322–24, 326
Waipaoa River, 90, 92–94
Waipara
   climate, 66–67, 338–41
   early wine industry, 10, 334–38, 354
   enterprises, 341–48
   regional vine distribution, 3, 39, 45, 336–38
   soil, 339
   varieties, 298, 341, 348–49
Wairarapa
   climate, 61, 64, 66, 80, 183–84, 308–9

   early wine industry, 10, 36
   enterprises, 312–20
   regional vine distribution, 39–40, 45, 310–11
   specialisation, 49–54
   varieties, 298, 309–12, 348–49
   yields, 311–12, 314
Wairau River Wines, 32, 230–34
Wairau Valley, 44, 63–64, 66, 71, 154, 188–95, 199, 202, 205, 209, 215, 217–23, 234, 238–39, 361
Waitakere, 17
Waitaki Valley, 67
Walters, Blair, 244, 280, 284
Wanaka, 248–49, 256–57, 261–62, 267–68
Wanganui, 35
Wattie's, 26, 90, 152
Webber, John, 205
Webster, Jim, 178
Weersing, Claudia and Mike, 345–46
Wellington, *see* Martinborough; Wairarapa
Wellsford, 36
Wentworth Estates, 259, 264
West Brook Winery, 301
West Coast, 64
Western Vineyards, 14–18, 20
Whanganui River, 34
Whangaroa, 34
Wheeler, Jenny, 331–34
Whenuapai, 110
White Cloud, 48
Whitecliffs, 121
William Hill Vineyards, 254–55, 257
Wilson, James, 4
Wine Institute of New Zealand, 13, 159, 181, 198, 202, 205, 243
Winegrowers, Gisborne, 117
Winegrowers, New Zealand, 13, 22, 98, 124, 126, 159, 181–82, 214, 265, 300, 304
Wines and Spirits Co. Ltd, New Zealand, 109
Wither Hills, 208, 219
Witters (growers), 96, 122
Wohnsiedler, Friedrich, 89, 95
Wohnsiedler winery, 26, 88, 96–97, 107
Wolf Blass, 203
Wolter, Mike, 258, 276–77
Wood, Gary, 97
Woodbourne vineyard, 199
Woodthorpe vineyard, 165–66, **168**
World Trade Organization, 7

Yealands, Peter, 210, 220
Yealands Estate, **220**
yeast varieties, **78**
yields, 8, 73, 85, 88–89, 100–2, 104, 223, 228, 276, 292, 311–12, 314, 331, 358–60
Yozin, M. B., **20**
Yugoslavs, *see* Dalmatians
Yukich, Frank, 18, 29, 41–43, 83, 95–97, 107–8, 110–11, 176, 187, 195–98, 357
Yukich, Mate, 18, 41, 108, 110–11, 195

Zame, Antonio, **85**, 89
Zinfandel, 143
Zweigelt, 325–26